INTER PERSONAL communication

AN OVERVIEW OF
BASIC PRINCIPLES
AND
CONTEXTS

Kendall Hunt
publishing company

EDITORS:

Todd Lee Goen, Kendra Knight, Linda D. Manning, and Alice E. Veksler

www.kendallhunt.com
Send all inquiries to:
4050 Westmark Drive
Dubuque, IA 52004-1840

Contents

chapter **3**   Nonverbal Communication   47

chapter **8**   Sustaining Relationships   195

chapter **12**   Family Communication   299

chapter **13** Health Communication   323

The History and Foundation of Interpersonal Communication
Examining the Roots

OBJECTIVES

- Provide three important reasons for the study of interpersonal communication
- Discuss Spitzberg and Cupach's Components Model of communication competence
- Define interpersonal communication and distinguish it from other types of communication (e.g., intrapersonal, small group, organizational)
- Identify and explain each of the thirteen basic principles of interpersonal communication (INTERPERSONAL)
- Describe the pivotal research and historical events that contributed to the development of the field of interpersonal communication
- Define communication competence
- Define theory and explain the four goals of a theory

© Andres Rodriguez, 2007, Shutterstock.

KEY TERMS

communication
  competence
knowledge
skill
motivation
mass communication
organizational
  communication
small group
  communication

intrapersonal
  communication
interpersonal
  communication
transactional content
  and relational
  components
process
shared meaning
  metacommunication

verbal and nonverbal
  component rules
symbolic
  interactionism
Maslow's Hierarchy of
  Needs
kinesics proxemics
Attribution theory
theory

OVERVIEW

Chances are most people have had a number of frustrating experiences with communication. Whether we are communicating with someone face-to-face or are using our computer to send messages, our communication skills often falter and we ask ourselves what went wrong. For instance, have you ever talked on the phone with a family member, hoping to have a meaningful conversation, but

Have you ever unexpectedly ended up in an argument over what you thought would be a good dinner conversation?

© fred goldstein, 2007, Shutterstock.

as you hung up, you wondered why nothing really important was said? Have you ever taken your relationship partner out for a romantic anniversary dinner, anticipating the chance to reminisce about happy times together; but instead, the night was spent arguing and the date ended abruptly? Experiences such as these may be connected to either underdeveloped communication skills or a lack of awareness of the communication tactics and behaviors needed to negotiate these situations. Interpersonal skills can, and should, be continually evaluated and improved, reinforcing the importance of learning more about interpersonal communication. In this chapter we explore reasons for taking an interpersonal communication course, offer a definition of interpersonal communication, and distinguish it from other types of communication. Additionally, we identify key interpersonal communication principles, provide a brief overview of the history of interpersonal communication, and discuss the significance of communication theories.

WHY STUDY INTERPERSONAL COMMUNICATION?

Researchers and practitioners from an array of disciplines often describe interpersonal skills as absolutely essential for success in their professional fields. Regardless of the profession you enter, it is very likely that effective communication skills are required for your success. For example, successful journalists note that there appears to be a strong relationship between a writer's conviviality and his creativity. Most individuals employed in this field agree that success at work is often contingent on one's ability to relate well to fellow journalists (Manssour 2003). Similarly, Steve Bauman (2003), an employee of NASA Glenn Research Center, notes that in a recent survey conducted in the engineering profession, oral communication skills were cited as one of the most important skills needed for recent engineering graduates. Individuals from all types of health care fields and services are encouraged to participate in interpersonal skills training to improve their ability to treat patients (see, for example, Rath et al. 1998). When health care providers communicate more effectively, patient satisfaction and motivation often increase

Why would it be especially important for health care providers to have strong interpersonal skills?

© dasilva, 2007, Shutterstock.

(Thompson 1986; Wanzer, Booth-Butterfield and Gruber 2004). Not surprisingly, nurses of all levels of ability are expected to possess strong interpersonal communication skills in order to excel in their vocation (Crosby et al. 2003; Utley-Smith 2004). There are innumerable professions that demand strong interpersonal skills as a means of relating well to colleagues and clients, and to achieving and maintaining one's position within the organization. In fact, it is probably more difficult to identify a field or profession that does *not* demand strong interpersonal skills than it would be to list all those that do.

Developing strong interpersonal skills is more necessary than ever to negotiate in today's "bigger is better" business environment (Myers and Tucker 2005). Organizations have undergone radical changes resulting in a more diverse workforce, a greater ability to obtain and process information through the Internet, and an expanding global marketplace which makes doing business with people from other cultures easier than ever before. According to management professors Laura Myers and Mary Tucker, as these changes occur, more emphasis is being placed on "people skills" in business programs across the nation and the specific "soft skills" which distinguish effective from ineffective managers. Effective managers must be able to deliver constructive criticism, manage conflicts between employees, persuade and influence individuals at all levels, provide support and guidance and exhibit appropriate leadership behaviors. Others, such as Daniel Goleman (1995), agree that in addition to possessing interpersonal communication skills, a strong sense of self and other awareness is what distinguishes successful from unsuccessful professionals.

The job interview is an excellent example of a situation that demands effective interpersonal communication skills. A recent survey of personnel interviewers confirmed the importance of interpersonal communication skills during the interview process. The survey highlighted areas of improvement for potential job candidates (Peterson 1997). Marshalita Sims Peterson conducted a survey of approximately 500 personnel interviewers and found that while ninety percent of personnel interviewers indicate that strong communication skills are needed for success in corporate settings, only sixty percent feel that applicants exhibit effective communication skills during job interviews. The five most frequently identified verbal and nonverbal communication skill inadequacies exhibited during interview situations were: lack of eye contact, topic relevance, response organization, listening skills, and response clarity (Peterson 1997, 289). Several chapters in this textbook are intended to help you to become a more effective interviewee, particularly the chapters on verbal and nonverbal communication, perception and listening, and organizational communication.

What interpersonal skills are important to exhibit during a job interview?

Additional and equally important reasons for taking a course in interpersonal communication include the indisputable links between effective communication and health, and between effective communication practices and relationship satisfaction. Having rewarding communication and relationships with others is closely connected to both mental and physical health (Burleson and MacGeorge 2002; Omarzu, Whalen, and Harvey 2001). Knowing that others will "be there" for us during stressful or traumatic times in our lives offers us a sense of perceived social support, which correlates to mental well-being (Burleson and MacGeorge 2002). In his new book, *Social Intelligence: The New Science of Human Relationships*, Daniel Goleman (2006) provides additional support for the relationship between the quality of one's interpersonal relationships and one's mental and physical well-being. More specifically, this groundbreaking work focuses on the notion of a social brain that is biologically "wired to connect" with those around us. According to Goleman (2006) "our social interactions even play a role in reshaping our brain, through "neuroplasticity," which means that repeated experiences sculpt the shape, size, and number of neurons and their synaptic connections" (p. 11). Stated more simply, the ongoing relationships that we establish can shape the intricate "wiring" or neural circuitry of our brain. To further emphasize the link between our relationships and our health, Goleman describes unhealthy or abusive relationships as "toxic" to our social brain and healthy relationships are described as "vitamins." Thus, when we are around individuals that love and support us, this experience is analogous to taking vitamins that assist in the functioning of our social brain (Goleman 2006).

Many interpersonal communication scholars would agree that healthy communication is essential to achieving healthy relationships. When communication between individuals deteriorates or ceases to exist, relationships are often doomed for failure. A significant body of research focuses on the relationship between specific communication patterns or practices, such as emotional communication, and relationship satisfaction and longevity (see for example, Burleson and MacGeorge 2002; Burleson and Samter 1996; Metts and Planalp 2002; Noller and Feeney 1994; Roloff and Soule 2002). Interpersonal communication researchers have studied nearly all aspects of romantic and platonic relationships, including how people come together to form meaningful relationships (Knapp and Vangelisti 2000), how they maintain these relationships (Canary and Stafford 2001), the factors individuals consider when deciding to terminate a relationship, and the methods used to disengage these relationships (Baxter 1982; Cody 1982). Learning about effective communication practices can assist individuals throughout every stage of relationship development, from the beginning stages when individuals are uncertain about how to proceed, to the relational maintenance stage, or to the end of a romantic relationship. In this textbook we provide you with several chapters that focus on the stages of relationship development (initiating, maintenance, growing dark, and terminating) as well as the communication practices that both contribute to and detract from a relationship's reported "health."

The following sections of this chapter highlight the broad learning objectives to be addressed throughout this textbook. While there are specific learning objectives and key terms for each chapter, the following three primary objectives are the overall purpose of this textbook.

1. Students will be exposed to and become familiar with a wide range of communication concepts and theories that are central to the process of interpersonal communication.

In this chapter we define interpersonal communication and distinguish it from other forms of communication. Also, in an effort to better understand the "roots" of interpersonal communication, we discuss its history, with an emphasis on classic research and on the historical events that stimulated interest in this topic. Throughout the entire textbook you will see numerous bold-faced terms, concepts, and theories that we consider central to understanding the process of interpersonal communication. Our hope is that you will be able to define these terms and concepts and relate them to your own experiences.

2. Students will become more competent communicators.

We suspect that many of you are taking this course to improve your ability to send and receive messages from others, also known as communication competence. **Communication competence** is defined as the ability to send messages that are perceived as appropriate and effective (Spitzberg and Cupach 1984). The model most often used to describe communication competence is the Components Model advanced by Spitzberg and Cupach. This model highlights three key components of communication competence: knowledge, skill and motivation. The **knowledge** component of this model refers to understanding what reaction or action is best suited for a particular situation. Taking a class in interpersonal communication is the first step in acquiring knowledge and information about the process of forming relationships with others. The

skill component of this model addresses one's ability to utilize the appropriate behaviors in a situation. It is important to remember that there is a difference between *knowing* how to do something (e.g., knowledge of interpersonal models, theories, and concepts) and actually *being able* to do it. For example, a person may understand the principles and concepts associated with managing conflict in relationships. However, when the time comes to put that knowledge to use, it may be difficult to engage in the appropriate behaviors. The final component of the model, **motivation**, refers to one's desire to achieve results in a competent manner. It is not enough to have knowledge and skills. You must also have a desire to achieve communication competence. To assess your current level of communication competence, we suggest you complete the Communication Competence Scale found in the final pages of this chapter at the onset of the course, and then again at the end of the semester.

While we can address the knowledge and skill aspects of communication competence, it is up to you to become more motivated and make attempts to achieve your interpersonal goals. Many of the chapters in this textbook offer valuable information about the communication process and emphasize specific communication behaviors linked to interpersonal communication competence. For example, in Chapters Three and Four we focus on the highly complex process of sending and receiving verbal and nonverbal messages. By calling attention to certain important aspects of nonverbal messages such as dress, body movements, gestures or eye contact, we hope students will hone in on the specific skills needed to communicate more effectively. Our chapter on perception and listening also highlights specific communication behaviors associated with effective communication. We often forget to focus on the process of message reception, which is why listening is often referred to as the "forgotten" communication skill.

3. Students will achieve rewarding personal and professional relationships.

People communicate and ultimately establish different types of relationships to satisfy three universal human needs: control, inclusion and affection (Schutz 1966). We communicate with others and establish relationships to control or manage our surroundings, to be part of a group, and to fulfill the need to feel liked. Virtually every chapter in this textbook explains interpersonal communication concepts and theories that will help you understand how relationships work. By teaching you the important communication concepts that are central to understanding the process of interpersonal communication, and by helping you acquire the skills needed to communicate more effectively, we are certain that our third and final goal will be met. And so we begin our journey by clarifying what we mean when we use the term interpersonal communication.

WHAT EXACTLY IS INTERPERSONAL COMMUNICATION?

Communication researchers continue to study many forms of communication, including

- Mass or mediated communication
- Organizational communication
- Small group communication
- Intrapersonal communication
- Interpersonal communication

© Emiliano Rodriguez, 2007, Shutterstock.

We all want to successfully communicate with others and establish good relationships.

Mass or Mediated Communication

The study of mediated or **mass communication** involves communicators that are typically separated in both space and time and who send and receive messages indirectly. Mass communication typically occurs when a small number of people send messages to a large, diverse and geographically widespread population (Cathcart and Gumpert 1983; Kreps and Thorton 1992).

Organizational Communication

Communication scholars also study **organizational communication,** which is recognized as communication that occurs within businesses or organizations. Organizational communication takes place between organization members within a clear hierarchical structure; individuals are typically encouraged to adhere to roles and rules established within this structure. In this text, we will examine the role of interpersonal communication in organizations, and different types of relationships in this context will be discussed.

Small Group Communication

Small group communication, another area frequently studied by communication scholars, is defined as "interaction among a small group of people who share a common purpose or goal, who feel a sense of belonging to the group, and who exert influence on one another" (Beebe and Masterson 1997, 6). Small group communication is complex and often occurs between three or more people who are interdependent and working to achieve commonly recognized goals or objectives.

Intrapersonal Communication

Intrapersonal communication, the most basic level of communication, takes place inside one's head and is silent and repetitive (Kreps and Thorton 1992). Many of us talk to ourselves which often affects our interpersonal communication decisions. Think about a time when you rehearsed a conversation in your mind before actually engaging in interpersonal communication. Perhaps it was a situation where you were building up the courage to ask someone on a date, or maybe you planned out a conversation with a colleague regarding a project at work.

What are some of the benefits of working in small groups?

© Yuri Arcurs, 2007, Shutterstock.

Interpersonal Communication

Interpersonal communication, sometimes referred to as *dyadic* communication, is often loosely described as communication that occurs between two individuals. While most agree that interpersonal communication typically involves at least two people (Knapp, Daly, Albada and Miller 2002), there is great disparity in the actual definitions advanced by interpersonal communication researchers.

"In some respects, the construct of interpersonal communication is like the phenomenon it represents—that is, dynamic and changing" (Knapp et al. 2002, 8). It is not easy to develop a definition for this concept that is widely agreed upon, although there are certainly some similarities and overlap in the different ways interpersonal communication is typically defined by communication researchers. For example, Booth-Butterfield (2002) says "Interpersonal communication is when we interact on an individual-to-individual basis with someone, and we get beyond the roles in the situation" (p. 3). Similarly,

DeVito (2001) defines interpersonal communication as "the communication that takes place between two persons who have an established relationship; the people are in some way connected" (p. 5). Capella (1987) describes interpersonal communication as one person influencing another person's behavior, above and beyond that explained by "normal baselines of action" (p. 228). All of these definitions mention an exchange of some kind, typically between two individuals. These exchanges can potentially occur face-to-face, over the telephone or via the computer.

Interpersonal communication connects us in our relationships

One area where there appears to be great variability in definitions of interpersonal communication is the "nature of interaction units," or type of interaction, where interpersonal communication typically occurs (Knapp et al. 2002, 9). Similar to Booth-Butterfield and DeVito, we argue that interpersonal communication typically occurs between individuals whose relationship has evolved beyond that of strangers or even acquaintances. Additionally, we agree with Miller and Steinberg (1975) who argue that the extent or degree of "interpersonalness" in a relationship often varies greatly, based on the type of information exchanged between the source and receiver. On any given day, you connect with a variety of people which may include business associates, family members, and relationship partners. We recognize that the communication occurring between a store clerk and a customer is less intimate, or personal, than the communication that occurs between a mother and daughter. For this reason, we note that interpersonal communication occurs along a continuum, with one end representing a type of interpersonal communication often described as "impersonal," and the other end representing a type of interpersonal communication described as "intimate." When we are able to adapt our messages to meet the specific attitudes, beliefs, values, or personality traits of the receiver, our communication is described as exhibiting a higher degree of intimacy. Alternatively, when we communicate with someone at a basic level and have only cultural or sociological information about the receiver, the communication is often described as less interpersonal or impersonal (Knapp et al. 2002). Thus, the communication that occurs in the relationship will often determine whether the relationship is described as impersonal or intimate, or something in between.

We define **interpersonal communication** as a process which occurs in a specific context and involves an exchange of verbal or nonverbal messages between two connected individuals with the intent to achieve shared meaning. While there is a wide range of definitions available, we chose one that emphasizes the importance of communication as a process that consists of both verbal and nonverbal components and results in shared understandings between the interactants. In the following section, we take a closer look at aspects of this definition and important principles of interpersonal communication.

AN OVERVIEW OF THE BASIC PRINCIPLES OF INTERPERSONAL COMMUNICATION

To help you remember some basic principles and terms associated with the process of interpersonal communication, we created the acronym, INTERPERSONAL.

Table 1.1	Basic Principles of Interpersonal Communication
I	Irreversible
N	Not communicating is difficult
T	Transactional
E	Evolving
R	Relational/content components
P	Process
E	Effectiveness important
R	Relationship building
S	Shared meaning/metacommunication
O	Other-oriented
N	Nonverbal messages
A	Abide by rules
L	Learned skill

Irreversible

First, interpersonal communication is irreversible. This means that once you say something, you cannot take it back. It is permanent. You cannot recover by saying, "Oh, forget I said that." Do you remember the last time someone asked you, "How do I look?" The slightest pause or facial expression on your part cannot be taken back once it is detected by the receiver. Once we communicate something, verbally or nonverbally, we must build from it.

Not Communicating Is Difficult

Communication scholars often say that one cannot not communicate because intentional messages are often perceived when sources exhibit nonverbal behaviors such as eye contact, gestures and body movements, facial expressions and touch. It is often the case that receivers perceive these nonverbal behaviors exhibited by sources as intentional nonverbal communication. Picture someone sitting in an apartment, staring straight ahead, her arms across her chest. Her friend walks into the room and asks why she is angry. The friend perceived the staring and crossed arms as the message "I am angry" when, in actuality, the person sitting was daydreaming about getting an extra-large cheese pizza.

Transactional

Next, interpersonal communication is a transactional exchange of verbal and nonverbal messages. **Transactional** refers to the fact that even as we are sending messages, we are receiving them as well. When you talk to your friend, she may smile at you and simultaneously nod her head to show that she is actively listening. At the same time, you notice her new glasses and raise your eyebrows while commenting, "Cool specs! I never knew you wore glasses!" As she listens to your comment, she glances at an attractive male walking past while responding, "I usually wear contacts, but I was too lazy to put them in this morning." In this simple conversation, several verbal and nonverbal messages are being sent and received simultaneously.

Just by looking at their expressions and gestures, can you tell what these individuals are feeling?

Evolving

Since communication in interpersonal relationships is constantly evolving, each time we speak with someone, we are building on previous messages. We are developing a history with this person and, therefore, our communication reflects this change. Think about the conversations you have with your closest friends. Because you have probably spent countless hours discussing family, friends, career goals and other mutual topics of interest, it is not necessary to revisit these conversations in detail each time you see each other. Instead, you may make quick references to previously discussed events in your conversations. You may ask your friend questions such as "How is your brother recovering from his skateboarding accident?" or "Why do you think Bob ended your relationship by saying, 'Let's just be friends'?" Asking these types of questions illustrates how conversations and relationships evolve over time.

Relational/Content Components

Each message exchanged between interactants is made up of two types of meaning: content and relational (Bateson 1951). The **content,** or informational component of a message, is the verbal message you send, the words you choose. The **relational component** of a message, which includes nonverbal messages such as eye contact, gestures, and vocal inflection, tells the receiver how you would like the message to be interpreted. Consider the following situation.

> A mother is waiting for her son to come home from an unexpected late night out with friends. She is quite angry because her son has been out two hours after his curfew. The mother is standing guard by the front door with her arms crossed and teeth clenched. As soon as her son comes home, he opens the door and sees her standing right inside the front door looking very frustrated. She says, "Where have you been? Why didn't you call me to tell me you were running late?"

The content information is simply her questions. The relational information is unique to the relationship between the mother and son. How does the speaker want the receiver to interpret the message? How do they feel towards each other? These feelings are conveyed through the nonverbal actions of the speaker such as the mother's clenched teeth, crossed arms, and angry tone of voice. In order to interpret messages accurately, it is important to pay close attention to both the content and relational components of messages.

Process

Interpersonal communication is often described as a **process** because it is continuous, or ongoing (Berlo 1960). While verbal messages may have clear beginnings and endings, nonverbal messages do not. Whether or not we are aware of it, we constantly send messages to others about our attitudes, moods, and personalities through our clothing choices, facial expressions, bodily movements, and gestures. Communication is also described as a complex process that involves many different steps. For example, the listening process involves receiving the message, selecting components or aspects of the message to process, interpreting the message, responding to the message, and remembering important aspects of the message at a later date.

Effective Communication Is More Important than More Communication

We must remember: we determine the effectiveness of our interactions based on the quality of our communication, not the quantity or amount of words exchanged between individuals. Sometimes it is important to adhere to the "less is more" principle when engaging in communication with others. Consider taking a road trip with a friend. Would you rather be driving with someone that never stops talking or with someone that does not speak as much, but when he does, tells a funny, meaningful story, or shares some interesting news? Being appropriate with our communication is much more important than talking all the time.

Effective interpersonal communication builds trust and establishes relationships between people.

© Andrew Gentry, 2007, Shutterstock.

Relationship Building

An essential function of interpersonal communication is relationship building. We use interpersonal communication to self-disclose, listen, build trust, and establish relationships. It is impossible to form healthy relationships without effective communication.

Shared Meaning

Shared meaning is the goal of our interpersonal communication interactions. We do this by collaborating during the communication process in an effort to reduce ambiguity about what verbal and nonverbal messages mean. Although we may never share exactly the same understanding with someone, we work to find common experiences and, at the same time, increase our chances for successful interpersonal exchanges. Often people engage in what Gregory Bateson (1972) conceptualized as **metacommunication,** "communicating about communication," when they want to clarify a message's meaning. A friend might say to her roommate, "What did you mean when you said 'I am fine' in that tone of voice?" Or a man might ask his significant other, "I think we need to talk about why you've been so quiet lately." Meta-communication is used during social interaction to increase our shared meaning and to reduce uncertainty about the status of our relationships.

Other-Oriented

Interpersonal communication should be other-oriented. We need to create messages in a way that ensures our audience will understand them. Using appropriate language in a given context is critical to our success as communicators. Have you ever had professors who lectured over your head? Perhaps they used terminology that was unfamiliar to the students, or moved quickly without considering whether students understood the material. Unfortunately, professors like this do not realize how important it is to alter their messages to accommodate the different perspectives and levels of student learning. Regardless of what a professor might intend to say, what matters most is what the students actually perceive. This is why feedback, listening, and dual-perspective taking are critical to effective communication. These concepts will be discussed in greater detail in Chapter Five.

© Galina Barskaya, 2007, Shutterstock.   © Zsolt Nyulaszi, 2007, Shutterstock.   © Bartosz Ostrowski, 2007, Shutterstock.

What can you learn about these people by reading their nonverbal messages?

Nonverbal Messages

Communication is often defined as the process of sending verbal and nonverbal messages to a receiver. The **verbal component** consists of the words we choose. The **nonverbal component** comprises everything other than the words including, among other behaviors: eye contact, hand gestures, facial expressions, volume, and tone of voice. There are many times when the verbal component of our message suggests one idea, while the nonverbal component indicates a quite different message. When there is a contradiction between the nonverbal and verbal messages, we tend to believe the nonverbal message because it is often perceived as involuntary, or less controllable. Because we know that individuals place more weight on the nonverbal component of a message, we will often use nonverbal messages strategically to contradict the verbal message. For example, a person says sarcastically, "Yeah, I just loved the movie *Gigli* with Jennifer Lopez and Ben Affleck," while he rolls his eyes. The verbal message suggests he does indeed like the movie, while the nonverbal message suggests exactly the opposite.

Nonverbal Messages Are More Believable

Nonverbal messages tend to be taken more seriously than verbal messages in our culture. The well-known phrase "actions speak louder than words" is based on this principle. Verbal and nonverbal messages are discussed in much greater detail in Chapters Three and Four.

Abide by Rules When Interacting with Others

Another principle of interpersonal communication is that we abide by rules when interacting with others. In fact, much of our communication is governed by *rules*. What are some examples of appropriate guidelines, or **rules,** for communicating in the classroom? When we ask students this question, they often point out the importance of paying attention in class, not talking while the instructor is lecturing, and turning off cellular phones during class time. We learn rules like these through interacting with others, a trial and error process. While it may seem unlikely that the same rules apply to everyone regardless of individual differences such as sex, age, culture, and personality, it is important to realize that people are not completely random in their behavior. We recognize that there is no magic formula or single rule that will work with everyone in every situation; however, we are interested in the research findings that significantly contribute to the interpersonal communication literature. In this textbook, we identify common themes from interpersonal communication research that can help predict successful or unsuccessful communication outcomes.

Learned Skill

Finally, interpersonal communication is a learned skill. We are born with the capability to communicate, but we must work at improving our communication skills to reduce misunderstandings with others. It is through repeated social interactions, taking courses like this one, and reading about communication processes that we learn the most appropriate and effective ways to send and receive messages. Although some people may seem to be "naturals" when it comes to relating to others, virtually everyone struggles with certain types of communication situations. By completing this course you should develop a more sophisticated understanding of communication concepts, theories, and research, which are central to the study of interpersonal communication. Interpersonal communication students should be able to identify and implement communication skills associated with communication competence and to understand relationship development processes. It is also important for students to understand the history of this academic area and identify significant research and historical events that have contributed to this field. In the following sections, we present a brief overview of what some interpersonal scholars view as the history of interpersonal communication (Knapp, Daly, Albada, and Miller 2002).

HISTORY OF INTERPERSONAL COMMUNICATION

In order to completely understand an academic area, you must start at its roots. In the *Handbook of Interpersonal Communication*, Knapp, Daly, Albada and Miller (2002) provide an overview of the historical foundations of the field of interpersonal communication. The introductory chapter of the *Handbook* is dedicated to providing a framework for tracing the development of the field. Readers are presented with a timeline highlighting the accomplishments of scholars who have made prominent contributions to the understanding of relational communication.

According to Knapp and his colleagues (2002) one of the most influential studies for providing a framework for both interpersonal and organizational communication was the result of research conducted by Elton Mayo from 1927 until 1932 at the Western Electric Hawthorne Works in Chicago. Mayo, a professor at the Harvard Business School, originally designed the study to examine the impact of fatigue and monotony on work production. But while the study was designed to focus on one aspect of the work process, an interesting thing happened. Mayo discovered that social relationships and, more specifically, interactions between co-workers and supervisors, resulted in higher productivity. The Mayo study is an excellent example of how researchers sometimes stumble upon unexpected results that change the way we view phenomena.

During the 1930s, a series of research studies was conducted by scholars in other disciplines. These would provide the groundwork for the field of interpersonal communication. Researchers had begun to systematically study children's interactions to learn more about patterns of social interaction and role taking behavior (see, for example, Piaget 1926). Also during this time period, George Herbert Mead, a philosophy professor from the University of Chicago, studied the relationship between the meanings that result from our interactions with others and our sense of self. Mead is often credited with the theory which came to be known as symbolic interactionism.

Herbert Blumer, a colleague from the University of California-Berkeley, actually coined the term **symbolic interactionism** and described this concept as a "label for a relatively distinctive approach to the study of human group life and human conduct" (Blumer 1969, 1). One of the first premises of this theory is that people form meanings based on the symbols used in interactions. These symbols include words or messages, roles that people play, gestures, and even rules that exist for interactions. The theory of symbolic interaction is significant because it recognizes the importance of our responses to symbols or words and the impact this has on the development of self. Consider your current role as a college student. It is likely that you gained the self-confidence to pursue a college degree as a result of the encouragement you received from parents and teachers, as well as the expectations that you and your family members have for your future education. Perhaps when you were in high school, someone asked you which college you planned to attend. All of these symbols helped shape your perception of self.

Also during this period, Abraham Maslow, a psychology professor at Brooklyn College, strove to understand the forces that cause humans to engage in certain behaviors. Beginning in 1939, he conducted research that specifically focused on human needs, resulting in the pyramid that has become widely known as **Maslow's Hierarchy of Needs.** Many of these needs have been identified as forces which motivate people to form interpersonal relationships with one another. Once the basic physiological and safety needs have been fulfilled, humans seek to fulfill the love and belonging needs by interacting with other individuals. As a result of our interactions with others, self-esteem needs, the fourth level of Maslow's hierarchy are addressed. Messages received from others are influential in forming one's self-esteem and tackling issues of identity (Maslow 1943).

Progressing into the 1950s and 60s, new scholars produced significant research that began shaping and defining the field of interpersonal communication as it evolved into its own discipline. In the 1950s, anthropologist Ray Birdwhistell (1952) created the term **kinesics** to refer to the use of body movements and gestures as forms of communication. In the late 1950s and early 60s, anthropologist Edward T. Hall focused on the role of space, or **proxemics,** in shaping and influencing our interactions with others (1959). While the study of nonverbal behaviors has evolved as an intriguing aspect of interpersonal interactions, additional studies during this time contributed to our understanding of the role of self and others in relationships.

In 1959, sociologist Erving Goffman published *The Presentation of Self in Everyday Life.* His work has served as the foundation for communications scholars' understanding of the role that impression management plays in our interactions with others. Goffman's work has been influential in shaping many subsequent theories of self-versus-other perceptions in interpersonal relationships. During this same time, Fritz Heider, a psychologist who taught at the University of Kansas, published work that addressed how attributions shape our interactions with others (Heider 1958). **Attribution theory** has been influential in interpersonal studies because it addresses the judgments that we make when we communicate with others. Research on relationship initiation has drawn from Heider's work to explain the evolving process of attributions as we make decisions to pursue interactions.

While these prominent scholars provided a solid foundation for our current approaches to investigating interpersonal relationships, you may have noticed that they are not communication researchers. Scholars often cross boundaries and build on ideas initiated by researchers in other fields. Recognizing the contributions that scholars in the fields of psychology, sociology and anthropology have made to the communication discipline is critical to understanding the interdisciplinary nature of our work. It is fascinating to explore human relationships from such a variety of perspectives! In fact, as you take classes in other disciplines, you may learn about some of the same theories and concepts that were presented in your communication classes.

While the study of communication has existed for decades, it was not until the late 1960s and into the 70s and 80s that interpersonal communication scholars began to carve out their own niche in the study of human communication and to clearly define the study of interactions in relationships. Increasing political and social unrest in the late 60s and early 70s caused scholars to direct their attention to individuals and their relationships. Significant historical events like the Civil Rights movement and the Vietnam War stimulated research activity in such areas as group dynamics, decision-making, and conflict resolution. In 1967, *Pragmatics of Human Communication* was published (Watzlawick, Beavin, and Jackson) and was one of the first books to adopt an interactional approach to communication. In the first chapter of the book, the authors acknowledge that each communication situation involves a "frame of reference." Two key concepts that have become central to the study of interpersonal communication are addressed in this initial chapter–the relationship between communication partners and the function of the communication interaction. As a result of this groundbreaking text, colleges and universities added courses focusing specifically on the dynamics of interpersonal communication. Other textbooks soon followed (Keltner 1970; McCroskey, Larson, and Knapp 1971; Giffin and Patton 1971).

As the level of interest in interpersonal communication mushroomed, scholars in the discipline turned their attention to research studies designed to explain the dynamics of relationships. Professional associations at the international, national, and regional levels formed interest groups and divisions devoted to interpersonal topics. By the late 1970s, interpersonal communication had become firmly established as a prominent field of study. During the early 1980s, it was difficult to open an issue of any leading communication journal and not find an article pertaining to research on interpersonal communication. Scholars began directing their attention to developing and testing theories directly related to interpersonal interactions.

INTERPERSONAL COMMUNICATION THEORY

Many significant theoretical contributions are provided in the historical foundations of interpersonal communication. While you may experience a heightened sense of anxiety when your instructor mentions "theory," the concepts are actually quite simple and very useful. A **theory** is nothing more than a set of statements about the way things work. Julia Wood (2000) recognizes theories as "human constructions—symbolic ways we represent phenomena" (p. 33) and notes that we use theories to achieve one of four basic goals. The four widely recognized goals of a theory are: (1) to describe phenomena, (2) to explain how something works, (3) to understand, predict and control occurrences, and (4) to make social change (Wood 2000). As students of communication, you will find theories to be useful tools for explaining interactions or categorizing behaviors.

Over the past thirty years, interpersonal communication scholars have truly made their mark as a core focus in the field of communication studies. While the seeds for many of today's prominent interpersonal theories may have been planted by experts in the fields of psychology, sociology and anthropology, the discipline has grown into an area that interpersonal researchers have defined as their own. In fact, scholars who study communication in other contexts (i.e., instructional communication, organizational communication, intercultural communication) are now applying interpersonal theories as the foundation for studying interactions in other areas.

Many different theories will be discussed throughout this text as we explore key components of interpersonal communication in a variety of contexts. Here is an overview of some of the prominent theories and their corresponding chapter or chapters.

- Attachment Theory (2, 11)
- Attribution Theory (5, 9)
- Covariation Theory (5)
- Equity Theory (7, 9)
- Family Communication Patterns Theory (11)
- Interpersonal Deception Theory (8)
- Leader-member Exchange Theory (12)
- Nonverbal Expectancy Violation Theory (4)
- Relational Dialectics (12)
- Self-determination Theory (9)
- Social Comparison Theory (2)
- Social Exchange Theory (6, 9)
- Social Identity Theory (5)
- Social Penetration Theory (6)
- Symbolic Interaction Theory (11)
- Systems Theory (11)
- Uncertainty Reduction Theory (3, 6)

OVERVIEW OF THE TEXTBOOK

The organization of this book is three-fold. Part I provides an overview of the basic concepts and theories which are central to the understanding of inter-personal communication. Chapter One will introduce the background, fundamentals, and key components of interpersonal communication. In Chapter Two we will explore self identity formation and the role individual differences play in our communication style with others. Chapter Three discusses how verbal communication is used to shape meaning in others and examines how certain words provoke certain responses. Chapter Four identifies several dimensions of nonverbal communication and their functions. The last chapter in Part I, Chapter Five, provides an overview of perception (selection, organization and interpretation) and listening. This chapter also addresses the significance of listening as part of the communication process and offers suggestions for improving our listening skills.

Part II of the textbook will explore how relationships typically develop, discussing communication practices exhibited during the outlined stages that either facilitate or hinder relationship growth and development. Chapter Six identifies characteristics that draw us to others and examines how we communicate in initial interactions. In Chapter Seven, relationship maintenance strategies are offered and conflict management is discussed as a natural progression of relationships. If conflict is not managed properly, it may turn dark. Chapter Eight discusses the dark side of communication: jealousy, deception, power and obsession. The last chapter in Part II, Chapter Nine, provides a detailed overview of the relationship termination process. This chapter walks you through the process of relationship disengagement, decision making, and strategies for moving on.

Part III of our text is devoted to what Knapp and Daly (2002) identify in the *Handbook of Interpersonal Communication* as trends that communication scholars are paying increasing attention to in their research. Some of these trends include: an increased emphasis on the role of cultural differences in interpersonal interactions; an examination of interpersonal communication in applied settings such as health, family and organizations; and the impact of technology on interpersonal communication. Chapter Ten addresses communication with diverse populations and highlights important areas of miscommunication between individuals of different ages, sexes, races and/ or cultures. Next, Chapter Eleven examines one area of applied communication research, family communication. The family communication chapter will discuss communication issues that occur across the family lifespan and across family relationships. Sibling, marital, and parent-child relationships will also be addressed in this chapter. In addition, Chapter Eleven will identify productive communication strategies and difficult communication situations that occur within the family. Communication in the workplace is another applied communication area that continues to be a popular research area for scholars. Chapter Twelve will introduce the unique aspects of organizational communication such as the development of superior-subordinate relationships, peer relationships, friendships, mentoring, and romantic relationships. Another type of applied communication that has received much attention in the literature is health communication. In Chapter Thirteen we identify situations that produce anxiety, typical responses to these health-related situations, and how we can improve our communication during these situations. Our final chapter will examine the impact of technology on our interpersonal relationships. Chapter Fourteen will provide an overview of the computer-mediated communication research. People rely heavily on various forms of online communication to form and maintain relationships with others. Consider the impact of technology on your own communication with friends and family members. Technologies such as the Blackberry and Pocket PCs have enabled colleagues to communicate with one another beyond the confines of the office walls. These and other computer-mediated communication issues will be addressed in the final chapter, Chapter Fourteen.

SUMMARY

This chapter provided a framework for the interpersonal communication discipline. We defined interpersonal communication and distinguished it from other types of communication. We identified key interpersonal communication principles and even developed an acronym to help you remember them! Finally, we provided an overview of the history of interpersonal communication to help you understand the roots of this discipline and contributions from scholars in others fields. Now it is time to embark on your interpersonal journey. As you read through the following chapters in Part I, you will explore other fundamental concepts of interpersonal communication. Part II will trace interpersonal relationships from initiation to termination. The final chapters, found in Part III, will examine interpersonal communication across contexts such as intercultural, family, organizational and computer-mediated communication. Bestselling author, Father John Powell said, "Communication works for those who work at it." Go work at it!

ACTIVITIES

Activity #1:   **Complete the Communication Competence Scale**

Place the number on the line that best describes your agreement with the items below, using the following scale:

Strongly Agree	Agree	Undecided	Disagree	Strongly Disagree
5	4	3	2	1

_____ 1.   I find it easy to get along with others.
_____ 2.   I can adapt to changing situations.
_____ 3.   I treat people as individuals.
_____ 4.   I interrupt others too much.
_____ 5.   I am rewarding to talk to.
_____ 6.   I can deal with others effectively.
_____ 7.   I am a good listener.
_____ 8.   My personal relations are cold and distant.
_____ 9.   I am easy to talk to.
_____ 10.   I won't argue with someone just to prove he/she is right.
_____ 11.   My conversation behavior is not "smooth."
_____ 12.   I ignore other people's feelings.
_____ 13.   I generally know how others feel.
_____ 14.   I let others know I understand them.
_____ 15.   I understand other people.
_____ 16.   I am relaxed and comfortable when speaking.
_____ 17.   I listen to what people say to me.
_____ 18.   I like to be close and personal with people.
_____ 19.   I generally know what type of behavior is appropriate in any given situation.
_____ 20.   I usually do not make unusual demands on my friends.
_____ 21.   I am an effective conversationalist.
_____ 22.   I am supportive of others.
_____ 23.   I do not mind meeting strangers.
_____ 24.   I can easily put myself in another person's shoes.
_____ 25.   I pay attention to the conversation.
_____ 26.   I am generally relaxed when conversing with a new acquaintance.
_____ 27.   I am interested in what others have to say.
_____ 28.   I don't follow the conversation very well.
_____ 29.   I enjoy social gatherings where I can meet new people.
_____ 30.   I am a likeable person.
_____ 31.   I am flexible.
_____ 32.   I am not afraid to speak with people in authority.
_____ 33.   People can come to me with their problems.
_____ 34.   I generally say the right thing at the right time.
_____ 35.   I like to use my voice and body expressively.
_____ 36.   I am sensitive to others' needs of the moment.

Note: Items 4, 8, 11, 12, and 28 are reverse-coded before summing the 36 items.

Human Communication Research by INTERNATIONAL COMMUNICATION ASSOCIATION. Reproduced with permission of BLACKWELL PUBLISHING, INC. in the format Republish in a book via Copyright Clearance Center.

Evaluating Your Communication Competence

Activity #2:

Type: Self-Reflection Exercise

Recall the three components to communication competence: knowledge, skill, and motivation. Identify your strongest component and discuss why.
Identify your weakest component and discuss why.

Exploring Interpersonal Communication across Contexts

Activity #3:

Type: Class Discussion

Think about the different types of interpersonal communication relationships you have. Fill in the following chart by identifying specific interpersonal relationships that exist across the contexts. Then provide a sample dialogue of communication topics for each.

Interpersonal Context	Interpersonal Relationship	Dialogue Sample
Organizational (example)	Manager to employer	"Denise, let's meet after lunch to discuss your progress."
Health Communication		
Computer Mediated		
Intercultural		
Family		

REFERENCES

Bardwell, C. 2001. Making the transition from college to the world of work. *Black Collegian*, April, 1–2.

Barnlund, D. C. 1970. A transactional model of communication. In K. K. Sereno and C. D. Mortensen (Eds.), *Foundations of communication theory* (pp. 83–102). New York: Harper and Row.

Bateson, G. 1951. Information and codification: A philosophical approach. In J. Ruesch and G. Bateson (Eds.), *Communication: The social matrix of psychiatry.* New York: Wiley and Sons.

———. 1972. *Steps to an ecology of mind.* New York: Ballantine Books.

Bauman, S. 2003. Design engineers evaluate their education. *AIAA Bulletin*, B5.

Baxter, L. 1982. Strategies for ending relationships: Two studies. *The Western Journal of Speech Communication, 46*, 223–241.

Beebe, S. A., and J. T. Masterson. 1997. *Communicating in Small Groups (5th ed.).* New York: Addison-Wesley Longman.

Berlo, D. K. 1960. *The process of communication.* San Francisco: Rinehart.

Birdwhistell, R. L. 1952. *Introduction to kinesics: An annotation system for analysis of body motion and gesture.* Washington, DC: U.S. Department of State, Foreign Service Institute.

Blumer, H. 1969. *Symbolic interactionism: Perspective and method.* Englewood Cliffs, NJ: Prentice-Hall.

Booth-Butterfield, M. 2002. *Interpersonal essentials.* Boston, MA: Allyn & Bacon.

Burleson, B. R., and E. L. MacGeorge. 2002. Supportive Communication. In M. L. Knapp, and J. A. Daly (Eds.), *Handbook of Interpersonal Communication* (pp. 374–424). Thousand Oaks, CA: Sage.

Burleson, B. R., and W. Samter. 1996. Similarity in the communication skills of young adults: Foundations of attraction, friendship, and relationship satisfaction. *Communication Reports, 9*, 127–139.

Canary, D. J., and L. Stafford. 2001. Equity in the preservation of personal relationships. In J. H. Harvey and A. Wenzel (Eds.), *Close romantic relationships: Maintenance and enhancement* (pp. 133–151). Mahwah, NJ: Lawrence Erlbaum.

Cappella, J. N. 1987. Interpersonal communication: Definitions and fundamental questions. In C. R. Berger and S. H. Chaffee (Eds.), *Handbook of communication science.* Newbury Park, CA: Sage.

Cathcart, R., and G. Gumpert. 1983. Mediated interpersonal communication: Toward a new typology. *Quarterly Journal of Speech, 69,* 267–277.

Chelune, G. J., E. Waring, B. Yosk, F. Sultan, and J. Ogden. 1984. Self-disclosure and its relationship to marital intimacy. *Journal of Clinical Psychology, 40,* 216–219.

Cody, M. 1982. A typology of disengagement strategies and an examination of the role intimacy, reactions to inequity, and relational problems play in strategy selection. *Communication Monographs, 49,* 148–170.

Crosby, F. E., J. D. Dunn, M. D. Fallacaro, C. Jozwiak-Shields, and A. M. Maclsaac. 2003. Preadmission characteristics of advanced nursing practice students. *Journal of the Academy of Nurse Practitioners, 15,* 424–431.

DeVito, J. 2001. *The Interpersonal Communication Book (9th ed.).* New York: Addison Wesley Longman Inc.

Giffin, K., and B. R. Patton. 1971. *Fundamentals of interpersonal communication.* New York, NY: Harper & Row.

Goffman, E. 1959. *The presentation of self in everyday life.* Garden City, NY: Doubleday.

Goleman, D. 1995. *Emotional Intelligence: Why it can matter more than IQ.* New York: Bantam.

Goleman, D. 2006. *Social intelligence: The new science of human relationships.* New York, NY: Bantam Dell.

Gottman, J. 1979. *Marital interaction: Experimental investigations.* New York: Academic Press.

Hall, E. T. 1959. *The silent language.* Garden City, NY: Doubleday.

Heider, F. 1958. *The psychology of interpersonal relations.* New York, NY: Wiley.

Keltner, J. W. 1970. *Interpersonal speech-communication: Elements and structures.* Belmont, CA: Wadsworth.

Knapp, M. L., and A. Vangelisti. 2000. *Interpersonal communication and human relationships.* Boston: Allyn & Bacon.

Knapp, M. L., J. A. Daly, K. F. Albada, and G. R. Miller. 2002. Background and current trends in the study of interpersonal communication. In M. L. Knapp and J. A. Daly (Eds.), *Handbook of Interpersonal Communication* (pp. 3–20). Thousand Oaks, CA: Sage.

Kreps, G. L., and B. C. Thorton. 1992. *Health Communication: Theory & Practice.* Prospect Heights, Illinois: Waveland Press.

Manssour, A. B. B. 2003. Interpersonal communication and creativity in journalistic telework. *Cyberpsychology & Behavior, 6,* 41–48.

Maslow, A. H. 1943. A theory of human motivation. *Psychological Review, 50,* 370–396.

McCroskey, J. C., C. Larson, and M. L. Knapp. 1971. *An introduction to interpersonal communication.* Englewood Cliffs, NJ: Prentice-Hall.

Metts, S., and S. Planap. 2002. Emotional Communication. In M. L. Knapp and J. A. Daly (Eds.), *Handbook of Interpersonal Communication* (pp. 339–373). Thousand Oaks, CA: Sage.

Miller, G. R., and M. Steinberg. 1975. *Between people: A new analysis of interpersonal communication.* Chicago: Science Research Associates.

Montgomery, B. M. 1988. Quality communication in personal relationships. In S. Duck (Ed.), *Handbook of personal relationships: Theory, research, and interventions.* (pp. 343–362).

Myers, L. L., and M. L. Tucker. 2005. Increasing awareness of emotional intelligence in a business curriculum. *Business Communication Quarterly, 68,* 44–51.

Noller, P., and J. A. Feeney. 1994. Relationship satisfaction, attachment and nonverbal accuracy in early marriage. *Journal of Nonverbal Behavior, 18,* 199–222.

Omarzu, J., J. Whalen, and J. H. Harvey. 2001. How well do you mind your relationship? A preliminary scale to test the minding theory of relating. In Harvey, J. and A. Wenzel. (Eds.), *Close romantic relationships: Maintenance and enhancement* (pp. 345–356). Mahwah, NJ: Lawrence Erlbaum.

Peterson, M. S. 1997. Personnel interviewers' perceptions of the importance and adequacy of applicants' communication skills. *Communication Education, 46,* 287–291.

Piaget, J. 1926. *The language and thought of the child.* New York: Harcourt Brace.

Rath, D., P. Poldre, B. J. Fisher, J. C. Laidlaw, D. H. Cowan, and D. Bakker. 1998. Commitment of a cancer organization to a program for training in communication skills. *Journal of Cancer Education: The Official Journal of the American Association for Cancer Education, 13,* 203–206.

Roloff, M. E. and K. P. Soule. 2002. Interpersonal conflict: A review. In M. L. Knapp and J. A. Daly (Eds.), *Handbook of interpersonal communication* (pp. 475–528). Thousand Oaks, CA: Sage.

Rusbult, C. E., D. J. Johnson, and G. D. Morrow. 1986. Impact of couple patterns of problem solving on distress and nondistress in dating relationships. *Journal of Experimental Social Psychology, 19,* 274–293.

Schramm, W. L. 1954. *The process and effects of mass communication.* Urbana, IL: University of Ilinois.

Schutz, W. 1966. *The interpersonal underworld* (pp. 13–20). Palo Alto, CA: Science and Behavior Books.

Shannon, C. E., and W. Weaver. 1949. *The mathematical theory of communication.* Urbana, IL: University of Illinois.

Spitzberg, B. H., and W. R. Cupach. 1984. *Interpersonal communication competence.* Beverly Hills, CA: Sage.

Thompson, T. L. 1986. *Communication for health professionals.* Lanham, MD: University Press of America.

Utley-Smith, Q. 2004. Needed by new baccalaureate graduates. *Nursing Education Perspectives, 25,* 166–170.

Wanzer, M. B., M. Booth-Butterfield, and K. Gruber. 2004. Perceptions of health care providers' communication: Relationships between patient-centered communication and satisfaction. *Health Communication, 16,* 363–384.

Watzlawick, P., J. Beavin, and D. D. Jackson. 1967. *Pragmatics of human communication.* New York: Norton.

Wood, J. T. 2000. *Communication Theories in Action.* Wadsworth: Belmont, CA.

Verbal Communication
Words of Wisdom

OBJECTIVES

- Define verbal communication
- Understand the characteristics of verbal communication
- Distinguish between connotative and denotative meaning
- Differentiate between relational and content levels of meaning
- Explain the difference between constitutive and regulative rules
- Describe the four functions of verbal communication
- Explain the Sapir-Whorf hypothesis
- Explore how uncertainty reduction is associated with verbal communication
- Discuss the difference between direct and indirect verbal communication styles
- Clarify the difference between informal and formal messages
- Distinguish between powerful and powerless language
- Provide examples of sexist language in our culture
- Define hate speech
- Understand verbal immediacy and how it contributes to confirming or disconfirming messages
- Identify how the life span factor impacts verbal communication
- Recognize gender differences in verbal communication
- Recall three verbal communication "Best Practices"

© PhotoCreate, 2007, Shutterstock.

KEY TERMS

verbal communication
rules
constitutive rules
regulative rules
symbols
—concrete
—abstract
semantics
denotative meaning
connotative meaning
subjective
relationship level of
   meaning
content level of
   meaning

context
jargon
cognitive function
Uncertainty Reduction
   Theory
self-disclosure
linguistic
   determinism
linguistic relativity
Sapir-Whorf
   hypothesis
direct/indirect
formal/informal
clarity
equivocation

powerful language
powerless language
credibility
competence
character
goodwill
status
sexist language
hate speech
immediacy
verbal immediacy
confirmation
Messxage Design
   Logics (MDL)
—expressive

—conventional	Predicament of Aging	report talk
—rhetorical	Model	concreteness
Communication	rapport talk	

OVERVIEW

Words are, of course, the most powerful drug used by mankind . . .
—Rudyard Kipling

Like a drug, the words we use in our interpersonal interactions can alter and influence relationships. Depending on our goals, verbal communication can be used to enhance our relationships or to destroy them. We have the power to make others feel competent, attractive, and strong. On the other hand, we know how to upset and annoy others, and to make them feel weak. This chapter discusses how the words we use impact our interpersonal relationships.

We begin by defining verbal communication and examining several of its distinct features and functions. We continue by examining factors that impact our verbal communication and how it is perceived by others.

DEFINING VERBAL COMMUNICATION

Verbal communication refers to the words we use during the communication process. We use words strategically to relate to the outside world and to create meaning. Have you ever played the game charades and attempted to convey a message to others without using words? Have you ever tried to communicate with someone who did not speak your language? These two examples illustrate how difficult it can be to express ourselves without relying on verbal communication. The words we use have a strong impact on our interpersonal relationships. What we say initially often determines whether we will have future interactions with others. There are four key characteristics of verbal communication. These include: rules, symbols, subjectivity, and context.

What constitutive rules do parents and children have for communicating mutual respect?

© digitalskillet, 2007, Shutterstock.

Rules

It is important to realize that there are certain rules we must follow when using language. **Rules** are agreed upon and provide a structure for what is socially acceptable communication in our culture. You follow certain rules when talking with your friends that are quite different than when you talk with your grandparents. There are two basic types of rules that relate to verbal communication: constitutive and regulative (Cronen, Pearce, and Snavely 1979; Pearce, Cronen and Conklin 1979). **Constitutive rules** help define communication by identifying appropriate words and behaviors. For example, how do you show respect in a classroom? Students follow constitutive rules in the classroom when they address their professors formally, using Dr., Mr., or Mrs. Constitutive rules are also in effect when students avoid using slang or swear words. Failure to understand appropriate rules can be detrimental to a student's success as an appropriate and effective interpersonal communicator. Can you think of the constitutive rules you would follow during a business interview?

Regulative rules control our communication by managing communication interaction. Who are we supposed to talk with and how should we speak to this person? What topics are acceptable? For how long should we talk? Think about the regulative rules in the classroom. Students greet each other when they enter the classroom, they do not interrupt the professor, and they take turns speaking. These rules are context-bound, that is to say, the rules will change depending on the audience and context. Our verbal communication is governed by constitutive and regulative rules and through language structure. This makes it possible for us to create shared meaning and have a common understanding of appropriateness across contexts.

What regulative rules do you practice in the classroom?

Symbols

A second feature of verbal communication is that it is symbolic. **Symbols** are socially agreed upon representations of phenomena and range between being concrete and abstract. **Concrete symbols** are more likely to resemble what they represent. **Abstract symbols** are arbitrary and nonrepresentational. For example, a chair is used to sit on and is a concrete symbol. However, the printed word "chair" is abstract and arbitrary. The more concrete (and therefore less abstract) a symbol is, the more it is associated with its meaning. Verbal communication is made up of abstract, arbitrary, and agreed upon concrete symbols or words.

It is difficult to discuss symbols without discussing **semantics**, or the meaning, we attribute to each word or symbol. When people interpret words they focus on both the denotative and connotative meanings. The **denotative meaning** refers to the universal meaning of the word, or the definition you would find in the dictionary. The **connotative meaning** refers to the personal meaning that the source has with that word. For example, the word "fireplace" connotes hospitality and warmth. Connotative meanings are difficult to explain because they can be different for everyone. This leads us to the third characteristic of verbal communication, subjectivity.

Subjectivity

Because everyone has a unique worldview, the way we use and interpret verbal communication is strongly influenced by individual biases. Verbal communication is **subjective** because we interpret the world through our own experiences, historical perspective and cultural upbringing, our physical environment, and the socio-emotional nature of relationships. Our perceptions are distinct and limited to our own personal field of experience and developed schema.

The subjective meanings we place on our verbal communication have relationship and content levels of meaning. The **relationship level of meaning** is highly sensitive to the people involved in the conversation and the process of communicating, whereas the **content level of meaning** is primarily related to the topic at hand.

Consider the following conversation:

Samantha: Do you want to come to my mom's birthday party?

Edgar: Well, it is in an hour and I am in the middle of working on the house.

Samantha: So, you don't want to come?

Edgar: Well, the contractor is coming tomorrow so I have to get this done.

Samantha: You missed my sister's birthday party, also. I am starting to think you just don't want to spend time with my family.

Edgar: That is not true. I just have to get this work done.

Samantha: I cannot believe you are going to miss the birthday party.

Edgar: Do you want me to drop everything and come?

Samantha: I shouldn't have to tell you what to do; you should know what the right thing to do is.

Edgar: I am sorry, but I have to finish this project before the contractor comes.

The conversation above illustrates a common problem in interpersonal relationships: one party is focused on the content level of meaning and the other is interested in the relationship level of meaning. Edgar is focused on the content or the information in the message, while Samantha is concerned with how the communication process is affecting the relationship. Edgar is determined to finish working on the house and cannot understand why Samantha would be upset. Samantha feels Edgar is not really listening to what she is saying and does not understand. The content level of meaning is found in the words we use and the relationship level of meaning is often interpreted through our nonverbal behaviors, through how something is said. Because of Edgar's past behavior and concern for the house, Samantha perceived his nonverbal behavior as insincere. Edgar, however, heard Samantha complaining about not going to the birthday party and offered a valid reason for not attending. When one individual is relying on content level of meaning and the other is focused on the relationship level of meaning, often a source of conflict is the result. Overall, verbal communication is widely subjective and a function of our personal associations and the meanings we place on words, situations, and experiences. In order to improve our communication with others, it is important to seek clarification of ambiguous messages, identify areas of miscommunication, and talk about ways to improve communication. Relationship partners need to engage in productive metacommunication, which means that they need to talk in greater detail about both the quality and quantity of messages exchanged.

Context

The final feature of verbal communication is the contextual framework. The **context** refers to the environment, situation, or setting in which we use verbal communication. The context may influence the interpretation, meaning and appropriateness of the communication. For example, we may use a particular greeting with our roommates such as, "What's up?", while we may choose alternative words when we are greeting our grandparents, such as "Good morning, Grandfather!" The interpretation of our words changes when we consider the context in which they are used. In the last section of this textbook, we will review five general contexts in which interpersonal communication occurs. These are: intercultural communication, family communication, organizational communication, health communication, and computer-mediated communication.

In the following section of this chapter we review three specific examples in which researchers have focused on the context of the verbal communication to better understand our overall communication behaviors. These contexts include: African American English or Ebonics, organizational jargon, and communicating affection.

The dialect known as Black English, or Ebonics, developed within the African American community. Robert Williams coined the term Ebonics by merging the words "ebony" and "phonics" in his 1975 book *Ebonics: The True Language of Black Folks.* The term was not widely known until 1996 when the Oakland Unified School District in California recognized the legitimacy of Ebonics, or African American English (AEE), starting a media frenzy (Weldon 2000). Weldon argues that dialects are socially constructed linguistic systems that are rule-governed and natural. Dialects are neither inferior, nor genetically constructed, rather, they are socially determined. Although the linguistic system Ebonics is well-defined and sound, individuals often place prejudices, biases, and value on this particular dialect. Although it is dismissed by some as "bad English," Ebonics has a well-documented and rich cultural and historical background (see Rickford 1999; 2000; Dillard 1972).

Jargon is defined as a specialized vocabulary that is socially constructed and regularly used by members of a particular trade, profession, or organization. Jargon will differ greatly in different organizations and workplaces. Oftentimes jargon is used in technical and scientific fields to refer to concepts and terms in a universal manner. One category of jargon is the development of acronyms/abbreviations. Members of the military may use jargon such as MRE's, PCD's, MEO, and CDC when communicating with each other. What is the purpose or function of jargon? These verbal shortcuts can enhance communication by increasing precision and speed during social interaction (Hirst 2003). This specialized language may be abused when individuals use it with receivers who are not familiar with the vocabulary, and the speaker may be perceived as being pretentious (Nash 1993). For example, most of us prefer our health care providers to communicate clearly with us, avoiding the use of jargon and technical language. Organizational jargon or "shop talk" is contextually bound and may be considered rude or pretentious when communicating with individuals outside of the organization.

© Laurence Gough, 2007, Shutterstock.

A person who doesn't work in the lab would have a difficult time understanding the scientists' jargon.

Another example of contextually bound verbal communication is expressing affection. Many of us reserve special terms for our most intimate relationships. Consider the last time you told someone "I love you." You may have contemplated these three little words for quite a while before actually saying them. That is because these few words have large implications. These expressions of affection often initiate or accelerate relational development (Floyd 1997). We often save particular words or phrases for special individuals that impact or influence us. Communicating affection is risky. When the receiver is not on the same page as the sender, the communicative attempt may have a negative outcome. It is important that the sender consider the trust level, reciprocity, and future interactions, as well as the length of the relationship. If the receiver does not feel the same way, he may feel manipulated or perceive the sender as imposing confusing relational boundaries (Ebert and Floyd 2004). Once again, our verbal communication is bound by the context of the situation.

Now that we have defined verbal communication and provided its features, we can discuss the functions verbal communication serves.

FUNCTIONS OF VERBAL COMMUNICATION

There are four functions that help explain how we use our verbal communication. They are: cognitive function, social reality function, group identity function and social change function. Each is discussed below.

Cognitive Functions

The **cognitive function** of verbal communication can be defined as how we use language to acquire knowledge, to reason, and to make sense of the world. The cognitive function of verbal communication maintains a strong connection with culture. The culture we are raised within greatly influences how we use language. Growing up in a small town versus a large city or as part of a quiet family versus a loud family, or being raised in the South versus the North will influence the type of language we use.

We use verbal communication to acquire information. One way we acquire information about our interpersonal relationships is through uncertainty reduction.

Charles Berger proposed that the main purpose of verbal communication is to "make sense" out of our interpersonal world (as cited in Griffin 2003). Berger developed **Uncertainty Reduction Theory,** which suggests that human communication is used to gain knowledge and create understanding by reducing uncertainty and, therefore, increasing predictability. The more we ask questions and learn about someone new, the more we are reducing our uncertainty about him. For example, when we are first introduced to people, there are high levels of uncertainty. We may ask ourselves: Who is this person? Where are they from? Are they like me? Consider the last time you met someone new. Chances are the conversation went something like the one found below.

James: Hi, I'm James. What is your name?

Erica: My name is Erica. Where are you from?

James: I'm from New York, and you?

Erica: I am from Florida, but I am here studying communication.

James: That is my major also. Are you interested in broadcasting?

Erica: No, I am studying communication studies. I am interested in going to law school.

This example demonstrates how we use verbal communication to acquire knowledge through uncertainty reduction. Through the process of **self-disclosure,** or purposefully revealing personal information about ourselves, we are able to decrease the ambiguity of a situation. This is an example of how our verbal communication serves the cognitive function of acquiring knowledge and making sense out of the world. We will examine the concept of self-disclosure and its role in relationship initiation more closely in Chapter Six.

Social Reality Function

"The language used in everyday life continuously provides me with the necessary objectifications and posits the order within which these make sense and within which everyday life has meaning for me. I live in a place that is geographically designated; I employ tools from can openers to sports cars which are designated in the technical vocabulary of my society; I live within a web of human relationships from my chess club to the United States of America which are also ordered by means of vocabulary. In this manner, language marks the co-ordinates of my life in society and fills that life with meaningful objects." (Peter L. Berger. The Social Construction of Reality. New York: Doubleday, 1966, p. 22.).

In this quote from *The Social Construction of Reality,* the authors suggest that reality is socially constructed through our language and vocabulary. In other words, what appears to be real in society is socially agreed upon through our communication with others. Consider the words that have evolved in the U.S. culture across previous decades. In the 1970s, the terms "Watergate," "test-tube baby," and "Rubik's cube" became words which were widely understood by members of the U.S. because of events or products that had been introduced during that time period. Similarly, the words "AIDS" and "compact disc" were added to dictionaries in the 1980s. As the reality of the culture evolved, new words were created to explain and describe the changing society. Thus, our verbal communication serves to create our social reality.

Two American linguists, Edward Sapir and Benjamin Lee Whorf, were interested in how humans used language as a tool to make sense of the world. They developed the concept of **linguistic determinism,** which suggests that "language *determines* thought" (Whorf 1956; Sapir 1956). Although this groundbreaking and extreme perspective has few supporters today, many do share the belief that thought *influences* language. Sapir and Whorf also conceptualized **linguistic relativity,** which states that distinctions encoded in one language are unique to that language alone, and that "there is no limit to the structural diversity of languages" (Whorf 1956; Sapir 1956). By comparing the vocabulary of Inuit and Aztec peoples they found that the Inuit have many different words for "snow." There are different words for falling snow, powdery snow, slushy snow, packing snow, and icy snow, and there are even more. On the other hand, in Aztec there is only one word for snow, one word for cold, and one word for ice. In addition, Sapir and Whorf were fascinated by the fact that the Hopi language did not distinguish between past, present, and future time. Time is not considered multidimensional in their culture, whereas time is a fundamentally critical concept in Western society. Think about how we use time in such fields as physics and engineering. Also, our culture is embedded with daily planners, calendars, and appointments that rely heavily on our shared meaning of time. The **Sapir-Whorf hypothesis** suggests that the language we learn, as well as the culture we are exposed to, is used to shape our entire reality.

Group Identity Function

Another function of verbal communication is to serve as a symbol of group solidarity. Because we have similarities in language at work, in our family, and throughout our interpersonal relationships, verbal communication provides an identity function. Think about the cliques that were formed in high school. There were students who played in the band, athletes, theater members, and student council members. Students often describe and define themselves based on their affiliations or social groups. Within the different groups, shared "codes" develop that only members understand. These codes may be in the form of inside jokes, nicknames, abbreviations, or other specialized vocabulary. Their purpose is to form a sense of group identity. In other words, this function of verbal communication serves to distinguish one group from others and to provide a sense of similarity for its members.

Families can be considered a type of group. Think about your family. Are there inside jokes that get repeated over and over? You may hear something like, "Remember the time that Mom made Julie walk across the kitchen to get an apple, because she did not believe she had a broken leg? Or the time Shawn lied to Mom and Dad about that 'hit and run' so he could get a new bike?" We choose to let others "in" on the joke when we allow new members to enter into the group. From outside the group, non-members may interpret the stories, jokes, and nicknames as inappropriate, inconsiderate and not humorous. However, group members who use verbal communication for this function feel a sense of belonging. Verbal communication that is used to form group identity is used to maintain the group's rituals and celebrate the history of the group.

This boy may describe himself as a baseball player because of his group identity.

© Glen Jones, 2007, Shutterstock.

Social Change Function

Language can "imprison us" or it can "set us free." This is how Ting-Toomey and Chung (2005) describe the social change function of language. In other words, language can inhibit our abilities to perceive the world in unique ways or it can dynamically change habits and prejudices. We often try to avoid offending others by using politically correct language. Political correctness stems from the convergence of several factors, three of which are the Sapir-Whorf hypothesis, the Civil Rights Movement, and language reform. The Sapir-Whorf hypothesis provided a theoretical framework that suggested language can be used to attempt social change and influence reality. In addition, the feminist and racial equality movements altered our language system by eliminating gender-based and racial-based terms from our vocabulary. It is suggested that a more sensitive language will reflect a more caring society.

The Global Language Monitor (GLM) is a San Diego-based company that tracks and analyzes trends in the English language. The GLM staff monitors the evolution and demise of language, word usage, word choices, and their impact on the various aspects of culture. GLM suggests that the September 11 attacks on America have changed forever the way we speak and interpret various words. Currently, they suggest, the numbers 9/11 are the official shorthand for the 2001 terrorist attacks and *ground-zero* stirs up thoughts of a sacred burial ground where the twin towers once stood. Also since the attacks, the word *hero* includes police, firefighters, EMTs, and any type of first responders who place their lives on the line for the public good.

Now that we have explored the cognitive, social reality, group identity, and social change functions of verbal communication, we turn our attention to the different types of verbal communication styles.

VERBAL COMMUNICATION STYLES

Everyone has his own unique style of communicating. In this section, we have designated four common verbal communication styles. They have been labeled: direct-indirect, informal-formal, clarity-equivocality, and powerful-powerless. There are a number of different strengths and weaknesses associated with each of these verbal communication styles. These individual differences exist on a continuum and are not to be viewed as dichotomous groups. In other words, you will not necessarily be "one or the other" but you may be closer to one end of the spectrum than the other. While most people place themselves in the middle of the spectrum, you may be more likely to describe yourself as using a particular verbal style more consistently.

What strategy do you think he is using to end this relationship?

Direct/Indirect

Direct communication style explicitly verbalizes inquiries and comments in a straightforward manner, while the **indirect** communication style relies on a more roundabout or subtle method of communicating. Individuals who rely on indirect communication often use nonverbal communication such as facial expressions and eye contact, more often than verbal communication to convey a message.

Leslie Baxter refers to the extent to which individuals are direct and indirect in her theory of relationship dissolution. She suggests individuals have different styles when it comes to ending relationships. Withdrawing, being annoying or hurtful, or suggesting "being friends" would be considered indirect strategies. But an individual may rely on direct strategies to end a relationship. A simple statement that "It is over" or a fight where each partner blames the other would be examples of direct strategies. Baxter suggests that apprehensive people are more likely to use indirect strategies (as cited in Littlejohn 1992). It is important to point out that individuals will often intentionally choose a more indirect communication style over a direct style to save face for the receiver. Picture yourself at a boring party. Instead of telling the host you are bored and are ready to leave, you may engage in a more subtle approach. Perhaps you start to yawn and hint that you did not get much sleep last night. Engaging in an indirect communication style is sometimes more considerate than expressing your true feelings directly.

Indirect
(subtle)

Direct
(straightforward)

Informal communicative styles are most often used when speaking with peers and co-workers.

© Suhendri Utet, 2007, Shutterstock.

Informal/Formal

The formality of a communicated message refers to the extent to which it is official and proper. A **formal** style of communicating is typically used when you are communicating with someone of higher power, such as a parent, grandparent, teacher, boss, or health professional. It is used to show respect. **Informal** communication refers to using a relaxed, casual, and familiar verbal communication style. This is typically used with your peers and co-workers.

Choosing between informal or formal communicative styles can be tricky in intercultural situations. People who live in the United States, Canada, Australia, and Scandinavia tend to be more informal in their communication styles, whereas people of Asian and African cultures tend to be more formal. Adler and Rodman (2006) suggest that there are different degrees of formality for speaking with old friends, acquaintances, and strangers. The ability to use language that acknowledges these differences is the mark of a learned person in countries like South Korea. Whenever you are uncertain about a situation, it is better to be formal than informal, since most cultures value formality. Adopting a more formal communication style will demonstrate respect on your part.

Informal (casual) ⟷ Formal (proper)

Clarity/Equivocation

Another aspect of verbal communication involves the extent to which you express yourself with clarity, as opposed to equivocality. While **clarity** refers to the simplistic, down-to-earth, and understandable nature of the communication, Bavelas and his colleagues (1990) define **equivocation** as "nonstraightforward communication . . . [that] appears ambiguous, contradictory, tangential, obscure, or even evasive" (28). In other words, equivocation involves communicating by choosing specific words that may not demonstrate the whole truth. Equivocation allows an individual the possibility to deny events after the fact. Former President Bill Clinton denied having "sexual relations" with Monica Lewinsky. Later, Clinton stated he interpreted the agreed upon definition of sexual relations to exclude his receiving oral sex. This example demonstrates how someone uses equivocation to protect themselves by intentionally not revealing the entire truth. However, like indirect communication, individuals may choose to act in an equivocal manner to protect someone else's feelings. For example, you may tell your date, "This lunch was very thoughtful," even though you have no intention of going on another date with this person. Be aware that sending mixed messages may lead to confusion and awkward discussions in the future.

Communicating in a clear manner obviously has many benefits. In the classroom, researchers found that students taught by teachers with a clear communication style learned more than those taught by teachers with a less clear communication style. Students reported less receiver apprehension, less fear of misinterpreting, and less fear of inadequately processing information. Finally, students indicated that they were more favorably disposed towards clear teachers and reported more positive affect for both the professor and the course material (Cheseboro 2003).

Clarity (simple and clear) ⟷ Equivocality (ambiguous)

Powerful/Powerless Language

The final verbal communication style that we will discuss is the extent to which your language is powerful or powerless. In our society, **powerful language** is associated with positive attributes such as assertiveness and importance and it can be influential, commanding, and authoritative. Powerful language is a combination of using proper English, clear thoughts, organized ideas, and a persuasive structure. **Powerless language,** on the other hand, is associated with negative attributes such as shyness, introversion, timidity, nervousness, and apprehension. Avoiding linguistic features that suggest powerless language may positively impact the way we are interpreted. Types of powerless speech include hesitations, hedges, tag questions, polite forms, intensifiers, and disclaimers (see table 2.1).

Some researchers described powerless language as "feminine" or "women's language" (Lakoff 1973; 1974). In her work, Lakoff recognizes women's subordinate position in society by the language they use. She suggests women avoid powerless language if they want to move toward political and social equality. More recent research suggests that anyone who relies on powerless language, regardless of class or gender, should be aware of the judgments that might be attached (Rubin and Nelson 1983).

The use of powerful language has also been studied in the classroom. Haleta (1996) examined students' perceptions of teachers' use of powerful versus powerless language. Findings suggest that students' initial perceptions of powerful teachers were significantly higher in perceptions of dynamism,

▶ Table 2.1   Powerless Language, Interpretation, and Examples

Powerless Language	Interpreted as	Example
Hesitation	Uncertain, nervous, timid	*"I think . . . well, yeah . . . I saw someone take, errr, your notebook."*
Hedges	Less absolute, qualifying phrases	*"I guess that would be a good idea."*
Tag questions	Weak assertion, less absolute	*"That was a good idea, wasn't it?"*
Polite forms	Subordinate	*"Please pick up your dishes."*
Intensifiers	Unsuccessful attempt to make words sound stronger	*"It's really, really easy."*
Disclaimers	Diversion of responsibility, fault, truth	*"Remember, this is just what I heard . . ."*

status, and credibility than those teachers who used powerless language. Students' level of uncertainty was significantly higher with those teachers who used powerless language.

Powerful   Powerless

PERCEPTIONS AND VERBAL COMMUNICATION

Research has shown that we need to hear only ten to fifteen seconds of an individual's speech to form initial perceptions (Entwisle 1970). The next section is designed to give you some insight on some typical perceptions of verbal communication. First, we explore how language choices can impact perceptions of credibility and status. We then discuss types of communication considered biased. We also explore the concept of verbal immediacy as it relates to confirming and disconfirming messages. An overview of different types of message design logics is also included in this section.

Credibility and Status

We can demonstrate credibility in our interpersonal relationships through our verbal communication messages. **Credibility** or believability can be defined as having three dimensions: competence, character, and goodwill (McCroskey and Young 1981; McCroskey and Teven 1999). **Competence** refers to your knowledge or expertise, while **character** is the extent to which you are trustworthy. The third dimension, **goodwill,** refers to your ability to care or feel concerned.

Typically, we base our perceptions of credibility on the perceived status of an individual. **Status** refers to the level of position an individual has when compared with others. This may be social, socio-economic, and/or organizational status. In addition to nonverbal behavior, we can gain an understanding of credibility through an individual's verbal comments. The degree of formality, vocabulary, accent, rate of speech, fluency of language, and articulation all play a role in our perceptions of credibility and status. Our perceptions also affect our ability to listen. We tend to listen more attentively to persons of high status rather than to someone we perceive as having low status.

Bias Communication through Language

In the beginning of this chapter we said that the words we choose can be used to strengthen relationships or to destroy them. When we use biased, sexist, racist, and offensive language we are choosing to cause harm to others.

Recall the following riddle:

A doctor and a boy are fishing. The boy was the doctor's son, but the doctor was not the boy's father. Who was the doctor?

The answer is: The doctor is the boy's mother. The punch line of this riddle is relying on the fact that we would initially assume that the doctor was male. Researchers have agreed that sexist language ultimately reinforces a sexist community. **Sexist language** refers to any speech that is degrading to males or females. Most of the research examines how females are subordinate figures in the male-geared vocabulary, with words like chairman and fireman illustrating the masculine focus of our language structure. To avoid sexist language, researchers suggest using gender-neutral words. For instance, The National Council of Teachers of English (NCTE) suggests several guidelines (see table 2.2).

Verbally attacking individuals on the basis of their race, ethnic background, religion, gender or sexual orientation is considered **hate speech** (Pember 2003). As with sexist language, hate speech is used to degrade others. Hate speech includes racist language or words that dehumanize individuals from a particular ethnicity. Anthony Hudson argues, "The use of language to achieve and or perpetuate the subordination of a group of people is well documented. Whether it be Jews in Nazi Germany, African Americans in the U.S., or slaves in Mauritania, language has been and continues to be a vital tool in the oppression and abuse of minority groups" (2003, 46).

We need to be aware that the words we choose to express ourselves with may have powerful implications. We all have a responsibility to have a zero tolerance for these types of speech acts. Bobbye Persing succinctly states, "Meanings are in people, not in words, and if certain words create negative images in the receivers, we should stop using these words. . . . If we deny the importance of words we are denying the very fiber of our stock . . . communication" (1977, 19).

Table 2.2   Suggestions for Avoiding Sexist Language

National Council of Teachers of English Guidelines

Examples	Alternatives
mankind	humanity, people, human beings
man's achievements	human achievements
man-made	synthetic, manufactured, machine-made
the common man	the average person, ordinary people
man the stockroom	staff the stockroom
nine man-hours	nine staff-hours
chairman	coordinator, moderator, presiding officer, head,
businessman	business executive
fireman	firefighter
mailman	mail carrier
steward and stewardess	flight attendant
policeman/woman	police officer
congressman	congressional representative

EXAMPLE: Give each student his paper as soon as he is finished
ALTERNATIVE: Give students their papers as soon as they are finished.
EXAMPLE: The average student is worried about his grade.
ALTERNATIVE: The average student is worried about grades.

Adapted from http://owl.english.purdue.edu/handouts/general/gl_nonsex.html.

VERBAL IMMEDIACY

It makes sense to say that we approach things we like and avoid things we do not. Albert Mehrabian and his colleagues used this approach-avoidance theory as a basis for the concept of immediacy in the late 1960s. Mehrabian describes **immediacy** as the process of using communication behaviors purposefully to reduce psychological and physical distance (1969). Researchers have found many benefits to engaging in immediacy behaviors, including increased perceptions of liking and attraction. Immediacy may be enacted verbally and non-verbally, but we will focus on the verbal features in this chapter.

Verbal immediacy refers to using specific word choices and syntactic structures to increase perceptions of psychological closeness. Something as simple as using words such as "we" and "our" are considered more immediate than "I" and "yours." Consider this the next time you confront your roommate about the apartment being cluttered. You might say, "We should clean this apartment before dinner. Our stuff is everywhere," instead of "You should clean the apartment. I cleaned last time."

Gorham (1988) examined verbal immediacy in the classroom. She suggests that instructors can gain a psychological closeness with their students and enhance their humanness by engaging in a variety of verbal immediacy behaviors such as using humor, self-disclosing, utilizing students' names and viewpoints throughout lecture, incorporating student suggestions into the course, and showing a willingness to work with students outside of the classroom. Teachers' use of verbally immediate messages was correlated with perceived cognitive and affective learning outcomes. Utilizing verbally immediate messages with friends, family members and co-workers has been proven to result in the benefits of both learning and the perceptions of liking and attraction.

One way to portray verbal immediacy is through confirming messages. Research suggests we discover and establish our identity through confirming **messages** in interpersonal relationships (Buber 1957). **Confirmation** is the process in which individuals feel recognized, acknowledged, valued, and respected (Laing 1961). Conversely, disconfirming messages communicate a sense of insignificance and worthlessness and act to invalidate the source (Watzlawick, Beavin, and Jackson 1967). Research in this area has found that our self-esteem is tied up in these confirming and disconfirming messages (Cissna and Keating 1979).

Cissna and Sieburg (1981) state that there are four functions of confirming messages: (1) to express recognition of the other's existence, (2) to acknowledge a relationship of affiliation with the other, (3) to express awareness of the significance or worth of the other, and (4) to accept or endorse the other's self-experience. In table 2.3 we have listed the four functions of confirming messages, stated what is being intrinsically expressed to the other person for each function, provided examples of how to verbalize the confirming messages in interpersonal relationships, and described possible outcomes of communicating in this manner.

Conversely, there are three groupings of disconfirming messages: indifference, imperviousness, and disqualification of the message or speaker. See table 2.4 for a complete list of types and examples of these messages. Be aware of the extent to which you may rely on these behaviors. It may be the cause of unsatisfying relationships and ineffective communicative patterns.

Table 2.3 Confirming Messages

Function of Confirming Message	Expresses	Example of Confirming Message	Outcome
To express recognition of the other's existence	"To me, you exist."	"Certainly, that is upsetting."	This recognizes and validates the speaker's feelings
To acknowledge a relationship of affiliation with the other	"We are relating."	"Wow! That happened to me, too."	This recognizes that you can relate to the speaker
To express awareness of the significance or worth of the other	"To me, you are significant."	"What happened to you is terrible!"	This suggests you are attentive to their situation
To accept or endorse the other's self-experience	"Your way of interpreting the world is valid."	"Sure, I can see how you thought that."	You are increasing perceptions of value and respect

Table 2.4 Types of Disconfirming Messages

Disconfirming Message	Type	Example
Indifference response	Denying the presence of the other	Being silent when a response is expected, looking away, withdrawing, engaging in unrelated activities
	Denying the relation or involvement of the other	Using impersonal language by avoiding using the first person, avoiding feeling statements or disclosures, using nonverbal "distancing," avoiding eye contact and touch
	Rejecting the communication of the other	Talking "over" another, interjecting irrelevant comments
Imperviousness or lack of accurate awareness of others perceptions	Denial or distortion of others self-expression	"You don't really mean that," or "You are only saying that because . . ."
	Pseudo-confirmation	"Stop crying, there is nothing wrong with you," or "Don't be silly, of course you are not scared."
	Mystification	"No matter what you say, I know you still love me," or "You may think you feel that way now . . ."
	Selective responses	Rewarding speaker with attention and relevant responses only when he communicates in an approved fashion, while becoming silent or indifferent when the communication does not meet the responder's approval
Disqualification	Messages that disqualify the other person by direct disparagement	Insult, name-calling, or indirect disparagement (verbal or nonverbal),
	Messages that disqualify another message by transactional disqualification or tangential response	Using the speaker's remark as a starting point for a shift to a new topic to accomplish your own agenda
	Messages that are self-disqualifying	Being unclear, incomplete, ambiguous, or sending incongruent verbal-nonverbal messages

Message Design Logic (MDL)

Another way to portray verbal immediacy can be seen through our message design logics. In the late 1980s, Barbara O'Keefe linked cognitive complexity with communication and suggested people possess their own personal implicit theories of communication. There are three theories, known as **message design**

logics, which individuals use to interpret how communication works (O'Keefe 1988). The message design logic you are working under will determine how you understand, and ultimately use, communication. Perceptions of message design logics also have great implications.

Individuals working within the **expressive** design logic believe that "language is a medium used for expressing thoughts and feelings" (O'Keefe 1988, 85). These people will say whatever is on their mind and work under the premise that if everyone communicated openly and honestly we could understand and relate to each other better. Success, as defined by the *expressive,* is the extent to which individuals can disclose openly, clearly, and truthfully. Regardless of the situation, they feel that they have no choice but to express their genuine thoughts and feelings.

Individuals working within the **conventional** design logic suggest that communication is socially constructed, rule guided behavior. These people take into account the context of the situation and personal goals when deciding to go forward with what they consider is appropriate communication. They work under the premise that each circumstance has an appropriate response depending on what your goal is for the situation. Within the conventional design logic, O'Keefe (1988) suggests, "propositions one expresses are specified by the social effect one wants to achieve, rather than the thoughts one happens to have" (86). Success is defined by cooperativeness and appropriateness.

Individuals working within the **rhetorical** design logic believe communication is a function of co-constructing reality with the parties involved. These people view communication as "the creation and negotiation of social selves and situations" (O'Keefe 1988, 85). Success is defined by the extent to which you use your verbal behavior, character, and social setting to create a desired social reality. They create in-depth messages that serve multiple goals and are multi-dimensional in nature. They are truthful, appropriate, sensitive, harmonious, and unanchored by context.

Consider the following example:

It is your senior year and you live off-campus with a new roommate. After getting out of class early, you decide to meet your friends at the gym to burn some calories before dinner. You stop by your apartment to get your sneakers and after searching your entire apartment, you cannot find them anywhere. Where could they be? Your friends call your cell phone to find out where you are. You explain that you cannot find your sneakers. They laugh at you and say they just saw you wearing them yesterday. Annoyed, you hang up the phone and continue searching. Ten minutes later, the door of your apartment swings open and your roommate comes bouncing in wearing your sneakers.

How would you respond?

The *expressive design logic* individual may react by saying:

"You are so inconsiderate . . . what are you doing wearing my sneakers? I was supposed to meet my friends twenty minutes ago at the gym and I have been searching all over for them. I can't believe you would use my things without asking. Do not touch *anything* of mine ever again."

The *conventional design logic* individual may react by saying:

"Are those my sneakers? You cannot take my things without asking. I have been searching everywhere for those sneakers because I thought

I misplaced them. When you want to use something that is mine, you need to ask me."

The *rhetorical design logic* individual may react by saying:

"I realize we are new roommates and I would really like us to continue out the year not only as roommates, but as friends. So, I think it is important for us to communicate if we are going to be borrowing each other's property. It is okay if you use my things, just text me or leave me a note, so I'll know."

Past research has shown **expressive** message producers have significantly more negative perceptions than the other message design logics. It is plausible to suggest that because they are more likely to be insensitive, inappropriate, threatening and offensive to their audience, they may be witness to more negative responses from them. O'Keefe and McCornack (1987) found that judges rated expressive messages as less effective and expressive sources less attractive than individuals that used conventional and rhetorical message design logics. More recently, research found expressives to be more cynical than people who use conventional and rhetorical message design logics (Edwards and Shepherd 2004). Also, in the organizational setting, individuals in superior-subordinate relationships with expressive message producers tended to feel less supported, more burned out, and more stressed than when they are working with conventional and rhetorical message producers (Peterson and Albrect 1996). Both the conventional and rhetorical message design logics consider the context of the situation when communicating and this research reinforces the importance and positive outcomes of considering the contextual influences.

Factors such as age, sex, and context influence the words that we choose to use when communicating as well as how we interpret verbal messages from others.

FACTORS AFFECTING VERBAL COMMUNICATION

Life Span

One factor that influences how we choose to verbally communicate and how others interpret those communicative acts is age. This includes how our communication changes and is interpreted over time. From perceptions of control in mother-daughter relationships (Morgan and Hummert 2000) to the meaning of friendships (Patterson, Bettini, and Nussbaum 1993), our communicative patterns differ over our lifetime. The meaning behind any communicative act is inherently a function of the point in one's life in which this communicative act occurred (Nussbaum 1989). From infants to the elderly, Jon Nussbaum and his colleagues have conducted a considerable amount of research on the relationship between life span factors and communication behaviors (see Williams and Nussbaum 2001 for a more recent review). In the next section we offer three examples of how our verbal communication with different age groups has an impact on our lives.

How we respond to our children may impact how they view themselves. For example, those parents who are controlling and critical may threaten a child's self-esteem. As discussed in Chapter Two, self-esteem is the value we place on ourselves. Some research indicates that having high self-esteem has

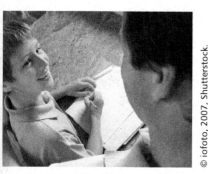

What kinds of confirming messages do parents give to their children?

been associated with several positive attributes such as competence, assertiveness, and attractiveness. Although the concept is still developing, many parents struggle to establish environments where children have the opportunity to develop a heightened view of self. Some research has shown that children with low or unstable self-esteem levels reported significantly more instances of critical and psychologically controlling parent-child communication (Kernis, Brown, and Brody 2000). When parents are less likely to acknowledge their children's positive behaviors or show approval in value-affirming ways, children are more likely to develop low self-esteem. To improve children's perceptions of self, parents should attempt to occasionally use confirming messages and avoid disconfirming messages. Confirming messages will express recognition of the child's existence and the worth of the child. These findings suggest that parent-child verbal communication effectiveness can impact a child's level of self-esteem.

What parents choose to talk about with their teens and what they choose to ignore may have serious impact on their teen's behavior. Recent research on parent-child communication indicates that the extent to which parents communicate with their teens about sex, birth control, and sexually transmitted diseases will directly impact the teen's sexual behavior. Specifically, research by Whitaker and Miller (2000) found that parents who spoke to adolescents about sex reduced the associations the adolescents made about their own behavior with perceptions of their peers' sexual behavior. Whitaker and Miller also found that communicating to teens about condom use correlated with adolescents' safer sexual behavior.

The **Communication Predicament of Aging Model** (Coupland, Coupland, and Giles, 1991; Ryan, Giles, Bartulucci, and Henwood, 1986; Ryan, Hummert, and Boich, 1995) suggests that when young people communicate with the elderly they often rely on negative stereotypes. These negative stereotypes imply that the elderly have declined in cognitive, perceptual, and emotional competence. As a result of these faulty perceptions, young people overcompensate by engaging in "patronizing communication" with the elderly. These patronizing communicative behaviors include: (1) speaking in short sentences, (2) using simple words, (3) using high volume, (4) speaking at a slow rate, and (5) exaggerating articulation. This patronizing talk may contribute to unsatisfactory intergenerational interactions.

Although it is important to be able to communicate across age groups, it is often difficult because of the lack of homophily, or similarity. These three examples offer some insight on the problematic symptoms and implications of verbally communicating outside of your age group.

How can intergenerational interactions be improved?

Sex Differences in Verbal Communication

When it comes to communicating, are men really from Mars and women from Venus? Maltz and Borker (1982) theorize that the way in which girls and boys play at a young age impacts their speech later in life. Let us look at the type of games young children play.

Girls often enjoy games that rely on cooperative play, such as house, Barbie, or school. In these types of play there needs to be a negotiation of rules. Questions like who will be Barbie and who will be the teacher need to be answered. After all, it would be difficult to play school if everyone wanted to be the teacher and no one wanted to be the students. During these childhood games, girls focus on their own and others' feelings, attitudes, and emotions. In addition, girls often discuss taking turns and decide on imaginary scenes. Therefore, girls encourage talk, collaboration, and sharing. They value cooperativeness and discourage aggressiveness.

Boys, on the other hand, tend to be more competitive in their childhood games. Cops and robbers, war, sports, "king of the hill," and hide-and-seek are just a few examples of boy's games. Typically in these games, there are set rules, so there is less negotiation and, therefore, less talk. Discussions are usually driven by reiterating the rules or reinforcing them. Boys value competitiveness and aggressiveness because their games center on a clear winner and loser. They value assertiveness, direct communication, and having a clear purpose.

Typical girls' games focus on feelings and sharing.

It is difficult to discuss sex differences without mentioning Robin Lakoff, one of the first women to publish theories on gender differences in communicating. In the early to mid 1970s she suggested that women lack a sense of humor, use senseless adjectives (divine, lovely), use more hedges, "sort of" or "kind of," use more polite forms of communicating ("Would you mind if . . ." or "I would appreciate it if you . . .") and have more words for things like colors. A student of Lakoff was Deborah Tannen, who became a professor at Georgetown University and the author of several best-selling books, including *You Just Don't Understand: Women and Men in Conversations.* Tannen proposes that women engage in **"rapport talk,"** or talking for the sake of talking. In other words, women talk for pleasure and to establish connections with others. In contrast, men engage in **"report talk,"** or talking to accomplish goals. Males talk to solve problems and are more instrumental in their approach to communication. Over the last twenty years, Tannen has identified a number of differences in male and female perspectives in regard to communication and relationships. She emphasizes that no one approach or style of communication is better than the other, just different. To improve male-female communication, it is important to understand the differences in perspective as well as the reasons they exist.

Boys tend to favor games that end with a clear winner and loser.

This section provides some insight into how men and women may be socialized to communicate differently. This is not to say that throughout your experiences, you have not met males that engage in rapport talk and females that engage in report talk. We acknowledge that these are research generalizations and they certainly do not apply to everyone.

Contextual Differences

In addition to age and gender, the context of the verbal communication will impact the outcome of the message. We identified context as a characteristic of verbal communication in the beginning of this chapter. We believe this is a

Women's conversations often revolve around rapport talk.

© Dmitriy Shironosov, 2007, Shutterstock.

key feature when determining appropriate verbal communication. Therefore we have provided a more in-depth examination into how to communicate effectively within specific contexts, including within intercultural relationships (Chapter Ten), our families (Chapter Eleven), our co-workers and boss (Chapter Twelve), and with health care professionals (Chapter Thirteen). Furthermore, we will discuss how appropriate communication is used in initiating (Chapter Six), maintaining (Chapter Seven) and terminating (Chapter Nine) friendships and romantic relationships.

BEST PRACTICES: AVOID VERBAL PITFALLS

Oftentimes our verbal communication is misinterpreted. This may be due to connotative meanings, sex differences, or varying verbal styles. Therefore it is important to be clear, appropriate, and concrete.

Clarity

When you are composing a message, keep in mind the KISS acronym: Keep It Short and Simple. Be clear and succinct. Often we think that by using large words, we will be perceived as more intelligent, but you do so at the risk of confusing your audience. Using ambiguous terms is risky. Direct and clear language will increase your chances of reaching shared meaning—your ultimate goal.

On the other hand, when you are on the receiving end of the message, it is important to ask questions to clarify verbal responses. Paraphrase, summarize, and ask direct questions to clarify, even when you think you understand what is being said. These concepts and others will be discussed in more depth in Chapter Five: Perception and Listening.

Appropriateness

Targeting your verbal responses will increase your communication competence. Ask yourself, "What is the best way to send this message to this particular receiver?" The only way to get better is to try different approaches and see how they work. Most people will appreciate your genuine effort to "reach" them.

Concreteness

Concreteness refers to being able to communicate thoughts and ideas specifically. In other words, choose your words wisely. By avoiding jargon and tangential words you will keep the receiver of your message "on track." Avoid superfluous words—they are not necessary. Intentionally choosing words your receiver will understand and relate to will increase your chances of being understood.

SUMMARY

Research on verbal communication dates back to Aristotle and continues to this day. We are fascinated with how individuals learn and use words because their impact is so powerful and significant. Catastrophes such as 9/11 and Katrina affect our language and change it forever. Television and movies also introduce new words and phrases, such as "Vote for Pedro" and "Welcome to Hollywood," into our vocabulary. In this chapter we presented definitions, features, functions, and perceptions of verbal communication. The goal of this chapter was to increase student understanding of verbal communication and how certain verbal styles are perceived by others. Heightening awareness of our own verbal communication as well as the verbal communication used by others will ultimately improve our understanding of interpersonal relationships.

APPLICATIONS

Discussion Questions

A. Gender Differences and Rules: Are there gender differences in regulative and constitutive rules? Do men and women follow different rules? When? Where? When is it socially acceptable for a male to violate a rule? What about a female?

B. Political Correctness: Has it gone too far?
Below are some proposed politically correct words:

Misguided Criminals vs. *Terrorist* (to strip away all emotions).

Thought Shower vs. *Brainstorming* (offensive to those with brain disorders).

Deferred success vs. *Fail* (to bolster self-esteem).

C. How do the words we choose affect our perceptions?

ACTIVITY

Instructional Findings: Confirming/Disconfirming   Activity #1:

In the classroom, it was found that students felt more confirmed when they perceived their teacher engaging in confirmation behaviors (Ellis 2000).

DIRECTIONS: Complete the scale below by choosing the number on the line that most accurately describes the extent you believe the following statements about your instructor. This measures whether your instructor uses confirmation behaviors.

Strongly Agree	Agree	Neither agree nor disagree	Infrequently	Never
5	4	3	2	1

_____ 1. Spends time to thoroughly answer students' questions.
_____ 2. Tries to become acquainted with students.
_____ 3. Responds sarcastically to some students' remarks or questions in class.*
_____ 4. Makes it known that students' remarks or questions are welcome in class.
_____ 5. Pays attention to selected students only in class and ignores everyone else.*
_____ 6. Acts in a pompous manner.
_____ 7. Shows interest by listening closely when students offer remarks or ask questions in class.
_____ 8. When students ask for extra help from the teacher, he/she criticizes.*
_____ 9. Patronizes students.*
_____ 10. Bullies students.*

_____ 11. Says that he/she knows that the students are capable of succeeding in the class.

_____ 12. Mocks students in front of the class.*

_____ 13. Plays favorites.*

_____ 14. Is willing to answer questions outside of class.

_____ 15. Teaches by encouraging feedback from students.

_____ 16. Is willing to use different methods to help students comprehend concepts.

_____ 17. While lecturing, makes an effort to have eye contact with students.

_____ 18. He/she can improvise if needed to answer questions during a lecture.

_____ 19. Offers a smiling face in class.

_____ 20. Makes sure students comprehend material before continuing.

_____ 21. He/she asks students their opinion of how class is progressing, including homework.

_____ 22. Lectures integrate exercises if possible.

_____ 23. Students who don't agree get no response from the teacher.*

_____ 24. Assignments receive oral or written encouragement.

_____ 25. Tells the students that he/she can't spare the time to meet with them.

---

*Four aspects: instructor's response to student remarks/questions, apparent interest in student learning, method of teaching, absence of disconfirmation

Source: Adapted from: Ellis, K. 2000. Perceived teacher confirmation: The development and validation of an instrument and two studies of the relationship to cognitive and affective learning. _Human Communication Research, 26,_ 264–291.

REFERENCES

Adler, R. B., and G. Rodman. 2006. _Understanding human communication._ New York: Oxford University Press.

Bavelas, J. B., A. Black, N. Chovil, and J. Mullett. 1990. _Equivocal communication._ Newbury Park, CA: Sage.

Berger, P. L., and T. Luckmann. 1966. _The social construction of reality: A treatise it's the sociology of knowledge._ Garden City, New York: Anchor Books.

Buber, M. 1957. Distance and relation. _Psychiatry, 20,_ 97–104.

Cheseboro, J. L. 2003. Effects of teacher clarity and nonverbal immediacy on student learning, receiver apprehension and affect. _Communication Education, 52,_ 135–147.

Cissna, K. N., and S. Keating. 1979. Speech communication antecedents of perceived confirmation. _The Western Journal of Speech Communication, 43,_ 48–60.

Cissna, K. N., and E. Sieburg. 1981. Patterns of interactional confirmation and disconfirmation. In C. Wilder-Mott & J. H. Weakland (Eds.), _Rigor and imagination: Essays from the legacy of Gregory Bateson_ (253–282). New York: Praeger.

Coupland, N., J. Coupland, and H. Giles. 1991. _Language, society and the elderly._ Oxford: Basil Blackwell.

Cronen, V. E., W. B. Pearce, and L. Snavely. 1979. A theory of rule structure and forms of episodes, and a study of unwanted repetitive patterns. Communication Yearbook III, Transaction Press (225–240).

Dillard, J. L. 1972. _Black English: Its history and usage in the United States._ New York: Random House, Inc.

Ebert, L., and K. Floyd. 2004. Affection expressions as face threatening acts: Receiver assessments. _Communication Studies, 55,_ 254–270.

Edwards, A., and G. J. Shepherd. 2004. Theories of communication, human nature, and the world: Associations and implications. _Communication Studies, 55,_ 197–208.

Ellis, K. 2000. Perceived teacher confirmation: The development and validation of an instrument and two studies of the relationship to cognitive and affective learning. _Human Communication Research, 26,_ 264–291.

Entwisle, D. R. 1970. Semantic systems of children: Some assessments of social class and ethnic differences. In F. Williams (Ed.), _Language and Poverty,_ New York: Sage.

Floyd, K. 1997. Communicating affection in dyadic relationships: An assessment of behavior and expectations. _Communication Quarterly, 45,_ 68–80.

Gorham, J. 1988. The relationship between verbal teacher immediacy and student learning. *Communication Education, 37*, 40–53.

Griffin, E. 2003. *A first look at communication theory.* Boston: McGraw-Hill.

Haleta, L. 1996. Students perceptions of teachers' use of language: The effects of powerful and powerless language on impression formation and uncertainty. *Communication Teacher, 45*, 16–28.

Hirst, R. 2003. Scientific jargon: Good and bad. *Journal of Technical Writing and Communication, 33*, 201–229.

Hudson, A. 2003. Fighting words. *Index on Censorship, 32*, 45–52.

Kernis, M. H., A. C. Brown, and G. H. Brody. 2000. Fragile self-esteem in children and its associations with perceived patterns of parent-child communication. *Journal of Personality, 68*, 225–252.

Laing, R. D. 1961. *The self and others.* New York: Pantheon.

Lakoff, R. 1973. Language and woman's place. *Language in Society, 2*, 45–80.

Littlejohn, S. W. 1992. *Theories of communication* (4th ed),. Belmont, CA: Wadsworth Publishing Company.

Maltz, D., and R. Borker. 1982. *A cultural approach to male-female miscommunication,* In J. Gumperz (Ed.), *Language and social identity,* Cambridge: Cambridge University Press (196–216).

McCroskey, J. C., and J. J. Teven. 1999. Goodwill: A reexamination of the construct and its measurement. *Communication Monographs, 66*, 90–103.

McCroskey, J. C., and T. J. Young. 1981.Ethos and credibility: The construct and its measurement after three decades. *Central States Speech Journal, 32*, 24–34.

Mehrabian, A. 1969. Some referents and measures of nonverbal behavior. *Behavioral Research Methods and Instrumentation, 1*, 213–217.

Morgan, M., and M. L. Hummert. 2000. Perceptions of communicative control strategies in mother-daughter dyads across the life span. *Journal of Communication, 50*, 49–64.

Nash, W. 1993. *Jargon: Its uses and abuses.* Oxford: Blackwell Publishers.

Nussbaum, J. F. 1989. *Life-span communication: Normative processes.* Hillsdale, NJ: Lawrence Erlbaum.

O'Keefe, B. 1988.The logic of message design: Individual differences in reasoning about communication. *Communication Monographs, 55*, 80–103.

O'Keefe, B. J., and S. A. McCornack. 1987. Message design logic and message goal structure: Effects on perceptions of message quality in regulative communication situations. *Human Communication Research, 14*, 68–92.

Patterson, B., L. Bettini, and J. F. Nussbaum. 1993. The meaning of friendship across the life-span: Two studies. *Communication Quarterly, 41*, 145–161.

Pearce, W. B., V. E. Cronen, and R. F. Conklin. 1979. On what to look at when studying communication: A hierarchical model of actors' meanings. *Communication, 4*, 195–220.

Pember, D. 2003. *Mass media law.* Boston: McGraw-Hill.

Persing, B. 1977. Sticks and stones and words: Women in the language. *Journal of Business Communication, 14*, 11–19.

Peterson, L. W., and T. L. Albrecht. 1996.Message design logic, social support, and mixed status relationships. *WesternJournal of Communication, 60*, 291–309.

Rickford, J. 1999. *African American Vernacular English.* Malden, MA: Blackwell Publishers, Inc.

Rickford, J., and R. Rickford. 2000. *Spoken soul: The story of black English.* Hoboken, NJ: John Wiley.

Rubin, D. L., and M. W. Nelson. 1983. Multiple determinants of a stigmatized speech style: Women's language, powerless language, or everyone's language. *Language and Speech, 26*, 273–290.

Ryan, E. B., H. Giles, G. Bartolucci, and K. Henwood. 1986. Psycholinguistic and social psychological components of communication by and with the elderly. *Language and Communication, 6*, 1–24.

Ryan, E. B., M. L. Hummert, and L. H. Boich. 1995. Communication predicaments of aging: Patronising behavior towards older adults. *Journal of Language and Social Psychology 14*, 144–166.

Sapir, E. 1956. *Language, Culture and Personality.* D. G. Mandelbaum (Ed.). Berkeley and Los Angeles: University of California.

Ting-Toomey, S., and L. C. Chung. 2005. *Understanding intercultural communication.* Los Angeles, CA: Roxbury.

Watzlawich, P., J. H. Beavin, and D. D. Jackson. 1967. Pragmatics of human communication: A study of interactional patterns, pathologies, and paradoxes. New York, NY: W. W. Norton & Company.

Weldon, T. L. 2000. Reflections on the Ebonics controversy. *American Linguist, 75*, 275–278.

Whitaker, D. J., and K. S. Miller. 2000. Parent-adolescent discussions about sex and condoms: Impact on peer influences of sexual risk behavior. *Journal of Adolescent Research, 15*, 251–273.

Whorf, B. L. 1956. J. B. Carroll (Ed.), *Language, thought and reality.* Cambridge, MA: MIT Press.

Williams, A., and J. F. Nussbaum. 2001. *Intergenerational communication across the life span.* Mahwah, NJ: Lawrence Erlbaum.

Nonverbal Communication
It's Not *What* You Said; It's *How* You Said it

© Anatoliy Babiychuk, 2007, Shutterstock.

OBJECTIVES

- Define nonverbal communication
- State the differences between nonverbal and verbal communication
- Explain Nonverbal Expectancy Violation Theory
- State the similarities between nonverbal and verbal communication
- Explain the eight types of nonverbal communication
- Explain the four functions of nonverbal messages
- Describe three functions of facial communication
- Explain and provide examples of the five categories of kinesics
- Explain and provide examples of the four types of space
- Provide examples of personal and environmental adornment
- Explain and provide examples of the five categories of touch
- Distinguish between monochronic and polychronic time orientations
- Discuss how we use nonverbal communication to regulate our conversations
- Define the term immediacy
- Advance a definition of the direct effects model of immediacy
- Advance four suggestions for improving our ability to send and receive nonverbal messages
- Describe electronic paralanguage and discuss how it differs from verbal paralanguage

KEY TERMS

nonverbal communication
continuous
  multi-channeled
constitutive rules
Nonverbal Expectancy
  Violation Theory
physical arousal
cognitive arousal
culturally bounded

facial communication
oculesics
kinesics
emblems
illustrator
regulator
affect displays
social referencing
adaptors
haptics

functional-professional
social-polite
friendship-warmth
love-intimacy
sexual-arousal
proxemics
markers
paralanguage
physical appearance
homophily

endomorph	polychromic repetition	encoding
mesomorph	complementing	decoding
ectomorph	accenting	immediacy
artifacts	regulate	communication
personal adornment	turn-yielding	apprehension (CA)
environmental adornment	turn-maintaining	electronic paralanguage
environmental factors	back-channeling cues	emoticons
chronemics	turn-requesting	acronymns
monochromic	turn-denying	flaming
	emotions	

OVERVIEW

Originally performed by Keith Whitley, the song "When You Say Nothing at All" captures the power of nonverbal communication, communicating to others without using words. The lyrics in this song illustrate that certain nonverbal behaviors create meaning for others. For example, to this particular person the smile communicates "you need me," and the eyes suggest "you will never leave me." Even the "touch of your hand" implies safety. Finally, the song suggests that these nonverbal behaviors are more significant than words by stating, "You say it best when you say nothing at all." We address these characteristics of nonverbal communication throughout this chapter. First, we define nonverbal communication and discuss how it is similar and dissimilar to verbal communication. Next, eight types of nonverbal communication and their functions are offered. In the final sections, we explore how to improve your nonverbal communication and identify potential pitfalls.

DEFINING NONVERBAL COMMUNICATION

Beyond these song lyrics, the popularity of nonverbal communication in today's culture is immense. There has been a vast amount of research done in this area. Scholars have examined everything from the importance of physical attractiveness on the job interview (Watkins and Johnston 2000) to the implications of creating positive impressions by using certain nonverbal behaviors during the physician-patient interaction (Street and Buller 1987). In addition, there are entire courses devoted to the awareness and impact of nonverbal communication at both the undergraduate and graduate levels. Furthermore, several hundred books and websites address the repercussions of using appropriate versus inappropriate nonverbal communication. We are fascinated by the impact nonverbal messages have on our day-to-day interactions. From something as obvious as our physical appearance to something as subtle as a pause during a conversation, we are captivated by the meanings created by others' nonverbal behaviors. While it is impossible to put a numerical value on the amount of meaning created through nonverbal and verbal communication, we know that the majority of meaning is created through nonverbal communication. Researchers have estimated that the nonverbal behaviors exhibited by a source (e.g., body movements, gestures, vocal

© Galina Barskaya, 2007, Shutterstock.

How do you think these women feel about each other?

qualities, etc.) can explain sixty-five (Hickson, Stacks, and Moore 2004) to ninety-three percent (Mehrabian and Ferris 1967) of any given message's meaning. This makes sense if you think about the amount of time you spend communicating nonverbally versus verbally. Even when we are not speaking we are constantly sending nonverbal messages to others. Consider all of the nonverbal messages you sent to your instructor today while you were sitting in class listening to the lecture.

The popular phrases "It is not *what* you said, it is *how* you said it," or "actions speak louder than words" are examples of the emphasis our culture places on the nonverbal portion of communicating. While verbal communication refers to the words we use to express ourselves, **nonverbal communication** refers to all aspects of communication other than the words we use, including but not limited to: facial expressions, body movements and gestures, physical appearance, and voice.

As explained in Chapter Three, each message we send has two components: the content level of meaning and the relationship level of meaning. While the content level of meaning is usually conveyed through the words we use, the relationship level of meaning is often created through *how* we say those words. Therefore, understanding nonverbal communication will play a critical role in understanding the relationship level of meaning in our messages.

Throughout the remaining sections of this chapter we isolate specific types of nonverbal communication and discuss relevant research findings. However, before we do this, it is necessary to first distinguish nonverbal communication from verbal communication.

HOW IS NONVERBAL COMMUNICATION DIFFERENT FROM VERBAL COMMUNICATION?

The first characteristic that is unique to nonverbal communication is that it is **continuous.** While there is a clear distinction between when we begin verbally communicating and when we stop, nonverbal communication continues beyond our words. Recall our discussion of the definition of communication provided in Chapter One and the statement; *you cannot not communicate.* We continuously send nonverbal messages which are being perceived by others. Even in the absence of others, we are sending nonverbal messages. For example, think about a high school friend you have not spoken to in a long time. She may perceive your silence and distance in several ways. Perhaps she thinks you are extremely busy or maybe that you are upset with her. What else might she think?

Our nonverbal messages may conflict with our verbal messages. We may say one thing, but behave inconsistently with our verbal message. For example, you might tell Aunty Lucy you liked the knit scarf she made for you. However, your facial expressions might tell another story as you pull the purple-and-red polka dot knit scarf out of the package. When our nonverbal and verbal messages contradict each other, research has shown that we tend to believe the nonverbal messages. Therefore, a second unique feature of nonverbal communication is that nonverbal is more believable than verbal communication. Although our nonverbal communication often supplements our verbal communication, such as raising our eyebrows to help stress or emphasize certain words, we tend to believe the nonverbal more than the verbal when there is a discrepancy between the two. While Aunt Lucy heard you say you liked the scarf, she will probably interpret your facial grimace as a stronger indicator of whether it will actually become a part of your wardrobe.

While verbal communication relies solely on the words we exchange with others, nonverbal communication has many different outlets. Therefore, a third distinct feature of nonverbal messages is they are **multi-channeled.** We can use several senses to communicate something nonverbally. Doctors dress professionally, maintain eye contact, listen attentively, and hang their diplomas on the wall in an attempt to establish credibility with their patients. Likewise, day spas manipulate lighting, music, and aroma to communicate a relaxing and calm atmosphere. Because we use multiple cues to send the same message, it makes sense that we will have a higher chance of nonverbal effectiveness. Although it may seem that nonverbal and verbal messages are quite different, they do have similar characteristics. Let us discuss three similarities between verbal and nonverbal communication.

HOW IS NONVERBAL SIMILAR TO VERBAL COMMUNICATION?

Just like verbal messages, nonverbal messages are rule-guided. As mentioned in Chapter Three, there are certain rules we must follow to be socially appropriate and these rules are culturally defined. In regard to nonverbal communication, **constitutive rules** refer to the behaviors we enact to help define the appropriateness of our communication. For example, if we asked you to generate a list of nonverbal behaviors that would communicate respect in a job interview, could you do this? We can demonstrate respect and professionalism in a job interview through our choice of clothing and use of certain gestures and facial expressions. Also, we adhere to specific rules when it comes to regulating or monitoring our communication with others. In the same way we use words to start, maintain, or end our conversations with others, we also use nonverbal communication to control or regulate our conversations. Eye contact (or lack of), specific hand gestures, paralanguage, and nods are all examples of nonverbal signals that we use to indicate turn-taking cues in conversation. Later in this chapter we will discuss three specific ways to use nonverbal communication to regulate our conversations.

Judee K. Burgoon (1978) developed **Nonverbal Expectancy Violation Theory** to help understand rule-guided behavior. The theory suggests that individuals hold expectancies for nonverbal behavior and when these expectations are violated (or the rules are not abided by) there are two common reactions, **physical arousal** and **cognitive arousal.** If you are in an elevator alone and the door opens and a stranger enters, the nonverbal expectancy is that they will stand as far away from you as possible (in order to maximize each other's personal space). If this stranger stood directly next to you, this would be a violation of the space rule. In response to this space violation you probably would consider stepping away (physical arousal) and also might consider the person odd (cognitive arousal) for not abiding by the "elevator rules."

Another similarity between nonverbal and verbal messages is that they are **culturally bounded.** The rules we follow during social interaction are socially constructed and are restricted to a specific culture. Nonverbal gestures in the United States that imply certain meanings are not universally understood. In the United States, when we touch our forefinger to our thumb to create a circle and spray the other three fingers upward we are signaling to others "okay." In France, this same gesture means "zero." In Japan it signals "money" and in Germany it is considered an obscene gesture. As with our verbal language, nonverbal messages are culturally bounded and do not necessarily translate to other cultures. Even within the United States, there are several subcultures that attribute their own distinct meanings to particular nonverbal behaviors. Consider gang members and their particular signs of inclusion, or social groups such as fraternities that have specific handshakes. Nonverbal communication can be unclear and confusing and may lead to many misinterpretations. Therefore, it is important to be aware of how we enact these behaviors and be sure to confirm their meaning by asking questions when messages are perceived as ambiguous.

Finally, both verbal and nonverbal messages are contextually restricted. As we previously mentioned, we must consider the situation, environment and setting we are in when deciding on appropriateness. Depending on the context of the nonverbal communication, it may influence the interpretation, meaning, and appropriateness of the communication. When we are pitching a new idea to our boss, we tend to dress more formally and manipulate our posture to appear more professional. However, can you imagine how surprised your friends would be if you continued this behavior while you were relaxing at home? Just like the words we use, our nonverbal behaviors should be modified to fit the situation. To gain a better understanding of these specific nonverbal behaviors we will introduce eight types of nonverbal communication.

EIGHT TYPES OF NONVERBAL COMMUNICATION

We have grouped nonverbal communication into eight types: facial communication, kinesics, haptics, proxemics, paralanguage, physical appearance, artifacts, and chronemics. In this section we will explain each type and provide insight on how the particular nonverbal behavior influences meaning during social interaction.

Facial Communication

Let us begin with **facial communication.** This includes any expression on the face that sends messages. Think about the thousands of different expressions you can make with your face by raising or lowering your eyebrows, shutting or opening your eyes, wrinkling your nose, and protruding your lips. Three functions of facial communication are to *display emotion,* to *supplement the verbal communication,* and to *compliment the verbal communication.* Our face is the primary channel for expressing emotions. The most basic emotions displayed through our facial expressions are often referred to by the acronym SADFISH which stands for sadness, anger, disgust, fear, interest, surprise, and happiness.

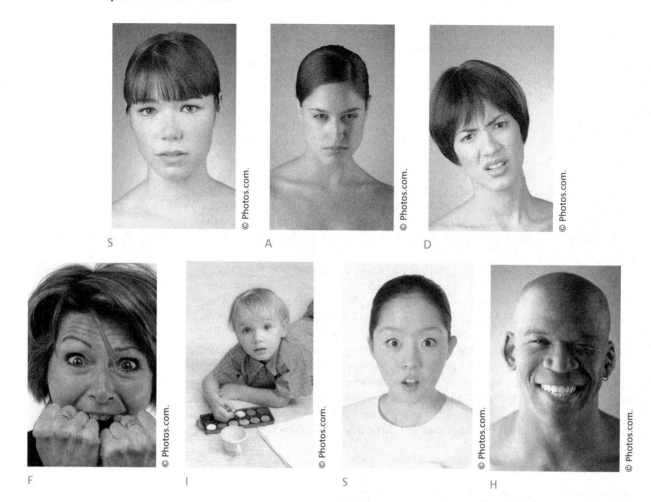

The second function of facial expressions is to supplement the verbal communication. Individuals reveal their attitudes toward certain subjects through their facial expressions. Think about how we analyze facial expressions when someone opens a gift from us. We can typically tell if they like the gift by the type of facial expression revealed. In addition, we use facial communication to complement our verbal message. For example, when we want to emphasize a word we tend to raise our eyebrows and open our eyes wide. This type of facial display matches the verbal portion of the message. Overall, our facial movements communicate emotions, attitudes and motivation.

One type of facial communication that has received a great deal of attention in the literature is oculesics. **Oculesics** is the study of eye behavior. Researchers are fascinated by oculesics and how it influences meaning. Eye behavior in the United States is very particular and is often perceived as an important means of showing attention, interest and respect to others. We often encourage our students to engage in eye contact during interviews for internships or jobs. However, if someone provides too much direct eye contact, it can be interpreted as disturbing and frightening. Eye contact is a perfect example of a nonverbal behavior that

What is this emblem conveying?

is culturally defined. Direct eye contact in Asian cultures is considered rude, disrespectful, and intimidating while in the United States, eye contact during conversation is expected.

Kinesics

Another type of nonverbal communication often associated with facial expressions is **kinesics,** or body movements. Ekman and Friesen (1969) classify kinesics into five categories: emblems, illustrators, affect displays, regulators, and adapters. Let us examine each of these. **Emblems** are specific nonverbal gestures that have a particular translation. For example, extending your forefinger over your lips means to be quiet. Or if you wanted to signal to someone to "come here" you would wave your hand toward your body. Because these emblems are context-bound, they are often misinterpreted when communicating with individuals from other cultures. Kitao and Kitao (1988) explain that the emblem for "okay" in the United States is the emblem used for "money" in Japan. They write, "An American and a Japanese man wanted to meet some friends. The American called from a pay phone and signaled to the Japanese man the American emblem for "okay," indicating that the friends would be able to meet them. The Japanese man interpreted the emblem as meaning that more coins were needed for the pay phone and rushed over to put in more money" (89). Although this is a lighthearted example, you can imagine how misinterpretations during business exchanges might not be humorous and may even be costly.

© Bartosz Ostrowski, 2007, Shutterstock.

Indicating something with a body gesture is an illustrator.

Illustrator is the label used to indicate when you use your body to help describe or visually depict something. You have probably heard someone say, "I caught a fish this big!" while indicating the size of the fish with their hands. This is an example of an illustrator. We use illustrators to visually demonstrate how big our nephew is or to point someone in the right direction when he is lost. Illustrators are more universal and less ambiguous than emblems.

Regulators are any type of body movement that is used in conversation to control the communication flow. Sometimes one person is monopolizing the conversation and you want to signal to him that you have something to say. What would you do? You have many options such as leaning forward, opening your mouth, nodding, and using your hand to gesture.

We can demonstrate our emotions nonverbally through affect displays. **Affect displays** are overt physical responses to our emotions that can be either positive or negative. Positive affect displays are constructive and encouraging. Patting or rubbing a close friend on the back when he is sad is an example of an affect display. Hugging and kissing are additional ways to display positive affect towards another. What about negative affect

© Miroslav, 2007, Shutterstock.

Positive affect displays are constructive and encouraging.

Do you have any nervous habits that you do unconsciously?

displays? Recall the last time someone asked you why you were angry. Perhaps it was because you were clenching your teeth or glaring with your eyes. In what ways have you physically manifested feelings of boredom, frustration, or sadness?

It is amazing how quickly infants and young children pick up on these displays. These learned behaviors are typically modeled by the infant's parent or caregiver through a process called social referencing. **Social referencing** refers to the process by which individuals will rely on those around them to determine how to respond to unfamiliar stimuli (Campos and Stenberg 1988). For example, when an infant is introduced to someone or something new they look to the parent for reassurance. When the parent responds with a positive affect display, like a smile, she sends a message to the infant that this new stimuli is comforting and not threatening. It is not long before the child displays more complex emotions through nonverbal affect displays. He may roll his eyes because he is annoyed or stomp his feet and cross his arms in disgust.

Adaptors are body movements that are enacted at a low level of awareness and usually indicate nervousness, anxiety, or boredom. Individuals may display these types of behaviors in situations that evoke anxiety such as public speaking classes or other types of public performances. Sometimes students are not aware that while they are giving their speech they are also engaging in behaviors such as tapping a pen on the podium, cracking their knuckles, and fixing their hair. When they watch themselves on videotape later, they are surprised because they were often unaware that they were exhibiting these adaptors. Outside of the classroom, individuals who work in human resource departments are often trained to look for adaptors during interviews and screening processes. Interviewee behaviors such as a bouncing knee, playing with paper, and postural changes are examples of adaptors that are often exhibited during interviews and considered a sign of nervousness or weakness.

Haptics

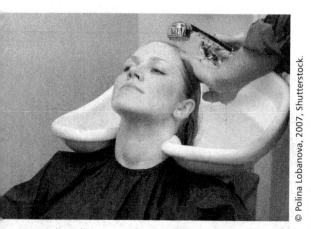

Hair stylists use a functional-professional touch in their work.

An additional type of nonverbal communication is **haptics,** or touch. The amount of touch in interpersonal relationships is related to liking and status. Anderson and Sull (1985) suggest that individuals who like each other will touch more often than those who do not. In fact, if individuals are not fond of each other they will actively avoid touching. Individuals with higher status, such as your boss or professor, typically choose whether to initiate touch into the relationship. They also may use touch to maintain control. For example, a middle school teacher may lead a student by physically directing them towards the corner of the room while saying, "Let's move over here." This type of touch is considered role-bound because the teacher and student are working within specific positions. The type of touch and who it is by is determined by the level of the interpersonal relationship. Thayer (1988) offers categories of touch based on people's roles and relationships. **Functional-professional** are touches that occur while accomplishing a specific task which is performed by those working within a specific role. For example, a barber, doctor, or nail technician will perform tasks which involve touch as part of their occupation. Functional touch also includes any touch that is done while trying to accomplish a goal. Helping a player off the ice when you are playing hockey or assisting an elderly woman across the street would both be situations employing functional touch. **Social-polite** are touches that occur between business partners, acquaintances and strangers. These include greetings and salutations, such as a handshake. **Friendship-warmth** are touches that occur between extended family members, close business associates, and friendly neighbors. This type of touch signals caring, concern and interest between interactants. A hug and a pat on the back are examples of this type of touch. There are some gray areas between this type of touch and the "love intimacy" category which may be a cause of great misinterpretation. **Love-intimacy** are touches that occur between family members and friends where there is affection and a deep level of caring. Extended hugs and holding hands are often examples of this type of touch. **Sexual-arousal** occurs within sexual/erotic contexts. Kissing is an example of this type of touch. Sometimes we use touch to initiate permission to enter into a "deeper" relationship with someone. If there is a discrepancy between the level of touch and your interpretation of the level of the relationship, it is important to be assertive and direct in your communication about this discrepancy with your relationship partner. Touch is the most intimate type of nonverbal communication and is also the most ambiguous. We interpret touch differently depending on the context. At a crowded club, party, elevator, or subway, touch is not interpreted as intrusive. However, within different contexts, when people intentionally enter our "space" we may view it as a violation. Now, let us discuss how our use of personal space contributes to nonverbal communication.

© Miroslav, 2007, Shutterstock.

Love-intimacy touches occur between family members and friends where there is affection and a deep level of caring.

Proxemics

The fourth type of nonverbal communication is space, or **proxemics**, which refers to the invisible bubble we place around our bodies. Often this space is considered our "comfort zone." Americans are highly conscious of our space and our territory. We allow certain individuals into our space, depending on the context of the situation. Edward T. Hall (1966) defined four types of space as listed on the next page.

Although this chart provides us with a general idea of how individuals use space, perceptions of appropriate personal space differ among individuals. In the United States we are generally very concerned with others infringing on what we consider to be "our space" and are very protective of it. We may even go so far as to place physical objects, or **markers**, between ourselves and others. Similar to the ways in which animals mark their territory, we may claim the territory around us by using markers to show others that this is our space. Think about all of the different ways that you may protect space that you consider yours. Have you ever spread out your books, bag, and articles of clothing in the library to purposefully take up more space? Have you ever spread out your

Table 3.1	Space, Context, and Nonverbal Communication	
Type of Space	**Distance**	**Individuals/Groups**
Intimate	0 to 18 inches	Reserved for those that are closest to us (e.g., boyfriend, girlfriend, spouse)
Personal	18 inches to 4 feet	Reserved for family members and close friends
Social	4 to 10 feet	The distance that we feel comfortable conductingeveryday social situations with strangers, acquaintances, and business partners
Public	10 feet and farther	The distance reserved for large audiences

belongings at the lunch table to discourage others from sitting next to you? Do you know anyone that intentionally takes up more than one parking space to deter anyone from parking "too close" to his vehicle? Males in our classes often admit they leave a seat between themselves and their friends at the movie theaters to increase their personal space. You may recall the popular *Seinfeld* "close-talker" episode; individuals who invaded someone's space while conversing were considered annoying and inappropriate. These are all examples of how our use of space influences meaning.

Paralanguage

The fifth type of nonverbal communication is **paralanguage,** which means everything beyond the words in the verbally communicated message. Paralanguage, or vocalic components of messages, includes pitch, rate, volume, pronunciation, inflection, tempo, accents, and vocal fillers such as ahh, ummm, and ya know. Hesitations and "sounds such as grunts, screams, laughs, gasps, sighs, and even silence fall under the purview of vocalics" (Hickson, Stacks, and Moore 2004, 258). Have you ever thought about the ways you use silence? You may use silence to show disgust, to keep a secret, to reveal a secret, or to enhance the importance of your message. As compiled by Knapp and Hall (2002), silence serves the following five functions: (1) to punctuate or emphasize certain words or ideas; (2) to evaluate or provide judgment of another's behavior (showing favor or disfavor, agreement, disagreement, attacking); (3) to hide or to reveal; (4) to express emotions: the silence of disgust, sadness, fear, anger or love; and (5) to engage in mental activity: show thoughtfulness, reflection, or ignorance (Bruneau 1973; Jaworski 1993; Jensen 1973). Because silence serves several functions, it is important to understand that it is often misunderstood. Can you recall a time when your silence was misconstrued?

Physical Appearance

The sixth type of nonverbal communication is **physical appearance,** which includes our body, clothing, make-up, height, size, and hair. Much of the literature on physical appearance examines the attractiveness of individuals. The literature (see, for example, McCroskey 1992) on this topic recognizes three different types of attraction: physical attraction (how visibly pleasing someone is), task attraction (how pleasing some is to work with), and social attraction (how pleasing someone is to interact with). We will focus primarily on physical attraction in this section.

What is perceived as attractive in the United States may be quite different from what is considered attractive in Thailand or Egypt. Likewise, what you might find attractive, your neighbor may find repulsive. However, we know that individuals are more attracted to physically attractive people than to physically unattractive people (Sprecher 1989). But perhaps this has more to do with **homophily,** or how similar we consider the target to be to ourselves. Although we cannot develop a global list of physically attractive attributes, we do know that there are benefits to being attractive. Watkins and Johnston (2000) found that when screening job applicants, attractiveness had no impact when the quality of the application was high. But attractiveness was a significant advantage when the application was mediocre. A more in-depth discussion of the three types of attraction will be examined in Chapter Six.

Physical Appearance

Research Brief

In the early 1980s some scholars even examined female bust size as it relates to perceptions of physical appearance. Researchers found that women with large bust sizes were evaluated as being relatively unintelligent, incompetent, immoral, and immodest, while women with small bust sizes were evaluated as being more intelligent, competent, modest, and moral (Kleinke and Staneski 1980).

Body size is one aspect of physical appearance that has been studied by researchers and is linked to how we form impressions of others. Body size is the relationship between an individual's height, weight, and muscular build and has received considerable amount of attention in the nonverbal communication literature. In 1942, Sheldon and Stevens theorized that there was a link between a person's physical attributes and personality traits. After collecting data on male body types and temperament, they distinguished between three primary body types: endomorphs, mesomorphs, and ectomorphs (see Hickson, Stacks and Moore for a more in-depth discussion).

The **endomorph** body type is described as being short, round, and soft. Researchers have associated the endomorph body type with being lazy, better-natured, more old fashioned, less good looking, more agreeable, and more dependent on others compared to the other body types. One study found that self-perceived endomorphs had significantly stronger intentions to smoke cigarettes compared to the other body types (Tucker 1983). But are all individuals with this body type lazy? Certainly former NBA player Charles Barkley, who was at one time referred to as "The Round Mound of Rebound," is not described as lazy, dependent, or even overly agreeable. It is important to be aware of our tendency to inaccurately stereotype individuals based on their appearance.

The **mesomorph** body type is described as being physically fit, muscular, average height and weight, and athletic. Researchers have associated this body type with being stronger, better looking, more adventurous, younger, taller, and more mature compared to the other body types (Sheldon, Hartl, and McDermott 1949). The mesomorphic body type was perceived by college students as an ideal body type for both males and females (Butler and Ryckman 1993). Even professional clinicians have been found to stereotype based on body type. Fletcher and Diekhoff (1998) found that therapists judged more muscular males, or male mesomorphs, as more mentally healthy than endomorphs and ectomorphs.

The **ectomorph** body type is described as being tall, thin and frail. Characteristics associated with this body type include being more tense, nervous, quieter, taller, younger, introverted, more afraid of people, lacking confidence, and being less social when compared with the other body types (Sheldon, Hartl, and McDermott 1949). Not all perceptions of this body type are negative. For example, our culture certainly seems to value a thin or ectomorphic body shape, especially in women. The media has been criticized for only displaying images of thin women and contributing to the problem of eating disorders in young women. In an effort to reduce the number of eating disorders in young women, the modeling industry has adopted healthier standards for their models' body weight.

Portnoy (1993) examined whether perceptions of body types differed across the lifespan by measuring senior citizen perceptions of same-sex cohorts. The researcher found that endomorphs were rated significantly more negatively on measures of physical attraction, social attraction, task attraction, and communication desirability than the other body types. This research illustrated that perceptions of different body types are similar for both younger and older populations.

In addition to body type, height has also been examined as a physical characteristic that influences meaning. Are taller people perceived as more competent? To date, Judge and Cable (2004) have designed the most comprehensive analysis between physical height and work success. Their meta-analysis found that while controlling for sex, age, and weight, there were significant positive relationships between height and social esteem, leader emergence, performance, and income. Therefore, not only are taller people perceived as more competent, they actually get paid more. How much more? Their findings suggest that someone who is six feet tall earns, on average, nearly $166,000 more during a thirty-year career than someone who is five feet, five inches.

Artifacts

The seventh type of nonverbal communication is artifacts. **Artifacts** are defined as "the physical objects and environmental attributes that communicate directly, define the communication context, or guide social behavior in some way" (Burgoon, Buller, and Woodall 1994, 123). We can think about artifacts in terms of personal adornment and environmental adornment. **Personal adornment** refers to how we use artifacts on our bodies. Tattoos, jewelry, branding, scarring, painting, makeup, glasses, and body piercing are all examples of artifacts that can be considered personal adornment. Two popular personal adornment artifacts addressed in the literature are tattoos and body piercing.

Although tattoos and body piercing are becoming more mainstream, there are still negative perceptions associated with these artifacts. Some of these perceptions may be founded, since Carroll, Riffenburgh, Roberts, and Myhre (2002) noted that participants with tattoos and body piercings were more likely to engage in high risk-taking behaviors such as disordered eating behavior, gateway drug use, hard drug use, sexual activity, suicide, and violence. Forbes (2001) also found that tattoos and piercings in college students are associated with more risk-taking behavior, greater use of alcohol and marijuana, and less social conformity. Another study found individuals with body modifications (tattoos or body piercings other than earlobes) reported more symptoms of depression and trait anxiety than individuals without body modifications (Roberti and Storch 2005).

Environmental adornment refers to artifacts that we use in our environment to identify ourselves. Consider how much you can learn about someone just by walking through their bedroom. Think about the artwork on the wall, the cleanliness, the type of objects on the dresser, and the clothes hanging in the closet. The MTV show *Room Raiders* capitalized on this phenomenon. Contestants decided who to go out with based solely on the contents of the bedrooms of the prospective dates. In addition to our bedrooms, we often use artifacts in our cars, offices, and other personal spaces to reflect our identity. Try to identify the environmental adornment artifacts the next time you are in your professors' offices. Do they have any artwork? Do they have photos of their dog or children? Can you figure out their alma mater?

Closely related to those artifacts are additional **environmental factors,** such as the context, room layout, lighting, and/or color. Environmental factors will influence how we interpret meaning. Consider the environmental factors inside a McDonalds. Think about the lighting, seating and colors—do they encourage you to eat fast? Fast food restaurants are interested in high turnover and do not typically want you to become too comfortable while eating your burger and fries. In contrast, high-end restaurants are more concerned with having their patrons relax, order more food and drinks, and stay for a long time in their establishment. These types of restaurants will often use candlelight, comfortable seating, and soft music to create an environment that says "stay awhile." Around the holidays, department stores often play specific music and try to create a certain mood in the store to encourage shoppers to spend more money. Be aware of the setting and environment around you. Do you respond to certain colors? Is there a reason why most classrooms have white walls and very little artwork? Does certain music put you in a certain mood? What types of smells make you hungry? What scents make you calm? Heightened awareness of the impact of environmental factors is critical to your success as a competent communicator.

Chronemics

The final type of nonverbal communication is referred to as **chronemics,** or how we use and perceive time. Our subjective view of time is contingent on our personal/psychological orientation and our cultural influences. Edward T. Hall (1976) suggests that each culture operates on a continuum from a monochronic orientation to a polychronic orientation to time. In general, Americans tends to be more **monochronic** because time is considered to be "linear" in nature. It spans across a "time line" and we can schedule appointments one after another in an orderly fashion. Think about how your daily planner is set up. (Or the fact that you *have* a daily planner.) You can segment time and schedule classes, appointments, and social events for each week, each day, and within each hour. Being punctual, scheduling appointments, and having strict adherence to starting times and ending times are all valued behaviors in the United States. During one of the authors' first day of graduate school, faculty stressed to the students, "Being on time is being late; being early is synonymous with being on time." This example reinforces the monochronic orientation that is valued in our culture. Being early in our culture is perceived as being organized, professional, prepared, and productive. Being late in our culture is perceived as being lazy, disorganized, uninterested, and unprofessional.

In contrast to monochronic, **polychronic** cultures perceive time as circular. This time orientation suggests that several things can be done at the same time. Polychronic cultures do not rely as heavily as monochromic cultures do on the clock. Meetings are viewed as time to cultivate relationships and it is more important to finish the conversation than to be "on time" for the next appointment. Time and activities are more fluid and things will "get done when they get done." Work time and personal time typically overlap in these cultures. Within the United States, this orientation has negative perceptions, such as being "nonambitious and a waste of precious time" (Hickson, Stacks, and Moore 2004, 316).

In addition to our cultural norms, we must also consider individual orientations. Consider how monochronic or polychronic your parents are. Did you grow up with a curfew? Did you have daily chores? Did you eat dinner at the same time each evening? Consider the extent to which you are monochronic. How punctual are you? Does it frustrate you when individuals do not accomplish tasks in an "appropriate" time? Do you consider "how long" things should take to accomplish?

FOUR FUNCTIONS OF NONVERBAL MESSAGES

Now that we have discussed the eight types of nonverbal communication, we will review four ways we use nonverbal behavior. The four functions of nonverbal messages are: (1) to facilitate our cognitive meaning, (2) to encode and decode emotions, (3) to express affection and support, and (4) to aid in impression formation/identity management.

Facilitate Cognitive Meaning

One primary function of nonverbal messages is aiding in cognitive meaning. We can use our nonverbal behavior in several ways to help create meaning. Ekman and Friesen (1969) specify five ways we aid our cognitive meaning. These include: repetition, contradiction, complementation, accent, and regulation. First, **repetition** refers to both verbal and nonverbal expressions made simultaneously to reinforce each other. The nonverbal message repeats the verbal message in order to increase the accuracy of the message. For example, when a police officer is directing traffic he may extend his hand and yell "Stop!" In this example, the cognitive meaning of the verbal message is repeated with the nonverbal emblem. We can use this function when we want to clarify or increase accuracy of the messages we send.

On the other hand, our nonverbal and verbal expressions may be contradictory. Oftentimes we say one thing and behave in a way that is inconsistent with our verbal message. When our nonverbal and verbal messages contradict each other, research has shown that we tend to believe the nonverbal messages.

Once again, we refer to the heuristic, "It is not what you said, but how you said it." If someone says, "I really like your new car," you will determine the sincerity of the message by dissecting the nonverbal cues. Was it said sarcastically? What do their facial expressions reveal? After scrutinizing the nonverbal and verbal messages, we will determine whether the verbal portion of the message was genuine. If there are any discrepancies between the two messages, we will rely on the nonverbal portion of the message.

Thirdly, **complementing** is a process by which our nonverbal communication is used in conjunction with the verbal portion of the message. We can determine the attitudes people hold when we examine the extent to which the verbal and nonverbal messages are complementing each other. If you want to make sure that your relationship partner knows that you are angry with her, you may glare at her and say, "I am so angry with you!"

The fourth way we aid our cognitive meaning, according to Ekman and Friesen (1969), is through accenting. **Accenting** is used when we want to stress or emphasize a particular word or phrase in our verbal message. If a friend says, "Please, do not be *late* to the party", and stresses the word "late," her use of accenting implies that it is important to her that you are on time for the party. Accenting can change the meaning of the original message, as well as the emotion conveyed (Anderson 1999). Consider how the meaning and the emotion of the same sentence changes slightly when we accent different words in the following statements:

> *George*, will you pick up fat-free milk from the store today?
> George, will you pick up *fat-free* milk from the store today?
> George, will you pick up fat-free milk from the store *today*?

The final way to aid our cognitive meaning is to **regulate** conversations. Duncan (1972) first introduced three ways we use nonverbal communication to regulate or negotiate our conversations. First, we engage in **turn-yielding** behaviors which signal to the listener that we are going to stop talking. Some examples of these signals include placing a drawl on the final syllable, placing emphasis on a final word, saying, "do you know what I *mean*?" displaying an open and direct body position, and leaning forward. Second, we can also engage in suppressing signals or **turn-maintaining** that suggest to the listener that we want to continue talking. These behaviors include talking more quickly and/or more loudly using hand gestures that suggest "wait a minute" or "one last point," and filling more pauses. **Back channeling cues** are used by listeners to signal that they are motivated to listen to us, they are not interested in "taking over the floor." Some nonverbal behaviors they may engage in include nodding their heads, and saying "I agree" or "ah huh." They are confirming interest in our message, but they are not interested in speaking themselves. Wiemann and Knapp (1975) added **turn-requesting** to the list of turn-taking cues. They suggest that listeners use buffers, short words or phrases such as, "But uhhh . . ." or "You know . . ." to signal to the speaker that they are interested in speaking. These buffers may be used while the speaker is talking or during a pause in conversation. If used properly, the speaker should finish his thought and relinquish the floor to them. Burgoon, Hunsaker, and Dawson (1994) identified an additional turn-taking cue referred to as **turn-denying.** Listeners use this cue when they are not interested in "taking over the floor." They may signal that they are not interested by increasing space between themselves and the speaker and/or avoiding direct eye contact with the speaker.

Encoding and Decoding Emotions

A second function of nonverbal communication is to display and interpret emotions. **Emotions** are subjective feelings such as happiness, anger, shame, fear, guilt, sadness, and excitement that produce positive or negative reactions that are physical, psychological and physiological. We often weigh the appropriateness of our outward reaction of emotion and judge whether it is desirable and/or acceptable (see Anderson 1999). Emotion is primarily communicated through nonverbal means. And typically, our most intense emotional experiences result from the formation, maintenance, and termination of our interpersonal relationships (Bowlby 1979).

Encoding emotions refers to an individual's ability to display feelings. Scholars have suggested as we get older we are better able to encode emotions such as happiness, anger, sadness, and fear (Mayo and LaFrance 1978). Furthermore, a seminal study found that regardless of gender, young children seem to express emotions quite similarly. However, as girls become older they become more accurate in detecting affective states in others and more expressive. Boys, on the other hand, are less accurate in detecting affective states in others and are less expressive encoders (Buck 1975). A more recent study revealed that women were more effective in encoding emotions than men (Wagner, MacDonald, and Manstead 1986). This research makes sense because it is more socially acceptable for women to express their emotions in the American culture. Men are more likely to suppress their feelings. In 1994, Kring, Smith, and Neale developed the Emotional Expressivity Scale (EES) to measure the extent to which individuals outwardly display their emotions. Complete the scale at the bottom of the next page to determine your own emotional expressivity.

Decoding emotions refers to the ability to accurately read and interpret the emotional states of others. Most scholars agree that individuals who are skilled encoders are also skilled decoders (see Burgoon, Buller, and Woodall 1994). Therefore women tend to be better decoders than men (Wagner, MacDonald, and Manstead 1986). However, research has shown that men tend to improve their sensitivity to facial expressions with individuals over time (Zuckerman, Lipets, Koivumaki, and Rosenthanl 1975). Test your decoding abilities by trying to interpret the emotions of the following facial expressions and vocalics.

© Junial Enterprises, 2007, Shutterstock.
© Edyta Linek, 2007, Shutterstock.
© digitalskillet, 2007, Shutterstock.
© Rade Pavlovic, 2007, Shutterstock.

What are these facial expressions saying?

Express Affection and Support

A third function of nonverbal communication is to provide affection and support. Oftentimes we will display nonverbal comforting strategies in our interpersonal relationship when someone is going through a difficult or stressful time. Dolin and Booth-Butterfield (1993) identified twelve nonverbal comforting strategies that college students employ to lend support to others.

Their study revealed that females reported more nonverbal comforting strategies and more diverse comforting responses than males. This means that females not only use nonverbal comforting strategies more frequently, but they also use several different types of strategies. Males were more likely to use emotional distancing behaviors than females. This strategy was negatively related to all the other strategies and the authors suggest it could be considered a comforting avoidance response. See Table 3.2 above for a complete list of comforting strategies and messages.

Aid in Impression Formation/Identity Management

Another significant function of nonverbal communication is creating first impressions. Typically, our initial perception of someone is based on

Table 3.2   Nonverbal Communication: Comforting Strategies

Comforting Strategy	Examples
Attentiveness (Showing you care)	Active listening behaviors and head nodding
Eye contact	Maintaining direct eye contact with the person
Crying	Referencing crying or weeping, either the other person's or the comforter's
Vocalics	Using one's voice to show concern, references to tone of voice, intensity, and speaking softly
Instrumental activity (Doing something for the other to show support person which may or may not be directly related to the distress)	Making dinner or running errands for the other person
Facial expression (Showing emotional reaction through one's face)	Adapting facial features to show empathy or simply looking concerned or sad
Proxemics	Using proxemics to close up the space without touching
Gesturing	Using hand and arm movements to show empathy, anger, and/or agitation about what the person is saying
Hugs	Directly hugging the person, either a whole or half hug
Pats	Touching arm or shoulder
Increased miscellaneous touch	Any type of increase in touching that does not fall into hugging or patting category
Emotional distancing (Comforting avoidance response)	Behaviors that are self-oriented and avoidant, intended to keep distance or to remain uninvolved

observing nonverbal behavior such as physical appearance, eye contact, and facial expressions. The information gathered through these first impressions is used to predict attitudes and opinions not yet revealed. This is referred to as proactive attribution. This information is also used for retroactive attribution, or to help explain the behavior of others in hindsight (Berger 1975). Although we gather this information quickly, it tends to remain stable over time—making these initial perceptions critical for future interactions. For example, research suggests that roommates whose initial impressions were positive had more satisfying subsequent interactions and used more productive strategies to solve conflict (Marek, Knapp, and Wanzer 2004). However, how often do you think our first impressions are inaccurate? We do not often provide second chances as we do not communicate long enough to find out if our first impressions were accurate.

BEST PRACTICES: AVOID COMMON NONVERBAL COMMUNICATION MISTAKES

To increase your effectiveness and appropriateness of receiving and displaying nonverbal communication in your interpersonal relationships, we offer suggestions in four areas. This section provides suggestions on how to monitor and adapt your nonverbal messages to your audience and context.

Common Areas of Miscommunication

First, nonverbal messages are often perceived as ambiguous and open for misinterpretation. The cultural barriers attached to many nonverbal behaviors can inhibit our interpretation of the meaning. Additionally, we do not usually have an extended period of time to create first impressions, which may have lasting results. Therefore, it is important to reinforce that nonverbal communication is not clear and is often misinterpreted. The more time we spend with others, the more we can interpret their nonverbal behavior accurately. Remember, nonverbal communication is multi-channeled and we can increase our chances of accurately interpreting others' behavior if we take all of the cues into consideration. Similarly, if we want to become more successful at getting our messages across to others, we will employ a number of different nonverbal behaviors that reinforce or clarify our verbal message. Therefore, if you want to make sure that your roommate knows that you are really angry with his behavior, you would look directly at him, fold your arms across your chest, lean forward, and accent certain words for emphasis while describing the reason you are angry.

Nonverbal Messages and Social Influence

Have you ever caused someone to change a behavior or attitude without intending to do so? Can you recall a specific time when you unintentionally influenced another person's attitudes or actions by displaying certain nonverbal behaviors? The two examples below illustrate how we can unintentionally influence others through our nonverbal behaviors.

1. Perhaps you broke eye contact with your sibling while she was telling you about something that happened to her at school. As a result of this behavior, your sister stopped talking and walked away from you. When you asked her later why she walked away from you, she told you that she could tell that you were not interested in her story.

2. Several years ago a famous supermodel cut her long hair quite short and, as a result of this choice, many other women did the same. In an interview the model stated that she certainly did not intend to influence others to cut their hair short.

These examples illustrate how we may influence others' attitudes or behaviors through our nonverbal messages without intending to do so. Thus, it is important to monitor our nonverbal behaviors closely and consider how our actions may influence others. Be aware that we may unintentionally influence someone else's behavior or attitude through our nonverbal behaviors.

Of course there are also many times when we intend to influence others by exhibiting certain nonverbal behaviors. For example, each time you dress professionally for a job interview you attempt to influence the interviewer's perceptions of you as a viable job candidate. Communication researchers have had a longstanding interest in learning more about how certain verbal and nonverbal behaviors influence those around us. Much of the research in this area suggests that you can influence individuals by displaying nonverbal behaviors associated with power and authority or kindness and liking, or both. Individuals can give the impression of authority and expertise through nonverbal cues such as wearing uniforms (e.g., military), name tags which include titles (e.g., manager), and personal artifacts. Military personnel, police officers, doctors, or managers in a retail store all have control over certain resources, and have power to reward or punish. We are more likely to obey a police officer's suggestion to move our car than the suggestion made by a stranger on the street because the officer wearing the uniform has the power to give us a ticket. Other nonverbal messages that project an image of authority and power are eye contact, touch, voice, and space. We often can tell who has the most power in an organization by the size of his or her office. Other persuasive tactics involve liking and kindness. We can persuade others by our charismatic tone, physical attractiveness, and smile. Nonverbal immediacy behaviors have been shown to be associated with social influence.

Nonverbal Immediacy in the Classroom

Research Brief

Research on nonverbal immediacy has exploded in the last twenty-five years. McCroskey and his colleagues have specifically explored nonverbal immediacy in the educational context. They have found that a teacher's nonverbal immediacy behavior is highly related to student affect for the teacher (McCroskey and Richmond 1992; McCroskey, Richmond, Sallinen, Fayer, and Barraclough 1995), student affective learning (McCroskey, Fayer, Richmond, Sallinen, and Barraclough 1996), student cognitive learning (McCroskey, Sallinen, Fayer, Richmond, and Barraclough 1996) and student motivation toward studying (Christophel 1990; Richmond 1990). Therefore, it appears that teachers who enact nonverbal immediacy behaviors provide many benefits to their students.

Immediacy refers to the psychological and physical closeness we have with one another. Mehrabian (1971) developed this principle that suggests we are drawn to people and things that we like, prefer, and value highly. Nonverbal immediacy behaviors can indicate inclusion, approachability, involvement, warmth, and positive affect. Some examples of nonverbal immediacy behaviors that individuals might use during social interaction include: eye contact, decreasing distance, appropriate touch, positive facial expressions, open body positions, varying pitch and tempo, and spending time with another person. In general, nonverbal immediacy behaviors produce direct, positive effects on other people (Mehrabian, 1971, 207). This direct-effects model suggests that individuals who engage in immediacy behaviors are more likely to be perceived as warmer, friendlier, more intimate, and more attractive (Anderson 1999). Although immediacy behaviors seem to be ultimately a good thing, can you think of a circumstance where enacting nonverbal immediacy behaviors may be detrimental to your interpersonal relationships? In other words, can you think of a time when you might want to increase the psychological space between yourself and a relational partner? Anderson (1999) suggests that in less positive relationships immediacy behaviors can be perceived as suffocating and threatening.

Practice Sending and Receiving Nonverbal Messages

As mentioned previously, it is often quite difficult to interpret the nonverbal behavior of others. Therefore, we need to supplement our observations with questions. We can clarify our perceptions of other's nonverbal messages. Simply by asking questions such as: "Are you upset?" "Were you being sarcastic?" and "Are you serious?" are easy ways to clarify nonverbal signals from others. Remember that not all nonverbal communication is intentional. Typically, the intentional nonverbal signals are emphasized. Subtle nonverbal behaviors may not be intentional. To accurately interpret others' nonverbal messages it is important to pay attention to all of the behaviors exhibited and seek clarification when verbal and nonverbal messages are contradictory.

Furthermore, be aware of the potential impact of the nonverbal messages you send to others. Because the assumption is that all nonverbal messages are intentional, we must be aware of the nonverbal messages we send. How do others interpret your facial expressions, use of space, and touch? We may never find an answer to this question unless we ask others for feedback.

Recognize Differences in Nonverbal Communication Perceptions

Sometimes individual differences can influence an individual's nonverbal behavior. One example of this is the extent to which individuals have communication apprehension. Recall our discussion of **communication apprehension (CA)** in Chapter Two. **CA** refers to the level of fear or anxiety an individual has that is associated with real or anticipated communication with another person (McCroskey 1977). McCroskey (1976) proposes that high CA's avoid communication situations and actively try to decrease communication attempts. Therefore, he predicts that high CA's are more likely than low CA's to have increased space, to avoid eye contact, to be averse to being touched, to have less vocal variety, to have fewer kinesic movements, and to have longer pause times in conversation. The degree of CA an individual has will determine the nonverbal impact on their interpersonal communication situations.

Age is another factor that may impact how we interpret nonverbal behavior. Life span refers to how our communication changes over time. Just as our verbal communication changes over time, so does our nonverbal behavior. Because we learn most of our nonverbal communication through cultural exposure, it is common for children to lack knowledge in what is considered socially appropriate nonverbal expression. As adults, we have a good time laughing at young people when they make mistakes like making a disgusted face when they taste grandma's signature soup. We do not expect them to have mature social skills, since those skills are acquired over time, although research has shown that throughout our life span we tend to express emotions such as SADFISH, similarly. In other words, the way a child would act surprised is similar to how a ninetyyear-old woman would—by opening her eyes, raising her eyebrows, and dropping her jaw. While initially we may have similar ways of expressing emotions, as we grow older we tend to engage in more self-monitoring techniques, become more aware of the rules regarding nonverbal behavior, and modify our behavior to fit these socially appropriate rules.

To send and receive nonverbal messages effectively, it is important to take into consideration the ambiguous nature of nonverbal messages. To make sure that the intended message is effectively communicated to your receiver, be sure that the verbal message is accompanied by multiple nonverbal behaviors that are consistent with the verbal message. Also, be aware of the fact that you can influence others both intentionally and unintentionally by exhibiting nonverbal messages. When you are confused about the nonverbal messages someone is sending, ask questions to clarify the message's meaning. Finally, when interpreting others' nonverbal messages, always consider the impact of individual differences such as personality, age, and culture on message delivery.

FUTURE DIRECTION FOR NONVERBAL COMMUNICATION: ELECTRONIC PARALANGUAGE

Current research has explored how we compensate for the lack of nonverbal cues during electronic communication. Nonverbal communication researchers know it is difficult to express emotions verbally. This is why in face-to-face situations we rely on a certain glance, smile, wink, or even tears to express our emotions. During computer-mediated communication we do not have the luxury of traditional nonverbal cues. Therefore we rely on electronic paralanguage to express emotions and regulate our conversations.

Electronic paralanguage includes emoticons, acronyms, abbreviations, and flaming. **Emoticons** are symbols made up of combinations of keyboard keys that convey emotions. For example, :) refers to a smiley face, while a :(refers to a frown face and ;) refers to someone winking. In addition, text messages and instant messages may insert actual artwork, such as ☺ or ☹.

Table 3.3   Nonverbal Communication: Electronic Paralanguage

Purpose	Text Messaging Shorthand
To express emotions	LOL, laugh out loud WYWH, Wish you were here
To regulate conversations	TTYL, talk to you later BRB, be right back L8R, later PMFJI, Pardon me for jumping in OMPL, one moment, please GGFN, gotta go for now
To provide feedback	IGTP, I get the point J/K, just kidding ISWYM, I see what you mean

Acronymns or text messaging shorthand are used to express a variety of nonverbal cues. Three functions are explored in Table 3.3 above.

Flaming refers to anti-social electronic behavior, such as swearing, firing insults, or shouting. Shouting or expressing anger in computer-mediated communication is usually indicated by typing in all capital letters (Krohn, 2004).

One difference between face-to-face nonverbal communication and engaging in electronic paralanguage is that emoticons are more deliberate and voluntary (Walther and D'Addario 2001). In traditional face-to-face situations, our nonverbal behavior is often unintentional. However, it is impossible to insert these emoticons without intent. Research has found that emoticons may serve the function of complementing the "written" statements, but they do not necessarily enhance them (Walther and D'Addario 2001).

SUMMARY

In this chapter we have introduced nonverbal communication and highlighted the importance of nonverbal communication in our everyday lives. We identified similarities to verbal communication and characterized the unique features of nonverbal behavior. Our hope is that you will heighten your awareness of how you use and interpret the eight types of nonverbal communication and understand how they function in your interpersonal relationships. By increasing your understanding of nonverbal communication, we hope you will avoid the communication problems that often accompany our nonverbal behavior. Remember that individuals are more likely to believe our nonverbal messages, regardless of intent. Therefore it is critical we understand the messages we are sending to others and how we interpret the nonverbal communication behaviors of others.

APPLICATIONS
Discussion Questions

A. Nonverbal Expectancy Violations: In what circumstances has someone violated your nonverbal expectancies? How did you respond? Under what circumstances would violating someone's expectations be considered favorable? Could there be benefits of violating someone's expectations?

B. Are our emotions innate or are they learned behaviors? This has been debated for the last 100 years. Charles Darwin's theory of facial expressions argues that our emotions are inherited (1965). This makes sense when we analyze babies and their expression of emotions. They have had little time to "learn" behavior and yet have universal signals (e.g., screaming) to express emotions. Other researchers suggest that our emotions have both genetic and biological origins because they are consistent among cultures (Ekman 1993; Izard 1992). What would you argue?

C. Discuss how instant messaging, text messages, email, and other computer-mediated methods of communication contribute to a polychronic culture.

D. Develop a list of regulative and constitutive rules for communicating online. How do you determine turn-taking? Is there such a thing as "interrupting" online? How do you demonstrate liking, professionalism, support, and/or anger? What is considered a rule violation online? How do you react to violations?

REFERENCES

Anderson, P. A. 1999. *Nonverbal communication: Forms and functions.* Mountain View, CA: Mayfield Publishing.

Anderson, P. A., and K. K. Sull. 1985. Out of touch, out of reach: Tactile predisposition as predictors of interpersonal distance. *Western Journal of Speech Communication, 49,* 57–72.

Berger, C. R. 1975. Proactive and retroactive attribution processes. *Human Communication Research, 2,* 33–50.

Bowlby, J. 1979. *The making and breaking of affectional bonds.* London: Tavistock.

Bruneau, T. J. 1973. Communicative silences: Forms and functions. *Journal of Communication, 23,* 17–46.

Buck, R. 1975. Nonverbal communication of affect in children. *Journal of Personality and Social Psychology, 31,* 644–653.

Burgoon, J. K. 1978. A communication model of personal space violation: Explication and an initial test. *Human Communication Research, 4,* 129–142.

Burgoon, J. K., D. B. Buller, and W. G. Woodall. 1994. *Nonverbal communication: The unspoken dialogue.* Columbus, OH: Greyden Press.

Burgoon, J., F. G. Hunsaker, and E. J. Dawson. 1994. *Human communication (3rd ed.).* Thousand Oaks, CA: Sage.

Butler, J. C., and R. M. Ryckman. 1993. Perceived and ideal physiques in male and female university students. *Journal of Social Psychology, 133,* 751–752.

Campos, J. J., and C. Stenberg. 1988. Perceptions, appraisals, and emotion: The onset of social referencing. In M. E. Lamb and L. R. Sherrod (Eds.), *Infant social cognition: Empirical and theoretical considerations.* Hillsdale, NJ: Erlbaum.

Carroll, S. T., R. H. Riffenburgh, T. A. Roberts, and E. B. Myhre. 2002. Tattoos and body piercings as indicators of adolescent risk-taking behaviors. *Pediatrics, 109,* 1021–1027.

Christophel, D. M. 1990. The relationship between teacher immediacy behaviors, student motivation, and learning. *Communication Education, 39,* 323–340.

Cortes, J. B., and F. Gatti. 1965. Physique and self description of temperament. *Journal of Consulting Psychology, 29,* 432–439.

Darwin, C. 1965. *The expression of emotions in man and animals.* Chicago: University of Chicago Press.

Dolin, D., and M. Booth-Butterfield. 1993. Reach out and touch someone: Analysis of nonverbal comforting responses. *Communication Quarterly, 41,* 383–393.

Duncan Jr., S. D. 1972. Some signals and rules for taking speaking turns in conversations. *Journal of Personality and Social Psychology, 23,* 283–292.

Ekman, P. 1993. Facial expression and emotion. *American Psychologist, 48,* 384–392.

Ekman, P., and W. V. Friesen. 1969. The repertoire of non-verbal behaviour: categories, origins, usage and codings. *Semiotics 1,* 49–98.

Fletcher, C., and G. M. Diekhoff. 1998. Body-type stereotyping in therapeutic judgments. *Perceptual and Motor Skills, 86,* 842.

Forbes, G. B. 2001. College students with tattoos and piercings: Motives, family experiences, personality factors, and perception by others. *Psychological Reports, 89,* 774–786.

Hall, E. T. 1966. *The hidden dimension,* NY: Doubleday.

Hall, E. T. 1976. *Beyond culture.* New York: Doubleday.

Hickson III, M., D. W. Stacks, and N. Moore. 2004. *Nonverbal communication* (4th ed.). Los Angeles, CA: Roxbury.

Izard, C. E. 1992. Basic emotions, relationship among emotions, and emotion-cognition relationships. *Psychological Review, 99,* 561–565.

Jaworski, A. 1993. *The power of silence: Social and pragmatic perspectives.* Newbury Park, CA: Sage.

Jensen, J. V. 1973. Communicative functions of silence. *ETC, 30,* 249–257.

Judge, T. A., and D. M. Cable. 2004. The effect of physical height on workplace success and income: Preliminary test of a theoretical model. *Journal of Applied Psychology, 89,* 428–441.

Kitao, S. K., and K. Kitao. 1988. Differences in the kinesic codes of Americans and Japanese. *World Communication, 17,* 83–103.

Kleinke, C. L., and R. A. Staneski. 1980. First impressions of female bust size. *Journal of Social Psychology, 110,* 123–134.

Knapp, M. L., and J. A. Hall. 2002. *Nonverbal communication in human interaction.* United States: Wadsworth.

Kring, A. M., D. A. Smith, and J. M. Neale. 1994. Individual differences in dispositional expressiveness: The development and validation of the emotional expressivity scale. *Journal of Personality and Social Psychology, 66,* 934–949.

Krohn, F. B. 2004. A generational approach to using emoticons as nonverbal communication. *Journal of Technical Writing and Communication, 34,* 321–328.

Marek, C. I, J. L. Knapp, and M. B. Wanzer. 2004. An exploratory investigation of the relationship between roommates' first impressions and subsequent communication patterns. *Communication Research Reports, 21,* 210–220.

Mayo, C., and M. LaFrance. 1978. *On the acquisition of nonverbal communication: A review.* Merrill-Palmer Quarterly, 24, 213–228.

McCroskey, J. C. 1976. The effects of communication apprehension on nonverbal behavior. *Communication Quarterly, 24,* 39–44.

McCroskey, J. C. 1977. Classroom consequences of communication apprehension. *Communication Education, 26,* 27–33.

McCroskey, J. C. 1992. *An introduction to communication in the classroom.* Edina, MI: Burgess Publishing Division.

McCroskey, J. C., J. M. Fayer, V. P. Richmond, A. Sallinen, and R. A. Barraclough. 1996. A multi-cultural examination of the relationship between nonverbal immediacy and affective learning. *Communication Quarterly, 44,* 297–307.

McCroskey, J. C., and V. P. Richmond. 1992. Increasing teacher influence through immediacy. In V. P. Richmond and J. C. McCroskey, (Eds.), *Power in the classroom: Communication, control and concern* (101–119). Hillsdale: NJ: Lawrence Erlbaum Associates.

McCroskey, J. C., V. P. Richmond, A. Sallinen, J. M. Fayer, and R. A. Barraclough. 1995. A cross-cultural and multibehavioral analysis of the relationships between nonverbal immediacy and teacher evaluation. *Communication Education, 44,* 281–291.

McCroskey, J. C., A. Sallinen, J. M. Fayer, V. P. Richmond, and R. A. Barraclough. 1996. Nonverbal immediacy and cognitive learning: A cross cultural investigation. *Communication Education, 45,* 200–211.

Mehrabian, A. 1971. *Silent messages.* Belmont, CA: Wadsworth.

Mehrabian, A., and S. R. Ferris. 1967. Inference of attitudes from nonverbal communication in two channels. *Journal of Consulting Psychology, 31,* 248–252.

Portnoy, E. J. 1993. The impact of body type on perceptions of attractiveness by older individuals. *Communication Reports, 6,* 101–109.

Richmond, V. P. 1990. Communication in the classroom: Power and motivation. *Communication Education, 39,* 181–195.

Roberti, J. W., and E. A. Storch. 2005. Psychosocial adjustment of college students with tattoos and piercings. *Journal of College Counseling, 8,* 14–19.

Sheldon, W. H., and S. S. Stevens. 1942. *The varieties of temperament; a psychology of constitutional differences.* Oxford, England: Harper.

Sheldon, W. H., E. M. Hartl, and E. McDermott. 1949. *The variety of delinquent youth.* Oxford, England: Harper.

Sprecher, S. 1989. Premarital sexual standards for different categories of individuals. *Journal of Sex Research, 26,* 232–248.

Street, R. L., and D. B. Buller. 1987. Nonverbal response patterns in physician-patient interactions: A functional analysis. *Journal of Nonverbal Behavior, 11,* 234–253.

Thayer, S. 1988. Close encounters. *Psychology Today, 22,* 30–36.

Tucker, L. A. 1983. Cigarette smoking intentions and obesity among high school males. *Psychological Reports, 52,* 530.

Wagner, H. L., C. J. MacDonald, and A. S. R. Manstead. 1986. Communication of individual emotions by spontaneous facial expressions. *Journal of Personality and Social Psychology, 50,* 737–743.

Walther, J. B., and K. P. D'Addario. 2001. The impacts of emoticons on message interpretation in computer-mediated communication. *Social Science Computer Review, 19*, 324–347.

Watkins, L. M., and L. Johnston. 2000. Screening job applicants: The impact of physical attractiveness and application quality. *International Journal of Selection and Assessment, 8*, 76.

Wiemann, J., and M. Knapp. 1975. Turn-taking in conversation. *Journal of Communication, 25*, 75–92.

Zuckerman, M., M. S. Lipets, J. H. Koivumaki, and R. Rosenthanl. 1975. Encoding and decoding nonverbal cues of emotion. *Journal of Personality and Social Psychology, 32*, 1068–1076.

Formation and Maintenance of Identity

OBJECTIVES

- Identify and explain the different stages of identity development.
- Identify the factors that contribute to each stage of identity development.
- Understand the unique interaction between psychological, sociological, and communicative processes during identity development.

KEY TERMS

accommodation
active vocabulary
animistic thinkers
assimilation
conservation
daydreaming
difficult infants
dyadic interactions
easy infants
egocentrism
fast mapping
gonads

holophrases
identity
imaginary audience
imaginary playmate
infancy
intuitive thinking
magical thinking
object concept
operations
passive vocabulary
personal fables
play

protowords
psychosocial
    development
puberty
pubescence
schemas
sensorimotor
slow-to-warm-up
    infants
socialization
temperament
transitive inference

INFANTS

The first stage of human development that is of major concern to communication scholars is infancy. Indeed, infancy is critical to the development of communication skills that you use on a daily basis.

Physical and Motor Development in Infancy

Human development is typically divided into various stages (Table 4.1): **Infancy**, which lasts until age 2, is the first of these.

One of the important developmental outcomes of infancy involves changes in motor abilities. Although newborn infants are almost unique among the earth's animal species in their inability to locomote within a short time of birth, they are among the few that eventually learn to walk on two legs. Other nonhuman primates who are capable of this same feat are usually more at home on all fours than on two; and the kangaroo, which does move on two legs, cannot run or even walk very well on those two legs, but must instead resort to hopping.

But the newborn does not hop, does not even crawl. In fact, the newborn's first movements are largely uncoordinated and purposeless. But these movements are a way of exercising and developing control over muscle systems. Gradually, they become more purposeful. At first the infant can only stare at an interesting object, waving hands and arms wildly, clearly excited but incapable of coordinating action with intention. Learning to reach and grasp, like learning to walk, is not an easy matter.

In time, infants do learn to walk—and eventually, like the kangaroo, to hop. But first they go through a relatively predictable sequence of motor achievements: learn to lift the head, to turn over on the back, to direct hand movements, to sit, to crawl, to stand, to walk, and finally, to hop.

Perception in the Newborn

For a long time, psychologists believed William James's (1890/1950) claim that the infant's world is "one great blooming, buzzing, confusion," that, in particular, vision and hearing are so poorly developed as to be virtually useless. We now know that is not quite true. Infants are sensitive to light almost immediately after birth and are capable of visually following moving objects within a few days. When shown blurred or clear images of human faces, they show preference for the clear face (Berger, Donnadieu, Meary, Kandel, & Mazens,

Table 4.1   Major Stages in Human Development

Stages and Substages	Time Span
Prenatal	Conception to birth
Neonatal	Approximately first 2 weeks of life
Infancy	Until age 2
Childhood	2 to 11–12 years
Early Childhood	2 to 6–7 years
Middle Childhood	6–7 to 11–12 years
Adolescence	11–12 to 19–20 years
Adulthood	20 to the end
Early Adulthood	20 to 40–45
Middle Adulthood	40–45 to 65–70
Late Adulthood	65–70 to the end

2010). With respect to hearing, evidence suggests that, unlike the young of many species that are deaf at birth (dogs and cats, for example), the neonate is sensitive to a wide range of sounds and can also locate the direction of sounds (Volpe, 2008).

The smell system, too, is functional in newborns. When presented with unpleasant odors, newborns turn away (Porter & Rieser, 2005). In contrast, the smell of their own mother's milk, but not that of other mothers, has a calming effect on them (Nishitani et al., 2009).

The taste, system, too, seems to be relatively well developed in newborns. In fact, it seems that they can learn about different tastes even before they're born. Mennella, Jagnow, and Beauchamp (2001) had a group of pregnant mothers drink carrot juice during pregnancy. Their infants later showed stronger preference for carrot-flavored cereal than did other infants whose mothers had not drunk carrot juice while pregnant.

Cognitive Development in Infancy

So even before birth, newborns begin to learn, as is evident in their recognition of flavors to which their mothers have been exposed. But the fact is, they aren't born with a great store of knowledge and ideas and opinions. For the first three months of their infants' lives, Super and Harkness (1998) tell us, Kipsigis mothers in rural Kenya refer to them as *monkeys*; only later do they call them *children*.

Why? One plausible answer is that the newborn is much like a little monkey: It can respond to a small range of stimuli, it can cry and vomit, and it is heir to a handful of survival-related reflexes such as sucking and rooting. But it would surely die if its environment did not include adults devoted to its survival. There is much that the infant needs to learn, much with which it must become familiar, before it can stand on its own two feet—not only physically, but also cognitively.

We know that infants are born with an impressive array of cognitive tools—tools that will eventually allow them to know and understand things of which they cannot yet even dream. They can look and see; they can hear; they can smell and taste. And more impressive than anything else, they have an astonishing brain. In fact, they are remarkably ready to become familiar with all there is out there.

That infants begin to learn before and immediately after birth seems clear. As an example, Lipsitt (1971) conditioned infants' rooting reflex by stroking their cheeks when a tone sounded. (Rooting is the infant's reflexive head turning

Infants are born with an impressive array of cognitive tools. This tyke is learning more than just one thing at a time.

when the cheek or corner of the mouth is stimulated—an important reflex for finding nipples.) If they turned in the appropriate direction, they were reinforced by being allowed to suck briefly on a nipple. Within a half-hour of training, newborns who had initially turned in response to the tone an average of 25 percent of the time now turned 75 percent of the time. Perhaps even more striking, when a different tone was introduced and the newborns were not reinforced for turning in response to the second tone but were still reinforced for the first tone, they continued to respond to the second tone only 25 percent of the time. Thus, newborns can not only be conditioned, but they can also discriminate between different sounds.

Cognition and Language Development.   Discriminating the sounds of a language is essential for one of the most formidable and important of all cognitive tasks: learning to communicate with language. And, as we saw in Chapter 2, language is basic to thinking, to creating and participating in cultures, and to communicating.

The *prespeech* stage of language learning spans most of the first year. It entails learning to take turns, to use gestures, to discriminate among different sounds, to produce sounds, and eventually to produce words. A good set of wireless headphones with cleverly designed lessons might also help.

But communication and language are not quite synonymous. A dog that walks to its empty dish, looks its master in the eye, and begins to growl is communicating but is not using language. Language is the use of arbitrary sounds or symbols in a purposeful way to convey meaning; communication is simply the transmission of a message.

The infant's first communication system is not language but a complex system of sounds and gestures. To master this communication system, the infant needs to learn five things: turn taking, the use of gestures, sound discrimination, sound production, and words. All of these are basic to adult conversation. These accomplishments are part of the *prespeech* stage of language learning.

At around age 1, though sometimes much earlier or later, the first word appears. In all cultures, the first words tend to be nouns—simple names for common, everyday objects (Salerni, Assanelli, D'Odorico, & Rossi, 2007). Often, the earliest consistent sound made by an infant is not a recognizable word but has a clear meaning. Elizabeth, at a startlingly young age, repeatedly said "buh"—an expression that her parents eventually realized meant "light" or "turn the light on and off and on and off and on and off . . ." These sorts of consistent sounds are labeled **protowords**.

Holophrases are similar to protowords except that they are real words rather than just sounds. Holophrases are words or expressions that are sentencelike in that they contain a variety of sometimes complex meanings. Holophrases usually appear by the age of 12 months. They often express meanings that an adult could not easily communicate in less than an entire sentence. For example, the holophrase "up," uttered in an unmistakably imperious tone by 1-year-old Nathan, means "Pick me up right now and sing me a song or else I may do something really annoying."

By the age of 18 months, most infants have begun to join modifiers to nouns and pronouns to make two-word sentences. At this stage, speech is still highly telegraphic; complex meanings are squeezed into simple, and sometimes grammatically incorrect, two-word utterances. For example, the sentence "Mummy gone" may mean something as complex as "my dear mother is currently on a business trip in Chicago."

During this stage, there is ordinarily a tremendous spurt in vocabulary, common to all cultures. Whereas learning the first 100 or so words can take several months, the next hundred might be learned in just a few weeks (Yu, 2008). This type of learning is called **fast mapping**.

Note that in all early stages of language learning, children's **passive vocabulary** is much larger than their **active vocabulary**. That is, they understand far more words than they actually use in their speech.

Multiple-word sentences typically appear by the age of 2 to 2½. Although early preschool speech is still often telegraphic, it includes complex grammatical variations to express different meanings. By the late preschool years, it has become adultlike.

Although average ages are assigned to each of these developments, they are simply approximations. Here, as in all areas of human development, it is normal for some to display a behavior earlier or later. An average is not an expression of normality; it is simply a point around which observations are distributed. (See Table 4.2 for a summary of early language development.)

Table 4.2   Sequence of Infant Language Development

Developmental Stage	Main Accomplishments	Sample Utterances
Prespeech (before age 1)	Turn taking Using gestures such as pointing Discriminating and producing sounds	"Waaaaaa …" "Gooogoooogooogaaahgaah"
First words (around age 1)	Protowords (nonwords with consistent meaning) Holophrases (single words with sentence-like meanings)	"Bulla," meaning all umbrella-like things, including rhubarb leaves "Mama," meaning "Would you please come here mother and bring the milk with you …"
Two-word sentences (around age 18 months)	Vocabulary spurt Fast mapping (one-exposure learning)	"More milk" "Pretty horsie"
Multiple-word sentences (by age 2 to 2½)	Longer sentences; more grammatical variation; increasingly correct use of word classes	"Read again book" "I no can play" "I runned fast"

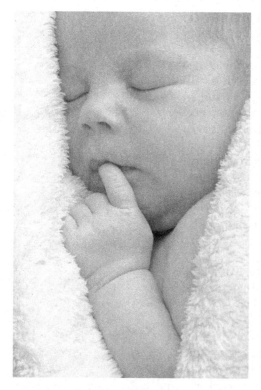

Social-Emotional Development in Infancy

Average vocabulary size at different ages is relatively easily calculated; uncovering average social and emotional characteristics is more challenging.

Erikson's Stages.   Erik Erikson (1963; 1968) describes eight major stages in human development over the lifespan. Each of these stages is identified by a basic conflict brought about by the need to adapt to the social environment—hence it is a theory of **psychosocial development**. And at each level, new competencies are required of the individual. The first two of these stages span infancy (all eight stages are summarized in Figure 4.6).

Trust Versus Mistrust.   The first task for the infant, Erikson explains, is learning to trust this bewildering and often frightening world—in the face of a strong tendency not to trust because everything is so strange and unfamiliar. The most important person in the infant's life at this stage is the principal caregiver. If that person is warm and loving, the infant soon learns that the world is a safe, warm, and predictable place. But if the caregiver is cold and rejecting, the child may grow up to be wary and anxious.

Autonomy Versus Shame and Doubt.   At first, infants cannot intend to carry out an action and then do so. They have to learn to coordinate and control activities according to intentions. As they begin to realize that they can *intend* and *accomplish* things, they develop a growing sense of autonomy. But always, there is the tendency to go back to a safer period, back to the comfort and security that marked the end of the previous period. Successful resolution of this conflict depends largely on caregivers giving the child opportunities to explore and to be autonomous.

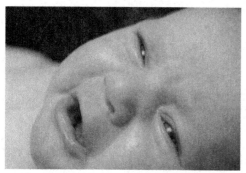

Sleep is the most common newborn state, occupying about two thirds of the day. Happily, crying is the least common state.

Infant States.   Clearly, however, not all infants develop in the same way and at the same pace. Even very early in life, we are sometimes very different from one another in our typical behaviors and reactions. These early differences might foreshadow differences among adults.

The most common *infant states* are described as regular sleep, disturbed sleep, drowsiness, alert activity (alert and actively responding to stimuli), alert inactivity (alert, examining environment, but inactive), and crying (Wolff, 1966).

Infants vary tremendously in the amount of time they spend in each state. For example, in a study of six infants, Brown (1964) found that although the babies spent approximately one third of their time sleeping, one infant slept 56 percent of the time, and another 22 percent of the time. One infant cried 35 percent of the time; another, 17 percent of the time. One was alert 40 percent of the time; another, 10 percent of the time (Figure 4.1).

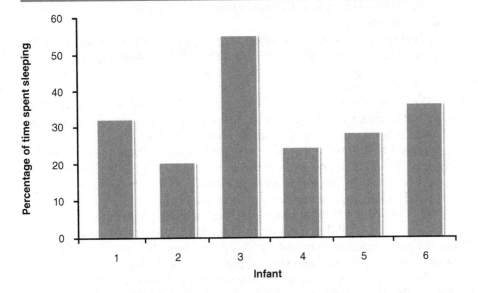

Figure 4.1 **Brown observed 6 infants for 1 hour about an hour after feeding, during the first week after birth. Shown here are the tremendous variations in the amount of time each spent sleeping. (Based on data from J. L. Brown, 1964.)**

Infant-Caregiver Interaction.   To understand what it is like to be a child, it is essential to know which child, when, and where. We have to be aware of children's contexts and of how these contexts have changed and continue to change. We also need to know something of the ethnic, cultural, social, and political realities in the child's life. Perhaps most important, to understand the lives of infants, we need to ask about interactions in the family, because the family usually defines the most important aspects of the child's physical and social context.

Traditionally, the emphasis has been on **dyadic interactions** (interactions involving two individuals)—especially the mother-infant dyad. Father-infant and infant-sibling interactions also need to be taken into account. More complex interactions are concerned with how infants affect parents and change the family, and how these changes in turn affect the infant. The contexts in which the family functions—social, political, economic, religious, and philosophical—are all important influences in shaping the child.

Infant Temperament.   Parental characteristics, such as patience or irritability, influence how parents interact with their children; so, too, do infant characteristics.

The infant's characteristic ways of behaving define **temperament**, a term that is somewhat different from *personality*. *Personality* indicates a degree of learning and experience that infants have not yet had; it is used to describe identifying traits of older children and adults. *Temperament*, on the other hand, implies an inherited predisposition to act and be a certain way. For example, some infants are habitually active, others quieter; some readily approach strangers, others hide behind their mothers; some are generally happy, others less so.

After looking at the typical behaviors of a large group of infants, Thomas and Chess (1977) found that certain infants seem to have remarkably similar patterns of characteristics. One group, the **difficult infants**, is characterized by irregularity in such things as eating, sleeping, and toilet functions; withdrawal from unfamiliar situations; slow adaptation to change; and intense and often negative moods.

In contrast, **easy infants** are characterized by regularity in eating, sleeping, and toileting; high approach tendencies in novel situations; high adaptability to change; and a preponderance of positive moods as well as low or moderate intensity of reaction.

Slow-to-warm-up infants are characterized by a low activity level, high initial withdrawal from the unfamiliar, slow adaptation to change, greater negativity in mood, and a moderate or low intensity of reaction.

Of the 141 children in Thomas and Chess's study, 65 percent could be classified as belonging to one of these three temperament types (40 percent easy; 15 percent difficult; 10 percent slow to warm up); the remaining 35 percent displayed varying mixtures of temperament (Figure 4.2).

Note that these temperaments don't exhaust all possibilities. Nor do all "easy" or "difficult" children always react predictably in a given situation. Even easy infants sometimes cry and fuss; and the most difficult of little urchins might occasionally laugh and seem approachable and adaptable.

The long-term implications of infant temperament are intriguing. For one thing, following a study of some 7,695 families, Jokela (2010) reports that the probability of parents having a second child is significantly affected by the temperament of the first. Parents whose first child adapts easily to novelty and

Figure 4.2 Infant temperaments. Approximate percentage of children with each temperament. Based on data reported in Thomas, A., & Chess, S. (1977). *Temperament and development.* New York: Brunner/Mazel.

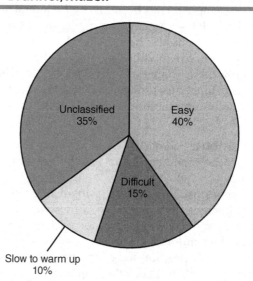

Unclassified 35%

Easy 40%

Difficult 15%

Slow to warm up 10%

is alert, intelligent, and sociable are more likely to have a second child than are parents of more difficult children.

Several longitudinal studies also indicate that infants rated as *difficult* are at somewhat higher risk of displaying psychiatric symptoms in adolescence (Kapornai et al., 2007). And Kagan's (1997) research with infants classified as highly *reactive* (fearful of the unfamiliar; easily distressed) or *nonreactive* (relaxed in the face of the unfamiliar; not easily frightened) shows that these classifications might have implications for later developmental outcomes. In his sample, about one third of the highly reactive infants continued to be highly fearful in strange situations at the age of 14 to 21 months. In contrast, the majority of the nonre-actives were calm, outgoing, and confident. And these patterns, though less clear, were still evident in some children at the age of 4 ½ years.

Note, however, that infant temperament is not always easy to classify accurately. Furthermore, for many infants, tempera-ment may be quite variable, especially during the first 2 years of life; after age 2, it appears to be far more stable.

The majority of children are classified as "easy" or of mixed temperaments. About 10 percent are "slow to warm up." Some take comfort behind a parent's leg; others rely on the bear.

CHILDREN

By the age of 6 or 7, the uniqueness that will mark the indi-vidual throughout life has become increasingly apparent. Four-year-old Robert sits at the Thanksgiving table as his dad explains the meaning of this day and how the pilgrims could not just run to the store to buy their food, how they made do with what they could grow. "If you were a pilgrim," says his dad, "what would you plant?"

"Corn," his older brother says. "And peas, and potatoes, and turnips."
"And what would you plant, Robert?"
Robert glances cleverly at his plate. "I'd plant turkeys," he answers.

That's the way Robert is: clever and entertaining. He has a wonderfully inventive mind, seldom limited by the rules that constrain our thoughts. His thinking is, as Pearce (1977) puts it, **magical thinking**; it does not always need to be checked against reality. In these early years, thinking is wishful and fan-tastic. It somehow assumes that reality can be changed by a thought. Thus it is that a magic spell can produce a witch or a princess, a silver thread or a pot of gold; a dream can be real, and perhaps reality too can be a dream; and a wish can make a race car of a stone, a cave of a small corner, a giant sailing ship of a discarded matchbox.

Cognitive Development in Childhood: Piaget's Theory

But, Pearce tells us, we do not gladly accept—perhaps we don't even under-stand—the magical child. Our approach to children and our scientific research ask instead: "How can the child be made to attend to reality?" or "How can we make the child abandon magical thinking?" (p. xv). The Swiss psychologist, Jean Piaget, provides some fascinating insights that have become a lasting part of the child development puzzle.

Mechanisms of Adaptation.

Piaget was first trained as a biologist, and he brings a biologist's perspective to the questions of development. Development, he explains, is a process of adaptation. Children are not born knowing how to cope with external reality; they're born with a handful of reflexes that are crucial for biological survival (sucking, sneezing, and swallowing, for example). These ready-made responses allow the child to *assimilate* important aspects of the environment. Piaget defines **assimilation** as the use of previously acquired or innate activities without having to modify these activities.

But from the very beginning, the infant's reflexes are not always suited to the demands of the environment. For example, differently placed and shaped nipples require changes in the infant's behaviors. These changes define **accommodation**. Accommodation implies changes in the child's thought and behavior in response to environmental demands.

Throughout life, assimilation and accommodation are the two ways we have of interacting with the environment. We make use of aspects of our environment for certain activities that we already know (assimilation); and we modify our activities to be able to make use of certain aspects of the environment (accommodation).

Schemas.

Children are born with a limited repertoire of unlearned abilities (sucking, for example). Mental representations of these abilities are labeled **schemas** (also called *schemata* or *schemes*). As a result of interacting with the environment through assimilation and accommodation, schemas (mental representations) change. In other words, mental growth takes place through assimilation and accommodation.

The Stage Theory.

As children develop, their primitive schemas give way to more advanced representations of the world and to new ways of dealing with the world on a mental level. Piaget describes the progression of cognitive development in terms of four major stages and various substages (Table 4.3).

Sensorimotor Thought.   During much of the first 2 years of life, says Piaget, infants understand the world mainly in terms of the activities they perform and the sensations that result; hence the label sensorimotor. It is a world of sensation and movement, a world that is not represented in imagination and that therefore ceases to exist when it is not being perceived. If an attractive object is shown to a very young infant and then hidden, the child will not even look for it: The object does not seem to exist when it cannot be seen or touched.

One of the important cognitive achievements of this period is the realization that objects are permanent and independent. This realization, the **object concept**, is possible only when the infant can *symbolize*—that is, can represent internally. Internal representation makes it possible for the child to imagine, to begin to think, to imitate objects and people who are not immediately present, and eventually to develop language.

Preoperational Thought.   Piaget labels the years from 2 to about 7 *preoperational* because children don't develop the ability to deal with **operations**

Table 4.3	Piaget's Stages of Cognitive Development	
Stage	**Approximate Age**	**Some Major Characteristics**
Sensorimotor	0–2 years	Motoric intelligence World of the here and now No language, no thought in early stages No notion of objective reality
Preoperational **Preconceptual** **Intuitive**	2–7 years 2–4 years 4–7 years	Egocentric thought Reason dominated by perception Intuitive rather than logical solutions Inability to conserve
Concrete **Operations**	7–11 or 12 years	Ability to conserve Logic of classes and relations Understanding of number Thinking bound to concrete
Formal **Operations**	11 or 12–14 or 15 years	Complete generality of thought Ability to deal with the hypothetical Development of strong idealism

(logical thought processes) until around 7. Before then, thinking is full of contradictions and errors. As an example, Piaget describes his young son's reaction to a snail they see while out walking one morning. When they later see another snail, the boy exclaims, "Here it is again, the snail," absolutely convinced that this is the same snail. He does not yet understand that similar objects can belong to the same class but not be identical. Billy, who sees four different Santa Clauses in four places on the same day, still knows there is only one Santa Claus. He is a preconceptual thinker.

Preconceptual thinkers also tend to be **animistic thinkers**. "Does the sun move?" Piaget (1960) asks a young child. "Yes," the child answers, going on to explain how the sun, like the moon, moves when he walks, stops when he stops, turns when he turns, that it must surely be alive. But even among preschoolers, animism has its limits. If the sun and the moon are alive because they move, Bullock (1985) suggests to a 4-year-old, then surely a car, which also moves, must also be alive. No, the child is not so easily fooled. How can this thing of metal and plastic and rubber possibly be alive?

At around age 4, the child's reasoning becomes somewhat more logical, although it is still heavily influenced by appearances rather than by logic. It is not so much logical as **intuitive thinking**.

Intuitive thought, explains Piaget, is often marked by the type of **egocentrism** evident in this simple problem: An experimenter holds one end of a string in each hand so that a male and female doll, side by side on the string, are hidden behind a screen. He asks the child which doll will come out first if the string is moved toward the right. Whether the child is correct or not, the boy doll is moved out and hidden again. The procedure is repeated a number of times without variation so that the boy doll always comes out first. Eventually the child will predict

This 4-year-old's logic is intuitive, egocentric, and perception dominated. He is easily fooled by appearances. There are still many head-scratching puzzles out there.

that the other doll will come out. Why? "Because it's her turn. It isn't fair." The child interprets the problem only from a personal point of view, from an egocentric view.

Egocentricism is also evident in many preschool verbal exchanges:
Bill: I got a red one.
Sarah: My cat is sick.
Bill: Go. Go. RRRRRR.
Sarah: We don't have a dog.

A conversation? Not really, says Piaget: More a *collective monologue*. A real conversation requires the nonegocentric ability to adopt another's point of view.

Concrete Operations.   That perception tends to dominate the preoperational child's thinking is evident in this Piagetian demonstration: Michael, a 4-year-old, is asked to take a bead and place it in one of two containers. As he does so, a researcher places a bead in another container. They keep doing this until one of the containers is about half full. To confuse Michael, the researcher has put her beads in a shallow, flat dish whereas Michael's container is tall and narrow. The researcher now asks, "Who has more beads? Or do we both have the same number?" "I have more," says Michael, "because they're higher." Or he might just as easily have said, "You have more 'cause they're bigger around." In either case, his answers reflect his reliance on the appearance of the containers. This reliance on perception, even when it conflicts with logic, is one of the major differences between child and adult thought.

With the advent of *concrete operations*, children no longer make this mistake. They now rely on rules of logic rather than on intuition and perception. They know that quantity does not change unless something is added or taken away. In Piaget's terms, they have achieved **conservation**.

There are as many types of conservation as there are quantifiable characteristics of objects: There is conservation of number, length, distance, area, volume, liquids, solids, and so on. None of these is acquired before the stage of concrete operations, and even then some (volume, for example) will not be acquired until late in that period. Experimental procedures and approximate ages for different conservations are shown in Figure 4.3.

Strikingly, when faced with conservation problems, preoperational children can contradict themselves repeatedly without ever changing their minds. After the bead demonstration, for example, the experimenter can pour the beads back into their original containers and repeat the question. Michael now agrees the containers have the same number of beads; but as soon as the beads are again distributed into the tall and shallow containers, he changes his mind.

During the concrete operations period, children also develop new abilities relating to classification, seriation, and numbers. The seriation problem shown in Figure 4.4 would present insurmountable problems for a 3-year-old but would be ridiculously simple for an 8-year-old. Given the ability to classify and to seriate, understanding numbers becomes relatively simple.

By the end of the period of concrete operations, the child has acquired the ability to deal with a wide range of problems systematically and logically and is very much at home in the world of symbols. But there remain a number of limitations to thought during this period, the most obvious of which is the child's continued inability to deal with the hypothetical; hence the label

Figure 4.3   **Some tests for conservation with approximate ages of attainment.**

1. Conservation of substance (6–7 years)

A

The experimenter presents two identical modeling clay balls. The subject admits that they have equal amounts of clay.

A

One of the balls is deformed. The subject is asked whether they still contain equal amounts.

2. Conservation of length (6–7 years)

B

Two sticks are aligned in front of the subject. The subject admits their equality.

B

One of the sticks is moved to the right. The subject is asked whether they are still the same length.

3. Conservation of number (6–7 years)

C

Two rows of counters are placed in one-to-one correspondence. Subject admits their equality.

C

One of the rows is elongated (or contracted). Subject is asked whether each row still contains the same number.

4. Conservation of liquids (6–7 years)

D

Two beakers are filled to the same level with water. The subject sees that they are equal.

D

The liquid of one container is poured into a tall tube (or a flat dish). The subject is asked whether each still contains the same amount.

5. Conservation of area (9–10 years)

E

The subject and the experimenter each have identical sheets of cardboard. Wooden blocks are placed on these in identical positions. The subject agrees that each cardboard has the same amount of space remaining.

E

The experimenter scatters the blocks on one of the cardboards. The subject is asked whether each cardboard still has the same amount of space remaining.

Figure 4.4   To test children's understanding of seriation, they are asked to order a pile of dolls by height. The top row was arranged by a 3 1/2-year-old; the bottom, by an 8-year-old.

concrete. The logic of concrete operations is tied to real things. Children don't yet have the freedom made possible by the more advanced logic of formal operations.

Formal Operations.   According to Piaget, the single most important achievement of formal operations is the transition to a more advanced logic that deals with hypothetical states and events. Piaget illustrates this with the following problem: Edith is fairer than Susan; Edith is darker than Lilly. Who is the darkest of the three?

This problem of **transitive inference** is very difficult for the younger *concrete operations* child, not because it involves seriation, which has already been mastered, but because it is an abstract problem. If Edith, Susan, and Lilly were all standing in front of a 10-year-old, she could easily say, "Oh! Edith is fairer than Susan, and she is darker than Lilly—and Susan is the darkest." But when the problem is verbal rather than concrete, it requires thinking that is more formal (abstract).

Among the cognitive tools of adolescent thinking is a powerful logic that allows the adolescent to deal with the hypothetical rather than only the real. One of the important consequences of this newfound ability is an increasing concern with the ideal. Once children are able to reason from the hypothetical to the real or from the actual to the hypothetical, they can conceive of worlds and societies that, hypothetically, have no ills.

It should be noted, however, that the ability to deal logically with the hypothetical is not a characteristic that governs all adolescent and adult thinking. Rather, it is a form of thinking that is now *possible*, whereas it had previously been beyond the child's abilities. Although formal thought may be clearly evident in individual instances, it is by no means evident in all cases.

Evaluation of Piaget's Theory.   Piaget's critics typically agree on a number of standard complaints. One is that he used very few subjects in his research, which is true but not especially important unless studies with larger groups contradict his findings. In fact, as Fuson (2009) notes, of the thousands of studies that have followed Piaget's research, the majority support his description of the general sequence of intellectual development.

However, most critics also agree that Piaget underestimated the abilities of young children. That might be because Piaget's investigations, even with very young children, were largely verbal. When tasks are made simpler, children sometimes respond quite differently. For example, Charles and Rivera (2009) found that 5- and 6-month-old infants will often actively *look* for an object before they can actually reach for it. Looking for an object is a strong sign of some understanding of object permanence. Similarly, Aubrey (1993) points out that preschoolers have a far more advanced understanding of number than Piaget thought.

Critics also agree that whereas Piaget underestimated what younger children can do, he overestimated the capabilities of children at the stage of formal thinking. More recent studies often fail to find much evidence of formal operations thinking among adults, let alone adolescents (for example, Modgil & Modgil, 1982).

A final caution is in order: The stage aspect of theories such as Piaget's gives the impression that one day a child of a certain age is at stage X; the next day, the child wakes up at stage Y. But that, of course, is not really the case. The boundaries between stages are never entirely clear, and transitions are seldom entirely abrupt and irreversible.

Children's Social-Emotional Development

As we saw earlier, Erik Erikson describes eight stages of *psychosocial* development. The theory explains how, in the very beginning, parents are all-important. Not only are they essential for the baby's comfort and survival, but they provide for all of the newborn's psychological needs. They are the infant's source of love, and that is not a small four-letter word.

As children grow older, peers become progressively more important. But that does not mean that parents immediately become less important. Even in adolescence, peers and others outside the family don't ordinarily completely replace parents either as a source of love or as a source of profound influence on interests, values, and decisions. Two of Erikson's stages span childhood (see Figure 4.6).

Initiative Versus Guilt.   By the age of 4 or 5, Erikson explains, children have become relatively autonomous. They have discovered that they are capable and independent. Now they will spend the rest of their childhood trying to discover exactly who they are. In early childhood, they do this by trying to be like their parents—that is, by *identifying* with them. At the same time, their world expands beyond the family, and as they explore this wider environment, they're called upon to exercise initiative and to overcome the sense of inferiority that threatens.

Industry Versus Inferiority.   From about ages 6 to 11, children interact extensively with peers. It now becomes increasingly important that they be accepted as worthwhile. They need to discover that they are competent, that they can do things—in short, that they are *industrious*. During this stage, children are anxious to learn what their culture offers them and requires of them. Failing to do so can result in a lasting sense of inferiority.

Play.   The **socialization** of the child begins in the family and continues with peers, schools, and other social institutions. Through these, children become aware of the many implicit and explicit rules that govern behavior in their culture. Much of the child's early socialization occurs through play.

And what is **play**? Sadly, many of us have forgotten. We abandon ourselves reluctantly and guardedly to the joys of madness and the ecstasies of whimsy. We know too carefully what reality is, and we fear too passionately the possibility of confusing the imaginary with the real.

There is no such fear in the hearts of children. The games they play, unlike the games we play, are played solely for their enjoyment. They are designed neither to impress nor to deceive; neither to persuade nor to annoy.

Children's games may be classified into three broad categories: sensorimotor play, imaginative play, and social play. Many games obviously share characteristics of all three.

Sensorimotor Play.   *Sensorimotor play* is mainly physical activity such as skipping, hopping, jumping, running, and the countless solitary games of young children. It is the only type of play of which young infants are capable.

Imaginative Play.   *Imaginative* (or *pretend*) play begins very early, continues throughout life, and takes a variety of forms. Most obvious are the host of make-believe games and activities prevalent in the preschool years. Even infants as young as 1 can pretend, often by simulating common activities like pretending to eat or pretending to sleep. And by age 2, a wide range of make-believe games becomes possible as children learn to transform objects, people, and activities into whatever they wish. Many of these pretend games are suggested by the immediate environment, notes Jaffke (1996). Thus, a picture, a crooked stick, a broken teacup, a squished worm—each can inspire a new game.

Another type of imaginative play becomes increasingly common in the later preschool years and continues well into adulthood, although we spend little time talking about it.

Daydreaming is a normal and healthy form of play. Evidence suggests that daydreaming may be very important in the resolution of fears, anxieties, and a wealth of related problems (Barber, Bagsby, & Munz, 2010). It very likely contributes significantly to creative output (Singer, 2009) and probably is also centrally involved in the development of interpersonal skills, providing as it does an opportunity for the imaginary exercising of these skills.

There is, too, the **imaginary playmate** with whom as many as one third of all preschool children play constantly (Singer, 2009). These imaginary friends are loved, spoken to, taken on trips, dressed, and played with. Psychology has not yet interviewed any of them in depth. Most of them go away in the earlier school years and never come back.

Social Play. *Social play* is any type of play that involves interaction among two or more children. Thus, both practice and pretend play are social when they involve more than one child. Skipping rope alone in the darkness of one's basement is a solitary sensorimotor activity; skipping rope out on the playground with others turning the rope and chanting "salt, mustard, vinegar, pepper . . ." is a cooperative or social activity. Similarly, creating daydreams in the solitude of one's bedroom is private imaginative play, but playing "let's pretend—you be the veterinaman [sic] and I'll be the dog" is social imaginative play.

Note, too, that children play solitary games before they engage in more social games, and that even when two children are playing side by side, they are often playing independently. Piaget (1951) drew attention to this progression in children's games, pointing out that, prior to truly *social play*, there is *parallel play* where children play together (in the sense of being in physical proximity) but neither share the activities employed in the game nor follow mutually accepted rules.

True social play requires interaction between two or more children, the use of rules, and cooperation. It is hardly surprising that it is considered one of the most important means of fostering language growth as well as cognitive, social, and emotional development in children.

Earlier research had suggested that as children begin to play more socially, they engage in less solitary play. Solitary play among older children has sometimes been seen as evidence of social immaturity. Xu's (2010) research suggests that this is really not the case. She explains that cultural changes have resulted in an increasing amount of solitary play among today's children. These changes include smaller families, frequent social isolation in larger urban centers, the mushrooming availability of games designed for solitary play on computers and hand-held devices, and the enormous amount of time children spend watching television.

Three categories of children's play: (a) imaginative, (b) social, and (c) sensorimotor. Note that these forms of play are not mutually exclusive. A rope-tug competition can be every bit as sensorimotor as social. And playing cowboy roles may be highly social as well as imaginative.

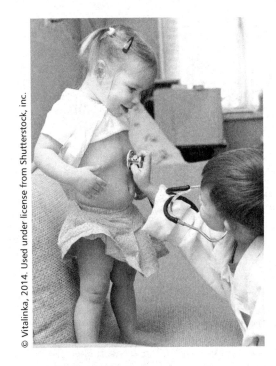

© Vitalinka, 2014. Used under license from Shutterstock, inc.

© Diego Cervo, 2014. Used under license from Shutterstock, Inc.

© Juriah Mosin, 2014. Used under license from Shutterstock, Inc.

The most important changes of adolescence are those that lead to sexual maturity. These changes occur very early for some and much later for others. Early maturation is sometimes associated with a higher likelihood of engaging in behaviors—and displaying hairstyles—of which parents don't approve.

© Olena Zaskochenko, 2014. Used under license from Shutterstock, Inc.

ADOLESCENTS

Social play continues through the transition from childhood to adolescence and beyond.

Physical and Sexual Changes

It is not always an easy transition, complicated as it is by the gap that often exists between newly achieved biological maturity and social maturity. Although biological maturation readies the adolescent for adult roles of mating and procreation, social constraints often delay the adoption of these roles.

Biologically, adolescence is the period from the onset of **puberty** (sexual maturity) to adulthood. Puberty is defined as the capacity to ejaculate semen for boys and the first menstrual period (**menarche**) for girls. The changes that result in sexual maturity define **pubescence**. These changes are initiated by a dramatic increase in hormones produced by the **gonads** (*testes* in boys and *ovaries* in females), culminating in the ability to produce mature ova and sperm. Other signs of pubescence include the appearance of pigmented pubic hair, breast enlargement in the girl, the growth of armpit and facial hair, and a lowering of the voice. There is also a dramatic increase in height and weight just before adolescence (the *growth spurt*). Puberty (sexual maturity) typically immediately follows the growth spurt.

Because of wide individual variations in the ages at which these changes occur (typically much earlier for girls than for boys), the beginning and end of adolescence are not easily defined. Age 12 is often used as an approximation for the beginning of adolescence and age 20 for the beginning of adulthood—although the "legal" age of adulthood varies widely in different jurisdictions.

Early and Late Maturation.   In North America, sexual maturity (puberty) is reached at around age 12.8 for girls and 14 for boys. However, some girls may reach sexual maturity as young as 9; others, not until age 16; some boys, as young as 11 or 12; others, not until age 18. Evidence suggests that sexual maturity has been occurring earlier across the United States, especially for girls. Herman-Giddens et al. (1997) looked at the age of menarche among more than 17,000 girls in the United States. They found that average age of sexual maturation has dropped from around 17 in the middle of the 19th century to just below 13 at present.

Research indicates that early maturation is sometimes an advantage for boys. Early-maturing boys are often better adjusted, more popular, more confident, more assertive, and more successful in heterosexual relationships. They are also likely to begin dating earlier and to have first sexual intercourse earlier (Kim & Smith, 1999). However, they are also more likely to use illegal drugs and to smoke cigarettes (Engels, 2009; Jaszyna-Gasior et al., 2009).

Early-maturing girls, too, are more likely to engage in behaviors of which parents don't approve, including an increased likelihood of drug use (Arim & Shapka, 2008). However, there is good evidence that most of the negative effects of early maturation disappear by young adulthood (Copeland et al., 2010).

Adolescent Egocentrism

And much of the adolescent's egocentrism will also have disappeared by then—with exceptions.

In Piagetian theory, egocentrism is not a derogatory term; it refers less to a selfishness than to a cognitive and emotional *self-centeredness*. Egocentrism is apparent in children's inability to be completely objective in their understanding of the world. For young infants, objects exist only when they are being looked at, tasted, felt, or smelled. And in the preschool period there is evidence of egocentrism when children focus on the perceptual features of objects and respond incorrectly to conservation problems. The egocentrism of the adolescent is of a different nature.

The Imaginary Audience and the Personal Fable.   When 15-year-old Rosa was getting ready to go to a concert, she agonized over her hair. It seemed that her mop had gone wild overnight, so now she was desperately trying to find some way of making it look decent enough that she would not be an absolute dork.

"Nobody'll notice, you look fine," said her mother.

"Everybody'll see," she retorted.

Her **imaginary audience** that night would consist of 30,000 people. *Everybody* would be watching; everybody would care. And Rosa is not exceptionally egocentric.

The adolescent's imaginary audience is an imagined collection of all who might be concerned with the adolescent's self and behavior. It is the "they" in all those expressions "they think . . ." "they say . . ." The imaginary audience is an expression of adolescents' belief that they are the center of attention.

In some ways, argue Bell and Bromnick (2003), the adolescent's imaginary audience is not entirely *imaginary*. In fact, there are important social and personal consequences attached to what people think of the adolescent's dress and behavior. And there may be negative consequences attached to ignoring the audience.

The imaginary audience, says Elkind (1967), is not a highly critical, but an admiring audience. It makes sense that adolescents' **personal fables** would include a supportive audience. Personal fables are fantasies adolescents invent in which, not surprisingly, they are the heroes. They're stories characterized by a feeling of being special and unique, as well as by a sense of power and invulnerability. Unfortunately, this feeling of invulnerability is often sadly inappropriate, as is evident in the fact that adolescents aged 16 to 19 are four times more likely to have vehicle accidents than older drivers (Insurance Institute for Highway Safety, 2009).

Identity Formation

A higher probability of accidents is just one of the risks of adolescence; there are others. As G. S. Hall claimed many decades

The adolescent's *personal fable* includes feelings of being special and powerful and invulnerable and, as this lad proves, capable of awesome bicycle feats. Not surprisingly, high-risk behaviors—and accidents—are more common in this age group.

ago, adolescence can be a time of storm and stress. And when there are storms in adolescence, they sometimes have to do with the problem of developing an **identity**, a sense of wholeness and purpose.

In Erik Erikson's theory of *psychosocial* development, the conflict that labels the stage descriptive of adolescence is *identity versus identity diffusion* (see Figure 7.13). During this stage, the adolescent is faced with the daunting task of developing an *identity*. This involves decisions and choices not so much about who one is but rather about who one can be among all potential selves. The source of conflict lies in the various possibilities open to adolescents.

While in the transition between childhood and adulthood, the adolescent's *identity status* typically changes as crises come and go and as the adolescent explores various options. Building on Erikson's work, Marcia (1966, 1980) identifies four distinct types of identity status on the basis of whether the adolescent has undergone or is currently undergoing a crisis and on whether a commitment has been made to a specific identity.

Identity Diffusion.

Adolescents in the state of *identity diffusion* have made no commitment and experienced no identity crisis. These are adolescents whose political, social, and religious beliefs are ambiguous or nonexistent and who have no vocational aspirations. It is a state that's very common in early adolescence.

Foreclosure.

Some adolescents, by virtue of religious, political, or vocational commitments, achieve a strong sense of identity without experiencing a crisis. This is often the case, for example, in close-knit religious communities where roles and beliefs are predetermined. It may also be the case when adolescents simply allow parents or others to make important identity-related decisions for them. The most striking characteristic of these adolescents, says Marcia (1980), is high adherence to authoritarian values (obedience and respect of authority).

Moratorium.

Erikson believed that one of the functions of adolescence was to serve as a *moratorium*—a period during which adolescents could experiment with various identities without having to make a commitment. Moratorium adolescents have vague, changing commitments; in this sense, they are in crisis. But it is a useful crisis because without it, there is a danger of premature commitment (as in the case of foreclosure) or of continuing lack of commitment (as in identity diffusion).

Identity Achieved.

Those who have gone through the moratorium and made a commitment are described as *identity achieved*. Marcia (1980) reports that identity achieved adolescents are more independent, respond better to stress, have more realistic goals, and have higher self-esteem than adolescents in any of the other three categories. However, he also emphasizes that identities are never static and absolutely permanent. Even when the adolescent appears to have achieved an identity, further changes often occur. For example, some college students move in and out of identity crises before finally achieving a permanent commitment (Figure 4.5).

Figure 4.5 **Marcia's four states of identity development.**

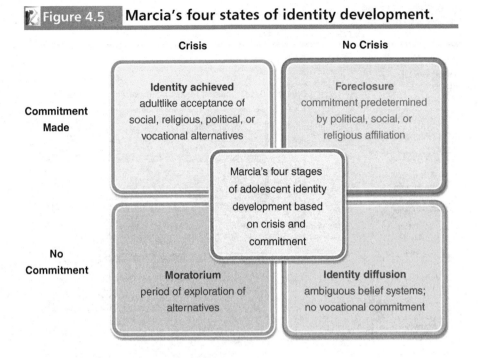

ADULTS

And even when they are adults, some never achieve any lasting commitment, never develop a strong sense of identity. They're recognizable later in life as the full-time "fun seekers," says Marcia (1980), or as disturbed, highly anxious individuals with low self-esteem and low confidence.

Erikson's Stages of Adulthood

As we saw, Erikson describes human development in terms of progression through a series of adaptations that the culture requires. At every developmental stage, growth and development require new competencies. And always, there are opposing tendencies. Thus, the infant must develop trust in a world that is initially strange and sometimes terrifying. If the opposing tendency, fear and mistrust, is not overcome, it is difficult for the toddler to go out into the world, to explore and learn and develop. And the main task of adolescence is to overcome the crisis that comes with conflicting choices and the need to make a commitment.

Adulthood brings with it a whole new set of challenges, each with powerful conflicting tendencies. Three of Erikson's eight stages of the human lifespan cover adulthood (Figure 4.6).

Intimacy Versus Isolation. One of the commitments that many adolescents and young adults are called upon to make requires forming intimate relationships, often, though not always, with someone of the opposite sex. But here, as in all stages of the lifespan, there is a conflict between the need to make a commitment and an unwillingness to do so. Often, says Erikson, there is a reluctance to give up or compromise the hard-won sense of identity that has been achieved. And, of course, in many cases, the search for identity and commitment goes on well into adulthood.

Figure 4.6   Erikson's developmental tasks. Based on Erik H. Erikson (1959).

Erikson's
Psychosocial
Stages

Principal Developmental Tasks and Important Infuences

Erikson's Psychosocial Stages	Age	Principal Developmental Tasks and Important Infuences
Trust vs mistrust	0–18 months	Develop enough trust in the world to explore it
Autonomy vs shame	18 months–2 years	Develop feelings of control over behavior. Realize that intentions can be acted out
Initiative vs guilt	2 or 3–6 years	Develop a sense of self by identifying with parents; develop a feeling of responsibility for own actions
Industry vs inferiority	6–11 years	Develop a sense of self-worth through interaction with peers
Identity vs identity	11 through adolescence	Develop a strong sense of self (identity); select among various vocational, political, religious, or lifestyle alternatives
Intimacy vs isolation	Young adulthood	Develop close relationships with others; achieve the intimacy required for long-term commitment
Generativity vs self-absorption	Adulthood	Assume responsible adult roles in community; contribute; be worthwhile
Integrity vs despair	Older adulthood	Face death; overcome possible despair; come to terms with the meaning of life

Generativity Versus Self-Absorption.   At every stage of the lifespan, there are different social demands placed on the individual. These can vary enormously from one person to another. What is common to most adults, says Erikson, is the expectation that they will form the sorts of caring and work relationships that will benefit their immediate family and friends, their community, and perhaps the world. The opposing tendency is to be self-absorbed and selfish, not willing to expend the effort required to be *generative*. Generativity can be evident in many areas: work, family, and wider social or political commitments.

Integrity Versus Despair.   The overriding psychosocial conflict in old age is one between despair at the thought that the end is at hand and the need to maintain a sense of *integrity*—a conviction that life has been useful and worthwhile. What the elderly need to do, says Erikson, is integrate the experiences of a lifetime, make sense of them, and achieve a feeling of acceptance and contentment. Failing that, the individual may be overcome with a sense of regret and despair and by the frustration that it is now too late to do anything further. We may never find those pieces of the puzzle not yet in place.

There is not always going to be a tomorrow.

MAIN POINTS

1. **Infants:** There is an enormous amount of motor and cognitive learning during the first 2 years of life, including locomotion and language. This learning is made possible by relatively well-developed perceptual systems coupled with an impressive brain. Infants vary in the amount of time they spend sleeping, crying, being alert, and being active. They also vary in terms of their predominant temperaments (easy, difficult, slow to warm up).

2. **Children:** A sort of *magical* thinking characterizes childhood. But as children adapt by assimilating (using previously learned responses) and accommodating (modifying responses), they become more closely attuned to reality and less given to magic. In Piaget's description, the *here-and-now* world of the infant gives way to the egocentric, perception-dominated, intuitive world of the preschooler, then to the reality-based, concrete-operations world of the young child, and finally to the more logical and idealistic world of the adolescent. Play has a fundamental role in the socialization of the child.

3. **Adolescents:** The transition from childhood to adulthood is defined by sex-related changes (pubescence) leading to sexual maturity (puberty). The adolescent's egocentrism is evident in the imaginary audience and the personal fable (which brings with it a sometimes dangerous sense of invulnerability). The principal task of adolescence is to arrive at a commitment (a decision regarding who one can and should be) and to overcome related crises.

4. **Adults:** Adulthood brings new challenges having to do with establishing intimate relationships, making worthwhile contributions (being generative in various spheres), and, in the end, reconciling one's life and developing a notion that it has been worthwhile.

Social Influence

OBJECTIVES

- Define persuasion and differentiate it from other forms of influence.
- Describe key characteristics of persuasion.
- Describe situations in which persuasion is commonly used.
- Consider the role of ethics in persuasion.

KEY TERMS

Assimilation
Attitudes
Authority heuristic
Behavioral intention
Beliefs
Central route
Cognitive complexity
Cognitive dissonance theory
Commitment and consistency
  heuristic
Constructivistic model
Controllability
Dogmatism
Door in the face technique
Ego-involvement
Elaboration likelihood model
Functional model of credibility
Inoculation theory
Latitude of acceptance
Latitude of noncommitment
Latitude of rejection

Liking heuristic
Machiavellianism
Multiple-act
Need for cognition
Need for social approval
Opinionated acceptance
Opinionated rejection
Perceived behavioural control
Perceived control
Peripheral route
Persuasibility
Reciprocity heuristic
Scarcity heuristic
Selective exposure
Self-efficacy
Self-esteem
Social proof heuristic
Subjective norm
Theory of reasoned action
Values

DEFINING CHARACTERISTICS OF PERSUASION

Persuasion has been defined in numerous ways, as is illustrated by the five definitions shown in Figure 5.1. Before we provide the definition to be used in this text, let's discuss some key characteristics that will help you understand why we define persuasion the way we do. First, **persuasion is a type of communication using a shared symbol system**. Persuasion uses messages in some kind of symbol system, and four of the five definitions in Figure 5.1 refer to communication. The one definition that does not directly refer to communication does imply communication. These messages may be verbal and involve language (e.g., English), or they may be nonverbal with symbols that have shared meanings (e.g., a smile, a picture of a flag). In either case, a message must be transmitted from a sender to a receiver in some commonly shared symbol system for persuasion to occur. All of Cara's influence situations clearly involve communication and a shared symbol system, so all have at least one characteristic of persuasion.

Second, **persuasion requires intent**. Without this requirement, we could argue that all communication is persuasive; however, only three of the five definitions in Figure 1.1 refer to intent in some way. When someone walks across campus and says "hello" to you, it is possible to interpret that as a persuasive intent to convince you that he or she is a friendly person and/or to convince you to respond in a friendly manner but, most often, it is nothing more than a greeting. A definition that doesn't require persuasive intent on the part of the sender doesn't help us distinguish persuasion from other related terms such as communication. The intent requirement means that persuasion focuses on messages that are intended to persuade the receiver. The first situation clearly

Figure 5.1   Definitions of persuasion.

Bostrom (1983)

"Persuasion is communicative behavior that has as its purpose the changing, modification, or shaping of the responses (attitudes or behavior) of the receivers" (p. 11).

Petty and Cacioppo (1981)

"… any instance in which an active attempt is made to change a person's mind because the word is relatively neutral and because one person's propaganda may be another person's education" (p. 4).

Larson (2013)

"… the process of dramatic co-creation by sources and receivers of a state of identification through the use of verbal and/or visual symbols" (p. 20).

Perloff (2010)

"… a symbolic process in which communicators try to convince other people to change their attitudes or behaviors regarding an issue through the transmission of a message in an atmosphere of free choice" (p. 12).

O'Keefe (2002)

"A successful intentional effort at influencing another's mental state through communication in a circumstance in which the persuadee has some measure of freedom" (p. 5).

involves intent, but is Cara the intended target? The students arguing about baseball teams clearly intended to influence each other, but did they intend to influence someone who overheard their loud conversation? Clearly Larry intended to influence Cara about the group project, and Kellie intended to influence Cara to join the rowing club. Did the newspaper story about armed robbers intend to influence student behavior? Does Dr. Kalibo intend to influence Cara to change her eating habits? Maybe. Assuming Cara's teacher, Dr. Kalibo, is like most other teachers, she wants Cara to learn specific information about nutrition and dispel myths and misconceptions about food and diet. But that doesn't mean Dr. Kalibo intends to change Cara's eating habits, particularly the changes that Cara made. We would really need to ask Dr. Kalibo if she intended to change her students' eating habits. If that indeed was her intention, then the situation would have the second characteristic of persuasion. If Dr. Kalibo simply wanted students to learn the content, and she left it up to the students to decide what to do with that information, then we would likely conclude that this really is not persuasion. Education and persuasion overlap in numerous ways, and the similarities and differences are further discussed later in this chapter. Intent is a necessary requirement for persuasion, but it isn't always easy to determine.

Third, **persuasion need not be successful to be considered persuasion**. When we see a television advertisement attempting to sell a product, or watch a politician's campaign speech, we view those messages as persuasion. Even if we choose not to buy the product or to vote for the political candidate, we are aware that an attempt at persuasion has been made. We don't have to wait months for the election to be held to decide what is persuasion, and we wouldn't define the losing candidate's speeches as anything but persuasive messages. Thus, it is critical that the message is intended to be persuasive rather than it necessarily be successful. Only one definition in Figure 1.1 refers to success. The other definitions are consistent with our approach that success is not required for a message to be considered persuasion.

Fourth, **persuasion involves two or more persons**. There has to be a sender and a receiver for persuasion to occur. Some have considered whether nonhuman animals can be involved in persuasion, whether individuals can persuade themselves through intrapersonal communication, and/or whether inanimate objects (e.g., a tree) can be persuasion agents. Although each of these arguments has supporters, the persuasion discussed in this textbook (and in most persuasion -research) refers to persuasion attempts between at least two persons. All of the previous influence situations involve at least two persons, so they all have this characteristic.

Finally, we need to consider the outcomes of persuasion. Miller (1980) argues that persuasion is intended to shape, reinforce, or change the responses of the receiver, and all of the definitions in Figure 1.1 refer to some type of change. We generally expect persuasive messages to involve attempts to **change** the beliefs, attitudes, and/or behavior of the receivers. For example, you have probably heard and seen numerous public service campaigns that want smokers to stop smoking. In our situations, we can see change in behavior. Cara changes her eating habits and intends to sign up for the rowing club. We also assume that Cara's beliefs about her diet changed, which led to a change in her behavior. We can also assume that Cara developed positive beliefs about the rowing club; otherwise, she wouldn't plan to sign up. On the other hand, we don't know what Cara thinks about the Yankees or the Red Sox. However, not knowing the outcomes doesn't mean that these were not attempts to change Cara's beliefs, attitudes, and/or behaviors.

Not all persuasive messages try to invoke change, however. Some attempt to **reinforce** currently held beliefs or attitudes and/or current behavioral practices. For example, Pepsi wants current Pepsi drinkers to remain loyal to the product. Political candidates speaking to members of their own party want members to remain loyal to the party and vote along party lines. Typically, speeches at the Republican and Democrat National Conventions focus on their supporters and use persuasive messages designed to reinforce current political views. Check out the 2012 convention speeches online to examine their focus. Another example is antismoking campaigns targeted at teens. Such campaigns are focused more on encouraging them *not* to start smoking than on altering current behaviors. Much of the persuasion surrounding us is attempting to reaffirm current beliefs, attitudes, and/or behaviors.

Finally, some persuasion tries to **shape** responses. These are messages targeted toward receivers who have not developed an attitude toward an object and who often lack knowledge on the issue. For example, when a company introduces a new product, it tries to shape positive responses to that product. When Procter and Gamble introduced Febreze®, a product targeted at removing odors from fabric, the company needed to inform consumers and wanted them to think positively about such a product. Because receivers had no prior knowledge of this product, the company wasn't trying to change anything, and there was nothing there to reinforce. When AIDS was identified, the government was most concerned with shaping responses to that information. Now, the government is more concerned with reinforcing positive behaviors (e.g., safe sex) and trying to change the behaviors of those who are at risk for transmission of the disease (e.g., those who engage in sex without condoms, those who share needles). Thus, depending on the situation, the intended outcome for persuasion may be change, reinforcement, or shaping of receiver responses.

Of course, you may be wondering what is meant by "receiver responses." Depending on the situation, the desired response from the receiver may involve attitudes, beliefs, and/or behaviors. For example, at times, attitude change is desired. A political candidate may want voters to share favorable attitudes toward key campaign issues. A religious organization may want to target beliefs in receivers so that they would be in alignment with the particular religion. Many times, however, behavior is the ultimate target of persuasion attempts. Advertisers ultimately want products to be purchased. Political candidates want votes and/or financial contributions. Social issue organizations often want to persuade the public about acceptable behavior (e.g., not smoking, wearing seatbelts, adopting healthy exercise and eating patterns). We often expect attitudes and/or beliefs to be the basis for behavior, so targeting attitudes and beliefs may be an avenue to influence receiver behavior. As a result, when considering receiver responses, we need to consider attitudes, beliefs, and behaviors. We examine attitudes, beliefs, and behaviors in more depth in Chapters 2 and 3.

Thus, when all of these criteria are taken into account, we come to the following definition of persuasion, which draws on the multiple perspectives represented earlier: **Persuasion involves symbolic communication between two or more persons with intent to change, reinforce, or shape attitudes, beliefs, and/or behaviors of the receiver.**

At this point, we have discussed the situations presented at the beginning of this chapter in relation to the key characteristics of persuasion, but we really haven't answered the question of which of these is persuasion and which are not. We determined that Cara's change of eating habits might not be a result of persuasion if Dr. Kalibo did not intentionally try to influence her eating habits. However, the situations involving Larry asking for group work and Kellie encouraging Cara to join the rowing club seemed to have all of the characteristics of persuasion. The situation involving armed robberies brings up another issue in distinguishing persuasion from other forms of influence: coercion. **Coercion** is social influence that involves force or threat of force. The robbers used a threat to force students to turn over their property. For this reason, this situation is a better example of coercion than it is of true persuasion; however, the difference between coercion and persuasion is not always clear. Perloff's (2010) and O'Keefe's (2002) definitions of persuasion in Figure 1.1 refer to the receiver having free choice or freedom. The continuum that follows has *free choice* on one end and *forced choice* on the other.

Free choice _____ Forced choice

Having a gun pointed at your head with a demand for your laptop is clearly a forced choice. Cara's behavior in signing up for the rowing club was a result of free choice. However, not all circumstances easily fit into one end of the continuum or the other. In the group project situation, Cara's grade appeared to be threatened by a negative peer evaluation if she did not comply with Larry's request. Is that coercion? Consider the class you are in. The teacher controls the awarding of grades. Instructors set grading policies, work and attendance expectations, and so on. Students may choose to complete the work or not; however, there is a consequence in terms of grade received for choosing not to complete the work. Is that a free choice, or is there an element of threat in this situation? Is the public service announcement in Figure 5.2 an example of persuasion or coercion? Are you being threatened? Do you have free choice when it comes to wearing a seat belt? Situations that fall toward the forced choice end of the continuum are considered more coercion than persuasion, whereas situations that offer more free choice are considered more persuasion than coercion. However, where choice ends and force begins is not clear, making many situations ambiguous.

WHY STUDY PERSUASION?

The question of why we study persuasion is one that students may ask advisers and that researchers ask themselves. There are three major reasons people have for wanting to know more about persuasion. The most common reason students have given us for taking a class in persuasion is a very practical one. We all engage in persuasion in multiple contexts in our lives, and many want to study persuasion in order to be **more successful persuaders** themselves. That desire for mastery of the art of persuasion may be career oriented. Regardless of what career path is sought, most people want to be able to convince organizations to hire them and supervisors to promote them and award raises. People want to be able to sell their ideas to those in power and want to influence the choices made in their organizations. Some career paths call for particularly strong persuasive skills, such as in sales, law, marketing, public relations, and politics. In these areas, the ability to do a good job relies on strong persuasive abilities.

In addition, we all use persuasion in our personal lives. You might work to convince parents to send money or to buy you a new car. You might try to persuade others to engage in social activities with you, follow you on Twitter, or to join causes you support. Perhaps you try to persuade faculty to admit you to classes or to give you a better grade. You might attempt to persuade a car

Figure 5.2   Public service announcement for safety belt use.

National Traffic highway safety.

salesperson to give you a better deal on your next vehicle or try to negotiate a better price for a new house. In short, because we engage in persuasion on a regular basis in multiple aspects of our lives, one good reason for studying persuasion is to be better at this process.

Another common reason for studying persuasion is so that we can be **better consumers of information**. As we discussed previously, we are all bombarded with a broad variety of persuasive messages daily. Understanding persuasion allows us to make choices about when to be influenced and when not to be. By understanding the strategies, tactics, and methods employed by others, we can be better prepared to deal with persuasive messages targeted at us. This is particularly important in a democratic society where we trust that the typical citizen is able to process huge amounts of material and competing persuasive campaigns in order to make rational decisions about voting. Participation in a democratic society involves both the production and consumption of persuasive messages.

Finally, some people study persuasion in an attempt to **better understand** what they observe happening around them. When we look at behavior that doesn't fit our expectations and seems at times irrational to us, we try to understand how this can happen. Cult members engage in mass suicide in the belief that a spaceship hidden in the tail of a passing comet will take them to heaven. Seemingly useless products such as singing toy fish sell out of every store on the block. Trends in fashion come and go. Political candidates are elected to office although experts said they had no chance of being elected. A nation supports a leader conducting unspeakable atrocities, such as what happened in Germany with the Holocaust under Hitler's leadership. Studying persuasion can give us insight into these puzzling events and help to make sense of them.

The study of persuasion and the value of exploring this realm is certainly not new. Persuasion was studied and written about more than 2,500 years ago by the ancient Greeks. Arguably the most famous scholar of persuasion from that time was Aristotle. His work, *Rhetoric*, laid out many concepts about persuasion that are still considered valid today (Freese, 1991). Aristotle observed human interaction and persuasive attempts and taught his students how to persuade others. We discuss some of Aristotle's concepts as we explore persuasion, and much modern research draws on Aristotle's basic principles. For example, in Chapter 10, we examine source factors that influence the success and failure of persuasion and draw on Aristotle's concept of ethos, which still guides how modern researchers define source credibility. Aristotle saw persuasion as a central part of society and human interaction then, and today we still ask questions and explore persuasion as a part of interactions.

WHERE AND WHEN DO WE PERSUADE?

We suggest in this chapter that we are immersed in attempts at influence every day. The daily lives of individuals often involve persuasion in interpersonal and small-group contexts as well as in myriad forms of mass media. Students try to persuade parents to support them financially and emotionally. Roommates try to persuade each other to clean living quarters and to respect each other's privacy. Students try to convince faculty to grade them more positively. Group projects involve persuasion about meeting times, locations, and the division of labor. The multiple forms of media, such as radio, television, smartphones, newspapers, magazines, Internet, posters, billboards, and corporate logos, surround us with messages constantly. It is hard to imagine a lack of persuasion in daily interactions for most people.

In addition, some segments of society depend on persuasion in order to achieve their goals. We have all been targeted as receivers by these segments, and some of you anticipate being senders in these contexts. We often think of advertising and marketing as bombarding us with persuasion. Certainly every form of media from television to newspapers to the Internet carries advertising, and it is clearly labeled as such. These advertising messages are open attempts to influence behavior, and they meet the criteria we established for persuasion. The messages are framed in words and nonverbal images that draw on culturally developed shared symbol systems. Persuasive intent is clearly involved in the purchase of advertising space, and the ads aren't always successful, but many are. The advertisements all have the purpose of changing, shaping, or reinforcing behavior toward the product or service being promoted.

Marketing encompasses advertising, but it moves beyond the purchase of advertising space in mass media outlets. Marketing can include promotional programs such as the popular, annual McDonald's Monopoly promotion. Consumers are encouraged to purchase McDonald's products in order to collect Monopoly game pieces for a chance at a variety of great prizes, including a million dollars. Although the odds against winning are great, McDonald's does great business during the promotion. Marketing can also include such promotional devices as hats or T-shirts with corporate logos, special events, direct mail, and more. In these cases, persuasion is operating and the receivers are generally aware that persuasion is being attempted. It still involves systems of verbal and nonverbal symbols, clear persuasive intent, varying degrees of success, and attempts to influence the purchasing behaviors of receivers.

Persuasion is also used in public relations and encompasses a broad range of activities such as media relations, special events, crisis management, grass-roots lobbying, and more. Here, receivers may be unaware that they are targets of persuasion. When reading a newspaper, readers often assume that more or less objective journalists write the articles. However, those articles are often influenced heavily by public relations materials that organizations have sent to the newspapers to influence content. The same is true for other forms of mass media, including news programming, talk shows, game shows, and situation comedies. These activities still meet the established criteria for persuasion. They all involve an agreed on verbal and nonverbal symbol system, intent is clearly present in the hiring of public relations professionals, the level of success varies, and the targeted result includes changing, shaping, and reinforcing responses from the receivers.

Although we often think of marketing and corporate interests as involved in persuasion, public health organizations and social issue groups also engage in persuasion. For example, the Surgeon General has launched efforts to reduce smoking, encourage better eating patterns, reduce drug use, and encourage safer personal behaviors to avoid the spread of AIDS. Other groups, both public and private, have launched public health campaigns around specialized issues. For example, Mothers Against Drunk Driving (MADD) has worked for years to reduce driving while under the influence of alcohol. Chances are good that one or more of the health campaigns has influenced choices you make about what to eat and how to live your life safely. Similarly, there are social issue groups that are attempting to get you to recycle more, donate to the homeless, or care about abandoned pets. These campaigns generally draw on approaches from advertising, marketing, and public relations and they all involve persuasion.

PERSUASION AS ONE OF MULTIPLE FORMS OF INFLUENCE

We have used both the terms *influence* and *persuasion*, and we have used them somewhat differently. At this point we want to clarify how persuasion is different from influence as well as to clarify some related terms. Influence is a very general term that refers to a power that affects something. Persuasion, as we have discussed, is the use of communication to intentionally change, reinforce, or shape another's attitudes, beliefs, and/or behaviors. Clearly, persuasion is a form of influence. **Coercion** is also a form of influence that we discussed that involves force. Persuasion doesn't rely on force, although persuasion may involve pressure to change. Another term is *propaganda.* Propaganda is a term we often use to refer to persuasion attempts by those we do not agree with. When we are engaged in influence attempts, we call it persuasion. But when others are engaging in influence attempts that we disagree with, we often label that propaganda. This perspective represents the connotative meaning propaganda has for many people. In Chapter 12, we examine various definitions of propaganda and develop a more complete definition of this concept. **Propaganda** has been defined as a type of persuasion that involves mass audiences with a purpose of achieving the goals of the persuader. It often involves emotional appeals, concealment of purpose, and a lack of sound support. Propaganda carries negative connotations and, as a result, there are ethical questions about the techniques used in propaganda messages. Chapter 12 explores propaganda in greater depth and develops different tactics and strategies that are used in this subset of persuasion.

Education is another form of influence that overlaps somewhat with persuasion and is illustrated on the following continuum with persuasion. Whether we consider influence to be education or persuasion is dependent on the intent of the source and the outcomes of the influence. If the source intends to change the receiver's attitudes, beliefs, or behavior (or to reinforce or shape receiver responses), it would be considered persuasion. Many view persuasion and education as opposites with no overlap, yet education and persuasion share several qualities of persuasion.

Education _____ Persuasion

The difference lies in the intentions and outcomes. Purists argue that education does not have a persuasive intent, but instead has the intent of sharing information or knowledge. In the case of Cara and her nutrition class, it is quite likely that sharing of information was Dr. Kalibo's primary intent. It would be rare, however, for educators to not care about how that information is used. Most educators want their students to adopt the information and use it in their lives, and that runs pretty close to shaping, reinforcing, and changing responses. Dr. Kalibo might well have been pleased by the changes in Cara's diet. Certainly the public health campaigns have the intent of doing more than sharing information. Those campaigns want to affect how receivers think about health issues, and most want specific health behaviors to be the result. Because of the overlap between education and persuasion, a continuum is a more appropriate way of viewing the relationship between the two. Purely informational intents fall into the *education* end of the continuum, whereas those clearly intending to influence individuals fall into the *persuasion* end of the continuum; however, there are many situations that fall in the middle.

We've stated several times that persuasion involves communication, but how is it similar and different from persuasion? Communication is a broad term that encompasses a variety of messages, including those that influence people. Communication has been defined in a variety of ways; however, our preferred definition was put forth by McCroskey and Richmond (1996), who define **communication** as "the process by which one person stimulates meaning in the mind(s) of another person (or persons) through verbal and nonverbal messages" (p. 3). Certainly the definition of persuasion developed previously refers to persuasion as a type of communication, and influence

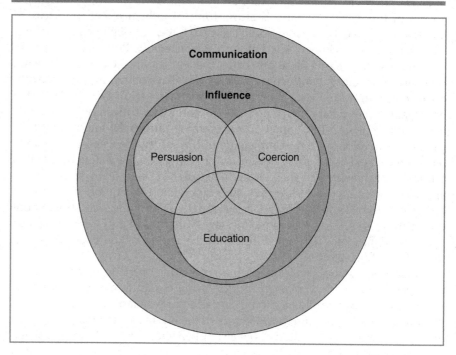

Figure 5.3   Venn diagram.

attempts involve communication. Thus, a hierarchy of terms would include communication as the umbrella term, influence next, with persuasion, coercion, and education fitting into the influence realm. The Venn diagram in Figure 1.3 illustrates the relationships among communication, influence, persuasion, coercion, and education.

ATTITUDES, VALUES, AND BELIEFS*

Beliefs. Inferences we make about ourselves and the world around us.

Values. Core beliefs or beliefs central to our cognitive system.

Attitudes. Collections of beliefs organized around an issue or event that predispose behaviour.

Integral to our frame of reference is the value and belief system upon which attitudes are based. One of the best explanations of human behavior and possibly the finest theory on attitude and attitude change was developed by Milton Rokeach. In this theory, beliefs are the fundamental building blocks of attitudes. Rokeach asserted that some beliefs are more central to an individual's cognitive system than others. These core beliefs, or values, are typically well-established and relatively stable. They are very difficult to change because they are most salient to the individual and his/her belief system. They function as "life guides," determining both our daily behavior and our life goals.

According to Rokeach, collections of beliefs organized around a focal point (like an issue, an event, or a person) constitute an attitude. He identifies two kinds:

1. attitudes toward **objects** and
2. attitudes toward **situations**.

The combination of these two kinds of attitudes will determine an individual's behavior in any given situation. Rokeach uses gardening as an example. The collection of an individual's beliefs—that gardening is fun, that it saves money, that it releases tension, and that it produces beautiful flowers—will result in a favorable attitude toward gardening. Given the absence of intervening attitudes, a person's collection of beliefs and resultant attitudes will motivate their gardening behavior.

For communications professionals to motivate behavior then, requires that they understand and tap into core beliefs and values that shape attitudes. In some cases, we may need to change beliefs and attitudes. Remembering that core beliefs are difficult to change, we may try to tap into a value and base the alteration of peripheral beliefs on that central belief. We may also need to motivate people to change the depth of a belief or value to help us build a foundation for attitude change. At any rate, it is important for us to recognize that people do not do something just because we want them to do it or because we think they should consider it in their self-interest. They behave in their own self-interest according to their own beliefs and attitudes. Changing behavior requires addressing those beliefs and attitudes.

Another set of theories that aids us in understanding how to change attitudes are the balance or cognitive consistency theories. This body of research has found that people are comfortable when their beliefs, attitudes, knowledge, and behaviors are consistent. The presence of conflict among those cognitive elements creates discomfort or dissonance. Leon Festinger contends that when the cognitive elements are in conflict, people tend to reduce or eliminate the dissonance by changing the elements or introducing new elements (like new information).

The classic example is that of a smoker. In today's environment with today's information, smoking behavior potentially causes great dissonance or conflict in the cognitive processes. The smoker will try to reduce the dissonance. One way would be to change one or more of the cognitive elements (like behavior) by stopping smoking. Another way would be to add a new element, like switching to a pipe which is perceived to be less harmful. A third way is to see the cognitive elements as less important than they used to be (i.e., longer life isn't such a desirable belief if I have to give up pleasure to achieve it). A fourth method would be to seek consonant information such as evidence contradicting the health hazard studies. Fifth, you might reduce the conflict among cognitive elements by distorting or misinterpreting (misperceiving) the information available on the ill effects of smoking. Finally, you have the option to flee the situation, or simply refuse to contemplate the conflict thereby avoiding the dissonance.

If we understand these cognitive processes, we are better able to work with people to bring about cognitive consonance. The process of changing the cognitive elements is the process of persuasion. We may conclude that the art of persuasion, to be effective in motivating behavior, must be implemented at the most basic level of public opinion: at the level of individual beliefs and attitudes.

Personality Traits and Persuasion*

Many communication studies have explored how personality influences communication, especially in persuasion situations. We will briefly survey some of the major personality traits that have been examined (for a review of this literature see Steinfatt, 1987).

PERSUASIBILITY.   Research reported in the book *Personality and Persuasibility* (Hovland & Janis, 1959) suggests that a personality trait predicts how much a person is influenced by persuasion attempts—regardless of the topic, source, or situation. This idea appears to be valid. Some people seem easy to persuade. They rarely resist pressure to move in one direction or another. This willingness to change can be viewed as **persuasibility**. Also, other individuals seem consistently difficult to persuade. They rarely budge on any issue. In essence, they seem resistant to persuasion.

The idea of a persuasibility trait appears to be an uncomplicated way to explain susceptibility to social influence. However, conceptually the matter is not so clear. Is there such a trait, or are there other personality traits sometimes related to persuasion that create the illusion of a general persuasibility trait? In that regard, the traits that follow have been found to be related to persuasion. The amount of persuasibility indicated by each trait, when viewed as a whole, could create the impression that there is a more global persuasibility trait.

Self-esteem refers to how favorably the individual evaluates self and is a trait related to persuasion.

SELF-ESTEEM.   Self-esteem refers to how favorably the individual evaluates self and is a trait related to persuasion. When individuals have low self-esteem, they lack self-confidence in general, and they have little faith that their positions on controversial issues are valid. They tend to be high in persuasibility. When told by a speaker that their positions should be changed, they tend to believe the speaker: "The speaker must know what is right on this, for I certainly do not know." High self-esteem, on the other hand, is thought to be related to low persuasibility. When people feel very good about themselves, they are also confident about their positions on controversial issues because opinions are a part of one's identity. Satisfaction with oneself usually discourages change. Therefore, individuals with high self-esteem tend to resist persuasion.

dogmatism The individual's willingness to consider other belief systems.

DOGMATISM.   Rokeach (1960) conceptualized dogmatism in terms of individuals' willingness to consider belief systems (what one associates with an object or issue) other than the ones they hold. Open-minded individuals are willing to consider other sets of beliefs, even if they feel very strongly about an issue. Dogmatic or closed-minded persons are unwilling to do so. They have a firm set of beliefs for an issue, and they do not want to be bothered by other belief systems.

Dogmatic people find it very difficult to separate a source from the source's message. Thus, if dogmatic people like a source, they tend to accept the source's message; if they dislike a speaker, rarely will the speaker's message persuade them. The open-minded person, however, has less trouble reacting differently to source and message—for example, "I can't stand the speaker, but he makes a good point." When the source is viewed as credible, dogmatism is associated with persuasion. This is especially true when the persuasion topic is not very important to the individual. Dogmatic people tend to be rather easy to persuade when given a credible source and a less important topic. This also suggests that open-minded persons are not necessarily easy to persuade. When the source is credible and the topic rather unimportant, open-minded people are more difficult to persuade than dogmatic individuals.

MACHIAVELLIANISM.   The trait of Machiavellianism refers to an orientation in which people believe that manipulating others is a basic strategy of social influence. Individuals who are high in Machiavellianism think it is ethical to tell people only what they want to hear, to use the receivers' doubts, fears, and insecurities to motivate action, and even to distort facts so they become more acceptable. Generally these people are willing to use whatever strategy works in persuasion; they are very pragmatic. High Machiavellians tend to act rather detached and to be less emotional than other people. They believe the end justifies the means. Persons with a high level of this trait have a strong need to influence others. They like leadership positions, and they are usually the dominant parties in their relations with other people.

Low Machiavellians, on the other hand, are very nonmanipulative in dealing with people. They want to avoid pressuring others, to allow others maximum freedom to decide for themselves. Low Machiavellians tend to have little need to dominate and influence others. They tend to be more emotional than high Machiavellians when discussing a controversial issue.

Machiavellianism An orientation in which people believe that manipulating others is a basic strategy of social influence.

COGNITIVE COMPLEXITY.   Cognitive complexity is sometimes conceptualized as a trait relating to our personal constructs. A construct is a bipolar pair of terms such as honest–dishonest or exciting–dull, which we apply to differentiate elements in our environment. People in a society learn a common core of constructs because of their shared culture, resulting in some fairly "standard" meanings. However, people also develop pairs of idiosyncratic constructs, opposites that are unique to the individual. The pair humorous–deadly would be an example of an unusual pairing. Individuals experience meaning in a situation depending on which constructs they apply and which pole of each construct they associate with the situation (for example, either *exciting* or *dull*). The basic idea is that people structure their reality based on their construct systems.

Someone who is cognitively complex has a greater number of constructs that are both more abstract and more interconnected than someone who is cognitively simple. Cognitive complexity is related to a number of important communication processes. The greater one's cognitive complexity, the better one is able to imagine how *other* people view a situation. Perspective-taking ability is a key determinant of successful communication. With this ability one is able to understand another person's concerns by seeing things from his or her perspective. This means the more complex person is better able to adapt a message to a particular receiver. If a message is not adapted to the audience, it seems impersonal, generic, and less relevant. Because the probability of success in persuasion is usually lower if the message is not tailored to the likes and dislikes of the receiver, cognitively complex sources should be better persuaders.

cognitive complexity
The complexity of one's construct system affects their persuasive ability.

NEED FOR SOCIAL APPROVAL.   People vary in their need for social approval and the extent to which they fear social disapproval. According to this idea, a source who offers social approval or threatens social disapproval when the receiver has a strong need for approval ought to be very persuasive. Various forms of opinionated language specified by Rokeach (1960) provide

need for social approval
A person's need for approval from others influences how they react to persuasive messages implying approval-disapproval.

opinionated rejection
Language that expresses an unfavorable attitude toward people who disagree with the speaker.

opinionated acceptance
Language that expresses a favorable attitude toward people who agree with the speaker.

a way to test this relationship. Opinionated acceptance language expresses a favorable attitude toward those people who agree with the speaker—for example, "Intelligent and responsible people will agree that my proposal is needed." Opinionated rejection language states a negative attitude toward those who disagree with the speaker's position—for example, "Only a bigoted fool would oppose this plan." Opinionated acceptance language represents social approval, whereas opinionated rejection constitutes social disapproval. Baseheart (1971) found support for the idea that opinionated language leads to more persuasion when people have a strong need for social approval. In such a circumstance, opinionated rejection was as successful as opinionated acceptance in stimulating persuasion. Having a strong need for social approval probably heightens a person's sensitivity to language that suggests the speaker is evaluating the receiver in some way.

Research on Message Variables

Throughout the last four decades, communication theorists have identified several message variables that appear to influence our reaction to persuasive messages (Sussman, 1973). Two will be examined here: fear appeals and evidence.

FEAR APPEALS.   The study of fear-arousing message content has its roots in antiquity. Aristotle discussed the use of fear and other emotions in the *Rhetoric*. Aristotle suggested that speakers must understand the emotional predispositions of their audience and then use that knowledge as one of the "available means of persuasion." Modern research considers fear appeals to be arguments that take the following form:

1. You (the listener) are vulnerable to a threat.
2. If you are vulnerable, then you should take action to reduce your vulnerability.
3. If you are to reduce your vulnerability, then you must accept the recommendations contained in this message.
4. Therefore, you should accept the recommendations contained in this message. (Boster & Mongeau, 1984, p. 371)

A typical fear appeal might be a variation on the following:

1. Smoking has been found to increase the chances for disease and death.
2. Because you do not want disease or death, you must do something to prevent them.
3. An effective way to prevent these outcomes is to stop smoking.
4. Therefore, you must stop smoking.

During an average evening, we may witness several fear-arousing messages in television commercials. From smoke detectors to life insurance, advertisers make frequent use of the fear appeal to influence consumers.

The contemporary study of fear in persuasion can be traced to the work of Irving Janis and Seymour Feshbach (1953). In their seminal study, high school students were randomly assigned to one of two experimental groups who heard messages on dental hygiene. For one group, a *moderate fear* appeal was used; for the other, a *high fear* appeal was created. A third group of students was also tested. They served as a *control group* and were exposed to an entirely different message on the structure and operation of the human eye. The high fear appeal urged dental care and recommended vigorous and proper brushing of the teeth; pictures of rotting gums and decaying teeth accompanied the message. In the moderate fear appeal, these pictures were omitted. Janis and Feshbach discovered that the moderate fear appeal was more effective than the high fear appeal in changing students' attitudes toward proper brushing and dental care.

These findings led to several decades of experimental research testing the relationship between the level of fear in a message and attitude change. Some studies discovered the opposite outcome: attitude change was more likely when a high fear appeal was used (Beck & Davis, 1978; see Miller, 1963, for a summary and analysis of the early research). Because experimenters sometimes arrived at different results when they studied fear appeals, scientists tried to reconcile these contradictions.

Boster and Mongeau (1984) reviewed six explanations of fear appeal effects. The *drive explanation* suggests that the fear aroused by a persuasive message creates a state of drive, which receivers find unpleasant. Individuals experiencing this state of drive are motivated to reduce it by changing their attitudes and/or behaviors. According to the drive explanation, the greater the amount of fear in a message, the greater the attitude change in the direction recommended by the message.

The *resistance explanation* finds that as perceived fear in a message decreases, individuals' attitudes and/or behaviors will move closer to those recommended in the message. The rationale is that receivers will pay attention to messages low in threatening content; they will resist more threatening messages. Low fear appeals are less threatening than high fear appeals. Thus, messages containing low fear appeals are more likely to be heard than messages containing high fear appeals.

According to the *curvilinear hypothesis,* when receivers are either very fearful or very unafraid, little attitude or behavior change results. High levels of fear are so strong that individuals block them out; low levels are too weak to produce the desired effect. Messages containing *moderate* amounts of fear-arousing content are most effective in producing attitudinal and/or behavior change.

The *parallel response explanation* suggests that fear-arousing messages activate fear control and danger control processes in listeners. *Fear control* is a coping process by which receivers strive to reduce the fear created by the message. *Danger control* refers to a problem-solving process in which listeners search for information on how to deal with the threat presented. These two processes interact to influence message acceptance. According to the parallel response explanation, when a fear-arousing message primarily activates the *danger control* process, a *high* fear appeal will most influence attitudes and/or behaviors. When a fear-arousing message primarily activates the *fear control* process, a *low* fear appeal is most influential.

The *protection motivation explanation* states that a receiver's attitude toward the topic is a result of the amount of "protection motivation" produced by the message. Protection motivation refers to receivers' drives to avoid or protect themselves from a threat. As protection motivation increases, conformity to attitudes and/or behaviors recommended in the message also increases. Thus, the greater the fear in a message: (a) the more likely a threat will occur; and (b) the greater the ability to deal with the threat by following the recommendations provided in the message; thus (c) the greater the attitude and/or behavioral change in the direction of the message.

The sixth explanation is labeled the *threat control explanation*. Reactions to fear appeals depend on logical, not emotional, factors. A fear-arousing message stimulates *response efficacy* and *personal efficacy* processes in listeners. Response efficacy refers to the receiver's perception of how effective the recommended attitudes or actions will be in reducing or eliminating the threat. Personal efficacy refers to whether or not the receiver is capable of taking the actions recommended by the message. These two responses combine to produce threat control. Threat control is a person's perceived probability of success in controlling the threat. This explanation suggests that, as threat control increases, listeners will adopt attitudes more closely corresponding to the recommendations of the message. As fear increases in a message, so too should the amount of attitude and/or behavioral change in the listener.

Boster and Mongeau concluded that all six explanations were less than adequate in explaining the results of experiments studying fear-arousing messages and persuasion. None of the six explanations was completely consistent with the evidence. Several problems were highlighted. First, researchers were not creating strong enough fear appeals. If manipulations of fear in messages were not strong enough to produce fear in listeners, then it was impossible for any relationship between fear and attitude or behavior change to emerge. Second, other demographic variables and personality traits interacted with fear appeals to affect attitudes and behavior. In particular, *age, trait anxiety* (see Chapter 5), and whether the participant *volunteers* for the study were offered as potential moderators of the fear–attitude relationship. Contrary to conventional wisdom, low-anxiety, older volunteers seemed to be more susceptible to fear appeals than high-anxiety, younger nonvolunteers.

Sussman (1973) similarly suggested the influence of mediating variables on the fear–attitude relationship. "Such variables as coping style, self-esteem, perceived vulnerability to danger, and chronic anxiety may mediate the response to a fear appeal" (p. 209). Despite the attention paid by researchers to understanding the fear–attitude relationship, additional theory and research are needed to uncover more satisfactory explanations. Because the use of fear appeals in messages is very common, the results of such research should be of interest both to applied communicators (for example, advertisers) and to scholars.

EVIDENCE IN MESSAGES.   When we hear the term *evidence,* images of attorneys arguing cases come to mind. Television shows such as *Law and Order* depict the powerful effects of good evidence. Clearly evidence is a critical component in any trial. Evidence is also an important verbal behavior variable in less-formal communication contexts. When we become the target of a persuasive effort, we usually challenge our adversary to *prove* the case to us. When a new drug claims to prevent baldness, all but the most desperate or trusting of souls require some type of evidence before they spend huge sums of money on it.

Communication theorists beginning with Aristotle have focused on evidence as a determining influence on individual belief systems. Evidence consists of "factual statements originating from a source other than the speaker, objects not created by the speaker, and opinions of persons other than the speaker that are offered in support of the speaker's claims" (McCroskey, 1969, p. 170). A slightly different definition is "any statement of fact, statement of value, or definition offered by a speaker or writer which is intended to support a proposition" (Florence, 1975, p. 151). Contemporary communication courses, especially argumentation and public speaking, stress the relationship between evidence and persuasion. However, the findings of almost two decades of communication research do not appear to support a direct, positive association between evidence and persuasion. It has not been conclusively shown, for instance, that an audience will be more easily persuaded if more evidence is presented.

After reviewing over twenty studies on the influence of evidence in persuasion, James McCroskey concluded that several variables interact with evidence to produce changes in attitudes or increases in perceived speaker credibility: *evidence and source credibility, evidence and delivery effectiveness,* and *prior familiarity of evidence.*

There is a relationship between the use of evidence and the credibility or believability of the speaker. If a speaker is already perceived to be very credible, including "good" evidence will do little to change attitudes or enhance speaker credibility. However, speakers who are perceived as low to moderate in credibility may increase their credibility by employing evidence. This increase in perceived credibility may in turn increase attitude change.

In several studies on evidence and message topic, McCroskey believed that other factors were influencing the evidence–attitude change relationship. By interviewing participants after the experiments, he discovered that the quality of the delivery made a difference. To investigate the relationship further, he conducted several studies using live, audiotaped, and videotaped versions of a well-delivered and a poorly delivered presentation. The amount and type of evidence were the same for each version in each medium. From these studies, he found that: (a) including good evidence influences attitude change very little if the message is delivered poorly; and (b) including good evidence can influence attitude change and speaker credibility immediately after the speech if the message is well-delivered, the speaker initially has only low-to-moderate credibility, and the audience has little prior knowledge of the evidence. Because the results were consistent for all versions, he concluded that the medium of presentation has little effect on the use of evidence in persuasion.

McCroskey also believed that prior familiarity with evidence should be considered when assessing the evidence–persuasion relationship. Postexperimental interviews led him to conclude that "old" evidence does little to influence listeners. "Old" evidence has already been heard and processed cognitively. If any dissonance had been created by the message, it was already resolved or defense mechanisms were created to prevent a recurrence. These assumptions are consistent with explanations derived from information theories and cognitive dissonance theory (discussed later in this chapter). For evidence to affect listeners' attitude change or perceptions of the source immediately, McCroskey found that the evidence must be "new" to the listener. Including evidence has little, if any, impact on receivers if they are already familiar with it. McCroskey concluded that although considerable information has been uncovered about the influence of evidence in persuasion, communication theorists should continue their research efforts.

One researcher examined the theoretical foundations of previous research and reformulated the existing theories concerning evidence and persuasion (Florence, 1975). According to these findings, evidence influences persuasion only if the proposal, idea, or policy it supports is *desirable* to the audience. Both the credibility of a source of evidence and the evidence itself influence the desirability of a proposal. More recently, Dale Hample (1977, 1979, 1981) developed a theory of argument in which evidence plays a major role. In this theory, the relative power of evidence was measured. Hample argued that the power of evidence is one of the best predictors of attitude change. Because evidence is a key verbal message variable in the communication process, researchers will no doubt continue to examine its influence in persuasion.

A number of other variables may affect credibility: energy (dynamism), sociability, power, impact, mental balance, cultivation, and charisma. If credibility is a list of factors, critics wonder about the length of the list. Does a longer list imply a better understanding of credibility? This raises the issue of whether a "laundry list" of factors really tells us anything. Does each new factor increase understanding or cause confusion? Another criticism of the factor approach is that the model does not specify whether a receiver uses all the factors in assessing a source's credibility. A plausible expectation is that in some persuasion situations some factors matter more than other factors; some receivers will find certain factors more relevant than will other receivers. Thus, the characteristics used to judge the source's credibility can change with different sources, situations, and audiences. These and other criticisms of the factor model have led to the development of two additional models of credibility.

THE FUNCTIONAL MODEL. The functional model of credibility views credibility as the degree to which a source satisfies the receiver's needs. Three simultaneous processes occur in a persuasive situation. First, the receiver becomes aware of the source's characteristics. Some, like height and voice quality, are observable; others, like education and social status, must be inferred. Second, the receiver determines criteria for judging the source in the situation. That is, the receiver becomes aware of the functions that the source could serve for the receiver (for example, to provide recent information, to entertain). Third, the receiver compares the characteristics with the functional criteria. An audience at a banquet might judge the extent to which a speaker has both informed and entertained them. The more needs that are fulfilled by the source, the more credible the source is. For example, the more the audience enjoyed the speech, the more credible they consider the speaker (Cronkhite & Liska, 1980).

> **functional model of credibility**   Credibility is determined by the extent to which a source fulfills the receiver's needs.

Another group of researchers developed a method for measuring credibility according to the functional approach and then compared the functional model to the factor model to determine which explains persuasion best. The two models performed equally well in explaining differences, so the test was inconclusive. However, because the factors did not explain persuasion better than a general measure of credibility, the functional model was judged to be promising (Infante, Parker, Clarke, Wilson, & Nathu, 1983).

THE CONSTRUCTIVISTIC MODEL.   Our earlier discussion in this chapter of constructivism and cognitive complexity as a trait related to persuasion is relevant to understanding the constructivistic model of credibility. The basic idea is that people use their personal construct systems to construct their reality. That is, reality is not something that exists where everyone experiences the very same thing. Two people viewing the same situation can have radically different conceptions of that reality because they have applied very different personal constructs to the situation. Personal construct systems involve bipolar judgments such as valuable-worthless. Some constructs are acquired from culture, others from family, friends, or school. Some constructs can be unique to the individual and highly idiosyncratic. For instance, an economically oriented person might see a situation mainly as having great potential for yielding investment profit, whereas a scholarly individual might mainly perceive how that situation could produce certain knowledge that will advance understanding of a problem.

> **constructivistic model of credibility**   How individuals use their personal construct systems to form, reinforce, and change impressions of sources.

These ideas can be applied to conceptualizing source credibility. Delia (1976) said understanding source credibility involves learning how individuals use their personal construct systems to form, reinforce, and change impressions of people in persuasion situations. Just as two people can have a very different conception of reality in viewing a given situation, they also can have very different impressions of the credibility of a given speaker. We need to determine which constructs the receiver of a message used in deciding to accept or reject the source's position on the object of persuasion. Although this seems to be a reasonable approach to understanding source credibility, a problem is that an appealing measurement model has not been developed. Whereas sets of rating scales have been used successfully for measuring credibility according to the factor approach, a comparable method of measurement has not been developed for the constructivistic approach. Research here typically has had the research subject write an impression of the communicator, which was then content analyzed later by researchers to determine the constructs used and how those identified constructs related to the degree of persuasion that took place (e.g., Delia, O'Keefe & O'Keefe, 1982). Not only is this a tedious, labor-intensive way to study credibility, but the results have not been promising enough to stimulate much further research. More progress in measuring source credibility is necessary, and if that is accomplished, it should have a very beneficial effect in stimulating future research.

Cognitive Dissonance Theory

Social psychologist Leon Festinger's cognitive dissonance theory (1957) is the most thoroughly researched of a family of cognitive consistency theories and therefore the one we shall discuss in this chapter (for a review of other consistency theories, see Kiesler, Collins, & Miller, 1969). Consistency theories of persuasion are based on the idea that inconsistency is psychologically uncomfortable. Inconsistency results when we believe A should have a certain relationship to B but does not, or when A has an unexpected, undesirable relationship with something. For instance, inconsistency would be felt if we see that a program to reduce poverty in our city is not reducing hunger among children as we had expected. Instead, the program is reducing hope and aspirations among poor people.

Cognitive dissonance theory assumes that two beliefs are related either in a state of consonance or dissonance. A state of **consonance** is characterized by consistency: "I like my sorority, and my good friend likes my sorority." **Dissonance** is marked by inconsistency: "I like my sorority, but my good friend does not like it." The idea is that it would "bother" us (we would feel dissonance) if our friend did not also value what we value, and we would be motivated to get rid of the uncomfortable feeling. A central tenet of the theory is: The more the mental discomfort (dissonance), the more we are motivated to change something to make things comfortable.

The theory identifies a number of factors that influence the amount of dissonance experienced. Perhaps the most important one is whether the person's self-concept is involved in the dissonant relationship. If one belief is, "I just said that I liked a task that I really hate" ("I lied"), and a second belief is, "I am an honest person," the dissonance involves self-concept—our mental picture of the kind of person we are. What will be done to reduce dissonance? Research suggests individuals tend to change so that their attitude toward the task is more favorable, "I actually do like that task." This change in attitude

cognitive dissonance theory Assumes that two beliefs are related either in a state of consonance or dissonance.

permits consistency with the belief, "I am an honest person." We try to protect our self-concepts by rationalizing our actions and decisions so we do not "look bad" to ourselves. Changing the second belief to "I am dishonest" would also have restored consistency: "I lied" and "I am dishonest." However, we seldom reduce dissonance by changing a favorable belief about ourselves.

This principle can be used to explain the results of a classic study by Aronson and Mills (1959). To join a very dull discussion group, individuals were required either to recite a list of sexual terms (mild initiation) or to recite a list of "obscene" words (severe initiation). The research participants were then asked how much they liked the group. Did the severe or the mild initiation lead to greater liking for the group? In line with the theory's prediction, persons given the severe initiation liked the group more. Why? Because they experienced more dissonance. Their beliefs could be characterized as: "I am efficient," so "I just put forth a great effort, and I got something worthwhile." To conclude that the group was worthless would force the belief about self to be: "I am inefficient" because "I just put forth a great effort for little reward." Individuals who experienced the mild initiation did not distort their feelings about the group. "I am efficient," and "I got little benefit from the discussion, but I did not put much into it, so I have not lost."

Dissonance can be reduced in many ways besides changing beliefs, as in the preceding example. Attitude change toward a speaker's proposal and attitude change toward the speaker are two basic methods of resolving dissonance. Attitude change toward the speaker might involve criticizing the source of the information: "I won't listen to the American Cancer Society public service announcement warning about the health risks of smoking because the American Cancer Society is biased against cigarette smoking." Other methods of reducing dissonance are not as obvious. Selective exposure involves seeking information that supports your opinion but avoiding information that is unfavorable toward your opinion. The listener can also misinterpret the speaker's position so that the speaker seems to agree with the listener. One could also consider the dissonant elements unimportant so that the dissonance does not really matter. "The new car I just bought has little pickup, but I really don't need power and speed in a car anyway." Another alternative is to add consonant elements to "drown out" the dissonance. "Besides, my new car has great lines, a beautiful interior, an excellent stereo, and perfect handling."

A basic idea about persuasion from dissonance theory is that to persuade people, you must cause them to experience dissonance, then offer your proposal as a way to get rid of the dissonance. A persuader might try to make receivers feel dissonance about energy policies in the United States and then present a proposal for developing alternative and renewable energy sources such as hydrogen fuel cells or solar energy to free the United States from dependence on foreign oil. When a speaker arouses dissonance, the receiver will try to reduce it, using one of the methods just listed. However, dissonance can also be reduced by adopting or agreeing with the speaker's proposal. Although there is no guarantee that the audience will reduce dissonance by changing their minds, the speaker does have a chance to achieve persuasion.

According to the theory, if no dissonance is aroused, there will be no persuasion. People do not change an attitude unless they feel they need to change it. Feeling dissonance provides the motivation to change. The theory predicts that to persuade someone, you must first "upset" the person (make them feel dissonance) concerning the topic of your proposal. If you fail to persuade the audience, perhaps the dissonance they felt was not great enough to motivate action.

selective exposure
Exposing oneself only to agreeable messages; avoiding situations, such as public speeches by a political opponent, requiring us to listen to those with whom we disagree.

Figure 5.4 Cognitive dissonance.

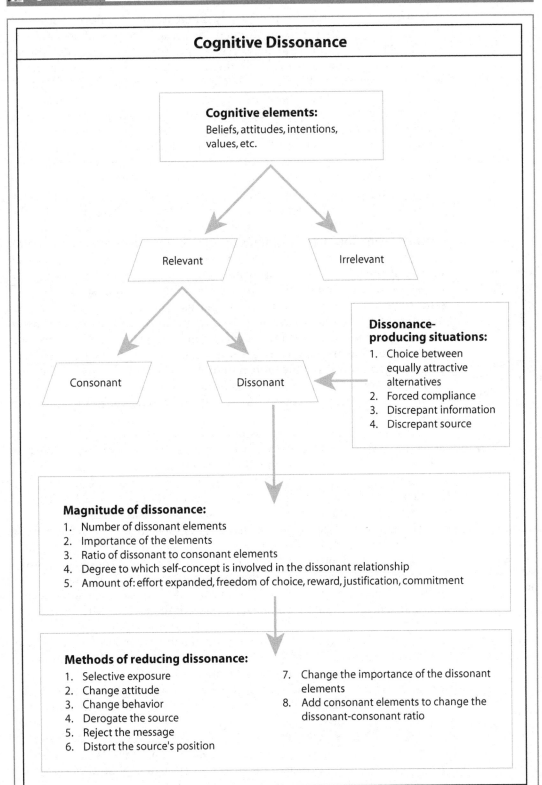

Cognitive Dissonance

Cognitive elements:
Beliefs, attitudes, intentions, values, etc.

Relevant

Irrelevant

Consonant

Dissonant

Dissonance-producing situations:
1. Choice between equally attractive alternatives
2. Forced compliance
3. Discrepant information
4. Discrepant source

Magnitude of dissonance:
1. Number of dissonant elements
2. Importance of the elements
3. Ratio of dissonant to consonant elements
4. Degree to which self-concept is involved in the dissonant relationship
5. Amount of: effort expanded, freedom of choice, reward, justification, commitment

Methods of reducing dissonance:
1. Selective exposure
2. Change attitude
3. Change behavior
4. Derogate the source
5. Reject the message
6. Distort the source's position
7. Change the importance of the dissonant elements
8. Add consonant elements to change the dissonant-consonant ratio

Ego-Involvement, or Social Judgment Theory

This approach to persuasion is distinctly different from cognitive consistency theories of persuasion. Ego-involvement or social judgment theory (Sherif, Sherif, & Nebergall, 1965) predicts successful persuasion by a message depending on how the message is related to the person's current beliefs. (The Sherifs were psychologists; Nebergall was a member of the communication discipline.) Research in physiological psychology indicates that if a person is given an "anchor" in making judgments, objects close to the anchor are seen as more similar to the anchor than they really are (they are assimilated). Objects far from the anchor are perceived as even more dissimilar than they really are (they are contrasted). If you were handed a bar and told it weighs 10 pounds, you would probably judge too low when asked to guess what a 12-pound bar weighs. You probably would judge the 12-pound bar as just about the same as the 10-pound anchor; you would assimilate it. Next, if asked to guess the weight of a 40-pound bar, you probably would judge it heavier than it really is. It would seem more distant from the anchor; the contrast effect would occur.

What does this have to do with persuasion? Ego-involvement or social judgment theory indicates that assimilation and contrast effects also occur in persuasion. Assimilation constitutes persuasion; a contrast effect represents a failure to persuade. In the case of persuasion, the receiver's position on the topic of the persuasive message serves as the anchor. If a speaker slightly opposes gun control and you moderately oppose it, you tend to interpret the speaker's position as basically the same as yours. On the other hand, the more you favor gun control and the more the speaker opposes it, the greater the likelihood that you will view the speaker's position as more extreme than it really is (that is, a contrast effect). Basically, we accept assimilated messages but reject contrasted messages.

Although interesting, the assimilation–contrast notion leaves several questions unanswered. Under what conditions are messages assimilated or contrasted? Why do two individuals with the same position on an issue react differently to the same message about the issue, one person assimilating the message while the other person contrasts it? The concepts of latitude of acceptance, rejection, and noncommitment are needed to answer these questions.

The latitude of acceptance consists of all statements the person finds acceptable, including the favorite position, the anchor. Figure 5.5 illustrates the latitudes of acceptance for two individuals on an issue with 11 positions. Notice that Chris and Pat have the same most acceptable position (A) or anchor belief: "Final exams should be optional for graduating seniors." Chris rejects statements 6 and 7, while Pat agrees with them. The latitude of rejection (r) consists of all of the positions on the issue the person rejects (finds objectionable). Pat and Chris have latitudes of rejection that vary in width. Pat rejects only statement 1, the position that final exams should be required of all students, whereas Chris rejects statements 1–7. The latitude of noncommitment (nc) consists of all positions the person neither accepts nor rejects. The person is noncommittal or neutral on these issues. Chris is neutral about statement 8; Pat is neutral about statements 2–5.

The latitudes of acceptance, rejection, and noncommitment determine whether a given person will assimilate or contrast a message. Messages falling in the latitudes of acceptance or noncommitment will be judged closer to the

ego-involvement Characterized by a wide latitude of rejection and narrow latitudes of acceptance and noncommitment.

assimilation   The degree to which a person accepts the influence of the new culture or environment.

latitude of acceptance Consists of all statements the person finds acceptable. This can include the favorite position or the anchor.

latitude of rejection Consists of all of the positions on an issue the person rejects.

latitude of noncommitment   Consists of all of the positions a person neither accepts nor rejects.

Figure 5.5 **Ego-involvement or social judgment theory.**

		Chris										
Topic Positions		1	2	3	4	5	6	7	8	9	10	11
		r	r	r	r	r	r	r	nc	a	A	a

		Pat										
Topic Positions		1	2	3	4	5	6	7	8	9	10	11
		r	nc	nc	nc	nc	a	a	a	a	A	a

A = most acceptable position
a = other acceptable positions

r = positions which are rejected
nc = positions on that the person is neutral

POSITION STATEMENTS

11. Final exams should be optional for all students.
10. Final exams should be optional for graduating seniors.
9. Final exams should be optional in elective courses.
8. Final exams should be optional for students with an A average.
7. Final exams should be optional for students with an A or B average.
6. Final exams should be optional for students with an A, B, or C average.
5. Final exams should be optional for students with a passing average.
4. Final exams should be optional at the professor's discretion.
3. Final exams should be required only of freshmen.
2. Final exams should be required only of freshmen and sophomores.
1. Final exams should be required of all students.

favorite position (anchor belief) than they really are (assimilated). Messages falling in the latitude of rejection will be judged farther away (contrasted). According to ego-involvement theory, a basic principle of persuasion is that to change a person's most acceptable position on a topic, the message must fall within the person's latitude of acceptance. A persuader can also attempt to widen the latitude of acceptance by advocating a position in the person's latitude of noncommitment. If successful, the persuader will widen the receiver's latitude of acceptance, thus creating a larger "target" for a second persuasion attempt.

The latitudes also indicate whether the person is ego-involved. According to the theory, high ego-involvement is characterized by a narrow latitude of acceptance (the person's own favorite position is about the only position accepted), a wide latitude of rejection (almost everything other than one's own position is rejected), and a narrow latitude of noncommitment (nearly all positions are either accepted or rejected; the person is neutral about very few positions). Low ego-involvement is the opposite. The latitude of acceptance is wide (people are able to accept several other positions on the issue besides their anchor position), the latitude of noncommitment is wide (there are many positions on the topic that the person is neutral about), and the latitude of rejection is narrow (there is not much left to reject if one accepts most positions and does not care about most of the remaining ones).

Chris is highly ego-involved, and Pat is not ego-involved with final exam regulations. According to the theory, even though they both hold the same most acceptable position (statement 10), they would react differently to a message that advocated position 6. Chris would contrast the message because it falls in the latitude of rejection; it would be "heard" as a more extreme message than it actually is. On the other hand, Pat would assimilate the message, perceive it closer to the anchor (position 10) than it really is because it is one of the acceptable positions. Thus, Pat would be persuaded by the message; Chris would not.

This theory permits us to conceptualize how persuasion can be achieved with a highly ego-involved individual. In our example, to persuade Chris to change from position 10 to position 2 would take many messages. One message would not be enough—it would be contrasted. Persuasion would require many messages over a long period of time, each gradually expanding the latitude of acceptance and slowly moving the favorite position (anchor belief). This probably is a realistic view of persuasion. It is very difficult to persuade someone who is very ego-involved in a topic. The theory represents this idea clearly. When a person is highly ego-involved, a "one-shot" attempt to persuade the individual is surely doomed to failure. A "persuasive campaign" composed of many messages over a period of time is a more realistic way to try to change someone who is ego-involved.

The Theory of Reasoned Action

theory of reasoned action
A theory of persuasion that is based on attitudes, belief strength, and the evaluation of the meaning of the belief.

The theory of reasoned action by psychologists Martin Fishbein and Icek Ajzen is included here because it has been used a good deal by communication researchers (e.g., see recent research by Edwards, 1998; Stewart & Roach, 1998; Park, 1998). It is also a good example of theory building. The theory was introduced in the 1960s and enhanced through the next two decades (for instance, see Ajzen, 1985; Ajzen & Fishbein, 1980; Fishbein & Ajzen, 1975).

The theory of reasoned action began with Fishbein's theory of attitude toward an object (an object could be a person, a physical thing, an idea, a social program, etc.); he conceptualized attitude as a sum of the beliefs that we have learned to associate with the object. Suppose we consider your attitude toward physical fitness. You might have learned to associate seven beliefs with physical fitness. The extent to which each belief contributes to your attitude depends on (a) belief strength and (b) evaluation of the meaning of the belief. You might have a belief that it is extremely likely (belief strength) that a physical fitness lifestyle results in a very favorable (evaluation) consequence, an attractive body shape. This belief would favorably affect your attitude toward physical fitness; you have a strong belief that the object produces something good. A second belief might be that you think it is slightly unlikely (belief strength) that you will get frequent colds if you are in good physical condition. This belief also is positive because it asserts that you will be less likely to experience something bad, but because it is not a very strong belief, it will have less impact on your attitude. If your remaining five beliefs followed the pattern of these two examples, you would have a moderately favorable attitude toward physical fitness. That is, if we add the degree of favorable feelings in your seven beliefs, the total would be much closer to the favorable end than to the unfavorable end of the attitude object continuum.

In the 1960s, psychology and sociology researchers found that attitude theories such as this one were poor predictors of a given behavior. For example, we could design a study to measure your attitude toward physical fitness. If your attitude was very favorable and we gave you a coupon for a free workout at a local gym, the prediction would be that you would use the coupon. Typically, that prediction would not be very accurate. In fact, flipping a coin might be just as accurate in predicting behavior as measuring attitude.

Fishbein, who was later joined by Ajzen, expanded the theory to deal with this problem of why attitude toward an object does not accurately predict a specific behavior relevant to the object. Fishbein declared that attitude does predict behavior, but not in the way that previous researchers had assumed that it should. The problem was the measure of behavior. A single act, observed once, was what most studies used as the criterion. This was a mistake because there is no theoretical reason why attitude toward an object should be closely related to a single behavior, unless there is only one behavior that is relevant to the object, which is seldom the case. Typically, many behaviors are relevant to an attitude object. When that is the case, attitude toward the object should be related to the total set of behaviors. Thus, one act, observed once, does not measure the entire set of relevant behaviors. The correct behavioral measure was what Fishbein called the multiple-act, repeated observations criterion. This means all the relevant behaviors should be counted; ideally, they should be observed more than once over a period of time.

multiple-act   A behavioural prediction in research based on a set of relevant behaviors ideally more than once over a period of time.

In terms of our example, then, your attitude toward physical fitness probably would not predict whether you will show up at the gym. We would be a bit more accurate if we could observe you showing up next week, the week after, and the next week, and so on (this would be a single-act, repeated measures criterion). An even better predictor would be observations of all other relevant behaviors, observed more than once. Two possibilities would be observing you eating a healthy diet each day for a month, or noting that you watched physical fitness shows on TV for a month. If we designated ten behaviors and observed them for a month, the total number of occurrences of the ten would constitute a multiple-act, repeated observations criterion. Research by Fishbein and others found an improved behavioral measure such as this is strongly related to attitude toward the object.

What this means in terms of persuasion, then, is if you succeeded in persuading someone who had an unfavorable attitude toward physical fitness to have a favorable attitude (probably by arguing successfully that several good things would likely follow), you should expect the total pattern of the person's fitness-related behaviors to change. However, any single behavior might not change. For instance, the person might go to the gym often, watch exercise shows on TV, attend fitness lectures, etc., but continue eating high-fat fast food. We might wonder at this point whether it is possible to target a single behavior not only for prediction but also for change in persuasion situations.

The theory of reasoned action was developed to deal specifically with the problem of predicting a single behavior, even if it is only observed once. Fishbein and Ajzen built on their earlier research. A core idea of the theory of reasoned action is that behavior is intentional; very little behavior is accidental. When people engage in a given behavior, it is because they formed intentions to do so, and they had reasons for their decisions to actualize their intentions. Thus, much of our behavior can be characterized as "reasoned action."

Attitude toward the specific act is one of two major components of a behavioral intention. The second is what has been called the *normative component*. Keep in mind that the Fishbein and Ajzen model works backward from a specific behavior. That is, a specific behavior is predicted or controlled by an intention to behave; that intention is predicted and controlled by two factors, attitude toward the act and the normative component. Each of these two components is controlled by particular factors.

Attitude toward the specific act is controlled by the beliefs that the person has about the consequences of performing the act. As with Fishbein's earlier theory of attitude toward an object, two aspects of each belief are important: belief strength and evaluation. Continuing with our gym visit example, suppose you have five moderately strong beliefs about five somewhat desirable consequences of accepting the offer for a free workout at a gym: the gym has superior equipment; it is easy to get to the gym because of its location; membership rates could be cheaper after a trial visit; a gym membership would increase motivation to exercise; you could meet interesting people there. At this point it might be tempting to predict that you probably will go to the gym. The five beliefs are reasons for action or inaction. In this case the reasons tilt somewhat toward action. However, there is more to the theory. The second determinant of an intention is the normative component, and we need to consider it before making a prediction about behavior.

The normative component is composed of our beliefs about what valued others expect us to do regarding the behavior. Each belief is weighted by our motivation to comply with the wishes of other people. In terms of our example, suppose one normative belief is that your good friend would not want you to join that gym, because he is planning on having a gym in the basement of his home and wants you to work out there so the two of you can motivate one another. Perhaps another normative belief is that your significant other does not like the manager of the gym and therefore is less than enthusiastic about the prospect of you being a member there. Suppose further that you have fairly strong motivation to comply with these normative expectations.

On the basis of these two components, attitude toward the act and the normative component, can we now offer a prediction of whether or not you will go to the gym for the trial workout? Often information about these two components is enough to make an accurate prediction, However, in a case like this where you are being pulled one way by one component and another way by the second component, more information is needed. The *subjective weights* of each component help evaluate conflicting influences. For some behaviors we feel that we can do whatever we feel like doing (i.e., we let our attitude toward the act guide us and feel no constraint from other people). For other behaviors we decide what we do must be compatible with the preferences of valued others (i.e., we look to the normative component for guidance).

In our example, suppose on a 1–10 scale your weight for attitude toward the act is 3 and your weight for the normative component is 8. In view of this data the theory would predict that you will not go to the gym for the trial workout. Suppose that the theory is accurate (as it has been most of the time), and you do not go to the gym. However, what would have happened if we had made a prediction based only on the first attitude that we considered, attitude toward physical fitness? Because the attitude in the example was moderately favorable, the prediction would have been that you would go to the gym. The prediction would have been wrong. If the prediction had been based only on attitude toward the act, once again it would have been wrong. An accurate prediction was achieved only when both components were considered and weighted. The theory became more accurate as it developed—an excellent illustration of the advantages of theory building. The theory of reasoned action has been a popular one in communication research because of its accuracy.

In addition to prediction strengths, the theory provides implications for persuasion. For example, if you want to influence a person to perform a specific behavior, do not devote much time to trying to change attitude toward the object. Instead, try to determine what the person's current attitude is toward that act and also the normative component. Importantly, how is each component weighted? Such analysis directs your focus for the persuasive attempt. The fundamental persuasion tactics would involve arguing the consequences of performing the act. For a favorable attitude toward the behavior you would claim good consequences would be likely and bad consequences would be unlikely. For an unfavorable attitude, the opposite would be argued (i.e., that good things would not happen, but bad things would occur). Influencing the normative component involves maintaining that persons valued by the individual either expect certain behaviors or do not want certain things to happen. Sometimes it could be necessary to convince people that they should have high motivation to fulfill the expectations of valued others. In other circumstances persuading people to perform a given behavior necessitates moving them to ignore the wishes of others and to act mainly on the basis of self-interest. This tactic could be especially difficult to accomplish because it is not unusual in persuasion situations for need for approval to be a major factor.

The Theory of Planned Behavior

As explained in the previous section, the core of Fishbein and Ajzen's theory of reasoned action is the notion of the behavioral intention; a person's intention of performing a given behavior is the best predictor of whether or not the person will actually perform the behavior. It may have occurred to you, however, that several factors can work against this behavioral intention → behavior sequence. Think about some examples where you, to use a cliché, "had the best intentions" to perform a behavior (e.g., taking your sibling to the mall to go shopping next Saturday morning) but certain personal limitations (e.g., you were too tired and overslept) and/or external obstacles (e.g., you didn't have a car available to you that day) prevented you from actually performing that behavior. The successful performance of a behavior also depends on one's ability to control factors that either allow or prevent performance of that behavior (Ajzen, 1988).

To resolve some of the difficulties in predicting behavior precisely, Ajzen (1985, 1988, 1991) proposed the theory of planned behavior (TPB), an extension of the theory of reasoned action (TORA). TPB is also based on the premise that the best predictor of an actual behavior is a person's behavioral intention. However, unlike its predecessor theory, TPB suggests that there are three, rather than two factors associated with a person's behavioral intention (see Figure 5.6).

In TPB, the first two factors associated with a behavioral intention are the same as in TORA: (1) attitude toward the specific act (or behavior), and (2) the normative component, our beliefs about what valued others expect us to do

behavioral intention
A person's intention of performing a given behaviour is the best predictor of whether or not the person will actually perform the behavior.

Figure 5.6   Theory of planned behavior.

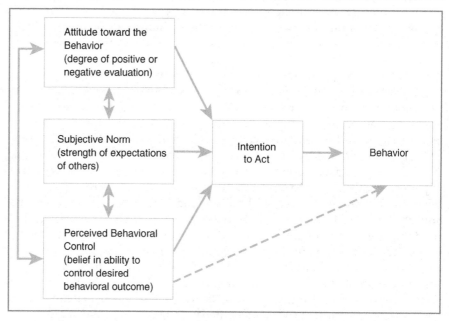

regarding the behavior in question. Ajzen (1985, 1988, 1991) added a third factor, perceived behavioral control, to TPB. Perceived behavioral control refers to "the degree to which a person believes they can control the behavior in question" (Roberto, Meyer, & Boster, 2001, p. 316)—how easy or difficult the person believes it will be to perform a given behavior.

TPB suggests that, in general, more favorable attitudes toward the specific act (or behavior), more favorable subjective norms (normative component), and greater perceived behavioral control (the ease of performing the behavior in question) strengthen the intention to perform the behavior. According to TPB, perceived behavioral control is directly related to behavioral intentions and to actual behavior.

Ajzen (2001) suggests that perceived behavioral control influences a person's confidence that they are capable of performing the behavior in question. Perceived behavioral control is, in essence, a combination of two dimensions, self-efficacy (ease or difficulty in performing the behavior or likelihood that the person can actually do it) and controllability (people's beliefs that they have control over the behavior, that the performance of the behavior is—or is not—up to them).

Returning to the physical fitness lifestyle example, let's say you want to predict whether a person will walk on a treadmill in a physical fitness center for at least 30 minutes each day in the next month (Ajzen, 2001). To assess the self-efficacy dimension of perceived behavioral control, you might ask the person to respond to an item such as, "For me to walk on a treadmill for at least 30 minutes each day in the forthcoming month would be" [impossible—possible]. To assess the controllability dimension of perceived control, you could ask, "How much control do you believe you have over walking on a treadmill for at least 30 minutes each day in the forthcoming month" [no control—complete control].

perceived behavioural control   The degree to which a person believes that they control any given behavior.

self-efficacy   The degree of ease or difficulty in performing the behavior or likelihood that a person can actually perform a behavior.

controllability   People's belief that they have control over the behavior, that the performance of the behaviour is-or-is not up to them.

Thus, if you want to assess more accurately whether a person will actually perform a given behavior, you will need to measure perceived control, along with an assessment of the person's *behavioral intention*, "I plan to walk on a treadmill for at least 30 minutes each day in the forthcoming month" [strongly disagree—strongly agree], their *attitude toward the behavior*, "I believe walking on a treadmill for at least 30 minutes each day in the next month is [harmful—beneficial, worthless—valuable], and their subjective norm, "Most people who are important to me think that [I should—I should not] walk on a treadmill for at least 30 minutes each day in the next month" (Ajzen, 2001, pp. 4–7).

When put to the test, TPB has been able to predict a number of health-related behaviors such as weight loss (Schifter & Ajzen, 1985), adolescent use of alcohol (Marcoux & Schope, 1997), and adolescent abstinence from sex and/or use of condoms during sexual relations (Basen-Engquist & Parcel, 1992). Communication researchers have recently adopted TPB to predict actual behavior. For example, Roberto, Meyer, and Boster (2001) used TPB to predict adolescent decisions about fighting. In their study, several hundred seventh-grade boys and girls were questioned about their participation in physical fights "where two or more people hit, punch, slap, push, or kick each other in anger" (p. 317). They completed a survey instrument that measured their actual behavior (e.g., "During the last month how many times did you get into a fight?), their behavioral intentions (e.g., "How many times do you think you will get into a fight in the next month?"), the perceptions of subjective norms (e.g., "Do most of the kids you know think you should get into fights?"), their attitudes toward fighting (e.g., very cool—very uncool), and their *perceived behavioral control* (e.g., "How easy or hard is it for you to stay out of fights," and "When someone tries to start a fight with you, how easy or hard is it for you to avoid the fight?").

The results supported several of the assumptions of TPB in that attitudes toward fighting and perceived behavioral control were both related to an individual's behavioral intentions. That is, those adolescents who felt they were more "in control" of their fighting behaviors and who expressed unfavorable attitudes toward fighting were less likely to get into fights. Both behavioral intentions and perceived behavioral control emerged as predictors of actual behavior (Roberto et al., 2001).

TPB has also been used to predict smokers' interests in participating in a smoking-cessation program (Babrow, Black, & Tiffany, 1990). TPB suggests that measuring a person's attitudes toward participating in a particular smoking-cessation program allow better prediction of participation in the program than attitudes toward smoking in general or attitudes toward quitting smoking in general. Intentions to participate (behavioral intentions), attitude toward participation, beliefs about the consequences of participating, perceptions of the subjective norm, and perceived behavioral control were measured ("how frequently would the following factors: flexibility of program hours, participation with other friends, convenience of location, etc. affect your ability to participate in this particular smoking-cessation program" [never—constantly]). Babrow et al.'s (1990) findings generally supported TPB. Beliefs about the consequences of participating in the program were related to attitude toward participation. Most important, attitude, subjective norm, and perceived behavioral control beliefs were strongly related to individuals' intentions to participate in the smoking cessation program.

perceived control The degree to which people believe that they have control over a situation or behavior.

subjective norm The pressure a person feels to conform to the will of others to perform or not perform a behavior.

The development of TPB in response to an earlier theory, TORA, allows us to see how theories are built by extension (see Chapter 2), where new theories emerge from expansion of existing theories. By adding new information, factors, and knowledge to existing theories, we can better explain, predict, and thus, control behavior.

Elaboration Likelihood Theory

We will now examine a theory that has been described as "the most promising recent theoretical development in persuasion research" (O'Keefe, 1990, p. 109). Social psychologists Petty and Cacioppo (1986) developed the elaboration likelihood model (ELM). They recognized that persuasion results primarily from characteristics of the persuasive message or from characteristics of the persuasion situation. ELM analyzes the likelihood that receivers will cognitively elaborate—engage in issue-related thinking—on the information presented in a persuasive message. Because of its focus on the conditions of certain types of thinking in persuasion, ELM fits the laws tradition of theories.

At times persuasion occurs because the receiver of a message considers the content of the persuasive message carefully and has favorable thoughts about the content. The favorable thinking about the message content causes a favorable attitude to form toward the object of the message. This represents one type of persuasion—the central route to persuasion, characterized by a good deal of persuasive, issue-related thinking. At other times persuasion occurs because the receiver is guided not by his or her assessment of the message but because the receiver decides to follow a principle or a decision-rule derived from the persuasion situation. The rule might be: "When everyone else goes along with the speaker's recommendation, I should too unless I have a very good reason to deviate from the group." This is an example of persuasion through a peripheral route.

According to Petty and Cacioppo, when persuasion takes a peripheral route, there is little or no elaboration of message content; that is, there is a lack of issue-related thinking. When a decision on a persuasive message is not based on the message itself, the receiver looks to other things to guide the decision, as in the preceding example. The persuasive situation provides many principles for evaluating a message if one does not want to engage in a critical assessment of the message content. We sometimes base message acceptance on the trustworthiness of the source, the expertise of the source, or even the physical attractiveness of the source. Also, a decision-rule can be based on rewards or punishments. "I will accept the source's position if I can realize a financial gain from it or if I can avoid a punishment such as higher taxes." Sometimes we are guided by our relationship with the persuader, as in "I need to return a favor."

The ELM is based on the idea that people realize their attitudes are important because attitudes guide decisions and other behaviors. This importance motivates people to form attitudes that are useful in their lives. Although attitudes can result from a number of things, persuasion is a primary source. When a persuasive message attempts to influence an attitude the receiver realizes is significant to his or her life, the likelihood increases that the receiver will cognitively elaborate on the content of the message. This process takes a good deal of effort, so it is avoided whenever possible. That is, people generally prefer not to have to work hard mentally and will follow the "easy way" whenever possible. This probably is due not so much to people being lazy as to the reality

elaboration likelihood model A model of persuasion that assumes persuasion results primarily from characteristics of the persuasive message or from characteristics of the situation.

central route The favorable thinking about the message content causes a favorable attitude to form toward the object of the message.

peripheral route When there is little or no elaboration of a message. Situational cues persuade people instead of the message.

of our cognitive limits. Our physical limits are pretty obvious. For instance, we cannot run a marathon as a sprint. The central route to persuasion is probably more like a "mental sprint." You can only do it for a limited period of time.

A peripheral route to persuasion is "easy" because not much thinking is necessary. All one has to do is realize an appropriate guiding principle and make a decision on the persuasive message based on the principle. "The source is a real expert so I can trust what she is saying." Little, if any, elaboration takes place when a simple principle, like this example, is used to guide assessment of a persuasive message.

It is important to note that persuasion, or lack of it, can take place with either route. What matters is the *cognitive product* of the process. When one takes the central route, thinking about the content of the message might result in unfavorable assessments of the source's arguments. This negative reaction would inhibit persuasion. Similarly, persuasion could fail to occur through a peripheral route when a receiver utilizes the negative side of a principle. "The source has no real credentials to speak on this topic, so I would not even consider changing my opinion."

Because elaboration or issue-related thinking is central to this theory, a good deal of research has explored the factors that influence how much we elaborate when we receive a persuasive message. Basically, two types of factors have been identified: (a) factors that influence our *motivation* to elaborate, and (b) factors that influence our *ability* to elaborate.

Motivation to elaborate has been investigated in terms of the receiver's involvement in the persuasive issue; the more the person is personally involved in the topic, the more likely he or she will elaborate on the message. Also, motivation to elaborate is increased when several sources present arguments on the topic. The variety of arguments presents a sense of conflict, and conflict tends to attract attention. The research also has discovered that some people are more likely than others to elaborate. Specifically, people who have a strong need for cognition (they enjoy thinking a lot) are more likely to elaborate on the content of a message.

The need for cognition trait is defined as "a stable individual difference in people's tendency to engage in and enjoy effortful cognitive activity" (Cacioppo, Petty, Feinstein, & Jarvis, 1996, p. 198). Cognitive activity refers to the degree of critical thinking a person engages in. People range from being high to being low in need for cognition. Individuals high in need for cognition enjoy thinking about abstract issues and often engage in contemplative thought, whereas people low in need for cognition tend to rely more on simple social cues that provide a shortcut to effortful thought. These cues can be things such as attractiveness and source credibility, as illustrated in the Elaboration Likelihood Model of Persuasion. That is, people who are high in need for cognition have a tendency to process information through the central route, whereas people low in need for cognition have a tendency to process information through the peripheral route.

Although it may appear that people high in need for cognition are somehow smarter than people low in need for cognition, this is not the case. Of course people high in need for cognition have to have a degree of critical thinking capacity. Sanders, Gass, Wiseman, and Bruschke (1992) compared Asian Americans, Hispanic Americans, and European Americans in need for cognition, argumentativeness, and verbal aggressiveness. The results of this study reveal that need for cognition was positively related to argumentativeness and

need for cognition
A stable individual difference in people's tendency to engage in and enjoy effortful cognitive activity.

negatively related to verbal aggressiveness. Further, Asian Americans reported being lower in need for cognition than both Hispanic Americans and European Americans. A similar link between need for cognition and argumentativeness was also observed by Mongeau (1989).

It is important to note that need for cognition is a motivational trait, not a behavior skill-related trait. Similar to the competing motivational tendencies that comprise the trait of argumentativeness, need for cognition simply suggests that we either enjoy abstract thinking or we do not.

You may be thinking, "Why is need for cognition in the Persuasion Approaches chapter and not in the Trait Approaches chapter?" The answer is that unlike other traits, need for cognition is an important motivational factor in the Elaboration Likelihood Model of persuasion. The need for cognition is a very important trait for researchers and theorists interested in a source-based factor that influences how people are persuaded.

The ability to elaborate is also influenced by several factors. Distractions are a key element. If people are distracted during the presentation of a message, they are less likely to elaborate on the content. They are more likely to take a peripheral route. For instance, distracting a friend by dining in a good restaurant while trying to persuade him or her makes it less likely that your friend will exert the cognitive effort to elaborate on the message (attention to the food subtracts from the attention available for message elaboration). In this example, it is again more likely that a peripheral route to persuasion will be taken. "Coming from so generous a friend, the message is probably valid." Knowledge of the topic also is a factor that influences ability to elaborate. Knowing little about the topic makes elaboration very difficult, and peripheral routes are welcomed when we find ourselves in such a circumstance. Similarly, the comprehensibility of a message influences elaboration. A very vague message or one that relies heavily on very difficult material reduces the ability to elaborate. However, this might not reduce persuasion if, instead of elaborating on the message content, the receiver relies on a principle such as "the speaker is such an expert that the message position surely is correct." Diverting receivers to a particular peripheral route at times could be a successful strategy of persuasion.

It should be noted that the two routes to persuasion are not mutually exclusive. Probably only one route is taken under circumstances of extremely high or extremely low elaboration. Thus, when elaboration of the message content is very extensive, no consideration might be given to a peripheral route. On the other hand, when there is no elaboration of the message, a peripheral route is taken exclusively. Between those extremes, however, probably both characteristics of the message and characteristics of the persuasion situation matter. For instance, after receiving a persuasive message, a person might say: "After thinking extensively about what was said, I must conclude that I am persuaded a bit, but not as much as I would have been if the speaker had been motivated less by self-interest." Research by James Stiff (1986) suggests people are influenced in persuasion not only by cues associated with the central route but also by cues pertaining to peripheral routes. Stiff demonstrated that, when they want to, people can "stretch" their capacity for processing information and process both message and situation information. Therefore, it is overly simplistic to view persuasion in an "either/or" (as in either a central or a peripheral route) sense. Allowing for both provides a richer explanation of persuasion.

We can avoid being overly simplistic also by saying that characteristics of sources (such as expertise or attractiveness) do not always pertain to peripheral routes. For instance, an actor's beautiful tan could be considered part of the persuasive message when trying to sell suntan lotion; the tan would constitute data (an example) for the claim that having a tan enhances physical attractiveness. In other circumstances, such as the actor talking about aiding the homeless, the tan would function as a component of attractiveness that, for some receivers, might be a peripheral route to persuasion.

O'Keefe's (1990) assessment of the ELM being most promising as a theoretical development is probably quite accurate. The theory is generating a good deal of research and is attracting the attention of a sizeable body of researchers. Although cognitive dissonance theory was the dominant theory of persuasion in earlier periods of persuasion research, the ELM might very well play a similar role in the future.

Compliance-Gaining Message Selection

A good deal of social influence research in the communication discipline through the 1980s focused on **compliance gaining**. Recall our earlier distinction that compliance gaining and persuasion are two different types of social influence (persuasion involves attitude change). The main emphasis of compliance-gaining research was on the various strategies that people use under different circumstances to influence another person to behave in a particular manner (see Dillard, 1990, for an analysis of this literature). This line of research had its beginning in the field of sociology, where Gerald Marwell and David Schmitt (1967) derived sixteen different compliance-gaining strategies from previous research and theory, which were later introduced to the communication field (Miller, Boster, Roloff, & Seibold, 1977). Figure 5.7 presents a definition of each strategy with an example from the Marwell and Schmitt study. Generally, research was conducted by presenting a hypothetical situation (for example, your roommate is playing the stereo too loudly). The set of compliance-gaining strategies was then presented, and participants were asked to rate the likelihood that they would use each strategy in the hypothetical situation. Another method was to ask participants to write what they would say in such a situation. Researchers then analyzed the written content to determine preferred strategies.

We will examine John Hunter and Franklin Boster's (1987) model of compliance-gaining message selection because it is a good example of the new direction taken in social influence theory building. The model posits that the source's selection of compliance-gaining messages is influenced greatly by the way the source thinks the receiver will react emotionally to the message. Emotional reactions to a message can range from extremely positive to extremely negative. Persuaders generally select messages that create a favorable emotional reaction in their receivers, and they would rather avoid messages that produce negative emotional states. However, this is a general pattern, and it does not apply to everyone. Some people are more willing than others to select messages that stimulate very unfavorable reactions in receivers. Some people only select messages that arouse positive emotions.

Willingness to select negative affect-producing messages is an individual difference, a variable from person to person. The persuader's willingness to stir

Figure 5.7   Compliance-gaining strategies: Family situation examples.

The situation analyzed here involved a father attempting to persuade his son, Dick, to study.

1. Promise
If you comply, you will be rewarded.
Offer to increase Dick's allowance if he increases his studying.

2. Threat
If you do not comply, you will be punished.
Threaten to forbid Dick the use of the car if he does not increase his studying.

3. Expertise (Positive)
If you comply, you will be rewarded because of "the nature of things."
Point out to Dick that if he gets good grades he will be able to get into a good college and get a good job.

4. Expertise (Negative)
If you do not comply, you will be punished because of "the nature of things."
Point out to Dick that if he does not get good grades he will not be able to get into a good college or get a good job.

5. Liking
Actor is friendly and helpful to get target in "good frame of mind" so that he will comply with request.
Try to be as friendly and pleasant as possible to get Dick in the right "frame of mind" before asking him to study.

6. Pre-Giving
Actor rewards target before requesting compliance.
Raise Dick's allowance and tell him you now expect him to study.

7. Aversive Stimulation
Actor continuously punishes target, making cessation contingent on compliance.
Forbid Dick the use of the car and tell him he will not be allowed to drive until he studies more.

8. Debt
Compliance is owed because of past favors.
Point out that you have sacrificed and saved to pay for Dick's education and that he owes it to you to get good enough grades to get into a good college.

9. Moral Appeal
You are immoral if you do not comply.
Tell Dick that it is morally wrong for anyone not to achieve good grades and that he should study more.

10. Self-Feeling (Positive)
You will feel better about yourself if you comply.
Tell Dick he will feel proud if he studies more.

11. Self-Feeling (Negative)
You will feel worse about yourself if you do not comply.
Tell Dick he will feel ashamed of himself if he gets bad grades.

12. Altercasting (Positive)
A person with "good" qualities would comply.
Tell Dick that since he is mature and intelligent, he naturally will want to study more and get good grades.

13. Altercasting (Negative)
Only a person with "bad" qualities would not comply.
Tell Dick that only someone very childish does not study.

14. Altruism
Your compliance is very badly needed, so do it as a favor.
Tell Dick that you fervently want him to get into a good college and that you wish he would study more as a personal favor to you.

15. Esteem (Positive)
People you value will think better of you if you comply.
Tell Dick that the whole family will be very proud of him if he gets good grades.

16. Esteem (Negative)
People you value will think worse of you if you do not comply.
Tell Dick that the whole family will be very disappointed in him if he gets poor grades.

From Marwell & Schmitt, Dimensions of Compliance-gaining Behavior, 1967, pp.357–58..

negative emotional reactions in receivers serves as a "go, no-go" trigger for message selection. Sources are willing to use messages that stimulate negative reactions up to a certain degree. A given message is a candidate for use if it does not exceed the degree of negative arousal persuaders are willing to cause in receivers; it triggers a "go" response. If a persuader believes a particular message will exceed the amount of negativity the persuader is willing to stir, the message selection process triggers a "no-go." This means the source finds the message "unacceptable" as a means of persuasion.

Hunter and Boster reanalyzed the data from several earlier compliance-gaining studies and found considerable support for the idea that sources' anticipations about the emotional reactions of receivers to messages provide a foundation for the message selection process. According to this idea, a fundamental concern in persuasion theory involves understanding the persuader's willingness to use messages that cause negative affect. Hunter and Boster suggested that variability in willingness to create negativity might be explained by certain traits such as argumentativeness and verbal aggressiveness (these two traits were discussed in Chapter 5).

Hunter and Boster derived several speculations about how these traits might pertain to one's willingness to create negativity. For instance, high verbal aggressives may have a higher willingness because they like inflicting psychological pain on others. Thus, they should be more likely than other people to use compliance-gaining messages that threaten the receiver with some form of punishment. Low verbal aggressives, on the other hand, probably have a very low threshold for creating negative impact because they are very sensitive to others' self-concepts and try not to cause psychological pain. In terms of argumentativeness, it could be predicted that high argumentatives use a diverse group of messages (positive and negative) because they like arguing and will try numerous arguments to succeed. Low argumentatives, however, probably use few negative compliance-gaining messages to avoid an argument being instigated by such messages. Other research has supported these ideas (Boster & Levine, 1988; Boster, Levine, & Kazoleas, 1989; Infante, Anderson, Martin, Herington, & Kim, 1993).

Although a person's traits probably exert considerable influence on his or her willingness to create a negative emotional impact on receivers, a possibility is that factors in the particular persuasion situation also may have an impact. That is, situational influences may cause the willingness to create negativity to be a little higher or lower in some situations than in others. Although Hunter and Boster's model did not deal much with this idea, expanding the model to include situational influences seems like a natural development. Thus, we might speculate that there are several important situational factors. The nature of the receiver might influence the source's willingness to stimulate negativity. For instance, if the receiver is extremely stubborn, the source might become more negative than usual. The persuasive topic could be another factor. Persuaders might be willing to stir more negative reactions on some topics than on others. For example, willingness to cause negative emotional impact may be lower when the topic is a delicate, sensitive one. For some receivers, this might pertain to their religion, their physical appearance, or their sexual orientation. The emotional climate in the situation could alter the source's willingness to be negative. For instance, if the mood in a crowd of people turns very aggressive, the source's willingness might increase; the source might find negative messages more acceptable than at other times.

Although only a few studies have been based on Hunter and Boster's model, the focus on compliance-gaining message selection is of obvious relevance to communication theory. Moreover, the ideas that make up the model are intuitively valid and lead to interesting implications. Thus, it deserves continued attention from researchers.

Cialdini's Persuasive Heuristics

Robert Cialdini (1988) developed six principles of compliance gaining based on his experience in a variety of occupations, including advertising, public relations, and fund-raising. He defines compliance as "action that is taken only because it has been requested" (Cialdini, 1987, p. 165). He noted that there are consistencies across all occupations in terms of getting people to comply with a request, which he labeled "persuasive heuristics." The six heuristics consist of reciprocity, commitment and consistency, social proof, liking, authority, and scarcity.

The reciprocity principle assumes that when someone gives you something, you should give them something in return. The sense of owing someone something is believed to be a powerful compliance-gaining strategy. People are constantly being given things in an effort to enhance compliance. Whether it is free food samples in a supermarket, free mailing labels from a charity, or free Avon products, the feeling of obligation is powerful and transcends cultures. In a study of charitable solicitations, Cialdini and Ascani (1976) used the reciprocity principle to increase blood donation. A request was made for people to join a long-term blood donor program. When this initial request was rejected, the researchers then made a second smaller request of a one-time blood donation. This smaller request resulted in a 50% compliance rate as opposed to a 32% compliance rate for simply asking for the one-time donation. This compliance technique is also known as the door in the face technique.

The commitment and consistency principle assumes that when people take a stand on an issue, there is internal pressure to be consistent with what you committed to. For example, it is common practice in the toy industry to purposely understock the more popular toys around the holiday season. Parents promise their children the most popular toys for the holidays. When the parent goes to the toy store and finds that the promised toy is out of stock, other toys are purchased to make up for the promised toy. Conveniently, after the holidays there is an ample amount of the most popular toys. The parent, more often then not, will return to get the promised toy, thus increasing the toy stores' overall sales.

The social proof principle states that "we determine what is correct by finding out what other people think is correct" (Cialdini, 1988, p. 110). This is especially powerful when we are uncertain about what is correct behavior. To determine what is correct behavior, we look around us to see how other people are behaving. This serves as a guide as to what is correct. Consider your favorite television comedy. The producers will purposely include "laugh tracks" to cue the viewer when to laugh. It is common practice in churches to "salt" the collection plate (i.e., put a one or five dollar bill in the plate before it is passed to the parishioners). By doing this, it sets a standard amount for the donation. This also works in bars, where the bartender will "salt" the tip jar to indicate the standard rate of tipping.

The liking principle assumes that we comply with requests because we like the person. The police use this principle when interrogating suspects. If you have ever seen an episode of *CSI* or *Law and Order*, you most certainly are familiar with the "good cop/bad cop" interrogation technique. The principle behind this technique is that one interrogator will threaten and be aggressive to the suspect, and the other will be more understanding and calm. When the aggressive interrogator leaves the room, the suspect will have a greater tendency

reciprocity heuristic
A compliance gaining strategy that assumes when someone gives you something, you should give them something in return.

commitment and consistency heuristic
A compliance gaining strategy that assumes when people take a stand on an issue, there is internal pressure to be consistent with what you committed to.

social proof heuristic
A compliance gaining strategy that assumes that we determine what is correct by finding out what other people think is correct.

liking heuristic
A compliance gaining strategy that assumes we comply with requests because we like the person.

authority heuristic
A compliance gaining strategy that assumes people should be more willing to follow the suggestions of an individual who is a legitimate authority.

scarcity heuristic
A compliance gaining strategy that assumes people want to try to secure those opportunities that are scarce.

door in the face technique   A compliance gaining strategy that utilizes a large request followed by a smaller request. People are more likely to agree to the smaller request after rejecting the larger request.

to give information to interrogator that he or she "likes" more. It is a common practice in sales to build a relationship with your clients and then work toward the sale. It is well documented that **homophily**, or similarities of attitudes and backgrounds, increases liking (Byrne, 1971; Stotland & Patchen, 1961). In a study of peace marchers, Suedfeld, Bochner, and Matas (1971) found that people were more likely to sign a petition if the person requesting the signature was similarly dressed.

The authority heuristic holds that "one should be more willing to follow the suggestions of an individual who is a legitimate authority" (Cialdini, 1987, p. 175). Our culture is filled with authority figures that tell us what to think, who to vote for, and what to buy. One study revealed that people were three and a half times more likely to follow a jaywalker into traffic when he wore a suit as opposed to just a shirt and pants (Lefkowitz, Blake, & Mouton, 1955). The authority heuristic, similar to that of social proof, is particularly effective in times of uncertainty. When we are uncertain, we look to authority figures to help us determine what is appropriate.

The final persuasive heuristic is scarcity. Ciladini (1987) defined this principle as "one should want to try to secure those opportunities that are scarce" (p. 177). The fact that something is offered for a limited time or in limited quantity makes the item that much more valuable. This concept is illustrated in television infomercials. It is a common tactic for vendors to put a counter in the corner of the television screen informing the viewer of how many units are left. This strategy gives the viewer the perception that once they are sold out of product, there will be no more available.

The persuasive heuristics developed by Robert Cialdini continue to represent one of the most comprehensive efforts in explaining the complex process of compliance gaining. Recall in the Elaboration Likelihood Model (ELM) of persuasion that people process messages either through the central route (critical thinking) or the peripheral route (cues in the environment). The persuasive heuristics presented here would be processed through the peripheral route of the ELM.

Preventing Persuasion

We turn now to theories that explain how to prevent persuasion. In emphasizing how to persuade people, it is easy to forget that the reverse is often our goal. It is not unusual for us to want another person to resist being influenced by a third party. We might want a wavering Democrat to resist appeals to vote Republican. In a sense, we try to "persuade" a person not to be persuaded. There have been five approaches in persuasion research to the problem of how to prevent persuasion.

The *behavioral commitment* approach advises public statements about positions. If you know that someone supports your proposal, you would want him or her to express that opinion publicly. When other people learn someone holds a given position, it is more difficult for that person to change the position. Because the position has been associated with the individual, "losing face" might result from changing what was previously declared.

The *anchoring approach* is based on the idea that someone will be less likely to change a position if the position is anchored or "tied" to things that are significant for that person. With this approach you would try to convince an individual who valued others (friends, family, etc.) to agree with a position by pointing out that other people and/or reference groups (religious, political groups, etc.) also agree. You might add that important values (freedom, for instance) are upheld by the position. Changing an opinion would involve disagreeing with family and friends, would violate group norms, and would undermine values.

A third approach is creating *resistant cognitive states.* People are more difficult to persuade when they are in certain frames of mind. The major research finding in this area is that when persons experience an increase in self-esteem, they are particularly resistant to persuasion because people who feel high self-esteem believe they are valuable; they are confident and therefore less likely to say they were wrong in holding a position that a persuader tries to change. It is relatively easy to raise or lower self-esteem in a research laboratory. The main technique for raising self-esteem is to lead individuals to believe they have succeeded at an important task. Conversely, believing they have failed lowers self-esteem. Because a person with low self-esteem is particularly easy to persuade, an ethical issue arises. Is it acceptable to try to persuade someone who has just experienced failure? The person may be especially vulnerable at that time, and attempting persuasion may be taking advantage of him or her (Infante, 1976).

Training in critical methods is an approach that has met with mixed results. The idea appears sound. Train people to think critically when listening to a speech, to recognize fallacies in reasoning, and to detect propaganda techniques; they will then not be so easily persuaded. In one study, students were trained in methods for critically evaluating speeches. Later they listened to a tape-recorded speech. Women in the study were persuaded less than the control group of women who had not been taught the evaluation methods. However, male participants were persuaded more than the control group of untrained men. American culture may have influenced men to be more dogmatic in their positions than women; therefore, men may pay less attention to opposing positions in the message. The training might have neutralized this cultural effect and made men more sensitive to the content of the message (Infante & Grimmett, 1971), thus yielding the variable results.

inoculation theory
Approach to preventing persuasion based on the biological analogy of preventing disease.

Inoculation theory from social psychology is the fifth approach (McGuire, 1964). This theory assumes that preventing persuasion is like preventing a disease. To keep a dangerous virus from causing a disease, the body can be inoculated with a weakened form of the disease-producing virus. The body's immune system will then create antibodies to destroy that type of virus. If the actual virus does invade the body at a later date, the defense will be in place and will prevent the disease. To prevent persuasion, according to this biological analogy, the person's cognitive system needs to be inoculated so a defense is in place when a strong persuasive message "invades the mind." How does *cognitive inoculation* work? The counterpart of the weakened virus would be weak arguments in support of an opponent's position. In theory, when an audience hears the weak arguments, they think of refutations for them. These refutations, like antibodies against a disease, form the foundation for attacking stronger arguments heard later. Thus, preventing persuasion from this approach involves "strengthening" the mind's defense systems so it will be able to destroy strong, attacking arguments.

Persuasion is an integral topic for communication study because the skill of the persuader in using verbal and nonverbal symbols affects the interaction. In this chapter, we defined persuasion as attitude change toward a source's proposal. Persuasion differs from coercion because audience members can choose to agree or disagree. In this framework, belief change leads to attitude change, which can then produce behavior change. Adapting to the audience and the situation makes persuasion more effective.

As we said at the beginning of this chapter, persuasion research has changed greatly in recent years. We think it is important for persuasion research to continue with the enthusiasm it has enjoyed in the past. Current researchers are especially interested in how people influence one another in interpersonal relationships. The advertising and public relations professions provide another important persuasive context for the application of communication theory.

Research that enhances our understanding of the persuasion process is inherently valuable. Of course, there are other ways of influencing another person's behavior. Two particularly distasteful methods are physical aggression and coercion. Persuasion is infinitely more desirable than these alternatives because the process of persuasion respects the dignity of others and their right to choose among alternatives based on their beliefs. Persuasion offers hope for people to resolve differences in a satisfying and constructive manner.

Interpersonal Conflict

OBJECTIVES

- Plan and conduct a conversation using the five stages of conversational development.
- Understand the cooperative principle and the benefits of dialogue.
- Recognize the importance of seeking productive conflict.
- Appreciate the variety and value of different conflict management techniques.
- Apply principles of confirmation and negotiation to work through conflict.
- Develop skills for handling difficult conversations and for de-escalating conflict situations.

KEY TERMS

Accommodating
Altercasting
Avoiding
Coercive power
Collaborating
Competing
Compromising
Confirmation
Conflict
Conversational disclaimers
Cooperative principle
Destructive conflict
Dialogic negotiation
Dialogue
Disconfirmation
Expert power

Facework
Feedback
Feedforward
Focus
Formal feedback
Informal feedback
Information/persuasive power
Legitimate power
Monologue
Negotiation
Phatic communication
Power
Principled negation
Productive conflict
Referent power
Reward power

Imagine you're discussing an upcoming presentation for this class with your instructor. Let's eavesdrop on part of that conversation.

"I'm lost on this assignment."

"What confuses you?"

"I just don't get it."

"Don't get what?"

"The whole thing. Your instructions are so unclear."

"The instructions are very explicit. Did you read them?"

"Of course I read them. You don't have to insult me. I'm leaving!"

Oh, dear! We just overheard a very ineffective conversation. The exchange might be fun to read, but it exemplifies significant, ongoing issues that affect our everyday communication. How often have you had a conversation that didn't go the way you wanted? Think of the worst date or social experience you ever had. Chances are that a major part of your disappointment began with a less-than-ideal conversation. We talk with each other all the time, yet too often we talk past each other, not connecting on deeper levels and failing to accomplish what we had hoped.

The first part of this chapter deals with the process of conversation, a form of communication we easily take for granted although it often forms the foundation of fulfilling relationships. A growing body of evidence suggests that everyday conversations play a key role in relationship satisfaction (Alberts et al., 2005). Research on same-sex couples confirms that conversational quality and relationship quality go hand in hand (Gottman et al., 2003).

The second part of this chapter focuses on conflict, which we can understand as situations where our goals, desires, or expectations differ from those of someone else. Agreement with others might seem more comfortable or easier than conflict, but too much agreement actually reduces creativity and productivity. Research has shown consistently that small groups where conflict and difference of opinion occur tend to be more productive and innovative than groups without significant disagreement (Likert & Likert, 1976).

We complete our tour of conversation and conflict with reflection on how to address some common challenges in both areas. We will probe some practical ways to prevent conversations and conflicts from getting out of hand. These recommendations can help you prepare for difficult communication situations and avoid communication breakdowns.

UNDERSTANDING AND ENHANCING CONVERSATIONS

Becoming a better conversationalist can be extremely beneficial. Skillful conversationalists find it easier to approach and interact with a wide variety of people, equipping them well for the highest positions in their profession (Murphy, 2005). Others increasingly approach you as someone who can engage in lively conversation. As a student and as a professional, your conversational skills will enable you to give and get more out of your talks with professors, supervisors, and colleagues.

If we know conversation skills are so valuable, why do we take them for granted? Perhaps we assume that we can converse effectively just because we have been communicating with others since we were very young. Unfortunately, we don't always recognize the importance of conversation until the conversation takes a negative turn or we end up hurting someone we care about. In this section, we will focus on understanding conversational structure and recognizing key elements of conversation. The best part about studying conversation is that you can put the principles and strategies into practice immediately.

A good way to begin understanding conversations is with their structure. We will track how to manage conversations by tracking stages adapted from DeVito (2005): opening, feedforward, focus (a stage DeVito labels "business"), feedback, and closing. We cover what happens within each conversational stage, offering ongoing examples from some of the most important conversations you can conduct as a student: consultations with your instructors. Through these examples, you will be able to gain a basic understanding of each stage of conversation as well as practical advice for appropriately handling conversations with instructors.

Opening

Although we often search for ways to begin a conversation, the very beginning is simple: Acknowledge the other person with a greeting. Surprisingly, many people forget this obvious step in e-mail messages. Instead of greeting the recipient with something as simple as "Hi, Cheryl," correspondents often simply dive right into a detailed message, which can disorient the recipient. During face-to-face conversations, the absence of an opening greeting is much more obvious. Consider this scenario. You are out with your significant other and a friend that you haven't seen or talked to in five years walks up and immediately asks you intimate details about your romantic relationship. You are likely stunned and not willing to disclose this type of information at this moment. You needed an opening greeting to help you and the friend ease into conversation.

Typically, a greeting leads to small talk that seems trivial but actually serves a vital social maintenance function. This small talk, known as **phatic communication**, simply keeps the lines of communication open, clearing a path for further interaction. Phatic communication works because it avoids controversy and does not require an emotional commitment, consequently inviting connection instead of conflict (Gill & Adams, 1998). Figure 6.1 provides examples of phatic communication.

Small talk has big consequences. Phatic communication acknowledges the presence of the other person, and this recognition reaffirms his or her value. In medical settings, phatic communication can make the difference between a patient feeling reassured or ignored by the nurses (Burnard, 2003). This is certainly not limited to the medical field, but important in all personal and professional interactions.

Figure 6.1   **Examples of Phatic Communication**

Common Phatic Communication Phrases

- "Hi, how are you?"
- "Nice day today, isn't it?"
- "Good to see you."
- "What's up?"

Sample Phatic Communication Between Instructor and Student

Student: "Hi, Dr. Doolittle, how are you?
Instructor: "I'm well, Biffy, and you?"
Student: "I'm doing pretty well."
Instructor: "Are you glad it's Friday?"
Student: "Yes, I'm looking forward to the weekend."

Another good way to begin a conversation is by referring to some shared knowledge or experience. You could note something about the other person or about what connects you. <u>Example</u> (at the gym): "Wow, we're working out at the same time again." An especially effective opener is to begin with an observation of something you have in common. This technique worked well for me one morning. An older gentleman at the gym caught my eye because he was wearing a sweatshirt from my alma mater. I approached him and said, "Oh, I see we're both Hawkeyes." He immediately warmed up to me, excited to encounter someone familiar with his beloved University of Iowa.

Feedforward

The second stage, **feedforward**, previews the content and tone of the upcoming conversation. Think of feedforward as the preview of main points in a speech or as a road sign alerting you to what lies ahead. Attention to feedforward can improve conversational quality by predicting the course of conversation and preparing participants to manage it appropriately. Feedforward often provides the preview of the conversational content, format, or emotional dimension. As with other oral communication, the preview should follow introductory material (the opening) that invites others to participate. Plunging directly into feedforward might disorient or antagonize your conversational partners, especially on a sensitive topic. Figure 6.2 provides examples of feedforward in a conversation between an instructor and a student.

Feedforward can set guidelines and boundaries. You might explicitly lay down the format of the conversation: "Each person will speak for five minutes"; "We will discuss the problem and then the possible solutions." Feedforward also can set limits to conversational topics or methods: "No interrupting"; "Everyone gets a chance to speak"; "Don't talk about anyone else's family."

We covered disclaimers in Chapter 4 as a form of powerless language. Now we can expand our understanding of disclaimers. In conversations, different kinds of disclaimers can serve more diverse purposes. Conversational **disclaimers** are statements that set guidelines to "regulate the impact of utterances" by warding off potential criticisms or channeling interpretations in a particular direction (Beach & Dunning, 1982, p. 178). Disclaimers can serve many purposes, such as the following:

- Warnings ("Anything you say may be used against you in a court of law").
- Image management ("Don't consider me homophobic when I say …").

Figure 6.2   **Examples of Feedforward**

Common Feedforward Phrases

- "Here's something that will really surprise/disappoint you."
- "I have some very good/bad news."
- "Let's try to understand why …"
- "We need to talk about …"

Sample Feedforward Between Instructor and Student

Student: "I have a few concerns about my performance in this class."
Instructor: "Okay, let's talk them through."
Student: "I will present my concerns and then ask for any ideas you might have."
Instructor: "I will be happy to do that."

- Establishing expectations or credentials ("This is just the opinion of an amateur," "As someone with vast experience on this topic …").
- Setting other conditions for interpreting what someone says ("Hypothetically speaking, what if …").

Used in these ways, disclaimers shape expectations about how the conversation should proceed.

Feedforward can include setting up the roles conversational participant play in relation to each other. **Altercasting**, or designating a role for the other person in the conversation, could help you accomplish your conversational goals (Weinstein & Deutschberger, 1963). Altercasting sets up the expected roles that will structure response. For example, I have had students altercast by saying, "I'd like your reaction as if you were my parent, not my professor." Altercasting can distinguish which among several possible roles someone should occupy. It also controls the direction of conversation if each participant responds in accordance with their role (Malone, 1995).

Focus

Now we will consider what to do in the heart of the conversation, or the **focus**. Each conversation will develop its own character depending on the topic, context, goals, and the people involved. Because there is not a specific set of statements that usually occurs during the focus of the conversation, this section offers some hints on ways to approach the substance of your conversations. Regardless of the topic, any conversation can improve by addressing some fundamental principles.

Cooperative Conversations. Paul Grice, a philosopher of language, observed that conversations operate on a **cooperative principle**, which calls us to be aware of the accepted rules and expectations of any conversation (1975). It isn't enough for someone just to be a lively conversationalist. Conversations proceed on mutual assumptions that each participant expects the other to fulfill (Bach, 2006). Conversations fizzle and spark conflicts or misunderstanding when these conditions are not met. Exactly what do we expect from each other in conversations? Grice identified four conversational maxims, shown in Figure 6.3. If we choose not to abide by the maxims, we might find ourselves in awkward situations or even worse—our conversational partner may leave. Understanding and following these maxims can invite productive participation in conversations.

Let's go back to the instructor–student relationship and apply these maxims to a conversation that may take place when you see your instructor at the local movie theater. You will need to consider the following issues:

- *Quantity:* Ask open questions that allow for both parties to expand on ideas. If you are asked a closed question, try to answer and then expand on your idea. Speak for a few minutes but don't continue talking for a long period of time.
- *Quality:* Speak about what you know and don't attempt to make things up or pretend to know something that you don't. Don't lie; after all, instructors are human beings and appreciate honesty.
- *Relation:* Try to recognize early (during feedforward) what you will discuss during this time. Will you talk about class? Will you talk about the movies you will be seeing? Just pick a topic or two and stay with it.

Figure 6.3   Grice's Conversational Maxims

Maxim	Explanation	Rationale	Example of Violation
Quantity	Contribute as much information as required, but no more than necessary.	Too little Conversation can't be sustained without interaction. Too much Conversationalists cannot process the flood of information.	Too little Conversation shuts down if one conversant only grunts or says "yes" and "no" Too much A "motormouth" who endlessly spews all possible information
Quality	Make statements that are true. Don't say false things. Don't say anything that lacks adequate support.	Conversation breaks down if we can't judge whether information is true or accurate.	False statements Lies, fantasies Statements without support Generalizations or extreme exaggerations
Relation	Stay relevant.	Conversations that wander from their focus accomplish little.	Random topic changes that interrupt the direction or focus
Manner	Remain clear. Avoid obscurity and ambiguity. Be brief and orderly.	We must enable others to interpret what we say.	Stream of consciousness babbling; saying one thing and meaning another; vague references

- *Manner:* Converse in a way your instructor can follow logically. Consider how to move the conversation progressively forward instead of randomly jumping from topic to topic. Achieve clarity by using a straightforward vocabulary instead of trying to impress your instructor with terms you don't understand.

Developing Dialogue.   Try answering the following questions:

1. Do you frequently use negative criticism and judgment?
2. Do you usually refuse to talk when others don't agree with you?
3. Do you often praise yourself and your accomplishments?

If you answered yes to these questions, you may often engage in a conversational style known as monologue. **Monologue** is communication in which one person does the majority of the speaking and maintains most of the attention. As we learned in Chapter 1, effective communication is transactional. This shared responsibility for communication would suggest that monologue may not be the best style for an effective conversation. Monologue prevents interaction and only allows for one individuals' goals and ideas to be heard.

Many philosophers, psychologists, communication theorists, and social activists note the advantages of moving conversations toward **dialogue** (Cissna & Anderson, 1994). When we discussed dialogue in Chapter 3 as part of listening, we noted that participants collaborate in conducting a conversation using honest, open communication based on mutual respect. Now we delve deeper into how to build dialogue through conversations.

Dialogues strive for shared understanding even if participants have different viewpoints. Engaging in genuine dialogue requires the willingness to cooperate with others to find common ground that enables participants to talk *with* each other rather than at each other. Dialogue isn't just about the personal satisfaction of self-disclosure, but of opening ourselves to what others have to offer (Arnett & Arneson, 1999). Participants in dialogue feel secure enough about the conversation and each other to advocate passionately and question assertively.

Exactly what does dialogue involve?

- *Turn-taking:* No one person or group monopolizes the conversation. Everyone has an equal opportunity to participate as a speaker and as a listener (even if some people choose to participate more or less than others).
- *Agreement on procedures:* Participants share basic rules or conversational practices that guide interaction and establish boundaries. Examples: no profanity, no yelling.
- *Sincerity:* All participants in dialogue feel "safe" enough in the conversation to speak honestly, expressing ideas and feelings genuinely. Examples: no "trick questions," melodrama, or refusal to engage others.
- *Equal power and status:* No one automatically gains a superior position simply because of who or what they are. Conversation proceeds without prejudice or privilege. Example: a first-year undergraduate and a university president in dialogue get an equal hearing.
- *Civility:* Everyone is respected, regardless of whether we agree with individual views. Each person has inherent value that he or she retains regardless of how the conversation goes.
- *Openness:* Dialogue requires openness to new viewpoints and willingness to concentrate on the strengths of ideas rather than tearing them down (Franco, 2006).

Not every conversation will exhibit characteristics of dialogue. In fact, few do. As we move closer toward achieving the characteristics of dialogue, we may find that our conversations become more interesting and rewarding.

Developing dialogue isn't easy, since dialogue isn't simply agreement and obedience (Arnett & Arneson, 1999). Indeed, "'dialogue' is not some saccharin-filled, consensual 'group-hug' affair! It refers instead to the ongoing tensionality of multiple, often competing, voices" that interplay in conversation (Baxter, 2007, p. 118). Approaching dialogue—even if we don't achieve it entirely—can move conversation to a more challenging but also deeper, more satisfying, and more productive level.

> **THAT'S DEBATABLE**
>
> Dialogue represents a conversational ideal. Like any ideal, it might fit some situations better than others. What are some examples of situations that might call for communication approaches in addition to or instead of dialogue? What might those approaches be? How should they be implemented?

Feedback

We saw as early as Chapter 1 that **feedback** is defined as the process of responding to the communication of others. Within any conversation, feedback reviews what has occurred. Certainly both verbal and nonverbal feedback occur throughout the stages of conversation; however, the feedback stage allows the speaker to see and hear how the bulk of the message has been interpreted. This type of verbal or nonverbal feedback is known as **informal feedback** and can

Figure 6.4   Examples of Conversational Feedback

Common Feedback Phrases

- "OK, so you're going to … and I'm going to …"
- "As I understand it, you are concerned about _____. Is that correct?"
- "Thank you for sharing your story with me. I hear that …"

Sample Feedback Between Instructor and Student

Student: "So, based on what I have heard, you believe that I have been writing strong papers; however, I need to continue to work on my oral presentations."
Instructor: "Yes, I believe you can improve your performance on presentations."

be as simple as a smile or frown. Often feedback used to review or summarize what has been said or what the participants will do as a result of the talk. Based on the feedback received, the speaker can determine whether the conversation has accomplished its goal. If not, return to feedforward to set a new agenda. Figure 6.4 provides examples of feedback.

Some entire conversations revolve around feedback, and these they can have a big impact. These conversations represent **formal feedback**. If you have not already experienced a performance review at your job, you will likely engage in one of these conversations in your future career.

For now, let's consider a formal feedback conversation that may happen in any of your college classes. If your professor requires meetings with students to review progress in the course and discuss grades, you might feel anxious, uneasy, or just unsure of what might happen. You might even have some of the following thoughts:

- "I must have done something wrong. Otherwise, why would I be meeting with my professor about my performance?"
- "If he says something bad about the work I've done after I've worked so hard this semester, I'll tell him a thing or two. I'll let him know just what a jerk he is."
- "Gosh, she's the professor and I'm the student. I guess I'd better just sit there silently the whole time, thank her, and then be glad it's over."

While you might have had the previous thoughts, they are actually all misguided and may harm the conversation. For this reason, it is important to prepare mentally before entering a feedback-oriented conversation. First, we need to eliminate negative and destructive thoughts such as those expressed in the examples above. Second, you will need to engage in positive mental preparation. Figure 6.5 lists some basic preparatory actions you can take before receiving feedback. For mental preparation to be effective, it has to be implemented, not just understood. You should actually be saying to yourself the kinds of statements that appear in the "self-talk" column of the list.

While receiving constructive feedback, be sure to demonstrate your effective listening skills and participate in the conversation. If any feedback is vague or confusing to you, ask for clarification. Effective feedback should leave you with clear indications of how your work can improve. Your questions should be courteous and presented in a tone that shows you value the person's comments, not that you are annoyed or want to retaliate.

DO ask questions such as …

- "As I understand it, you are concerned about _____. Is that correct?" (asks for verification, checks for proper interpretation)

Figure 6.5   Preparing for Feedback

Basic Mindset	Self-Talk	Actions
Constructive feedback evaluates performance, not the person. Regardless of what happens, feedback will not damage my personal worth.	"The other person is evaluating my performance, not judging my character."	Treat all comments as remarks about your work, not directed to you personally.
Constructive feedback focuses on ways to improve.	"Feedback is how I can become a better student."	Anticipate potential limitations of your own performance to avoid surprises.
Constructive feedback is a partnership among students and teachers to move toward better performance.	"My instructor and I have the same goal: for me to become the best student I can. If the instructor didn't care, I wouldn't be getting any feedback."	Treat the evaluator as someone trying to help you, not as an adversary.

- "Would you please help me understand which things I did that were not up to standards?" (moves toward getting precise targets for improvement)

  DO NOT ask questions such as …
- "So you're saying I'm a poor student, are you?" (leading question, sounds accusatory)
- "What do you mean my work was not up to standards?" (sounds challenging)

  DO ask questions such as …

- "Thank you for your comments. What would you suggest as the best ways to improve in these areas?"
- "If you were in my position, what would you do to perform better?"
- "What concrete actions can I take to do better next time?"

  DO NOT ask questions such as …

- "So, what do you want me to do?" (sounds as if you have no control over improving your own performance)
- "How am I supposed to do better with all this pressure and so little time?" (offers excuses, not a positive desire to improve)

Feedback can be a critical step in your personal and professional success. Generally, the higher the stakes in a feedback session, the more formal the feedback will be. Ordinarily formal feedback that is tied to determining job performance will be conducted in a performance appraisal interview. In such an interview, the supervisor typically meets personally with each employee to discuss strengths and areas for improvement. An employee cannot expect to advance by maintaining the same level of performance. Consistent improvement merits advancement in position, in pay, and in responsibilities. A major way supervisors determine improvement is to examine how well an employee implements suggestions from formal feedback sessions. It becomes vital to understand how to make the most of feedback.

Receiving feedback from various individuals with whom you interact is critical. Aside from receiving feedback from co-workers, feedback from clients has a major impact on employees. Many organizations have formalized the flow of feedback from clients by distributing comment cards or client satisfaction surveys. The practice of follow-up surveys to patients has become routine in many hospitals throughout the nation. Client feedback gives an important perspective to supervisors about how an employee is representing the organization to the public. A lot of positive feedback from clients (both formal and informal) about an employee can impress supervisors and ultimately enhance the employee's career. Conversely, a pile of client complaints can cause a worker to be reprimanded or fired.

Closing

Have you ever been conversing with someone and felt deep frustration that the person simply refuses to end the conversation? How about the guest who lingers on and on at a party or event you are hosting, ignoring every hint to leave? If these situations sound familiar, you know the value of conversational closure. Endless conversations can play havoc with schedules and disrupt plans, so we need to offer clear signs that the interaction has ended. Verbal signals of closure include remarks that call attention to time constraints. A closing may not explicitly reference time, but instead use the past tense to describe the interaction. Figure 6.6 provides some examples.

Regardless of the closing you use, remember to allow for the possibility of future interactions. "I'll text you" is just one common closing phrase that suggests a future interaction. Simply hanging up to end a phone call certainly closes the conversation, but it also may close the potential for more interaction. You can prepare for closure nonverbally, behaving in ways that signal your preparation to terminate the exchange: gather up books, close a briefcase or purse, put on a coat, take out your keys, or glance at a clock. All closures, however, should include some expression of appreciation. Conversation is a privilege, and anytime someone engages in conversation with us, we should consider it a gift. Remarks such as "I've enjoyed our conversation" or "This talk meant a lot to me" reaffirm the value of interaction.

Tech Talk: Managing E-mail Conversations

Because we cannot interact directly with others in computer-mediated communication, we must take extra steps to help conversations flow.

- **Include a subject heading as feedforward for every message.**
  A blank subject heading gives no clue how the receiver should process the message. Blank subject lines also invite the receiver to delete the message, suspecting it might be unimportant or spam (unwanted or "junk" e-mail).
- **Address the receiver directly, as in a personal letter.**
  Since you can't wave or shake hands through e-mail, you need a way to acknowledge the other person. Simply beginning with a greeting such as "Hi, Frodo ..." recognizes the other person as an individual.
- **Treat e-mail conversations as public communication.**
  Every e-mail is just one mouse click away from being forwarded to anyone with an e-mail address. Countless conflicts have arisen from supposedly "confidential" e-mails that (accidentally or intentionally) got into the wrong inboxes. For highly personal information, select more private media such as the telephone.
- **Remember to close the e-mail by referencing the next communication step**
  (e.g., "Please talk to me about this after class") or meeting time. You may even want to specify what type of feedback you are hoping to receive and when. Always sign your e-mails appropriately.

Figure 6.6 **Examples of Conversational Closure**

Common Closing Phrases

- "Well, you need to get back to what you were doing."
- "Too bad we can't continue our talk any longer."
- "I'll let you go now."
- "It's been nice speaking with you."

Sample Closing Between Instructor and Student

Student: "Well, I really appreciate your time and advice today."
Instructor: "I'm glad you came to talk to me."
Student: "I'll let you get back to your grading."
Instructor: "Great, and I'll see you tomorrow in class."

CONFLICT AND NEGOTIATION

When was the last time you saw a reality TV show or movie that included at least one conflict scene? You probably did not need to think too hard to recall several examples. It seems that many of us are drawn to these conflicts and we can't wait to see who will be yelling and cursing in the next episode of our favorite reality show or who finally "wins" the "fight" on any number of TV dramas.

Why are we so interested in conflict? A few reasons explain our focus on conflict (Melchin & Picard, 2008). First, war and violence have been prevalent during the twentieth and twenty-first centuries. From World War I to more recent wars in Iraq and Afghanistan, conflict has been a part of our present and past. Second, there is great concern about scarcity of our planet's resources. This crisis not only evokes strong feelings and emotions, but it also promotes competition and fear. Third, diversity increasingly surrounds us in our workplaces, homes, schools, and communities. While this diversity carries enormous benefits, differing opinions and lifestyles raise the potential for conflict.

In addition to world trends, the media frames our views and understanding of conflict. From TV to video games, we have created a world that appears to be full of conflict and competition (Brigg, 2008). Because of all of these factors, we often see "social and political life as saturated with difference and dissension" (Melchin & Picard, 2008, p. 3).

While we may be drawn to and surrounded by conflict, we often recognize this conflict as "difficult, complex, and frequently mismanaged" (Kellett & Dalton, 2001, p. 3). Despite the fact that conflict and competition can be frightening, it is unavoidable. In fact, some scholars suggest that it is not only inevitable but also necessary in human relationships (Kellett & Dalton, 2001). Conflict can cause damage, but we must separate violent attacks from productive disagreements. In work groups, for example, "while relationship conflicts based on personality clashes and interpersonal dislike are detrimental to group functioning, task conflicts based on disagreements regarding the specific task content are beneficial in many situations" (Jehn, Chadwick, & Thatcher, 1997, p. 287).

This inevitability of conflict explains why this chapter talks about "managing" instead of "eliminating" conflict. The choices we make concerning conflict management will undoubtedly affect our personal relationships and the greater society. The way we handle conflict can prove helpful or harmful to our relationships. This is why we must reflect on our individual experiences with conflict and work to develop effective strategies for managing conflict—even recognizing it as positive and constructive.

You might be asking yourself: "What is this thing called conflict that is so prevalent and what causes it?" or "Can't I just pretend I don't know something that I think might cause a conflict between me and a friend?" In the next few sections, we will address these questions and more.

What Is Conflict?

So, you and a friend are talking about your differing religious beliefs, or you and your parents are brainstorming different gifts that you might like to receive for your birthday. Are these examples of conflict? Probably not, although if the conversations escalate and both parties in the conversation begin to argue over competing views, it could become a conflict. **Conflict** can be defined as "an expressed struggle between at least two interdependent parties who perceive incompatible goals, scarce rewards, and interference from the other party in achieving their goals" (Hocker & Wilmot, 2006, p. 201). This definition recognizes that two people must be aware of the problem for conflict to occur, and it emphasizes the interconnectedness of both people. We can understand conflict as "a difference that matters" (LeBaron, 2003, p. 11). This definition allows us to focuses on the difference of opinions and beliefs that we often openly see during a conflict.

Now that we know what conflict is, we need to break it down a little further. You probably know from experience that conflict can be extremely destructive to a relationship. This **destructive conflict** usually "results in a worse situation and sometimes, harm to the participants" (Kellett & Dalton, 2001, p. 4). But another type of conflict might actually enhance a relationship. This type of healthy, or **productive conflict**, allows people involved to move "toward resolution" and protects the "psychological and relational health of the participants" (Kellett & Dalton, 2001, p. 4). Productive conflict may benefit the relationship and the people in it in several ways: (1) Conflict can create energy and motivation; (2) conflict can bring out different viewpoints and increase creativity; and (3) conflict can help people understand the argument and themselves as communicators (Walton, 1987).

So, what is required if we seek to have and manage productive conflict in our lives? Four suggestions can help you to continuously seek productive conflict and reduce destructive conflict (Kellett & Dalton, 2001). Figure 6.7 identifies these suggestions and provides an example of self-talk that might be helpful in achieving this.

Seeking productive conflict will not be a one-time event, nor is it something that you can do without hard work. As you notice from the previous suggestions, we should be asking deep questions about the nature of the conflict, prioritizing conflict and concerns, continuously learning, and continuously examining and inquiring about conflict and how it can best be managed. You will want to pay attention to your own needs and tendencies as well as those of your relational partners. This takes time and commitment—and of course, effective communication!

Figure 6.7   Four Ways to Seek Productive Conflict

Suggestion	Example
1. Ask deep questions about conflict experiences.	Why are we fighting? What are my beliefs and goals? What are the key negotiation principles I should remember? NOT: What's wrong with you?
2. Learn from your own and other people's conflicts.	I will focus on understanding this and not brush it under the rug or save it until later.
3. Make understanding conflicts a priority.	What has happened in the past that may have started this pattern? What happens with me during conflict?
4. Manage conflicts by continuously examining and inquiring.	How might forgiveness change our relationship? How might I manage my communication skills to prevent this from happening in the future?

Hopefully, you have chosen to invest the effort required for productive conflict; however, if it were as simple as choosing one type over another, we certainly would not be spending so much time studying this material. As with conversations, actually managing conflict in the moment is extremely difficult. We are often so emotionally invested and care so much that we forget that the other person is a human being and we use hurtful words, react inappropriately, and make the situation much worse than it originally was. The next section is designed to give you a few pointers for managing conflict and a strong foundation for understanding what is happening in that difficult moment.

How Can Conflict Be Managed?

Before we consider how to manage conflict, it will be important for us to openly recognize the misconceptions that often make conflict even worse. The follow examples illustrate common myths concerning communication and conflict (James, 1996):

- Myth: "If I communicate more, I will clarify everything."
- Myth: "I don't care what people say, there is an easy solution."
- Myth: "I'll just change what I am doing and it should fix everything."
- Myth: "If everything seems peaceful, that must mean there is no conflict."

Many of us have thought or said the previous myths. We need to consider why each of points is in fact a myth (Kellett & Dalton, 2001).

- First, as we noted in Chapter 1, "communication concerns quality, not quantity." The type of communication matters more than the amount of communication. Therefore, more communication is not always better and in fact sometimes makes conflicts worse.
- Second, conflicts are often deeply rooted in historical patterns and cultural beliefs. Even when we understand a conflict and work toward an agreement, the conflict does not always disappear. Furthermore, it takes time and hard work to move through many conflicts. Even with hard work, there are still times when you may need to "agree to disagree."

- Third, initially conflicts need to be understood. The understanding should always come before the action. Simply changing behavior will likely not address the root of the problem.
- Fourth, people often choose to avoid conflict or continue to be peaceful around one another even if there is a problem. This is why we must continue to utilize dialogue throughout relationships.

Now we know that we shouldn't handle conflict based on our assumptions and societal myths. The question becomes: How should we handle conflict? We will now focus on foundational conflict management styles, influential factors, and suggested ways to negotiate a conflict.

Conflict Management Styles

Now that we have a foundation for seeking productive conflict, let's consider five conflict management styles (Kilmann & Thomas, 1975). Each style is associated with its degree of cooperativeness or assertiveness and its concern for self or others. Figure 6.8 contains a breakdown of each style. We can use these management styles to improve our understanding of how we individually tend to handle conflict situations (Kellett & Dalton, 2001). While we may tend to prefer a particular conflict management style, it is also important to remain flexible when choosing a style to address a specific situation (Folger, Poole, & Stutman, 2005). Being an effective communicator often requires you to use different styles of conflict management. As you consider each of the following styles, try to determine which style of conflict you use most frequently, but also consider which styles you might use in specific situations.

Let's imagine that you and your best friend have just discovered that both of you are attracted to the same person—we'll name the object of your affection

Figure 6.8   Styles of Conflict Management

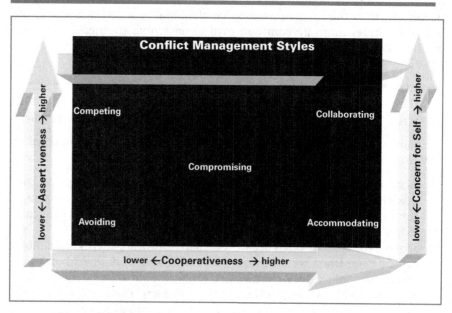

Sources: Folger, Poole, & Stutman (2005); Rahim, Antonioni, & Psenicka (2001)

Jordan. You really like Jordan and think there is potential for a relationship, but you also now know that your best friend feels the same way about Jordan. Both of you want to date Jordan. This has caused a lot of tension. Your friend suggests that the two of you talk. Assuming that Jordan likes both of you, what should you do? This will all depend on the style of conflict management that you choose. Let's look at the options.

Avoiding: You could choose a style that is not assertive or cooperative. Avoiding can be described as trying to ignore the fact that there is a problem. It is the most passive style of conflict management. You might say to yourself, "I'll just pretend that I don't know, and we will just let it blow over." You might choose to simply not respond to the request for conversation, or you may try to delay the conversation. Both of these strategies would suggest that you are avoiding the conflict. The pro of utilizing this style might be that you can side-step confrontation for the moment, but of course the con is that you are also eliminating the chance of working this out. Avoiding conflict is commonly recognized as a no-win style, and as you can see, it reflects low concern for your own needs or the needs of other people.

Accommodating: Your second style option is not assertive, but it is highly cooperative. Accommodating involves going along with what others want, just to appease them and keep everything conflict free. You might agree to the meeting and tell your friend, "I'll just let you date Jordan, you deserve this opportunity more than I do." If you don't openly give in to what your friend wants, you may find yourself continuously apologizing or excessively using disclaimers. Any of these strategies may be used to manage conflict through accommodation. The pro of accommodating might be that you make your friend happy, but the con is that you completely abandon your own needs and desires. Accommodating is commonly known as a lose-win style. It allows your friend to reap all the benefits, but you leave empty-handed.

Competing: Your third option is very assertive, but not very cooperative. Competing can be described as looking to achieve your own goals. If you choose to compete, you will likely agree to the meeting and try to use power, status, or force to convey your ideas. If you think or say something like, "We'll see who wins Jordan over," you are likely competing. The pro of competing might be that you get want you want, but the con is that you may hurt or silence others in doing so. Competing is commonly known as a win-lose style. It allows you to gain, but at someone else's expense.

Compromising: Your fourth option is moderately assertive and moderately cooperative. Compromising can be described as giving something to get something in return. If you choose to compromise, you might continuously restate your desires and summarize your friend's ideas. You might make statements like, "If you are willing to let me go out with Jordan on Friday, then I will let you go out with Jordan on Saturday." The pro of compromising is that both parties have some of their needs and desires met, and it is a quick way to come to a decision. Conversely, the con is that both parties have some needs and desires that remain unmet. For this reason, compromising is commonly known as a lose-lose style. Everybody sacrifices something in the process.

Collaborating: Your final option is highly assertive and highly cooperative. Collaborating can be described as seeking a mutually agreeable solution. You may find yourself deeply exploring a disagreement to see each other's perspectives and then openly sharing all concerns and desires in hopes that the underlying issues can be discovered and an appropriate solution can be implemented.

Suppose as a result of dialogue with your friend, you find that one of you wants Jordan as a date to a specific formal occasion while the other is interested in pursuing an ongoing romance. By sharing the rationales behind your attraction for Jordan, you can help each other. You might encourage Jordan to accompany your friend to the formal event, and during that event your friend could note how eligible you might be for longer-term companionship. The pro of collaborating is that everyone is validated and consensus is reached. The con of collaborating is the time and effort required. If managed effectively, collaborating is commonly known as a win-win style. All parties have their needs met.

So, it is time to choose your style. Figure 6.9 summarizes the five styles. Which approach do you normally use? Do you use this style in all situations? Let's consider a few more factors that may affect or confirm—or challenge—your decisions.

Figure 6.9   Comparison of Conflict Management Styles

Style	Approach	Explanation	Advantages	Drawbacks
Collaborating	Win/win	Seeks mutually beneficial outcomes, inclusive toward others; cooperative partnership	High level of buy-in from all participants; usually yields mutually satisfying outcomes	Time-consuming; requires mutual trust (rare and challenging to develop); requires willingness to share power
Competing	Win/lose	Zero-sum mentality: benefits to one party must come at the expense of others; style often involves dominating or coercing others	Maximizes personal benefits; can motivate high performance to "defeat" competitors	Encourages cutthroat practices; sets up conflict as antagonistic
Accommodating	Lose/win	Voluntary surrender; giving in to someone else	Maximizes generosity toward others; effective as showing obedience	May be seen as weakness; minimizes chance of personal gain; presumes other party is correct
Compromising	Lose/lose	Each party sacrifices something in order to gain something else; "give a little to get a little"	Does not insist on total "victory" for satisfactory outcome; highly flexible as each party can adjust what it gives/gets	All parties may remain dissatisfied; all parties must be willing to sacrifice; high degree of compromise may equal capitulation (e.g., appeasement of Hitler prior to WWII)
Avoiding	Don't play	Refusal to acknowledge or address conflict	Prevents pain and time expenditure of working through conflict	Fails to address root causes of conflict; unaddressed conflict can smolder and intensify

Source: Covey (1989)

THAT'S DEBATABLE

Of the five styles presented we might assume that compromising and collaboration are the best styles for managing any conflict. However, are there circumstances when avoiding, accommodating, and competing might be more appropriate? Furthermore, how can we effectively collaborate in an individualistic and often competitive society? What resistance might you encounter?

Factors Influencing Conflict Management

As we learned earlier, difference can spark and even define conflict. Certainly, various types of difference can influence your conflict management style and the potential for conflict in the relationship. Power, gender, culture, experience, and context are just a few factors that may highlight differences and consequently play a role in conflict and its management.

Power Factors.   Whether we realize it or not, power has the potential to be present in any relationship, and it can affect how conflicts are approached and managed. The classic types of social power originally discussed by French and Raven (1959) can apply to interpersonal conflict. **Power** here refers to the "resources that an influencing agent can utilize in changing the beliefs, attitudes, or behaviors" of someone else (Raven, 2001, p. 218). To illustrate how power operates during conflict, suppose you and your instructor are disputing a grade on an assignment.

   Referent power: When you have referent power, others identify with you. They look up to you or want to be like you. Referent power describes how someone can serve as a role model. Celebrities use their referent power when they endorse products or services. Example: Your instructor might have referent power because you admire this person's teaching style and connect with the examples and humor during class discussions. You might have referent power because you could represent the type of student the instructor used to be, so the instructor relates to you.

   Legitimate power: The power that results from a job title (e.g., president, CEO, military rank), appointment (e.g., the designated leader of a group), or role (e.g., "I'm the oldest") represents what is known as legitimate power. "Legitimate" here does not necessarily mean correct; it describes the way an official position entitles you to exert power. Example: The instructor has legitimate power (as part of the job's duties) to determine course policies and assign final grades. You have legitimate power as a student to communicate with your instructor and to ask questions.

   Expert power: The special knowledge or skill you possess can confer expert power. The saying "Knowledge is power" refers to expert power. Example: The instructor's expert power depends on proficiency in the subject matter, demonstrated by experience, education, publications, or other professional accomplishments. You might bring expert power to an assignment based on some specialized background you have in a particular topic.

   Reward power: This type of power enables you to provide someone with tangible or intangible incentives. If you have reward power, you can offer benefits to someone else for seeing things your way. Example: The instructor has reward power to write you a letter of recommendation in the future. You have the reward power to submit a positive evaluation of the instructor or to nominate the instructor for a teaching award.

Coercive power: Your ability to punish someone or withhold rewards constitutes coercive power. <u>Example</u>: The instructor could threaten to lower any grade that you challenge. You could threaten to lodge a formal complaint with the instructor's supervisor.

Information/Persuasive power: When a full explanation can justify something as desirable, information (also called persuasive) power is at play. You might have information power in a conflict if further information can clear up a misunderstanding. <u>Example</u>: The instructor's information power might lie in revealing details of the assignment that you had overlooked. Your information power might result from noting a portion of your work that the instructor accidentally skipped over while grading.

These types of power often operate together. Rarely does someone hold power in only one of the six dimensions. Understanding the types of power also reveals that while different degrees of power may be present in a conflict, no one is permanently powerless. A skillful communicator should understand how to adapt to each conflict by understanding the proportion of each type of power involved. <u>Example</u>: A teacher could approach conflicts in different classes by adapting power dynamics according to how students respond to various types of power (Tauber, 2007). Reward power might come into play more often with students who respond well to incentives. If students do not value academic credentials, the solution may be to cut back on legitimate power while exercising power in other dimensions.

Knowing the types of power you *can* wield opens up several questions to ask about the power components you *should* use within a conflict:

* Which dimension of power plays the most important role in this conflict? (The answer might be more than one type of power.)
* How do power differences between you and the other party affect your choice of conflict management styles? Which styles are you more or less likely to use given these power dynamics?
* How might different outcomes of this conflict affect the distribution of power? How could your relationship change if the power distribution shifts (with each party gaining or losing various types of power)?
* Which types of power are you willing to use in this conflict? What other sources of power might you choose? What effect might exercising different dimensions of power have on the relationship?

A few patterns have emerged in how the types of power play out during conflicts. Coercive power alone "is generally ineffective in influencing individual outcomes" (Rahim, Antonioni, & Psenicka, 2001, p. 195). The reason is that a threat of punishment might convince someone to avoid harm, but it fails to address the root of the conflict itself. Coercive power and reward power also tend to work best when the person who can punish or reward is present to check for compliance (Raven, 2001). After all, someone may comply with your wishes only to avoid punishment or obtain a reward, not out of respect for you or to resolve the conflict. The other types of power tend to exercise influence without the need for such constant monitoring.

If you are perceived to hold greater power in one or more key power dimension in a relationship, your relational partner may be more likely to avoid or accommodate. Consequently, whoever considers him- or herself more powerful in one or more key dimensions might be more likely to compete. If relational partners hold equal power, they may be more likely to collaborate or compromise. Of course, gaining and losing power may actually cause relational conflict to occur.

Gender and Cultural Influences.   Gender and culture may affect the way you express yourself and what you prioritize in conflicts. Everyone enters into conflicts and tries to manage them as "situated actors" (Avruch, 1998, p. 40), meaning that our group identities and cultural values affect our actions. Some researchers have claimed that gender seems to determine how people behave in conflicts (Gray, 1992; Tannen, 1990), but the situation is much more complex.

Gender does influence how people approach conflicts (Campbell, 1993), although it operates alongside other cultural factors (Wood, 2002). In the workplace, research shows that men gravitate toward more competing conflict management styles; however, a person's rank in an organization affects his or her choice of style more than gender (Thomas, Thomas, & Schaubhut, 2008). The more assertive styles (collaborating and competing) tend to be used by higher-ranking workers, while lower-ranking employees use less assertive styles (accommodating and avoiding). Women tend to opt for less competitive styles of conflict management, but gender alone does not explain which style someone will prefer in a specific situation (Folger, Poole, & Stutman, 2005; Shockley-Zalabak & Morley, 1984). Many assumptions about gender and conflict are too simplistic and lack sufficient evidence. For example, "no support was found from either population [students or non-students] for the perspective that females more than males prefer conflict styles requiring concern for relationship orientations or cooperativeness" (Shockley-Zalabak & Morley, 1984, p. 31).

The dimensions of culture we initially discussed in Chapter 2 have important connections with approaches to conflict. The cultural dimensions of individuality and achievement (masculinity) show stronger tendencies toward competitive styles (Mohammed, White, & Prabhakar, 2008). In high power distance cultures, those who occupy lower-power positions tend to avoid challenging those in positions of power or accommodate them. Highly individualistic cultures will gravitate toward styles that emphasize more concern for self, while more collectivist cultures will prefer styles that prioritize concern for others (Kaushal & Kwantes, 2006).

Confirmation and Disconfirmation

Now let's turn our attention to a few specific skills that can help you to manage conflict in the moment. In Chapter 12 we discussed the importance of confirmation for healthy relationships (Laing, 1961). **Confirmation** is simply a message that conveys the idea that an individual exists and matters. This type of communication would be especially beneficial during a conflict. Even if you disagree with someone's position, you still can recognize that person's inherent value. Certainly we would not want to utilize **disconfirmation**, or messages that suggest that an individual does not matter or even exist. Specific methods of confirmation can make a positive difference in conflict situations (Cissna & Sieberg, 2009).

Recognition.   This is the most basic type of confirmation, yet unfortunately we don't always remember to use it. If you have ever not responded to a text message or not acknowledged someone that you know when you see him or her in the store, then you may have missed an opportunity for confirming. By simply saying, "Hi," making strategic eye contact, or calling someone by name, we can recognize and confirm someone. Sometimes the failure to issue recognition can begin a conflict.

Acknowledgment.   One step up from recognition is acknowledgment. When we acknowledge someone, we intentionally summarize or reflect on the content or emotions that we hear. To practice acknowledgment we will need to listen actively, perhaps asking questions to clarify the message. We might also paraphrase the other person's ideas or note his or her feelings. <u>Example</u>: "I can see you find Jordan very attractive." In the heat of a serious conflict, acknowledgment immediately offers a point of agreement. No matter how opposed your viewpoints are, you and the other person can agree on what each of you is saying and feeling.

Endorsement.   The highest level of confirmation is endorsement. This means that we find something in the other's message that we agree with and share this with them. Endorsement does not mean we must agree with everything the person says, but we select at least one piece of the message to support. We might agree with the individual that the issue at hand is something we both need to address and take responsibility for, or we might agree that the problem is important.

If it sounds like you use confirmation in your daily interactions and during conflict situations, you are on the right track. Remember that like the opening of a conversation, confirmation is important for moving forward in the discussion.

Negotiation

Exactly how does the process of handling a conflict proceed? Here we move into the territory of **negotiation**, defined as "a process of communication between at least two parties, from individuals to states (in which case it goes by a special name, diplomacy). In negotiation, the two parties become interlocutors: they engage in an extended conversation about their dispute" (Avruch, 1998, p. 39). More specifically, negotiation refers to the strategic movement through concerns that involves a process of give and take to address the needs and values of all parties (Fisher & Ertel, 1995; Johnson, 1993). Fisher and Ury (1981) developed four foundational principles that have helped many people to work through conflict. These principles outline a method known as **principled negotiation**, which enables all parties to seek mutual benefit and helps them to develop and implement fair standards for evaluation. Figure 6.10 contains a basic overview of the four principles (Fisher & Ury, 1981, p.11).

The first aspect of principled negation to consider is to focus on the *people* and not the problem. Have you ever lashed out at your best friend or attempted to humiliate your significant other? If so, you were probably more focused on the problem than you were the people involved. We must remember to always recognize (beginning with confirmation) the individual perceptions

Figure 6.10   Principled Negotiation

Area of Concern	Basic Principle	Rationale	Example in Negotiations
People	Separate the people from the problem.	Personal attacks cause defensiveness and shut down open, honest communication.	Adopt a "nothing personal" rule for discussions: Criticize ideas but not the people who offer them.
Interests	Focus on interests, not positions.	Find potential connections among underlying values that can lead to solutions.	Ask what needs or core values the other party wants to fulfill through his or her positions.
Options	Generate a variety of possibilities before deciding what to do.	Maximize opportunities for finding desirable outcomes.	Entertain proposals that neither party had considered before.
Criteria	Insist that the result be based on some objective standard that does not favor one party over the other.	Everyone needs ground rules to determine what would be agreeable outcomes.	Settle on what a "good" outcome must include, preferably based on shared interests.

of everyo ne involved. We need to protect the feelings of others as well as ourselves and understand the emotions being expressed. Anyone who feels personally vulnerable to attack will not communicate openly and honestly in negotiations. Understanding emotions does not mean that it is appropriate to react without checking your emotions—so use your emotional intelligence (Cooper & Sawaf, 1997). Remain calm and focus on working jointly to build the relationship. The participants in negotiations operate best as partners trying to find solutions together, not as adversaries trying to beat each other (Nierenburg & Ross, 1985).

Recognizing individual *interests* and not just the positions that the parties are taking will be critical for negotiation. If you have ever viewed the people in a conflict as being on "two different sides of the coin," then you were probably focusing more on the position they were taking and not their interests. If you can determine the interests (or values) of each individual, then you should be able to define the problem. Consider not only what the other party wants, but why he or she wants it. There may be ways to satisfy those interests aside from the positions being taken. The goal here is to find shared interests. Remember that Maslow's hierarchy of needs showed we all have the same basic needs, so this might be a great place to start. Finding interests might require that you ask "why" someone is advocating a specific plan or seeking a particular goal.

Seeking *options* may sound fairly simple, yet the problem that many people encounter is not seeking enough options. On the surface it may seem that there are only two options: "We move to the mountains" or "We move to the beach." In reality, there are many more options. Just think of all of the different places to live in the world. As we learned earlier, there may not be only one solution, so remain open-minded. Be careful not to present options that simply solve the "current problem." Again, as mentioned before, there is a possibility that the most recent "fight" is a symptom of a deeper problem. Finally, use brainstorming methods and always avoid the trap of "either-or" think that assumes choosing one option excludes all others. Seek options that help both parties to benefit equally.

The principle that is often the most difficult, and overlooked, is *criteria*. Have you ever had a class assignment that included the criteria for earning a passing grade? Conflict negotiation can work in a similar way. Recall when one of your instructors assigned a paper with several requirements or rules (e.g., the paper must be between 8 and 10 pages; references must be cited in a certain format; it must contain a thesis, literature review, methodology, and discussion). Now, hopefully this has never happened to you, but what if you decided to ignore or overlook these requirements and instead created a fictional story with no references that was 20 pages long? My guess is that the outcome you had hoped for—a good grade—was not achieved. Now, what if you never had any criteria in the first place? There would be no way for you or your instructor to determine successful completion. What does this teach us? Just as we must have and follow criteria to create a product, we must do the same to have a strong negotiation process. The criteria that you create should not favor either party and recognize fair standards and procedures. All parties in the conflict must agree to abide by the criteria in choosing and implementing a solution. Then comes the hard part: Both parties must actually use the criteria during their discussion.

Principled negotiation is not the only negotiation method for managing conflict. **Dialogic negotiation** focuses on understanding the meaning of a conflict by understanding the ways the stories of participants intersect (Kellett, 2007). This strategy combines key elements of negotiation with the basic principles of dialogue. In dialogic negotiation, each party has the opportunity to explain his or her story of how the conflict originated and progressed. The stories include reflections on how the conflict affects each participant. Instead of telling "my side" or "your side," the participants commit to appreciating the feelings and needs expressed in each other's story—not simply advocating their own side. By revealing the stories that surround and ground the apparent conflict, each person can begin to understand how the other is constructing the meaning of the conflict. From that understanding, an approach to the conflict can emerge that addresses the values and meanings each person seeks from the conflict.

Dialogic negotiation can delve into the personal history each person brings into a specific conflict. This type of deep revelation requires a firm foundation of trust that enables open disclosure. Dialogic negotiation therefore may require a lot of time to develop, and it presumes everyone's readiness to risk telling how a conflict intersects with other aspects of their life. The reward, however, is that participants may find new and more permanent ways to connect with each other by noticing how the story of the conflict fits within larger life stories.

HONE YOUR SKILLS IN CONVERSATION AND CONFLICT MANAGEMENT

In previous sections of this chapter, we addressed specific aspects of conversation and conflict. But wait—didn't we say that perhaps the hardest part of managing conflict is actually developing skills and determining what you will say in the moment? The final section of this chapter is dedicated to helping you to (1) identify specific skills for difficult conversational moments and (2) recognize some ways to de-escalate conflicts that start to get out of control.

Skills for Difficult Conversational Moments

Because we now have a foundational understanding of conversation and the potential conflicts that may occur, we should consider specific challenging situations that we may encounter. For each of the situations that follow you will find specific suggestions for how to handle the difficult conversational moment.

How to Express Feelings.   Conversations about people, events, or things might not present much of a challenge; talking about how we feel is a different matter altogether. How do we express feelings honestly without letting our emotions run wild and possibly damage our relationships? Four steps can enable progress toward communicating feelings constructively (Fox-Hines, 2001; Gilles, 1974).

1. *Acceptance:* Accept that you are human, and humans have feelings and emotions *as well as* thoughts and ideas. Acknowledge your feelings and then consider what you want to do with them.
2. *Nondestructive expression:* Once you have acknowledged you do feel a certain feeling or combination of feelings, it is important to find some way to express those feelings ("good" and "bad") in a way that is safe and not harmful to yourself or to others. This might include physical and non-physical methods such as running, crying, writing feelings, or talking about feelings.
3. *Redirection:* After expressing feelings, it is often good to stop and take several nice, deep slow breaths. As relaxation increases, ask yourself: "What do I want to do about this?" "Are there any actions that would be helpful to take?" "What would be the most helpful, useful thing to do now?" "Do I want to talk to someone else about my feelings? Do I want to talk now?"
4. *Action:* After considering the facts, the situation, the consequences, etc., you are ready to put things into perspective make decision to act (make an assertive request, lodge an assertive complaint, leave a relationship) or to not act (truly let go of the feeling, decide that "in the great cosmic picture" it isn't worth your energy).

How to Handle Egocentric Communicators.   "It's all about me, me, me." "If I want your opinion, I'll give it to you."

The preceding statements describe the attitude of an **egocentric** communicator: someone who focuses on him- or herself while ignoring or dismissing others. This person is likely to engage only in monologue and not dialogue. What should you do when confronting an egocentric conversationalist? Several responses could rechannel the conversation to its proper focus:

* Reframe the conversation, establishing explicit guidelines. Example: "Let's approach the issue as something that affects both of us."
* Set procedural or content guidelines. Example: "Let's make a deal: Nobody uses the pronouns 'I' or 'me' in our conversation."

- Reciprocate by responding to each personal example or story with one of your own. Example: "OMG, that happened to me last week too." By contributing more of your own content to the interaction, you place yourself on a more equal footing within the conversation.

How to Revive Conversations.   We've all experienced those awkward moments of conversational silence. Luckily, you might be able to employ some tactics to restore lively interaction (Aaker, Kumar, & Day, 2007).

- *Chain reaction:* If you are in a group, ask each person to comment on an idea someone else expressed earlier. Not only does this tactic build on each person's contributions, but it encourages better listening because everyone has to connect what one person says to someone else's comments. Example: "We just heard from Hildegaard. Now, Rajiv, how would you react to her proposal?"
- *Devil's advocate:* Take an extreme position on an unexpected viewpoint to stimulate more reaction. The surprise might energize the entire conversation. Caution: Use this tactic carefully, since you must remain within the bounds of propriety for the conversation to continue. An extreme position also does not mean an offensive one. Example: "Our discussion of pesticide safety has reached an impasse. I think we should simply ban all pesticides and see what happens."
- *False termination:* Act as if the conversation has ended by offering closure and ask for final questions. Just as the "last call" at a bar generates a flurry of drink orders, this conversational "last call" might spur a slew of new ideas. Example: "I'm glad we've had this talk. Anything else before I go?"

Skills for Coping with Conflict

Sometimes you might find a conflict spiraling out of control. The dispute might threaten to become too nasty to permit any approach toward negotiation. A few communication tools might de-escalate a conflict so that everyone becomes more willing to manage the situation.

How to Deal with Anger.   In many settings, people operate under severe stress. While it is tempting to lash out at people who might complain or even verbally abuse you, remember that the distress of coping with fear, pain, or loss can make others edgy. When you feel your own anger building or encounter an angry person, the following techniques can help avoid a bitter dispute (Williams & Williams, 1994).

- *Validate the person's feelings.* Say that you understand and recognize that the person is angry. If you say, "I certainly see you're upset," you preserve the person's right to his or her feelings. You can accept that a person feels a certain way even if you do not agree with the reasons for his or her reactions.
- *Establish a connection with the other person.* If you find some basis for common ground, you will show that you and the other person are on the same side and can work together to solve the problem. A comment as

Anger and verbal aggression can undermine the productive aspects of conflict.

simple as "I also can't stand it when people give me the runaround" can show you are an ally, not an antagonist.

- *Maintain a calm tone.* Don't raise your voice, even if the other person rants and raves. Usually, someone who shouts will lower the volume quickly if the other person does not shout back. Since we tend to adapt to the communication behaviors of others, calmness breeds calmness.
- *Listen carefully and try to understand why the person is angry.* Sometimes dissatisfaction results from a simple misunderstanding. Don't interrupt, let the other person have his or her say, and then try to understand the other person's viewpoint.

How to Help Others Save Face.   The idea of **facework** deals with a communicator's attempt to maintain a positive sense of worth and dignity for themselves and others in public (Ting-Toomey & Kurogi, 1998). When we employ **face-saving** approaches to conflict, we communicate in ways that preserve the dignity and value of ourselves and others. Face-saving encourages respect for differing viewpoints and discourages personal attacks. **Face-detracting** communication robs someone of dignity, humiliating or shaming the person. To help others save face, you could try the following techniques:

- *Do seek understanding with others:* "I don't quite understand the question" or "I disagree with the premise of that question."
  Don't say: "That's a stupid question."
- *Do seek common ground:* "Let's see if we can find something we agree on."
  Don't say: "There are two approaches here: my way and the wrong way."
- *Do allow graceful exits:* "Could we agree to disagree?"
  Don't say: "We're going to continue until you admit everything was your fault."
- *Do value others:* "I understand your point, although I don't agree with it because…"
  Don't say: "There you go again. Blah, blah, blah. Yada, yada, yada."
- *Do use indirectness:* "Your proposal may not be among the most attractive options after we consider all the alternatives."
  Don't say: "Your proposal is absurd."

Saving face has important consequences in conflicts. "Repeated face-loss and face-threat often lead to escalatory conflict spirals or an impasse in the conflict negotiation process" (Ting-Toomey, 2007, p. 257). One way to separate the person from the problem in negotiations would be to commit to saving the face of the other party.

Saving face traditionally has played an important role in many Asian cultures. The government of South Korea expressed collective shame when it was disclosed that the murderer of 32 Virginia Tech students in April 2007 was a Korean American. South Korea is concerned with its public image (i.e., its face), and "its group-oriented culture means the achievements of the few are marshaled into rallying cries for the many" (Herman, 2007). We also must remember that high collectivism does not mean that every person will act or react the same way—only that each person feels more connected to other cultural cohorts.

Skillful management of conflict allows participants to save face even if they "lose." The sense of fair play in athletics practices face-saving by celebrating the efforts of all players, not just the winners. In conflicts, you can save face by appreciating the *process* of managing the conflict even if the outcome was not what you desired. Saving face includes being gracious to opposing sides in victory or defeat.

Throughout this chapter, we have presented both theoretical concepts and practical suggestions for creating effective conversations and managing productive conflict. Now it is your turn. The next time you need to have a conversation with one of your professors or a conflict arises with your best friend, try implementing some of the techniques we have discussed. You might find you not only get more accomplished, but you also might develop more satisfying relationships.

HIGHLIGHTS

1. Conversations proceed in several stages.
   a. The opening generally includes a greeting, phatic communication, and perhaps reference to something that connects the participants.
   b. Feedforward prepares for the conversation to follow. It establishes the rules and roles that govern the interaction.
   c. The focus of conversation is its substance. Cooperative principles guide our interactions. Dialogue can enrich participation and deepen understanding during conversation.
   d. Feedback offers information about the conversation. Some conversations are conducted primarily to exchange feedback.
   e. The closing concludes conversation while remaining positive about the interaction.
2. Conflict is common and unavoidable, but does not have to be destructive.
3. The five conflict styles represent different ways to deal with conflict.
   a. Avoiding is withdrawing from or ignoring the situation.
   b. Accommodating is giving in to appease others and keep peace.
   c. Competing is trying to gain an advantage at the expense of someone else.
   d. Compromising is sacrificing something in order to get something.
   e. Collaborating is cooperating with others to reach a mutually agreeable outcome.
4. Gender and culture will likely play a role in relational expectations and conflict management.
5. Confirmation is a key step in recognizing the other person during a conflict.
6. Principled negotiation allows you to focus on finding ways for both parties to benefit and find objective ways to solve the conflict.
   a. Separate people from the problem.
   b. Focus on interests and not positions.
   c. Seek a variety of options.
   d. Establish and follow objective criteria.
7. Dialogic negotiation focuses on creating shared meaning of the conflict in an effort to reach a mutually satisfactory outcome.
8. Difficult conversational moments require specific skills and considerations.
   a. Constructive communication of feelings links expressing emotions with deciding what to do about them.
   b. You can rechannel a conversation so egocentric communicators do not monopolize discussion.
   c. Conversations that lapse can be revived.

9. Communication techniques can prevent a conflict from escalating.
   a. Anger is best met with acknowledgment and not with further anger.
   b. Face-saving can preserve your own and the other party's dignity.

APPLY YOUR KNOWLEDGE

SL = Activities appropriate for service learning
🖳 = Computer activities focusing on research and information management
🎬 = Activities involving film or television
🎵 = Activities involving music

1. SL Identify a conflict that your community partner has encountered. Critically examine the nature of the conflict according to the following dimensions.
   A. What approach to "winning" did the primary participants take in the conflict? How productive was this approach?
   B. What conflict management style did each participant use? Provide specific examples from the conflict that support your assessment.
   C. In your opinion, what conflict management style or styles *should* the participants have used? What could these different styles accomplish in the situation?

2. Reflect on a conflict you have had with a friend or family member. Now, write out an effective conversation that would help you and your relational partner work through the conflict. Be specific and remember to implement confirmation and the principles of negotiation. Based on your new discoveries, what will you do differently to handle your next conflict with this individual?

3. 🖳 Track a current event that involves a conflict between nations or within a nation. According to your research in reliable news sources, what is causing the conflict? Describe how the conflict might be approached using each of the conflict styles discussed in this chapter. Which of these styles offers the best promise for managing the conflict? Why would this style make the best choice?

4. 🎬 🎵 Identify a movie, sitcom, or song that depicts two characters in dialogue. How are they upholding the requirements of dialogue? Are there any challenges or obstacles that may threaten their use of dialogue?

5. 🖳 Save all of the (non-confidential) e-mails you receive over the next few days. Examine these e-mails for effective or ineffective conversational techniques. What specific examples do you find of miscommunication in each of the following areas? How would you recommend the e-mails be altered to make better use of conversational techniques?
   A. Opening
   B. Feedforward
   C. Focus
   D. Feedback
   E. Closing

REFERENCES

Aaker, D. A., Kumar, V., & Day, G. S. (2007). *Marketing research* (9th ed.). New York: John Wiley and Sons.

Alberts, J. K., Yoshimura, C. G., Rabby, M., & Loschiavo, R. (2005). Mapping the topography of couples' daily conversation. *Journal of Social and Personal Relationships, 22,* 299–322.

Arnett, R. C., & Arneson, P. (1999). *Dialogic civility in a cynical age: Community, hope, and interpersonal relationships.* Albany: State University of New York Press.

Avruch, K. (1998). *Culture and conflict resolution.* Washington, DC: United States Institute of Peace.

Bach, K. (2006). The top 10 misconceptions about implicature. In B. J. Birner & G. Ward (Eds.), *Drawing the boundaries of meaning: Neo-Gricean studies in pragmatics and semantics in honor of Laurence R. Horn* (pp. 21–30). Amsterdam: John Benjamins.

Baxter, L. A. (2007). Problematizing the problem in communication: A dialogic perspective. *Communication Monographs, 74*(1), 118–124.

Beach, W. A., & Dunning, D. G. (1982). Pre-indexing and conversational organization. *Quarterly Journalof Speech, 68,* 170–185.

Brigg, M. (2008). *The new politics of conflict resolution: Responding to difference.* New York: Palgrave Macmillan.

Burnard, P. (2003). Ordinary chat and therapeutic conversation: Phatic communication and mental health nursing. *Journal of Psychiatric and Mental Health Nursing, 10,* 678–682.

Campbell, A. (1993). *Men, women, and aggression.* New York: Basic Books.

Cissna, K. N., & Anderson, R. (1994). The 1957 Martin Buber-Carl Rogers dialogue, as dialogue. *Journal of Humanistic Psychology, 34*(1), 11–45.

Cissna, K. N. L., & Seiberg, E. (2009). Patterns of interactional confirmation and disconfirmation. In J. Stewart (Ed.), *Bridges not walls* (9th ed.; pp. 429–439). New York: McGraw-Hill.

Cooper, R. K., & Sawaf, A. (1997). *Executive EQ: Emotional intelligence in leadership and organizations.* New York: Perigee.

Covey, S. R. (1989). *The seven habits of highly effective people: Restoring the character ethic.* New York: Simon and Schuster.

DeVito, J. A. (2005). *Essentials of human communication* (5th ed.). Boston: Allyn and Bacon.

Fisher, R. & Ertel, D. (1995). *Getting ready to negotiate: A step-by-step guide preparing for any negotiation.* New York: Penguin.

Fisher, R. & Ury, W. (1981). *Getting to yes: Negotiating agreement without giving in.* Boston: Houghton Mifflin.

Folger, J. P., Poole, M. S., & Stutman, R. K. (2005). *Working through conflict: Strategies for relationships, groups, and organizations* (5th ed.). New York: HarperCollins.

Fox-Hines, R. (2001). *Four steps in dealing with feelings.* Unpublished manuscript.

Franco, L. (2006). Forms of conversation and problem structuring methods: A conceptual development. *Journal of the Operational Research Society, 57,* 813–821.

French, J. R. P., Jr,, & Raven, B. H. (1959). The bases of social power. In D. Cartwright (Ed.), *Studies in social power* (pp. 150–167). Ann Arbor, MI: Institute for Social Research.

Gill, D., & Adams, B. (1998). *ABC of communication studies* (2nd ed.). Cheltenham, UK: Nelson Thornes.

Gilles, J. (1974). *My needs, your needs, our needs.* New York: Doubleday.

Gottman, J. M., Levenson, R. W., Gross, J., Frederickson, B. L., McCoy, K., Rosenthal, L., Ruef, A., & Yoshimoto, D. (2003). Correlates of gay and lesbian couples' relationship satisfaction and relationship dissolution. *Journal of Homosexuality, 45,* 23–43.

Gray, J. (1992). *Men are from mars, women are from Venus.* New York; Harper-Collins.

Grice, H. P. (1975). Logic and conversation. P. Cole & J. Morgan (Eds.), *Syntax and semantics, volume 3: Speech acts* (pp. 41–58). New York: Academic Press.

Herman, B. (2007, April 20). Sympathy and shame in South Korea. *Washington Post.* Retrieved April 20, 2007, from http://www.washingtonpost.com/wpdyn/content/article/2007/04/20/AR2007042001042.html

Hocker, J. L., & Wilmot, W. W. (2006) Collaborative negotiation. In K. Galvin & P. Cooper (Eds.), *Making connections* (4th ed.; pp. 201–208). Los Angeles: Roxbury.

James, J. (1996). *Thinking in the future tense: Leadership skills for a new age.* New York: Simon & Schuster.

Jehn, K., Chadwick, C., & Thatcher, S. (1997). To agree or not to agree: The effects of value congruence, individual demographic dissimilarity, and conflict on workgroup outcomes. *International Journal of Conflict Management, 8*(4), 287–305.

Johnson, R. A. (1993). *Negotiation basics: Concepts, skills, and exercises.* Newbury Park, CA: Sage.

Kaushal, R., & Kwantes, C. T. (2006). The role of culture and personality in choice of conflict management strategy. *International Journal of Intercultural Relations, 30,* 579–603.

Kellett, P. M. (2007). *Conflict dialogue: Working with layers of meaning for productive relationships.* Thousand Oaks, CA: Sage.

Kellett, P. M., & Dalton, D. G. (2001). *Managing conflict in a negotiated world: A narrative approach to achieving dialogue and change.* Thousand Oaks, CA: Sage.

Kilmann, R. H., & Thomas, K. W. (1975). Interpersonal conflict handling behavior as reflections of Jungian personality dimensions. *Psychological Reports, 37,* 971–980.

Laing, R. D. (1961). *Self and others.* New York: Pantheon.

LeBaron, M. (2003). *Bridging cultural conflicts: A new approach for a changing world.* San Francisco, CA: Jossey-Bass.

Likert, R., & Likert, J. G. (1976). *New ways of managing conflict.* New York: McGraw-Hill.

Malone, M. J. (1995). How to do things with friends: Altercasting and recipient design. *Research on Language and Social Interaction, 28,* 147–170.

Melchin, K. & Picard, C. (2008). *Transforming conflict through insight.* Toronto: University of Toronto Press.

Mohammed, U. K., White, G. R. T., & Prabhakar, G. P. (2008). Culture and conflict management style of international project managers. *International Journal of Business and Management, 3*(5), 3–11.

Murphy, P. (2005, May 7). How to master the art of conversation. *Ezine Articles.* Retrieved December 17, 2009, from http://ezinearticles.com/?How-To-Master-The-Art-of-Conversation&id=33622

Nierenburg, J., & Ross, I. S. (1985). *Women and the art of negotiating.* New York: Simon and Schuster.

Rahim, M., Antonioni, D., & Psenicka, C. (2001). A structural equations model of leader power, subordinates' styles of handling conflict, and job performance. *International Journal of Conflict Management, 12*(3), 191–211.

Raven, B. H. (2001). Power/interaction and interpersonal influence: Experimental investigations and case studies. In A. Y. Lee-Chai & J. A. Bargh (Eds.), *The use and abuse of power: Multiple perspectives on the causes of corruption* (pp. 217–240). Philadelphia: Psychology Press.

Shockley-Zalabak, P., & Morley, D. (1984). Sex differences in conflict style preferences. *Communication Research Reports, 1*(1), 28–32.

Tannen, D. (1990). *You just don't understand: Women and men in conversation.* New York: Ballantine.

Tauber, R. T. (2007). *Classroom management: Sound theory and effective practice* (4th ed.). Westport, CT: Praeger.

Thomas, K., Thomas, G., & Schaubhut, N. (2008). Conflict styles of men and women at six organization levels. *International Journal of Conflict Management, 19*(2), 148–166.

Ting-Toomey, S. (2007). Intercultural conflict training: Theory-practice approaches and research challenges. *Journal of Intercultural Communication Research, 36*(3), 255–271.

Ting-Toomey, S., & Kurogi, A. (1998). Facework competence in intercultural conflict: An updated face-negotiation theory. *International Journal of Intercultural Relations, 22,* 187–225.

Walton, R. E. (1987). *Managing conflict: Interpersonal dialogue and third-party roles* (2nd ed.). Reading, MA: Addison-Wesley.

Weinstein, E. A., & Deutschberger, P. (1963). Some dimensions of altercasting. *Sociometry, 26,* 454–466.

Williams, R., & Williams, V. (1994). *Anger kills: Seventeen strategies for controlling the hostility that can harm your health.* New York: Harper Perennial.

Wood, J. T. (2002). A critical essay on John Gray's portrayals of men, women, and relationships. *Southern Journal of Communication, 67,* 201–210.

Initiating Relationship

OBJECTIVES

- Identify three categories used to describe the nature of our relationships with others
- Explore four primary reasons people initiate interpersonal relationships
- Identify three types of attraction: physical, social, and task
- Understand the impact of age, gender, and culture on differences in perceptions of attraction
- Distinguish among social and task goals for relationship initiation
- Understand the three dimensions of similarity and four considerations that individuals make in assessing similarity to self
- Explore goals sought on a first date
- Understand the role of disclosure and reciprocal disclosure on relationship initiation
- Explore the relationship between social penetration and self-disclosure
- Identify the role of question-asking in reducing uncertainty in relationship initiation
- Explore the use of affinity-testing strategies in relationship initiation
- Identify five stages in the process of forming relationships
- Understand the impact of context on relationship initiation
- Explore the impact of technology on communication during relationship initiation
- Understand the four stages experienced by interracial couples in the relationship initiation process

© MaxFX, 2007, Shutterstock.

KEY TERMS

relationship
obligatory/involuntary
voluntary
duration
context
rules
role
interpersonal
  attraction

physical
  attractiveness
social attractiveness
impression
  management
self-monitoring
task attractiveness
proximity
similarity/homophily

demographic
  similarity
background
  similarity
attitude similarity
similarity to
  current self
complementarity
attachment security

similarity to ideal	social penetration	social exchange
view of self	theory	theory
false homophily	uncertainty	rewards
goals	reduction theory	costs
social goals	predicted outcome	initiation
task goals	value theory	experimenting
self-disclosure	liking	intensifying
reciprocal	affinity-seeking	integrating
self-disclosure	strategies	bonding

OVERVIEW

Many of you have probably heard of the movie *Jerry McGuire* and the line made famous by Renee Zellweger's character, "You had me at 'Hello.' " If only the process of initiating relationships with others was usually that easy! All of our relationships require a significant amount of time and energy. Consider the fact that *every* relationship we are involved in had to start somewhere. In this chapter we take a close look at how we define the term relationship, and how and why relationships are initially established. We also look at the communication behaviors and strategies used early in a relationship's development.

THE ROLE OF COMMUNICATION IN RELATIONSHIP DEVELOPMENT

The decision to begin a new relationship is filled with a myriad of emotions—confusion, excitement, anxiety, and anticipation. Consider the role played by many of the elements of interpersonal communication we have discussed up to this point. First, a person must decide whether to approach another person to initiate a relationship. Then the challenge involves figuring out how to make the initial approach. What opening line or verbal message should be used to make the all-important first impression? Let us not forget the impact of nonverbal messages as well; they have a tremendous impact on every stage of the relationship initiation process. We form assumptions about others based on such nonverbal clues as how they are dressed, whether they are standing with their arms crossed to communicate a closed body position, and whether they engage in eye contact with us. Of course, we also need to consider the role that self perception plays in the process. As discussed in Chapter Two, someone with a low level of self-esteem will face unique challenges when engaging in the relationship initiation process, as opposed to a person who has a positive self image.

As we begin our discussion of relationship development, it is important to first define what we mean by the term relationship. If you are involved in a relationship at this very moment, please raise your hand. Do you have your hand up? If not, you should probably reconsider how you define this term. When we have asked this question in our interpersonal communication classes, only a few students initially raise their hands. But after much prompting with questions such as, "Are you *sure* you're not involved in *any* relationships right now?" every member of the class has a hand up in the air. Our culture causes us to formulate stereotypes about what it means to be "in a relationship." Immediately, most people think of a "relationship" as involving romance. However, we are all involved in a number of different types of relationships at any given time.

RELATIONSHIP DEFINED

Messages about relationships surround us. A trip to the magazine section of a grocery store often involves exposure to multiple statements about the status of celebrity relationships. In the last two years writers for magazines have provided the public with the intimate details of budding relationships referred to only as, "TomKat" (Tom Cruise and Katie Holmes) and "Brangelina" (Brad Pitt and Angelina Jolie). The magazines *Cosmopolitan, People, Oprah,* and *Entertainment Weekly* also beckon you to learn how to attract members of the opposite sex with a sensuous new hairstyle, hip outfit, or clever banter. Even if you do not venture near the magazine sections or notice the magazine covers as you check out, take a moment to consider the most common themes of the songs played over the store loudspeakers while you shop. Many popular songs contain references to relationships. Messages about relationships are everywhere! While numerous magazine articles, movies and Web sites devote a lot of attention to romantic relationships, we encounter a variety of relationships throughout our lifetime. From family relationships to friendships and even work relationships,

Could this work relationship transform into a voluntary friendship?

we form communicative bonds with people across a variety of contexts. But how exactly do we define the term relationship? A **relationship** is a connection between two individuals that results in mutual interaction with the intent of achieving shared meaning. In this chapter, we focus primarily on voluntary relationships, which differ greatly from those described as either obligatory or involuntary. Relationships with family members and co-workers are often defined as **obligatory/involuntary** because they often occur by chance and not by choice. Our relationships with friends, roommates, and romantic partners are considered **voluntary** because we enter into them of our own volition. Some relationships, like those we form with co-workers, may start out as obligatory and transform into voluntary ones. We begin by describing important elements of voluntary relationships.

© Yuri Arcurs, 2007, Shutterstock.

The Nature of Relationships

We often use referents to describe the numerous relationships in which we are involved. Three categories often used to describe the nature of a relationship include references to duration, context, and roles.

Duration. **Duration** references are used to describe the length of time we have known the other person. Statements such as, "my friend from kindergarten," "my new co-worker," and "an acquaintance I met last week" are used to describe the duration of the relationship. These terms provide insight as to the amount of time that the relational partners have had to share information about one another.

Context.   In some instances, relationships are described by referring to the **context**, or setting, in which the relationship was initiated. "Friends from the soccer team," "committee members from the PTO," or "co-workers on a project team," provide information about the environment in which the relationship exists. By making reference to the relationship context, clues are offered with regard to the **rules** or expectations for communication. Rules may be explicitly stated. A boss may openly state to employees that there is an "open door" policy in the office, indicating that employees should feel comfortable walking in without an appointment to discuss issues. Some rules are implicitly understood. Teammates have a mutual understanding that emotions have an impact on how messages are created and interpreted on game day. If a teammate has a bad game, the unspoken rule is that it is probably not wise to discuss the errors that were made. It is important to note that rules regarding the appropriateness of topics and the acceptable depth of discussions may differ from context to context. While an individual may be comfortable disclosing her intimate feelings about her newest romantic partner with a family member, such information could be viewed as highly inappropriate in the workplace.

What role does the coach play on the team?

Role.   Finally, references to a person's **role** may be used to describe the nature of a relationship. Terms such as *mother, teacher, supervisor, colleague,* or *coach* are used to describe the role an individual plays in a particular relationship. It is important to note that role terms can also provide insight into the contextual nature of the relationship, and to shed light on the rules and expectations for interactions. More formality is needed when a student engages in an interaction with a teacher than when calling up a family member to discuss a bad grade on an assignment. By making reference to our relationships in terms of duration, context, or roles, we let others know what our initial expectations are for communication.

Deciding to Make the First Move: *Why* We Initiate Relationships

Think back to your first day in this class. As you walked through the door, you scanned the classroom and were faced with the decision of where to sit. Were there any familiar faces in the room? If not, you ended up sitting next to someone you had never met before. At that point, you had two decisions to make. Should you (a) initiate a conversation with that person, and if so, (b) how should you begin the interaction? As you reflect on that first day of class, consider how quickly some of these decisions were made. Even if the decision of where to sit was influenced by the fact that there were a limited number of seats available, you still had to choose whether to initiate a conversation, and thus, initiate a relationship with a fellow classmate. Every relationship has a unique history that includes an explanation of why we chose to initiate the relationship in the first place.

Over the years, scholars in the fields of communication, psychology and sociology have been fascinated by the question of *why* we initiate relationships. For example, when writing about why people initiate long-term romantic relationships, interpersonal communication researcher Anita Vangelisti (2002) describes the number of factors that contribute to mate selection as "daunting." Some research even indicates that the process of mate selection occurs by chance (Lykken and Tellegen 1993). While there appear to be many different reasons, years of research have identified four common explanations for why humans begin relationships. The four primary reasons we establish relationships with others are attraction, proximity, similarity, and purpose.

Not surprisingly, many decisions to initiate relationships are based on the attractiveness of another person. Second, scholars have discovered that we tend to initiate relationships with others on the basis of proximity. After all, it is much easier to begin a conversation with those who are physically close to us as opposed to those who are geographically distant. Third, relationships are typically initiated with those we perceive to be similar to us in some way. How we define similarity may differ from person to person. Relationships between adults may form because their children play on the same sports team. Students may form relationships because they are taking the same class or are in the same major. Finally, some relationships are initiated because they fulfill a purpose or a need. Consider the relationships that you have formed with coworkers or clients to fulfill a need at work. In the next sections, we take a closer look at each of the reasons for beginning a relationship.

Will these two students more likely become friends because they sit near each other in class?

© Simone van den Berg, 2007, Shutterstock.

DEFINING INTERPERSONAL ATTRACTION

Identifying the reasons for being attracted to one person and not to another is perhaps one of the greatest mysteries in life. Researchers have dedicated countless studies to exploring the phenomenon of initial attraction. After all, attraction is perhaps one of the most influential factors in setting the relationship initiation process into motion. While references to attractiveness are often assumed to be directed toward physical characteristics, **interpersonal attraction** refers to a general feeling or desire that impacts our decision to approach and initiate a relationship with another person. Many different forms of attraction influence our decision to begin relationships.

Attraction is one of the primary determining factors for choosing to initiate relationships, and it is the basis for forming initial impressions of others. While most people are quick to argue that forming first impressions of others based on their appearance is superficial and trivial, the fact remains that in the U.S. many of our decisions to initiate romantic relationships are rooted in our perceptions of the physical attractiveness of the other person. Consider a time when you were told that someone was beautiful. While you could argue that this could refer to either physical attractiveness or inner beauty, our first instinct is to assume that the statement is being made in reference to the individual's physical characteristics.

When asked to define attractiveness, most people tend to list physical characteristics associated with perceptions of attraction. While our initial impressions typically focus on the physical features associated with attractiveness, other factors can come into play as well. McCroskey and McCain (1974) identified three dimensions of attractiveness used when deciding whether to initiate relationships. These dimensions include: physical, social, and task attractiveness.

Physical Attractiveness

The dimension of attractiveness most often used in deciding whether to pursue a relationship is physical attractiveness. More often than not, we decide whether to initiate conversations with a potential relationship partner based on our perceptions of the partners' physical attractiveness (Vangelisti 2002). According to research by Reis and his colleagues (1980), we are more likely to perceive interactions as pleasant when we view the person we interact with as physically attractive. How do we determine whether someone is physically attractive? Judgments about what constitutes physical attractiveness are often answered by asking the question, "What do I think makes someone pretty or handsome?" When characteristics such as body shape or size, hair color or length, and facial features are used in making a determination of whether to initiate a relationship, this dimension is referred to as **physical attractiveness**. Aristotle recognized the value of physical attractiveness when he stated, "Personal beauty is a greater recommendation than any letter of reference."

Recall the discussion of perception in Chapter Five. The phrase "beauty is in the eye of the beholder" addresses the perceptual nature of physical attraction and provides insight as to why one person may be attracted to blondes while another is attracted to brunettes. Sometimes we are baffled as to how individuals who appear to be so completely opposite with regard to their physical appearance, could be attracted to one another. Our perception causes us to view physical characteristics in unique ways. Extensive research has concluded that romantic attraction is frequently related to the extent to which partners are physically attracted to one another initially (Curran and Lippold 1975; Goode 1996; Walster, Aronson, Abrahams, and Rottman 1966; Wilson, Cousins, and Fink 2006; Woll 1986). While some studies report that men may value physical attractiveness more than women (Buss 1989; Sprecher, Sullivan, and Hatfield 1994), it is clear that both men and women report physical attractiveness as a factor influencing their decision to initiate relationships (Hatfield and Sprecher 1986).

But why does physical attractiveness play such an important role in the early stages of relationship development? One explanation is that people tend to associate other positive and favorable characteristics with physical attractiveness. Take a moment to think about how much emphasis our culture places on physical attractiveness. An overwhelming amount of research (see, for example, Eagly et al. 1991) seems to support the bias that individuals have towards those perceived as physically attractive. One study found that people described as attractive were also perceived as kind, sexual, responsive, social, and sensitive (Dion, Berscheid and Walster 1972). In this same study, participants

Why is physical attractiveness important early in a relationship?

© iofoto, 2007, Shutterstock.

predicted that physically attractive individuals would experience more success in life, both personally and professionally. Other factors, such as age, gender and culture, influence our perceptions of physical attractiveness.

Age and Attractiveness.

Beginning at a very young age, we are taught that physical attractiveness is often rewarded or valued. After all, the princesses in Disney movies are always beautiful young women, while the evil characters are portrayed as being ugly. Hasbro's Barbie doll is presented to young children as an ideal image of female attractiveness. She has long, blonde hair and blue eyes, is big-breasted, tall and thin. Young children are able to identify her and many idolize her. But let's get real. Barbie's bra size has been estimated to be a DDD compared to the average C cup size of most women, and her body dimensions have been translated to the equivalent of 38-18-34 if she were a real woman. In fact, her tiny feet would not be able to support her busty upper body if she were a real woman. Nonetheless, young girls adore Barbie! They receive the message that being physically attractive, like Barbie, is associated with having friends and receiving more attention, not to mention a host of other rewards: cool clothes, cars, beach houses, and a "cool" life-style.

Even in the classroom, children receive messages regarding the importance of physical attractiveness. Research has shown that attractive children are perceived as being more popular with both classmates and teachers. Richmond (1992) states that elementary age students who are perceived as being physically attractive receive more attention from their teachers, while attractive high school and college age students receive higher grades than those who are perceived to be less attractive. Studies show that teachers provide higher evaluations and establish higher expectations for attractive students. Attractive people are perceived as being happier, more likeable, popular, and friendly (Berscheid and Reis 1998).

Even as we get older, physical attractiveness impacts our perception as well as the perceptions others have of us. Research has found that people under the age of thirty have been rated as being more physically attractive than people over the age of fifty (McClellan and McKelvie 1993), and faces perceived as being younger have been judged as being more pleasant compared to faces viewed as being older. Johnson and Pittinger (1984) discovered that physically attractive males and females aged 60 to 93 were rated more positively than those in the same age group who were perceived to be less attractive. Another study grouped males and females into age categories. These categories included participants aged 20 to 29, 30 to 39, 40 to 49, 50 to 59, and 60 to 69 years. Participants in the study were shown photographs of members of the opposite sex from the same age range categories and were asked to rate their physical attractiveness. Results of the study indicated that as males increased in age, they rated younger women as being more attractive than older women. However, the same was not true for women. Women in the older age categories rated males similar in age to be more physically attractive (Mathes, Brennen, Haugen, and Rice 1985).

Gender and Attractiveness.

While both men and women indicate that they view physical attractiveness as important in the initiation of romantic relationships, the intensity that each sex values attractiveness differs. For example, in a study by Hewitt and German (1987), women indicated a strong preference for men who were dressed more formally compared to those who were dressed informally. In the reality show *Queer Eye for the Straight Guy*, male participants receive a significant makeover that might include a new haircut, body waxing, grooming tips, a new wardrobe, and an apartment makeover. Friends, family members, and co-workers are asked to comment on the participant's new look. At the end of the show, relationship partners, who also happen to be women, typically respond very favorably to their partner's new hip, stylish and more formal clothing.

While many research studies point to the positive aspects of physical attractiveness, others have discovered potential pitfalls. In the workplace, physically attractive women often encounter biases *against* them when applying for administrative or executive positions (Zebrowitz 1997). The same is true of women who run for political office. While physically attractive women are often penalized for their appearance in these situations, the opposite was found to be true for attractive males seeking similar opportunities. Because of the increased attention on women's voting behavior in political elections, Lewis and Bierly (1990) examined the impact of female perceptions of male political candidates' attractiveness. Women rated physically attractive political candidates as being more competent than less attractive candidates.

Decisions to initiate dates are most often based on physical attractiveness. In a content analysis of more than 800 personal ads, Harrison and Saeed (1977) found that males are more likely to include descriptors of physical attractiveness as criteria for potential dates. In addition, men tend to indicate a strong preference for women who are younger than themselves. While women also included criteria such as *athletic, tall* or *attractive* in personal ads, references to a partner's status were included more often and emerged as a stronger predictor of attraction (Davis 1990).

To examine the impact of physical attractiveness in homosexual relationships, Sergios and Cody (1985) matched 100 men in dyads (pairs), based on ratings of physical attractiveness. Participants were told that they were being sent on a blind date that was matched through a computer. Physical attractiveness was the biggest predictor of liking and desire to seek a future date. This research is consistent with research on how heterosexual relationship partners select mates. Regardless of whether the relationship is a heterosexual or homosexual one, physical attraction plays a significant role in one's choice of a relationship partner.

Culture and Attraction.

Culture is an influential factor in our perception of physical attractiveness. Within our culture, media depict the accepted standards of beauty. Consider the appearance of typical movie villains such as the Joker or the Penguin from the *Batman* movies, and Ursula, the sea witch from *The Little Mermaid*. They are ugly and unattractive, whereas the hero is always handsome or beautiful. As the main characters in *The Exorcist* and *The Fly* turn evil, their external appearances transform from normal to unattractive. The timing of these changes seems to insinuate that there is a direct correlation between turning bad and turning ugly. We do not have to look that far or long to find messages about physical beauty in our culture. Images are found on television and billboards, in magazines, movies and books, and on the Internet.

Perceptions of physical attractiveness can differ across ethnic groups. A very curvaceous figure is often considered to be unattractive among Caucasian women, but African American women may not agree (Hebl and Heatherton 1998). In fact, African American women are perceived as more attractive by African American males if they have a curvaceous bottom, as opposed to being able to fit into a pair of size four jeans.

As we cross cultural boundaries, it becomes apparent that there are universal perceptions of beauty as well. One particular physical feature that has been judged across cultures as a focal point for physical attraction is the human face. In particular, the more "feminine" a face appears the greater its perceived level of attractiveness. In a study comparing the attractiveness of men and women by looking at close-up photographs of their faces, both Caucasian and Japanese participants rated pictures of men and women whose facial features had been "feminized" or softened as being more attractive (Perrett, Lee, and Penton-Voak 1998).

Social Attractiveness

Once we initiate a conversation with another person, it is likely that our attention shifts from the physical attributes, which drew us to start talking in the first place, to identifying commonalities. **Social attractiveness** can be defined as common interests or similar patterns of communication that cause individuals to perceive one another as someone they would like to spend time with. Questions used to identify the level of social attraction with another person might include, "Would I like to hang out with this person?" and "Is this someone who would fit in with my friends?"

What questions do you ask to determine your level of social attraction to someone?

© Galina Barskaya, 2007, Shutterstock.

While physical attraction has a substantial impact on our decision to initiate relationships with others, social attraction is equally important. Some people exert considerable effort to ensure that others perceive their social behavior favorably. **Impression management** is defined as the process of maintaining a positive image of self in the presence of others. Consider the time and energy dedicated to making sure our physical appearance is "just right" when we meet or approach someone for the first time. When interviewing for a job, it is essential that the suit is pressed, the shoes are polished, and the hair is neat and clean.

Individuals vary greatly in the extent to which they are self-aware. **Self-monitoring** refers to a personality construct that causes a person to respond to social and interpersonal cues for appropriate communication behaviors in a variety of situations. High self-monitors are constantly aware of behaviors others perceive to be appropriate in interpersonal situations, and continuously strive to control how they are portraying themselves. By contrast, low self-monitors dedicate little, if any, energy to responding to the cues of social appropriateness. They do not spend a lot of time worrying if they break the social rules by wearing jeans to an event where everyone else is dressed more formally, or by belching in front of a potential romantic partner. To examine the relationship of self-monitoring and relationship initiation, participants were given file folders containing photographs and descriptions of personal attributes of potential dates. High self-monitors dedicated more time to reviewing the photographs in the folders, while low self-monitors spent more time reviewing the personal descriptions (Snyder, Berscheid, and Glick 1985). Thus, it appears that high self-monitors place more emphasis on physical attraction when selecting a potential partner for a date, while low self-monitors focus more on social attractiveness.

Task Attractiveness

While physical and social attributes may be influential in the initiatory phase of relationships, as individuals pursue their professional goals, decisions based on attractiveness may take on a much different perspective. **Task attractiveness** refers to the characteristics or qualities that are perceived as appealing when initiating relationships in which the goal is to complete a task or assignment. Suppose your professor allows you to select the team members you wish to work with on a huge term project. Are you going to select the most physically attractive person to work with on this assignment? Possibly, if your goal is to get a date for Saturday night. Are you going to choose the funniest or most social person in the class to be on your team? Maybe, if your goal is to have plenty of laughs as you work on the project. Most likely, you will seek out people with characteristics and qualities that you know are essential to getting the job done. A question used to identify perceived task attractiveness might be, "Does this person have what it takes to help get the job done?" Depending on the task, the list of qualities used to assess task attractiveness might be very different. If you consider yourself to be "technologically challenged," you may seek someone who you consider to be proficient with computers. Suppose there is a strict timeline for the project. In such a situation, you will probably seek a person who is dependable and organized.

Proximity

Consider our earlier question regarding your decision to initiate a relationship with the person seated next to you in this class. In essence, the decision to begin the relationship was influenced by proximity. **Proximity** refers to the physical distance between two people. The fact that you sit next to the same person for an entire semester increases the chance that you will choose to form a relationship with one another. Segal (1974) supported this notion in a study that examined friendships formed in a college classroom. At the beginning of the term, students were given seat assignments. When asked to indicate the persons whom they considered to be friends in the class, most students reported that they were friends with those who were seated next to them.

So why is proximity such a strong predictor of interpersonal attraction? One explanation may be found in the decreased effort that is required to establish relationships with those who are close in distance. It is just easier to strike up a conversation with the person seated next to you in class, or to share stories with the co-worker whose cubicle is directly adjacent to yours. Much more effort is required to start relationships with those who sit on the other side of the room or who work on different floors. Many people believe that long-distance relationships are doomed, simply based on the physical distance separating relationships partners.

These childhood friends grew up together and share the same background.

© Monika Wisniewska, 2007, Shutterstock.

Similarity/Homophily

After initiating a conversation, identifying potential topics to discuss can be the next hurdle to overcome. The goal of our discussions at this phase in a relationship is to identify common interests between ourselves and the other person. Remember the phrase, "Birds of a feather flock together?" This phrase refers to an important element of interpersonal attraction known as **similarity**, or **homophily**. Research confirms that we seek out relationships with those who have common interests, backgrounds, and goals, and who are similar in appearance (McCroskey, Richmond, and Daly 1975). This phenomenon might explain why friendships are formed among people who go to the same gym to work out, or how romantic relationships begin between two people who meet in an Internet chat room dedicated to discussions of reality television. Both of these situations provide common topics for discussion. Our similarity with others can be categorized based on demographic, background, or attitude commonalities. **Demographic similarity** is based on physical and social characteristics that are easily identifiable. Consider the relationships that you have initiated with others who are of a similar age or are the same sex. **Background similarity** refers to commonalities that we share as a result of our life experiences. Chances are that many of your friendships began as a result of experiences that you had in common with others—going to the same summer camp, playing on the same athletic team, working in the same organization, or simply growing up in the same hometown. Finally, **attitude similarity** focuses on our perception of the attitudes, beliefs, and values that we hold in common. Some relationships are formed as a result of our cultural, religious or political affiliations. When two friends express similar attitudes towards music, movies, or sports, they are exhibiting attitude similarity.

In their examination of interpersonal attraction and similarity, Klohnen and Luo (2003) identified four dimensions of similarity that individuals consider in initial attraction. These include:

- Similarity to current self
- Complementarity
- Attachment security
- Ideal-self similarity

Similarity to current self refers to the belief that individuals are attracted to those who are similar to themselves. The dimensions we use to identify the congruence between ourselves and others differ from person to person. You may seek someone whose sense of humor is similar to your own, while another person may view similar levels of intelligence as being more important. The **complementarity** hypothesis explains the saying "opposites attract." It predicts that people will be more attracted to those whose personality characteristics complement their own. This may explain why persons who have a high level of communication apprehension seek romantic relationships with those who have low levels of apprehension. To someone who is apprehensive about communicating, it is attractive to have someone who will initiate and carry out interactions. **Attachment security** predicts that individuals will be most attracted to those who are secure. Thus, we find individuals who are confident and trusting more attractive than individuals who are preoccupied by emotions of jealousy, neediness, or worry. Finally, some individuals are most attracted to those whom they perceive to be **similar to the ideal view of self** (as opposed to their actual or current self). Those who are similar to our view of how we would ultimately like to be are rated more favorably.

While creating a favorable impression is a primary conversational goal during the initiation phase of a relationship, it is important to establish realistic expectations. Have you ever experienced the "Me, too!" phenomenon in a romantic relationship or friendship? In a recent episode of the situation comedy *'Til Death*, Jeff is angry with his wife Steph because she lied to him about her interest in ice hockey. Steph finally reveals that she does not like ice hockey and does not want to go to ice hockey games with him anymore. Jeff is angry and wonders what else Steph has lied about and whether he really knows her at all. In one scene, Jeff enters the kitchen and says, "Hi Steph—if that is your real name!" Steph realizes that Jeff is upset about the lie and tries to explain her actions. She tells him that when he asked her out for the first time he also questioned whether she liked ice hockey, to which she enthusiastically replied "Yes!" Steph explains that if she had not said yes, they may have never dated at all because he might prefer someone with more similar interests. Rather than continue to perpetuate the lie, Steph chose to tell Jeff the truth. How often does a situation like this occur in relationships?

When we attempt to portray ourselves as being more similar to the other person than we really are simply to appear more attractive, we run the risk of encountering a relationship pitfall known as false homophily. **False homophily** refers to the presentation of a deceptive image of self that appears to be more similar than it actually is. Claiming that you have interests or beliefs in common with another person just to appear more attractive creates unrealistic expectations in the relationship. While this strategy may be effective for gaining attention in the initial stages of the relationship, eventually the differences will emerge and could cause potential problems, as illustrated in the Steph and Jeff example from *'Til Death*.

One interpersonal context that places considerable emphasis on similarity as a reason for initiating relationships is the Internet. In the absence of the more obvious physical clues that are often used to decide whether to initiate a relationship, information about commonalities is sought to decide whether to interact with the other person. Baker (2005) points out that couples who initially meet via the Internet are explicit in delineating their interests in an attempt to find others with common interests. Typically they go to virtual chat rooms which focus on a specified topic to ensure that they will have something in common with others in the online community. Think about the process of posting information in an online personal ad. Match.com *(www .match.com)* provides several options to search for the ideal partner. Of course, some of the criteria that can be used to search for the ideal mate include physical characteristics, but additional criteria are available to narrow the focus on the basis of similarities. Questions regarding interests (sports, hobbies), lifestyle (job, smoking, drinking), and personal values (faith, education, politics) are included to identify similarities in relational partners.

What social and task goals do you find in classroom relationships?

© PhotoCreate, 2007, Shutterstock.

Goals

A fourth reason people choose to initiate relationships with others is to fulfill a purpose, or goal. Charles Berger (1995) defines **goals** as "desired end states toward which persons strive" (143). Many of our interpersonal interactions are initiated to fulfill two primary goals: social and task. **Social goals** refer to desired end states that fulfill the need for inclusion or affection. Both parties involved in the initial relationship can experience the fulfilled need. Consider the new kid in school. In order to ease some of the anxiety of starting a new school, the student might approach a table of students in the cafeteria and ask, "Is this seat taken?" One explanation for the initiation of this interaction is to fulfill a social goal—the student seeks to fulfill the need for inclusion at school. **Task goals** are defined as desired end states that fulfill the need for the completion of a task. Consider your current relationship with your hair stylist or barber. You initiated the relationship because the task of getting your hair cut needed to be fulfilled. A phone call was made to a local hair salon with the goal of finding a competent stylist to complete the task. As you initiated a conversation with the stylist, the initial task goal was to describe the hair cut you desired. Consider all of the relationships you have initiated to fulfill task goals. Relationships are initiated with teachers to fulfill the task goal of achieving your educational objectives, and teachers form relationships with colleagues to accomplish tasks associated with the job. Interpersonal communication is instrumental in achieving our goals.

Dillard (1990) points out that our goals serve three functions in interpersonal relationships. First, goals are used to take action and fulfill an interpersonal need. Individuals determine what need to fulfill, and the goal prompts the initiation of the relationship. If your social goal is to form new friendships at school, you will introduce yourself in an attempt to take action to fulfill the need. Second, goals assist us in defining the purpose for the interaction or behaviors. Suppose a woman asks a colleague to join her for a cup of coffee to discuss the upcoming presentation for an important client. She realizes that the purpose for the interaction is to accomplish a task goal. However, if she had a romantic interest in the colleague the ulterior motive for the meeting may have been prompted by social goals. Finally, goals provide us with a standard to judge the behaviors and outcomes of interpersonal interactions. We evaluate our interpersonal interactions with others and judge their effectiveness based on whether or not we accomplish our goals. After a blind date we typically evaluate the date as being *good* or *bad*, based on the interaction that took place. If conversation was forced and awkward, we are likely to evaluate the date negatively.

In a study of first date goals, college students identified eight primary reasons for going on a first date (Mongeau, Serewicz, and Therrien 2004). Table 7.1 compares the responses offered by men and women for their decision for first dates.

It is interesting to note the gender differences in the goals behind asking a person out for a first date. Males were more likely than women to pursue the goal of sexual activity during a first date, while women exclusively reported that their goal for going on the date was due to hedonistic reasons or guilt. Overall, women appeared to focus more attention on relational goals for the first date compared to men. In the past, our culture taught us that first dates should be initiated by men. "Nice girls" were supposed to sit patiently and wait for the male to contact them and arrange for a date. But this trend is changing. Mongeau and his colleagues (1993) reported that approximately eighty percent of men and sixty percent of women went on a date initiated by the female.

Online interactions can also be initiated to fulfill goals. Katz and Rice (2002) pointed out that sometimes Indian parents use the Internet as a source to seek suitable mates for their children as a modern extension of their traditional matchmaking processes. Signing up to post and browse online personal ads signals a social goal—the intent to form a romantic relationship.

Table 7.1   Frequencies of Goals for First Dates

Goal	Females	Males	Total
Reduce uncertainty (Get to know the other person better)	52	36	88
Relational escalation (Explore the possibility of pursuing a more intimate relationship)	48	25	73
Have fun (View dating as an enjoyable experience)	40	26	66
Companionship (Have someone to do things with)	16	7	23
Ego booster (Feel better about themselves)	6	6	12
Sexual activity	2	8	10
Hedonistic (Get something "free" from the date— concert ticket, fancy dinner)	8	0	8
Guilt (Avoid hurting the other person's feelings)	5	0	5

From "Goals for Cross-Sex First Dates: Identification, Measurement and the Influence of Contextual Factors" by Paul Mongeau in Communication Monographs, 2004. Reprinted by permission of the author.

INTERPERSONAL COMMUNICATION THEORIES: *HOW* WE INITIATE RELATIONSHIPS

While the decision to initiate a relationship may be based on attraction, proximity, similarity, or purpose, one of the key factors in beginning the interaction and taking the relationship to the next level can be explained by examining prominent communication theories. Theories and concepts such as social penetration theory, uncertainty reduction theory, predicted outcome value theory, liking, and social exchange theory address *how* we initiate relationships with others. Before we address relevant interpersonal theories and concepts, we address the importance of initial impressions and self-disclosure in establishing a relationship.

Starting the Conversation

To identify commonalities, we must first initiate a conversation. For some people, this is one of the most difficult tasks in a relationship. After all, we are often reminded that, "You never get a second chance to make a good first impression." Consider the last time you attempted to start a conversation. Figuring out the most appropriate way to break the ice and create a positive initial impression can be intimidating. Over the years, many of our students have shared "pick-up lines" or relational openers that have been used to initiate conversations with a potential romantic partner. Table 7.2 includes a list of the most interesting. It is important to note that they are not necessarily the most effective conversation starters, although they do succeed in getting one's attention. Our advice is that the next time you think about using one of these pick-up lines to begin a conversation, don't. Informal surveys of our students have revealed that the vast majority feel a simple and sincere introduction is the most effective way to initiate a conversation.

Table 7.2   Notorious Pick-Up Lines/Relational Openers

Excuse me, do you have a quarter? I want to call my mother and tell her I just met the girl of my dreams.

Do you have a map? Because I keep getting lost in your eyes.

You must be tired because you've been running through my mind all night!

Your eyes are blue like the ocean and I'm lost at sea!

Do you know karate because your body is really kickin'!

Is there a rainbow today? I've just found the treasure I've been searching for.

Are you from Tennessee? Cause you're the only "ten" I see!

Do you believe in love at first sight or should I walk by again?

Hey, I like a girl with some meat on her! **(We STRONGLY discourage use of this relational opener!)

Somebody better call God because he's missing an angel .

If I could rearrange the alphabet I'd put U and I together.

You must be a Snickers because you satisfy me.

Your lips look so lonely. Would they like to meet mine?

Do you know how much a polar bear weighs? Enough to break the ice.
Hi! My name is _____.

Were you in the Boy Scouts? Because you've sure tied my heart in a knot.

You're so sweet, you could put Hershey's out of business.

Apart from being beautiful, what do you do for a living?

Are you a parking ticket? Cause you've got "fine" written all over you.

So how does it feel to be the most beautiful girl in this room?

You must be a broom because you just swept me off my feet.

Self-Disclosure.   While it is difficult to determine which opening line should be used to initiate a conversation, taking the next step in the conversation can be an even greater challenge. Deciding what information to share about yourself, and what information you should seek from the other person can be viewed as a daunting task. During the early stages of relationship formation, partners will often self-disclose information in an effort to increase intimacy (Reis and Shaver 1988; Reis and Patrick 1996; Sprecher and Hendrick 2004). **Self-disclosure** is "the process of revealing personal information about oneself to another" (Sprecher and Hendrick 2004, 858). Self-disclosing is essential to relationship success and stability because it helps others learn who we are and what we want in a relationship. Aron (2003) validates this statement by noting that much of the process of becoming intimate with others involves disclosing information about the self and connecting the self to relevant others.

Typically, we disclose information more freely to those with whom we feel we have a close relationship. We are most likely to divulge information about ourselves to individuals we like and, as a result of this, tend to come to like those individuals even more (Kowalski 1999). However, in initial interactions the rules for disclosure are a bit more restrictive; we are more guarded in our disclosures. The task involves deciding what, and how much, information we should share. Have you ever heard a horror story of a first date where one person disclosed

How much information do you feel comfortable disclosing in a new relationship?

© Darren Green, 2007, Shutterstock.

their deepest secrets or declared their undying affection for the other person? Needless to say, the recipient typically reports being turned off by such intimate disclosures so early in the relationship. Consider what topics are "safe" when initiating a relationship. Would it be best to discuss and make comparisons to your most recent romantic relationship on a first date? Probably not. Similarly, discussing how much money you earn or asking the other person to discuss their greatest fears in life would be viewed as highly inappropriate. As a general rule, **reciprocal self-disclosure**, the notion that disclosure of information between two people, is best when it is similar in terms of topics discussed and depth of disclosure. Disclosures of information in the initial stages of a relationship are often met with similar disclosures. Consider the following initial disclosures between two classmates on the first day of class:

Sabina: Hi, I'm Sabina. Have you ever taken a class with Dr. Yost before?

Natalie: Hey Sabina, I'm Natalie. No, I haven't had a class with her, but my roommate took it last semester.

Sabina: Really, what did he say about it?

Natalie: He said she's tough but fair.

Sabina: Ouch! That's what I was afraid of. I have to take this class for my major and this is the only time that it fit into my schedule. If she's a difficult teacher then why did you take this class?

Natalie: Well, even though she's tough, I've also heard that you learn a lot that will help you down the road in other classes in the major.

Sabina: Oh, are you a communication major?

Natalie: Yes, this is my second year. What year are you?

Sabina: I'm a junior, but I just transferred into the major at the beginning of the semester. I feel like I'm so far behind. Everyone else has their schedules all planned out and they know exactly who and what to take.

Natalie: Don't stress yourself out about it. We've all been there before. If you have any questions about who you should take, just ask me. Have you met with your advisor yet? They're pretty good about helping you map out your long-term schedule.

Consider the reciprocity of disclosure in this initial interaction. Both women share information about their majors as well as their fears about the class. As one asks a question, the other answers it. When one woman discloses information, so does the other. In situations where others fail to disclose similar information, we become uncomfortable and may perceive them to be hiding something, or engaging in deceptive communication.

Cultural Differences in Disclosure.   Not all cultures approach or perceive self-disclosure in the same way. Nakanishi (1986) found that Japanese view limited levels of self-disclosure as being more appropriate in initial interactions with others. Most research supports the notion that Japanese individuals tend to engage in less self-disclosure than those from Western cultures. In a study comparing the disclosures of Japanese compared with Americans across a variety of relationships, Japanese were found to engage in fewer disclosures than their American counterparts. However, both Japanese and American students reported they preferred to disclose information to their same-sex friends as opposed to their opposite-sex friends, and members of both cultures reported engaging in more in-depth disclosures in romantic relationships than in friendships (Kito 2005). Consider the rules that your culture has for disclosure. These cultural norms may cause frustration when interacting with a person from a different culture. Recall the earlier discussion of reciprocal disclosures. If a person from the United States was disclosing information about financial difficulties with a friend from Japan, expecting similar disclosures, the result would likely be frustrating for the American. Whereas members of the U.S. culture tend to be very open in disclosures, those from Asian cultures tend to be more reserved.

Even within a particular culture, personal preferences for disclosure exist, depending on how familiar we are with the other person. In particular, bartenders and hair stylists report receiving surprising numbers of unsolicited self-disclosures from their clients. A recent *Newsweek* article described the tendency for individuals to disclose personal information to their hair stylists (Silver-Greenberg 2005). Twanda Hamilton, a cosmetologist from Wichita, Kansas was quoted as saying, "You get a client in the shampoo bowl and they just open up and tell us that they are being beaten. We hear so much in the salon that no one else hears." In response to these unsolicited disclosures, a program called Cut-it-Out was launched to train stylists to recognize the signs of domestic abuse.

Social Penetration Theory

Altman and Taylor (1973) created **social penetration theory** to address how information is exchanged during relationship development. This theory focuses on how self-disclosure changes as relationships move from one level to the next. In essence, their theory explains how and why we move from superficial topics of conversation in the initial stages of relationships to more intimate conversations as the relationship progresses. In the movie *Shrek*, Shrek uses the analogy of an onion to explain to Donkey that even though he is an ogre, he possesses many layers of feelings and emotions that need to be taken into consideration.

> **Shrek:** Ogres are like onions.
> **Donkey:** They stink?
> **Shrek:** Yes. No.
> **Donkey:** Oh, they make you cry.
> **Shrek:** No.
> **Donkey:** Oh, you leave 'em out in the sun, they get all brown, start sproutin' little white hairs.
> **Shrek:** NO. Layers. Onions have layers. Ogres have layers. Onions have layers. You get it? We both have layers. *(sighs)*
> **Donkey:** Oh, you both have layers. Oh. You know, not everybody like onions. (*Shrek* directed by Andrew Adamson and Vicky Jenson, 1 hr. 30 min., DreamWorks Animation, 2001.)

This analogy helps to illustrate Altman and Taylor's explanation of the levels of information we reveal as we move from one stage of a relationship to the next. There are three primary levels of information that we reveal as we progress. These include superficial, personal, and intimate. Superficial information is revealed in initial interactions. Communication focuses on safe topics such as one's major, occupation, or hometown. As the relationship intensifies, a layer of the onion is "peeled" away and more personal information is revealed. Personal communication focuses on topics of a more personal nature such as likes, dislikes, and experiences. As the relationship progresses to a more intimate level, so does the communication. Intimate communication focuses on topics that are personal and private. In order to reveal intimate information, a level of trust must be present. At this innermost core of the onion, topics of discussion include goals, challenges, values, and motivations.

As mentioned previously, it is important to adhere to self-disclosure norms or expectations when sharing information with a potential relationship partner. Some research indicates that individuals who self-disclose inappropriately by sharing private information early in a relationship are perceived as odd, deviant or even dislikable (Werner and Haggard 1985). Table 7.3 on page 166 offers some suggestions for both providing self-disclosure and receiving self-disclosure from others competently.

Uncertainty Reduction Theory

Consider the extensive use of questions throughout the interaction between Sabina and Natalie. **Uncertainty reduction theory** (Berger and Calabrese 1975) identifies questions as a primary communication strategy used for encouraging reciprocal disclosure and reducing levels of uncertainty. To test the relationship between initial attraction and the use of questioning or disclosure, Douglas (1990) asked pairs to engage in a six-minute initial interaction. He found that the majority of questions were asked in the initial two minutes of the conversation, and greater disclosures were made in the final two minutes of the conversation. Partners asked each other fewer questions as their answers required more detailed responses. Question-asking decreases as the questions require more in-depth responses. In the process of reducing uncertainty about the other person, individuals engage in a "strategy selection" process. This procedure requires them to maximize efficiency in gaining information about the other person while utilizing behaviors that are viewed as socially appropriate.

Predicted Outcome Value Theory

Once we have reduced our level of uncertainty about a new relationship, the next step involves deciding what we expect or want from the new relationship. **Predicted outcome value theory** focuses on the perceived rewards or benefits associated with the new relationship (Sunnafrank 1986). There is a shift from focusing on the need for more information about the other person to an analysis of the value obtained from the relationship. Consider when you meet someone for the first time. You probably engage in an analytical process to evaluate the potential for the future of the relationship. At that point a decision is made regarding whether to pursue the relationship, how the relationship should progress, and what type of relationship we should seek with the other person (e.g., friendship, romantic).

Liking

Our earlier discussion of uncertainty reduction theory discussed the strategy of information-seeking to decrease our level of uncertainty about the other person. However, an additional benefit of reducing our uncertainty is to increase liking between individuals. The more we know about a person, the greater the possibility that we will like one another. **Liking** is defined as the level of positive affect, or affinity, we feel toward another person. A critical factor

Table 7.3   Suggestions for Delivering and Receiving Self-Disclosures

DELIVERING

Begin by self-disclosing information on safe or neutral topics.

During initial conversations, talk about where you went to school, hobbies, talents, etc., before sharing any private information.

If possible, attempt to match your partner's disclosures in depth.

If your partner shares intimate information (e.g., fears, future goals, insecurities), he may expect you to reciprocate. Remember that reciprocal disclosures between partners often indicates trust and liking.

Before disclosing private information, ask yourself if this is someone you can trust.

If you feel you cannot trust this person or feel this person will share this information with others, it is probably not a good idea to share private information.

RECEIVING

Do not overreact when someone shares personal information with you.

Try not to become overly emotional or provide judgmental feedback when someone shares private information with you. For example, screaming, "YOU DID WHAT?" when a friend shares information is not recommended.

Provide verbal and nonverbal support.

Make an attempt to display warm receptive nonverbal cues during your conversation by maintaining eye contact, sitting near the person, nodding your head to indicate listening and, if appropriate, smiling. Engage in active listening behaviors which might include paraphrasing and appropriate empathic responses (e.g., I can see why you would be upset).

If you do not feel comfortable discussing a topic or issue, tell your friend or relationship partner.

Rather than avoid the person and risk damaging your relationship, tell the person why you are uncomfortable discussing the topic.

in deciding to initiate a relationship is reciprocal liking—each partner must perceive the other as having mutual positive affect. However, the trick often rests in obtaining information as to whether mutual liking is present. Douglas (1987) conducted a study to identify affinity-testing strategies used to identify the presence or absence of mutual liking. Participants in the study were asked to describe the things they do to find out how much somebody of the opposite sex likes them, being reminded to focus specifically on strategies they would use in initial encounters. Eight different affinity-testing strategies were identified in this study: confronting, withdrawing, sustaining, hazing, diminishing the self, approaching, offering, and networking. Participants were also asked to rate the efficiency and appropriateness of each of the affinity-testing strategies. Confronting, which involved asking the individual direct questions, was viewed as the most efficient strategy followed by approaching and sustaining; in the interest of time, it is best to be up front and direct when determining whether reciprocal liking is present. With regard to appropriateness, sustaining was rated as the most socially appropriate strategy. When individuals used the sustaining strategy they made active attempts to keep the conversation going by getting others to reveal information about themselves. This research supports the use of questions to reduce uncertainty. Hazing and diminishing the self were viewed as socially inappropriate. Both strategies involve "playing games" or using manipulative tactics to determine the level of interest in a relationship. When individuals use these affinity-testing strategies, they may be perceived as deceptive and unacceptable.

While Douglas (1987) examined how individuals determine whether mutual liking exists in romantic relationships, research by Bell and Daly (1984) identified the wide range of strategies used in platonic relationships to gain liking. Bell and Daly describe **affinity-seeking strategies** as verbal and nonverbal communication behaviors that are often used strategically to gain liking from others. In their seminal research they asked college students to identify all of the different tactics they used to gain liking from peers. A total of twenty-five different affinity-seeking strategies were identified from the students' descriptive responses. Examples of affinity-seeking strategies included: altruism, physical attractiveness, facilitate enjoyment, comfortable self, inclusion of other, nonverbal immediacy, and openness. Not surprisingly, affinity-seeking strategies are used in all types of relationships to increase liking. For example, a number of studies indicate that both students and professors use affinity-seeking strategies to improve their relationships (see, for example, Frymier 1994; Wanzer 1995; 1998).

Social Exchange Theory

Have you ever heard the phrase "on the market" to refer to a person who is single and searching for a new romantic relationship? While at first this reference may seem degrading, it actually fits quite well with the strategies used when considering new relationships. The process one experiences when evaluating the pros and cons of initiating a relationship is actually quite similar to shopping—we examine the options available and seek the best "deal" available. **Social exchange theory** (also known as interdependence theory) refers to an assessment of costs and rewards in determining the value of pursuing or continuing a relationship (Thibaut and Kelley 1959). **Rewards** consist of behaviors or things that are desirable, which the recipient perceives as enjoyable or fulfilling. By contrast, **costs** are perceived as undesirable behaviors or outcomes. As we exchange information in the initial stages of a relationship, decisions are made regarding the relative value of continuing to pursue the relationship further. While your initial conversation with the person seated next to you on an airplane may be rewarding in the sense that you felt comfortable discussing topics of interest and it helped pass the time on a three-hour journey, the costs of maintaining the relationship (effort involved in emailing and calling the person) may outweigh the benefits. Thus, you decide to shake hands at the end of the flight, exchange pleasantries, and go your separate ways. But suppose the person seated next to you is employed at the company you've always dreamed of working for. In that instance, the costs involved in continuing to communicate across the distance are minimal compared to the potential reward of having an inside connection when you apply for employment at the company in the future.

Stages of Relationship Development

Now that we have explored the reasons why we initiate relationships and some of the theoretical explanations for how we use communication, we turn our attention to understanding the process of progressing from one stage of a relationship to another.

Mark Knapp (1978) proposes a "staircase" model depicting the interactive stages of relationship development and dissolution. The first five steps of this model, known as Coming Together, will be discussed here. Chapter Nine will discuss Knapp's (1978) stages of relationship disengagement or, Coming Apart. Before discussing the stages of relationship initiation and development, it is important to note the following caveats about the movement from one stage to the next (Knapp and Vangelisti 2003):

- Movement from one stage of the model to the next is typically sequential. Moving sequentially allows us to make predictions regarding the future of the relationship.
- Movement may progress from one stage forward to the next. This movement involves an analysis of the potential benefits of continuing the relationship and increasing the level of intimacy in communication.
- Movement may revert to a previous stage. This is often due to a decline in the communication behaviors prescribed in the present stage.
- Movement through the stages occurs at different paces for each unique relationship. While one relationship may move very quickly from one stage to the next, another relationship may stall at one stage while the partners work through the communication challenges of the phase and make the decision of whether to progress to the next level.

Initiation.   **Initiation** occurs when one party decides to initiate conversation with another person. Communication during this phase typically consists of the polite formalities of introduction. Statements such as "How are you?" or "Is anyone sitting here?" are used to break the ice. Consider the role that variables discussed earlier in this chapter play in our decision to approach someone and initiate a conversation. For instance, we evaluate the person's attractiveness and scramble to come up with the perfect opening line. During this phase, impression management is essential. After all, we want to present ourselves in the most positive way possible. While some people may be tempted to use one of the pick-up lines discussed earlier in this chapter, the best strategy for making a good first impression is to be confident and sincere.

Experimenting.   You know that you have reached the **experimenting** phase when the communication involves excessive questions and discussions about topics such as classes, hobbies, or other demographic information. Whereas physical attraction has a strong influence on the decision to engage in the initiation phase, social attraction is discovered during the experimenting phase. Reciprocal disclosures are common, with one person asking questions such as, "So have you lived in Los Angeles your entire life?" and the other person responding with "No, I grew up in Chicago and moved to L.A. last year to escape the cold winters. Did you grow up in California?" Uncertainty reduction is the primary goal of this stage of relationship development.

Intensifying.   As we progress to the **intensifying** stage of the staircase model, our disclosures with one another increase in depth. Whereas in the experimenting stage we disclosed information on a variety of topics (breadth), during this phase the information shared becomes more personal and private (depth). Messages communicated between partners involve a lot of "tests" to determine the intensity or commitment felt by one another. Knapp and Vangelisti (2003) identify specific verbal characteristics that are common during the intensifying stage. These include using nicknames or terms of endearment to refer to one another (think "Hunny" or "Babe"), referring to one another through the use of first person plural pronouns ("*We* should go to the movies with Joe and Cara on Friday,") and making explicit references to the commitment like "I think about you all the time when you're not here."

Integrating.   The **integrating** stage is marked by a merging of personalities and identities. Not only do the partners see themselves as a couple, but others recognize and refer to them as a unit as well. Relationship rituals that occur during this stage include exchanging personal items such as clothing, pictures, and rings that can be worn or displayed to communicate their identity as a couple to others, engaging in similar verbal and nonverbal behaviors, and identifying common "property" that is identified as special to the relationship ("our" song or purchasing a pet together).

Bonding.   **Bonding**, the final stage of coming together, is viewed as a formal contractual agreement that declares to the world that the couple has made a serious commitment to one another. This stage can be marked by performing public rituals such as exchanging class rings to show that you are "going steady," or getting engaged, or that you have gotten married. It is important to note that while bonding can be viewed as a contract at any stage of the relationship, the message communicated between a couple during this stage is that there is a serious commitment that implies the goal of pursuing a long-term relationship.

Getting married demonstrates commitment to a long-term relationship.

© iofoto, 2007, Shutterstock.

Relationship Initiation Contexts

Another factor impacting the decision to initiate a relationship focuses on the setting in which the initial interaction takes place. In a study of college women, the actual settings where significant relationships began were examined (Jason, Reichler, and Rucker 1981). Five settings were identified by single women as the location where their significant relationships were initiated (see Table 7.4 below). Given that the women were currently enrolled in college classes, it should come as no surprise that they listed school as the place where

Table 7.4   Settings Where Most Important Relationships Began

Setting	Percentage
School	25
Work	20
Through friends	14
Bar	9
Party	9

The Journal of Psychology by HELDREFF PUBLICATIONS. Reproduced by permission of HELDREFF PUBLICATIONS in the format reuse in a book/textbook via Copyright Clearance Center.

their most important relationships began. While many would question the quality of a relationship that is initiated in a bar, women reported this as the initial location for nine percent of their significant relationships. In a study of relationship initiation in singles bars, researchers noted that a woman was approached by a man once every ten to twenty minutes. However, the average length of the interaction was approximately seven seconds (Glenwick, Jason, and Elman 1978). So while women may have many opportunities in single bars, it appears as though they choose not to pursue the majority of relationships initiated by men.

A study of preferred meeting places for gays and lesbians reveals a slight difference in setting choices. Gay bars are a popular place for initiating relationships given the fact that patrons of the bars are similar in terms of their sexual preference. Among lesbians, the second most preferred meeting place is at political functions, such as feminist or lesbian rallies (Huston and Schwartz 2003). It is important to note that some environments are not open or welcoming to the initiation of homosexual relationships. Thus, frustration in locating a common place to meet similar others is often reported by gay men and lesbians.

The Role of Technology in Relationship Initiation

Online Relationship Initiation.   As the number of people who form relationships online continues to grow, there is a greater need to understand the unique nature of interactions in cyberspace. In face-to-face interactions, the initial decision to approach another person is often based on physical characteristics. We see the person, make a decision of whether or not to approach him, and subsequently spend time getting to know one another by progressing through the relationship stages identified by Knapp and Vangelisti (2003). Online relationship initiation differs because of the absence of physical cues, which can affect the course of the relationship. Individuals meet via written messages or text. From there, they decide whether to talk with the other person via phone and, ultimately, in person. In essence, online relationship initiation could be considered a "test drive"—we can dedicate as little or as much time as we want getting to know the person before deciding if we want to meet face-to-face.

Baker (2005) developed a model delineating the characteristics of successful versus unsuccessful relationships which were initiated online (see Table 7.5).

While we might doubt the sustainability of relationships that are initiated online, research suggests otherwise. One study examined the stability of a variety of online relationships (acquaintances, friends, and romantic partners) over a two-year period and found seventy-five percent of respondents indicated that they were still involved in a relationship that had initiated online (McKenna, Green, and Gleason 2002).

Text-Messaging.   If you are a fan of *American Idol*, you have probably seen the commercials for AT&T Wireless in which Ryan Seacrest sends a text message to a woman named Jeanette, across a crowded bar to inquire if she is interested in meeting his friend, Dave. In the end, Jeanette declines the offer to initiate a relationship, but the scene depicted in the commercial is one that is all too

Table 7.5	A Model for Successful versus Unsuccessful Online Relationships	
Factor	**Positive/Successful**	**Negative/Unsuccessful**
Place met	Sites focused on specific interests	Sites focused on general interests
Physical appearance, degree of importance	Not viewed as being important	Considered very important or crucial
Hyperhonesty	Very honest online	Not honest in online interactions
Cybersex	Never or rarely engaged in cybersex	Frequently engaged in cybersex
Long-time communication before they met in person	Considerable time spent communicating online prior to face-to-face meeting	Little time spent interacting online prior to meeting
Relocation	At least one person willing to relocate	Neither partner is willing to relocate

From *Double-Click: Romance and Commitment Among Online Couples* by A. Baker. Copyright © 2006 by Hampton Press, Inc. Reprinted by permission.

Will this on-line relationship last?

© Zsolt Nyulaszi, 2007, Shutterstock.

familiar to those currently experiencing the dating scene. A popular channel for communicating in Europe and Asia for several years, text-messaging has achieved growing popularity in the United States as a means to communicate with others in relationships. When initiating new relationships, text messaging serves as a "safe" channel for reducing uncertainty and gaining information about the other person before meeting again face-to-face. The term *silent dating* has been used to discuss the strategy of exchanging text messages for a week or more in the initial stages of a relationship *(http://thescotsman.scotsman.com/index.cfm?id=290812004)*. Anna Close, a twenty-eight-year-old teacher from Glasgow, describes the value of text messages in initial relationships as: "Before text-messaging I'd meet someone and then not hear from him because he'd be too scared to actually go through the process of picking up the phone and having a conversation. But now, if a man is interested in you, he won't call, but he'll definitely text."

Relationship Initiation and Culture

While you might think that perceptions with regard to relationship initiation differ across cultures, you might be surprised to find out that we are more alike than different. Pines (2001) examined the role of gender and culture in initial romantic attraction by comparing Americans with Israelis. She asked participants to describe how they met their romantic partner and indicate what attracted them to the other person initially (see Table 7.6).

The only significant differences occurred when comparing U.S. and Israeli responses to questions relating to status, propinquity, and similarity. Eight percent of Americans reported that they were attracted by the status of their relational partner, while none of the Israeli respondents indicated this was a factor. Propinquity, or the proximity between partners, was listed as

Table 7.6   Attraction Variables (percent) by Country

Attraction Variable	USA	Israel
Appearance	63	70
Status	8	0
Personality	92	94
Need filled	54	6
Propinquity	63	46
Mutual attraction	41	40
Arousal	22	25
Similarity	30	8

Reproduced by permission from *European Psychologist* Vol. 6 (2): 96–102, © 2001 Hogrefe & Huber Publishers HYPERLINK "http://www.hogrefe.com" www.hogrefe.com

being more influential to Americans. Americans report being more attracted to partners who lived, worked, or studied at the same place, as compared to Israeli respondents. Similarity of partners was found to be more important to Americans. Having similar experiences, values, interests, attitudes, and personalities was rated as being far more important to Americans than to Israelis.

Interracial Dating.   As the number of interracial relationships increases, so does our need for understanding the stages of progression that are unique to this relationship context. Foeman and Nance (2003) enhance our understanding of these phases by presenting a model of interracial development. In this model, four stages are encountered by the couple. These include:

- Stage 1—Racial awareness
- Stage 2—Coping with social definitions of race
- Stage 3—Identity emergence
- Stage 4—Maintenance

Racial awareness focuses on the existence of multiple perceptions regarding the new relationship. In addition to each partner's perception of the relationship, interracial couples must also deal with the perceptions of the members of one another's racial groups. If the couple decides to move beyond the initiation phase and awareness, the next stage involves coping with society's definitions and reactions to the racially mixed relationship. Several communication strategies are considered during this phase. In addition to identifying how to respond to questions and statements regarding racial differences, the couple needs to decide when to avoid potentially negative interactions with others and when to confront them. During the third stage, identity emergence, the couple begins to define how they see themselves as an "interracial" couple. They work together to develop strategies and skills for addressing problems and often view themselves as being unique or trendsetting. Maintenance, the final stage of the model, involves occasional recycling through the stages of the model as new life events occur (such as the addition of children to the family) that generate new reactions to their status as an interracial couple.

SUMMARY

In this chapter we have answered some of the questions regarding *why* we form interpersonal relationships with others and *how* we use communication to initiate them. While each relationship is unique, the reasons we choose to interact with others are fairly similar. Our hope is that you have gained both an understanding of, and the confidence for, using effective communication behaviors to pursue new relationship journeys. Perhaps the most important piece of advice we could offer as you begin a relationship with another person, whether it is platonic or romantic relationship, is to just be yourself.

APPLICATIONS

Discussion Questions

A. Recall a time when you were successful at initiating a romantic relationship. Offer several suggestions or guidelines for individuals that want to be successful when initiating conversations or beginning a romantic relationship. What types of things should you avoid saying or doing during this critical time period?

B. Based on your experience, how prevalent is the silent dating phenomenon? Discuss several pros and cons of silent dating.

C. In what context or under what circumstances did most of your important relationships begin? Do you initiate different types of relationships in different contexts? Are there similarities and differences in the questions asked/strategies employed during the initiating stages of platonic and romantic relationship development?

D. In your opinion, what is the best way to gain liking from another individual? Bell and Daly identified twenty-five affinity-seeking strategies that individuals use to gain liking. Can you identify at least ten strategies?

REFERENCES

Altman, I., and D. A. Taylor. 1973. *Social penetration: The development of interpersonal relationships.* New York: Holt, Rinehart, & Winston.

Aron, A. 2003. Self and close relationships. In M. R. Leary and J. P. Tangney (Eds.), *Handbook of self and identity.* New York: The Guilford Press.

Baker, A. 2005. *Double click: Romance and commitment among online couples.* Cresskill, NJ: Hampton Press.

Bell, R. A., and J. A. Daly. 1984. The affinity-seeking function of communication. *Communication Monographs, 51,* 91–115.

Berger, C. 1995. A plan-based approach to strategic interaction. In D. E. Hewes (Ed.), *The cognitive bases of interpersonal interaction* (141–180). Hillsdale, NJ: Lawrence Erlbaum.

Berger, C. R., and R. J. Calabrese. 1975. Some explorations in initial interaction and beyond: Toward a developmental theory of interpersonal communication. *Human Communication Research, 1,* 99–112.

Berscheid, E., and H. T. Reis. 1998. Attraction and close relationships. In D. Gilbert, S. Fiske, and G. Lindzey (Eds.), *Handbook of social psychology (4th ed.)* (193–281). New York: McGraw-Hill.

Buss, D. M. 1989. Sex differences in human mate preferences: Evolutionary hypotheses tested in 37 cultures. *Behavioral and Brain Sciences, 12,* 1–49.

Curran, J. P., and S. Lippold. 1975. The effects of physical attraction and attitude similarity on attraction in dating dyads. *Journal of Personality, 43,* 528–539.

Davis, S. 1990. Men as success objects and women as sex objects: A study of personal advertisements. *Sex Roles, 23,* 43–50.

Dillard, J. P. 1990. A goal-driven model of interpersonal influence. In J. P. Dillard (Ed.), *Seeking compliance: The production of interpersonal influence messages* (41–56). Scottsdale, AZ: Gorsuch-Scarisbrick.

Dion, K. K., E. Berscheid, and E. Walster. 1972. What is beautiful is good. *Journal of Personality and Social Psychology, 24,* 285–290.

Douglas, W. 1987. Affinity-testing in initial interactions. *Journal of Social and Personal Relationships, 4,* 3–15.

———. 1990. Uncertainty, information seeking and liking during initial interaction. *Western Journal of Speech Communication, 54,* 66–81.

Eagly, A. H., R. D. Ashmore, M. G. Makhijani, and L. C. Longo. 1991. What is beautiful is good, but . . . A meta-analytic review of research on the physical attractiveness stereotype. *Psychological Bulletin, 110,* 109–128.

Foeman, A., and T. Nance. 2003. From miscegenation to multiculturalism. In K. M. Galvin and P. J. Cooper (Eds.), *Making connections: Readings in interpersonal communication (3rd ed.)* (pp. 166–170). Los Angeles, CA: Roxbury.

Frymier, A. B. 1994. The use of affinity-seeking in producing liking and learning in the classroom. *Journal of Applied Communication Research, 22,* 87–105.

Glenwick, D. S., L. A. Jason, and D. Elman. 1978. Physical attractiveness and social contact in the singles bar. *Journal of Social Psychology, 105,* 311–312.

Goode, E. 1996. Gender and courtship entitlement: Responses to personal ads. *Sex Roles, 34,* 141–168.

Harrison, A. A., and L. Saeed. 1977. Let's make a deal: An analysis of revelations and stipulations in lonely hearts advertisements. *Journal of Personality and Social Psychology, 35,* 257–264.

Hatfield, E., and S. Sprecher. 1986. *Mirror, mirror: The importance of looks in everyday life.* Albany, NY: SUNY Press.

Hebl, M. R., and T. F. Heatherton. 1998. The stigma of obesity in women: The difference is black and white. *Personality and Social Psychology Bulletin, 24,* 417–426.

Hewitt, J., and K. German. 1987. Attire and attractiveness. *Perceptual and Motor Skills, 42,* page 558.

Huston, M., and P. Schwartz. 2003. The relationships of lesbians and of gay men. In K. M. Galvin and P. J. Cooper (Eds.), *Making connections: Readings in interpersonal communication (3rd ed.)* (171–177). Los Angeles, CA: Roxbury.

Jason, L. A., A. Reichler, and W. Rucker. 1981. Characteristics of significant dating relationships: Male versus female initiators, idealized versus actual settings. *The Journal of Psychology, 109,* 185–190.

Johnson, D. F., and J. B. Pittinger. 1984. Attribution, the attractiveness stereotype, and the elderly. *Developmental Psychology, 20,* 1168–1172.

Katz, J. E., and R. E. Rice. 2002. *Social consequences of Internet use: Access, involvement and interaction.* Cambridge, MA: The MIT Press.

Kito, M. 2005. Self-disclosure in romantic relationships and friendships among American and Japanese college students. *The Journal of Social Psychology, 44,* 181–199.

Klohnen, E. C., and S. Luo. 2003. Interpersonal attraction and personality: What is attractive—self similarity, ideal similarity, complementarity, or attachment security? *Journal of Personality and Social Psychology, 85,* 709–722.

Knapp, M. L. 1978. *Social intercourse: From greeting to goodbye.* Boston: Allyn & Bacon.

Knapp, M., and A. Vangelisti. 2003. Relationship stages: A communication perspective. In K. M. Galvin and P. J. Cooper (Eds.), *Making connections: Readings in interpersonal communication (3rd ed.)* (158–165). Los Angeles, CA: Roxbury.

Kowalski, R. M. 1999. Speaking the unspeakable: Self-disclosure and mental health. In B. R. Kowalski and M. R. Leary (Eds.), *The social psychology of emotional and behavioral problems* (225–248). Washington, DC: The American Psychological Association.

Lewis, K. E., and M. Bierly. 1990. Toward a profile of the female voter: Sex differences in perceived physical attractiveness and competence of political candidates. *Sex Roles, 22,* 1–12.

Lykken, D. T., and A. Tellegen. 1993. Is human mating adventitious or the result of lawful choice? A twin study of mate selection. *Journal of Personality and Social Psychology, 65,* 56–68.

Mathes, E. W., S. M. Brennan, P. M. Haugen, and H. B. Rice. 1985. Ratings of physical attractiveness as a function of age. *The Journal of Social Psychology, 125,* 157–168.

McClellan, B., and S. J. McKelvie. 1993. Effects of age and gender on perceived physical attractiveness. *Canadian Journal of Behavioral Science, 25,* 135–142.

McCroskey, J. C., and T. A. McCain. 1974. The measurement of interpersonal attraction. *Speech Monographs, 41,* 261–266.

McCroskey, J. C., V. P. Richmond, and J. A. Daly. 1975. The development of a measure of perceived homophily in interpersonal communication. *Human Communication Research, 1,* 323–332.

McKenna, K. Y. A., A. S. Green, and M. E. J. Gleason. 2002. Relationship formation on the Internet: What's the big attraction? *Journal of Social Issues, 58,* 9–31.

Mongeau, P. A., J. L. Hale, K. L. Johnson, and J. D. Hillis. 1993. "Who's wooing whom?" An investigation of female-rinitiated dating. In P. J. Kalbfleisch (Ed.), *Interpersonal communication: Evolving interpersonal relationships* (51–68). Hillsdale, NJ: Lawrence Erlbaum.

Mongeau, P. A., M. C. M. Serewicz, and L. F. Therrien. 2004. Goals for cross-sex first dates: Identification, measurement, and the influence of contextual factors. *Communication Monographs, 71*, 121–147.

Nakanishi, M. 1986. Perceptions of self-disclosure in initial interaction: A Japanese sample. *Human Communication Research, 13*, 167–190.

Perrett, D. I., K. J. Lee, and I. Penton-Voak. 1998. Effects of sexual dimorphism on facial attractiveness, *Nature, 394*, August, 27, 884–886.

Pines, A. M. 2001. The role of gender and culture in romantic attraction. *European Psychologist, 6*, 96–102.

Richmond, V. P. 1992. *Nonverbal communication in the classroom*. Edina, MN: Burgess.

Reis, H. T., and B. C. Patrick. 1996. Attachment and intimacy: Component processes. In E. T. Higgins and A. W. Kruglanski (Eds.), *Social psychology: Handbook of basic principles* (523–563). New York: Guilford Press.

Reis, H. T., and P. Shaver. 1988. Intimacy as interpersonal process. In S. Duck (Ed.), *Handbook of personal relationships: Theory, research, and interventions* (367–389). Chichester: John Wiley & Sons Ltd.

Reis, H. T., J. Nezlek, and L. Wheeler. 1980. Physical attractiveness in social interaction. *Journal of Personality and Social Psychology, 38*, 604–617.

Segal, M. W. 1974. Alphabet and attraction: An unobtrusive measure of the effect of propinquity in a field setting. *Journal of Personality and Social Psychology, 30*, 654–657.

Sergios, P., and J. Cody. 1985. Importance of physical attractiveness and social assertiveness skills in male homosexual dating behavior and partner selection. *Journal of Homosexuality, 12*, 71–84.

Silver-Greenberg, J. 2005. Dying to know. *Newsweek, 146*, September, 11.

Snyder, M., E. Berscheid, and P. Glick. 1985. Focusing on the exterior and the interior: Two investigations of the initiation of personal relationships. *Journal of Personality and Social Psychology, 48*, 1427–1439.

Sprecher, S., and S. Hendrick. 2004. Self-disclosure in intimate relationships: Associations with individual and relationship characteristics over time. *Journal of Social and Clinical Psychology, 23*, 857–877.

Sprecher, S., Q. Sullivan, and E. Hatfield. 1994. Mate selection preferences: Gender differences examined in a national sample. *Journal of Personality and Social Psychology, 66*, 1074–1080.

Sunnafrank, M. 1986. Predicted outcome value during initial interactions: A reformulation of uncertainty reduction theory. *Human Communication Research, 13*, 3–33.

Thibaut, J., and H. Kelley. 1959. *The social psychology of groups*. New York, NY: Wiley.

Vangelisti, A. L. 2002. Interpersonal processes in romantic relationships. In M. L. Knapp and J. A. Daly (Eds.), *Handbook of interpersonal communication* (643–679). Thousand Oaks, CA: Sage.

Walster, E., V. Aronson, D. Abrahams, and L. Rottman. 1966. Importance of physical attractiveness in dating behavior. *Journal of Personality and Social Psychology, 4*, 508–516.

Wanzer, M. B. 1995. *Student affinity-seeking messages and teacher liking: Subordinate initiated relationship building in superior-subordinate dyads*. Unpublished doctoral dissertation, West Virginia University, Morgantown, WV.

Wanzer, M. B. 1998. An exploratory investigation of student and teacher perceptions of student-generated affinity-seeking behaviors. *Communication Education, 47*, 373–382.

Werner, C. M., and L. M. Haggard. 1985. Temporal qualities of interpersonal relationships. In M. L. Knapp and G. R. Miller (Eds.), *Handbook of interpersonal communication* (59–99). Beverly Hills, CA: Sage.

Wilson, G. D., J. M. Cousins, and B. Fink. 2006. The CQ as a predictor of speed-date outcomes. *Sexual and Relationship Therapy, 21*, 163–169.

Woll, S. 1986. So many to choose from: Decision strategies in video dating. *Journal of Social and Personal Relationships, 3*, 43–52.

Zebrowitz, L. A. 1997. *Reading faces: Window to the soul?* Boulder, CO: Westview Press.

Sustaining Relationships

© Kuzma, 2007, Shutterstock.

OBJECTIVES

- Discuss the four goals of relationship maintenance
- Explain the four essential components of successful relationships
- Explain equity theory and discuss how it is related to the process of relationship maintenance
- Explain the skill similarity model and relate it to the process of maintaining our relationships with others
- Describe the five most common relationship maintenance strategies
- Offer a definition of relationship maintenance
- Provide examples of additional types of relationship maintenance strategies (positive and negative) that emerge when relationship maintenance behaviors were studied in different types of relationships
- Identify the individual differences that affect relationship maintenance strategy choices
- Define CMC. Discuss the benefits and drawbacks of CMC as a means of maintaining our relationships
- Define conflict
- Identify the five key aspects of conflict episodes
- Differentiate between escalatory and de-escalatory conflict spirals
- Discuss the concept of conflict metaphors. Recognize examples of problematic conflict metaphors
- Distinguish between the three most common conflict management styles
- Describe the advantages and disadvantages for each conflict management style
- Explain the four most typical conflict responses
- Differentiate between productive and unproductive responses to conflict situations
- Identify examples of productive communication patterns that can be used during conflict episodes
- Recognize behaviors that should be avoided during conflict episodes

KEY TERMS

control mutuality
trust
liking or affinity
commitment
equity theory
skill similarity model
comforting skills
ego support
empathy
face-management
 skills
self-disclosure
relationship
 maintenance
 strategies
prosocial behaviors
ceremonial behaviors
communication
 behaviors
togetherness behaviors
positivity
openness

assurances
social networks
sharing tasks
joint activities
mediated
 communication
advice
humor
no flirting
avoidant
antisocial behaviors
computer-mediated
 communication
 (CMC)
exclusively Internet-
 based relationships
 (EIB)
primarily Internet-
 based relationships
 (PIB)
conflict
expressed struggle

interdependence
goal incompatibility
perceived shared
 resources
interference
escalatory conflict
 spirals
de-escalatory conflict
 spirals
conflict metaphors
conflict management
 styles
avoidance
competitive/distributive
collaborative/integrative
verbal aggression
exit
neglect
loyalty
voice
fair fighting

OVERVIEW

Relationships, like sharks, must constantly move forward or they will cease to exist. In Chapter Six we examined the process of initiating relationships. In this chapter we will examine how individuals maintain their relationships with others. While the process of *establishing* relationships is not without its own set of challenges, some people seem to have more trouble staying together. The difficulty in staying committed is best illustrated by the current divorce rate in the United States; approximately fifty percent of marriages will fail, and, sadly, most second marriages have an even greater chance of ending. Why is it so difficult

> *A relationship, I think, is like a shark, you know? It has to constantly move forward or it dies. And I think what we got on our hands is a dead shark.*
>
> *Annie Hall* directed by Woody Allen, 1 hr. 33 min., Rollins-Joffe Productions, 1977.

to maintain lasting relationships with others? What are some of the most effective ways to sustain our relationships? We will address these questions and take a closer look at some of the reasons it is often a struggle for individuals to maintain their romantic and platonic ties. Relationship maintenance strategies vary significantly depending on the relationship type. We use different strategies to maintain relationships with our romantic partners, friends, family members, and with colleagues at work. In this chapter we will explore the use of different strategies and examine their effect on relationship maintenance.

Computer-mediated communication, hereafter referred to as CMC, has emerged as a popular means for interacting with others. The majority of college students have access to computers. This enables them to interact with friends, roommates, romantic partners and family members via instant messaging, emails, or chat rooms. CMC is an important and frequently used means of maintaining relationships with others. In this chapter we will examine recent research that explores CMC as a means of sustaining relationships.

So what is the key indicator that a relationship is in trouble? Oftentimes it is the result of a poorly-managed conflict between relational partners. Conflict is inevitable, and in fact, all of us experience it at one time or another in our interpersonal relationships. To maintain relationships with those we care about, it is important to manage conflict appropriately. In the third section of this chapter, we present information on conflict in order to help you: (1) understand how conflict can be both good and bad in relationships, (2) approach and respond to conflict situations appropriately, and (3) consider how individual differences affect the way we manage conflict in our lives.

SIGNIFICANCE OF RELATIONSHIP MAINTENANCE

According to Steve Duck (1988), individuals involved in committed relationships spend much more time maintaining a relationship than in any other phase of the relationship. Relationship maintenance is not an easy task. It often takes a great deal of time, effort, and skill. To better understand the process of relationship maintenance, let us consider four common relationship maintenance goals as proposed by Dindia and Canary (1993). They state that individuals who are focusing on relationship maintenance have one of the following four goals in mind: (1) maintaining the existence of the relationship, (2) maintaining a desired state or condition in the relationship, (3) maintaining a satisfactory state in a relationship, or (4) repairing a relationship in an attempt to either restore it or sustain it in a satisfactory state (1993, 163). Let's consider each one of these definitions.

Maintaining the Existence of the Relationship

Have you ever had a friend whom you call only once or twice a year? Or perhaps there are friends or family members who send you an annual holiday card with a letter updating the events of the past year, and that is the only communication you have with them until the next Christmas card arrives? In both of these examples, the goal of relationship maintenance is to keep the relationship in existence, or to keep it from dying.

Maintaining a Desired State in the Relationship

The second goal, which focuses on maintaining the desired state of a relationship, can be explained by the relationship between characters in the television show *The Office*. Jim is attracted to his engaged co-worker, Pam. Rather than risk losing her friendship by revealing his true feelings, Jim communicates with Pam in "safe" ways to ensure that the current state of their relationship is maintained. This strategy of regulating the state of the relationship enables one partner to keep the relationship at a level that is satisfactory rather than dissolving the relationship altogether.

Maintaining a Satisfactory State

A third goal focuses on attempts made by both partners to maintain a level of relationship satisfaction that they find to be mutually agreeable. Depending on the type and status of the relationship, what partners define as "mutually satisfying" can differ from one relationship to the next. In the *Seinfeld* episode "The Deal," Jerry and Elaine are friends who consider engaging in a sexual relationship. In an attempt to maintain their current satisfactory relationship as friends, they agree on a set of rules that will enable them to enjoy being friends while enjoying a sexual relationship. However, Elaine soon becomes upset when Jerry gives her a birthday gift that she perceives as being insignificant. They soon discover that they are better off as friends, and they go back to the joking and sarcasm that were an essential part of their friendship in the first place. Thus, their focus is on maintaining the friendship that they both perceived as being satisfactory, abandoning their sexual relationship.

Spending time together helps friends reconnect and maintain their relationship.

© mihaicalin, 2007, Shutterstock.

Repairing a Relationship

Dindia and Canary (1993) point out that relationship maintenance is often an ongoing task. Just as you would seek routine maintenance to repair any issues that might keep your car from running smoothly, individuals engage in relationship maintenance to make sure that relationships run smoothly. Perhaps you realize that your relationship with a friend has become more distant since you started a new romantic relationship. In an attempt to maintain your friendship, you realize that you have to fix some things—namely, spend more time together and engage in more communication with one another. Dindia and Canary (1993) note that it is important to remember that some aspects of these four goals can overlap with one another. Further, they point out that a relationship can be maintained even though one or both partners find it to be unsatisfactory, and even satisfactory relationships end for a number of reasons.

WHY WE MAINTAIN SOME RELATIONSHIPS AND NOT OTHERS

So why is it that we choose to maintain some relationships and not others? There are numerous factors that are central to interpersonal communication and relationship maintenance, including: intimacy, immediacy, investment, attraction, similarity, liking, commitment, and affection (see, for example,

Burgoon and Hale 1984). Rather than providing an exhaustive list of all of the characteristics that have been identified as relevant to sustaining relationships, interpersonal scholars have narrowed the list to the four relational characteristics that are generally perceived as universal to most relationships: control mutuality, trust, liking, and commitment (Canary and Stafford 1994). Research has shown that relationships without these characteristics often lack substance, and as a result may not be able to be maintained. **Control mutuality** is defined as "the extent to which couples agree on who has the right to influence the other and establish relational goals" (Canary and Stafford 1994, 6). Relationships in which partners experience a high level of control mutuality are the result of both partners agreeing on who takes control in decision-making situations. Suppose two friends are planning a vacation to celebrate the end of the school year. If one of them is extremely organized, both friends may agree that he should be the one to plan their itinerary for the trip. Another example would be a couple agreeing that one partner should be in control of their finances since the other is not particularly savvy with money issues. **Trust** has emerged as an equally important relationship characteristic. Individuals are often reluctant to reveal information to those they do not trust, and a lack of trust in a relationship can be devastating. Recall the example of the *Friends* episode discussed in Chapter Five. Ross violated Rachel's trust when he decided to sleep with another woman on the same night that he and Rachel broke up. Regardless of the numerous apologies and promises that Ross offered, Rachel declared that she could no longer trust him and, as a result, they were unable to maintain their relationship. Another characteristic required for sustaining a relationship is **liking**, or **affinity**. Mutual liking, or expressed affect, is a universal feature of relationships. We prefer to be around individuals who know and like us. Not surprisingly, it is often very difficult for us to say no to requests that come from individuals we like (Cialdini 2003). Sometimes a friend or family member asks you for a favor and you really are too busy to help, but you do so anyway. You accept their request because you like them and want to maintain a pleasant relationship. A fourth and final characteristic of successful relationships is **commitment**, which refers to our desire to continue a relationship. When we say we are committed to a relationship, this is usually interpreted to mean that we are in it "for the long haul" and "for better or for worse." While commitment is important in romantic relationships for obvious reasons, it is also relevant to familial and platonic relationships. Can you remember a time when you became upset or frustrated because you felt that you were more committed to maintaining a friendship or family relationship than the other person? Commitment, trust, control mutuality and liking are characteristics that most of us desire in our communication and relationships.

In addition to understanding these relational characteristics, it is also important to recognize the theoretical explanations for why we choose to maintain relationships. **Equity theory** offers perhaps one of the most widely understood explanations for why some individuals engage in relationship maintenance activity and others do not (Canary and Stafford 1992, 2001). According to this theory, a relationship is considered equitable when the ratio of inputs to outputs is equal for both individuals involved. If, for example,

Committed relationships are in it "for the long haul."

you contribute more inputs compared to the outputs you receive from your partner, you will feel underbenefited in the relationship, possibly resulting in anger at getting less than you deserve. In the movie *The Break Up*, the character Brooke (Jennifer Aniston) becomes frustrated when her boyfriend, Gary (Vince Vaughn), spends more time watching television and playing video games than with helping her do various household chores. Her frustration with the inequity in their relationship becomes apparent toward the end of the movie when Brooke lists for Gary all the things that she has contributed to the relationship. Surprisingly, she states that she does not expect him to contribute equally to the relationship, but simply wishes that he would recognize the effort that she has made. Conversely, if your output to input ratio is greater than that of your relationship partner, then you will feel overbenefited. Some of you may wonder why those who are overbenefited in relationships report feeling dissatisfied. Is it possible that individuals who receive too much attention, affection, or gifts could possibly be unhappy in a relationship? Absolutely! Overbenefited individuals may be less satisfied in their relationships because they feel guilty about not contributing equally to the relationship. Can you recall a time when you felt guilty because you were not dedicating as much effort to a relationship as the other person? Perhaps you have a friend who is always the one who calls or writes. Eventually, you may feel so guilty that you fail to return their phone calls or email messages because you have failed at contributing equally to the relationship.

If we rank, in order, the level of satisfaction experienced in relationships, it is not surprising that partners who are in equitable relationships report the greatest level of satisfaction. Those who feel overbenefited are the next most satisfied, and the least satisfied individuals are those who report feeling underbenefited. Consider these questions: Are relationships perceived as equitable because both partners engage in relationship maintenance strategies equally? Or do relationship partners who already perceive their relationships as equitable engage in more maintenance behaviors? Researchers Dan Canary and Laura Stafford (2001) argue that individuals in equitable relationships are more likely to use relationship maintenance behaviors than those involved in a relationship that is perceived to be inequitable.

HOW WE MAINTAIN RELATIONSHIPS: THE ROLE OF COMMUNICATION

Now that you have a better understanding of the four relational characteristics associated with maintenance and the role that theory plays in explaining why we choose to sustain relationships, let us examine how we use communication to maintain our relationships.

Brant Burleson and Wendy Samter (1994) emphasize the importance of similarity in communication skills in maintaining relationships. They state, "similarity in the nature and level of partners' social skills may be more important to relationship maintenance than the absolute level of skill sophistication of the partners" (62). They propose a **skill similarity model** that portrays relationship maintenance as a process requiring the involvement of both partners. In particular, they note that while what one individual does for another is important, it is also necessary to examine what the partners do with one another. Consider the married couple whose lives have become so consumed with their children's activities that they fail to spend time alone. Perhaps they constantly do favors for one another to ensure that they can maintain their busy schedules, and they possibly even text message each other throughout the day. Eventually, they may discover that while they do things for each other, the lack of quality time with one another puts a strain on the relationship.

How do you comfort those who are close to you?

Burleson and Samter (1994) also argue that maintaining relationships with others is a skill that typically involves mastery of specific types of communication. Those who are able to master the communication skills that are viewed as valuable in a relationship are more likely to experience success. One communication skill that is valuable is labeled **comforting skill**, which is the ability to reduce another's emotional distress. Comforting can be communicated verbally ("I completely understand why you're so upset about this!") or via nonverbal channels, such as with a hug or an encouraging look. Another communication skill that is essential to relationship maintenance is **ego support**, which is described as the ability to make others feel positive about themselves. **Empathy** involves the ability to see things from the other person's point of view. Employing empathy communicates to others that their perspective is important in maintaining the relationship. Consider the relationship in which one partner is devoted to his religious beliefs, but the other partner may not have been raised to value religion. By respecting one another's differences in values and beliefs, maintenance is achieved. Perhaps they agree to attend church services together for particular events, and also agree not to force their beliefs on one another. **Face-management skills** are an essential part of relationship maintenance. In an earlier chapter, we defined face as one's self-perception that one wishes to present when interacting with others. Avoiding communication that could be perceived as face-threatening can strengthen a relationship. Examples of communication facework include: being polite, avoiding topics that could potentially cause embarrassment to another, and using disclaimers to help manage the other's perception of self (e.g., "I know I may be crazy to think that this means that you don't care …"). A final skill that is important to sustain relationships is **self-disclosure**. By engaging in appropriate disclosure and sharing our thoughts and feelings, we contribute an element that is valuable to the future of the relationship. Take a moment to consider your own relationships. Think about the role that each of these communication skills plays in their maintenance, and consider how different your relationship would be if the other person ceased to engage in these behaviors. Next, we will explore specific strategies that are necessary to help keep relationships going.

RELATIONSHIP MAINTENANCE STRATEGIES

When relationships possess the four qualities discussed earlier (control mutuality, trust, liking, and commitment) and are perceived as rewarding and equitable, individuals will seek out various ways to maintain these connections.

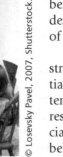

A big Sunday dinner is one ceremonial behavior for many families.

Because our relationships cannot sustain themselves, it is up to us to engage in behaviors that will prolong them. **Relationship maintenance strategies** are defined as the behaviors and activities used strategically "to sustain desired relational qualities or to sustain the current status of the relationship" (Canary and Stafford 2001, 134).

What are the most common relationship maintenance strategies that people use? Dindia and Baxter (1987) initially identified forty-nine different relationship maintenance strategies used by married couples. With these results they identified four categories of strategies: prosocial behaviors, ceremonial behaviors, communication behaviors and togetherness behaviors. **Prosocial behaviors** include being polite and cooperative in the relationship, while avoiding face-threatening communication. Recognizing the importance of rituals in sustaining relationships is the focus of **ceremonial behaviors**. Sharing Sunday dinner at Grandma's house, saying prayers with the children before going to bed every night, and bringing your friend her favorite Dairy Queen ice cream cake every year to celebrate her birthday are all examples of ceremonial behaviors. **Communication behaviors** involve the exchange of open and honest information. Telling your significant other that his or her recent behavior has disappointed you, or sending a text message to a friend when you hear a song that reminds you of the fun you had on summer vacation are examples of behaviors that sustain relationships. Finally, partners expect one another to dedicate time and energy to **togetherness behaviors** as a strategy of relationship maintenance. Watching a favorite television show together or sharing a cup of coffee while you catch up on one another's activities are examples of togetherness.

Researchers Laura Stafford and Dan Canary (1991) examined all of the studies that had focused on how partners maintain relationships, and identified the five most common types of relationship maintenance strategies: positivity, openness, assurances, social networks, and sharing tasks. **Positivity** involves being polite, acting cheerful and upbeat, and avoiding criticism. Is it not easier to maintain a relationship with someone who has a positive outlook on life and on the relationship than with someone who is always pessimistic? **Openness** refers to the open and ongoing discussions that partners have about the status of the relationship. When individuals employ openness, they share their thoughts and feelings about the relationship. **Assurances** refer to the expression of love and commitment as well as making references to the future of the relationship. Relationship partners also sustain relationships by spending time with the mutual friends and family members who create a **social network**. The fifth and final strategy, **sharing tasks**, focuses on the extent to which partners share the chores and responsibilities associated with the relationship. Depending on the type of relationship, these tasks could include sharing responsibility for exchanging emails or phone calls, or allotting household tasks. Recall our earlier example of the frustration experienced by Brooke and Gary in *The Break Up*. In one scene, Brooke is cleaning dishes after a dinner party while Gary plays PlayStation and "unwinds." When Brooke becomes frustrated, Gary points out that she said that she does not want him to help with the dishes. Brooke replies that she wants him to want to help with

Sharing different household tasks helps maintain a relationship.

the dishes—thus the role of sharing tasks becomes apparent to the maintenance of their relationship.

Since Stafford and Canary's initial investigation, there have been a number of follow-up studies exploring relationship maintenance strategies employed in a variety of relationships. For example, researchers have examined relationship maintenance in married adults (Dainton and Stafford 1993; Dainton and Aylor 2002; Ragsdale 1996), in gay and lesbian relationships (Haas and Stafford 1998), in dating couples (Dainton and Aylor 2002), in same sex (Canary et al. 1993) and cross-sex friendships (Messman, Canary, and Hause 2000) and in family relationships (Canary et al. 1993; Myers 2001; Myers and Weber 2004). Once researchers began investigating the use of maintenance strategies in the various types of relationships listed above, it became apparent that there were a number of taxonomies, or ways of classifying, relationship maintenance behaviors.

At this point, you will probably be happy to know that we are not going to cover all of the relationship maintenance strategies that exist. However, we will provide a brief overview of some of the additional maintenance strategies individuals might use with friends, romantic partners, family members, or coworkers such as: joint activities, mediated communication, advice, humor, no flirting, avoidance and antisocial behaviors (Canary et al. 1993). **Joint activities** refer to those behaviors relationship partners do together: "hanging out" with one another, watching television together, and going on trips with each other. Later in this chapter we will address the role that **mediated communication** plays in sustaining relationships. These behaviors include the exchange of email messages, letters, text messages, or phone calls to ensure a satisfying relationship. **Advice** typically involves disclosing personal information to the relationship partner or giving or seeking advice on some issue. **Humor** is also sometimes used as a means of maintaining relationships and might include the use of jokes and sarcasm in either positive or negative ways. A positive example of using humor would be "trying to make each other laugh," (Canary et al. 1993, 11) while a negative example of using humor might include being sarcastic or making fun of someone's appearance or personality.

Interestingly, there are also strategies individuals use to reduce the amount of intimacy in a relationship. One such strategy is labeled **no flirting** and includes behaviors such as "avoid flirting with him/her." Why do you believe this would be included under maintenance? The authors suggest that by not encouraging "overly familiar behaviors" we are able to help maintain relationships. How do you believe this works? The relationship maintenance strategies labeled avoidance and antisocial behaviors would initially appear to be antithetical to prolonging any type of relationship. When do individuals employ these types of "maintenance" behaviors? Strategies labeled **avoidant** include avoidance of "sore," or difficult, subjects that we should avoid discussing with our romantic partners, family members or friends, to steer clear of conflict. To maintain the quality of a relationship and, at the same time, preserve a sense of autonomy, it might also be necessary to establish times when we are away from our partners. Hence, relationship partners might have a "girls' night" or "boys' night" out. Partners also engage in either direct or indirect **antisocial behaviors**, which are described as behaviors which might seem unfriendly or coercive (Canary et al. 1993). To gain a relationship partner's attention or to signal that something is wrong in the relationship, one partner might act moody or difficult (indirect strategy) to gain the other person's attention. (Recall Brooke's behavior in *The Break Up*.) Olsen's (2002) research indicates that individuals might use verbally aggressive messages during conflict episodes to indicate that there is a significant relationship problem. Canary and his colleagues would describe this strategic use of aggressive communication as an antisocial behavior. Similarly, relationship partners might try to be more direct in their antisocial behaviors by being rude or mean to their partners' friends or family. These strategies may reduce the amount of closeness between relationship partners temporarily, and habitual use of these strategies might be detrimental to a relationship. However, for some individuals, avoidant and antisocial behaviors are perceived as valid ways of maintaining the relationship's health (Canary et al. 1993). See Table 8.1 for additional examples of relationship maintenance strategies.

As relationship partners become more connected, or interdependent, the use of relationship maintenance strategies generally increases (Canary and Stafford 2001). Not surprisingly, decreases in relationship maintenance behaviors by one or both partners often signals that a relationship is in trouble (Ayres 1983). Canary and Stafford's (1994) research indicates that the "use of positivity, sharing tasks, and offering assurance help sustain control mutuality, trust, liking and

Table 8.1   Relationship Maintenance Strategies

Strategy	Examples
1. Positivity	Engage in cheerful communication; Ask "How was your day?"
2. Openness	Solicit discussion on status of relationship; Ask partner to share feelings about the relationship
3. Assurances	Emphasize commitment to one another; Say "I love you" to one another
4. Social network	Express interest in spending time with mutual friends; Focus on building friendships that are mutual/shared
5. Sharing tasks	Help partner with various tasks, or household chores such as cooking and cleaning
6. Joint activities	Spend time hanging out with one another Go to the movies, football game, dinner
7. Mediated communication	Use email to communicate Call partner on the phone Send partner a card
8. Avoidance	Avoid talking about certain issues Avoid the relationship partner
9. Antisocial behaviors	Be mean or rude to him/her Act moody when around him/her
10. Humor	Call him/her a funny or silly name Use sarcasm when communicating
11. No flirting	Do not flirt with him/her Do not show any sign of romantic interest
12. Advice	Give/seek advice on variety of issues (e.g., love, relationships, school, future)

Source: Adapted from Canary and Stafford 1994; 1992; 2001, Canary et al. 1993; Messman et al. 2000.

commitment" (19). They also note that not all relationships will benefit equally from the use of these five strategies (positivity, assurances, etc.). Thus, it is important to examine research that summarizes how these strategies function in different types of relationships, paying special attention to the outcomes of their use.

RELATIONSHIP MAINTENANCE IN DIFFERENT TYPES OF RELATIONSHIPS

Are the tactics, or behaviors, that you use to maintain your friendships different from those you use to sustain your relationship with your romantic partner? They probably are. Researchers found that the use of relationship maintenance strategies differs depending on relationship type. While there is a vast amount of research available on relationship maintenance in different types of relationships, we will overview a small portion of it to understand how the frequency of relationship maintenance strategy use varies in different relationships. We also discuss the outcomes associated with the use of these strategies.

Relationship maintenance has been studied extensively in different types of romantic relationships (see, for example, Canary and Stafford 1992; 1993; Dainton 2000; Dainton and Stafford 1993). Researchers have investigated how relationship maintenance strategies differ based on (1) relationship length, (2) type of commitment, e.g., married or dating, (3) cultural differences, and (4) sexual preferences. Romantic partners use relationship maintenance strategies (e.g., positivity, openness, assurances, sharing tasks and cards/letters) more than friends (Canary et al. 1993). This finding is not particularly surprising since most of us put more energy into maintaining our romantic relationships. In another related study on married couples' use of relationship maintenance strategies, researchers found that married couples' use of relationship maintenance behaviors decreased over time (Dindia and Baxter 1987; Ragsdale 1996). Additionally, the use of relationship maintenance strategies in romantic relationships tends to become more routine and less strategic over time. In essence, we become comfortable with our partner and fall into a routine in which we use the same behaviors that have been proven to work in the past. In newer relationships, partners usually have to devote more time and energy to thinking about how they will strategically use assurances, positivity, or even openness as a means of stabilizing their relationship. Conversely, for individuals in long-term relationships, the use of these behaviors becomes part of the daily routine and is not something partners are always cognizant of doing. One example of this is the routine expression of affection through phrases such as "I love you." The husband of one of your authors routinely ends every phone conversation with her by stating, "Love you!" This phrase became such a routine part of their conversations that he inadvertently used it by mistake with a colleague at work. As he waited to leave a voicemail for the colleague, he thought about phoning his wife to discuss dinner plans. After the beep he left his message for the colleague, and absent-mindedly said, "Love you!" before hanging up. He quickly called back to leave a follow-up message explaining his behavior.

© Simone van den Berg, 2007, Shutterstock.

Do you think this couple's relationship has become routine?

Are some strategies more effective than others? It depends on the type of relationship and the individuals involved. Relationship partners' use of assurances has been linked repeatedly to relationship satisfaction and commitment (Dainton and Aylor 2002; Stafford and Canary 1991). There are very few of us who do not like to hear our relationship partner say, "I love you." When comparing relationship maintenance behaviors of married couples to dating couples, married partners use more assurances and social networks, while dating couples engage in more openness (Stafford and Canary 1991). Because partners in dating relationships are still getting to know one another, individuals must be more open and willing to share information with one another for the relationship to move from the experimenting to the intensifying stage of relationship development.

Is it possible that culture plays a role in the types of relational maintenance strategies we employ? If you answered yes to this question, then you are correct. When comparing impact of culture for marital partners, African American couples indicated using task-sharing as a maintenance strategy less often than European American couples (Diggs and Stafford 1998). Researchers explain this result by pointing out that, generally, African American males and females tend to be more focused on adopting egalitarian roles in their relationship when compared to their European American counterparts. The researchers speculate that task-sharing might be discussed more frequently by European American couples because they have struggled historically with creating more equity in their romantic relationships. This study illustrates that partners' individual differences, which might include factors such as culture, personality, age, or even maturity, may also affect the types of relationship maintenance strategies used.

In an attempt to examine strategies used by gay and lesbian couples, Haas and Stafford (1998) discovered that heterosexual and homosexual couples employ many of the same strategies in their relationships. Two strategies that are unique to gay and lesbian relationships include (1) being "out" as a couple when communicating with their social networks, and (2) seeking out social environments that are supportive of gay and lesbian relationships. Additional research by Eldridge and Gilbert (1990) points to the importance of perceived equity in relational power and high levels of emotional intimacy in enhancing relationship satisfaction in lesbian relationships. Gay men indicate a preference for low levels of conflict and high levels of cooperation as factors that help maintain a satisfying relationship (Jones and Bates 1978).

Relationship maintenance has also been studied in different types of platonic relationships. For example, in opposite sex friendships, partners might see potential for romantic connection but want to keep the relationship platonic. In such a situation, individuals employ maintenance behaviors strategically in order to stay friends. More specifically, research by Messman, Canary and Hause (2000) indicates that opposite sex friends frequently employ the strategies of giving/seeking advice, assurances, positivity, cards/letters, sharing activities, and openness in an effort to stay friends. One surprising finding was that opposite sex friends were least likely to use the strategies labeled no flirting and avoidance. When opposite sex friends flirted with one another, they often did so in a teasing and non-sexual way to send the message that the relationship was a platonic one. The researchers also noted that opposite sex friends seem to use strategies that express support and acceptance of one another (Messman et al. 2000).

More recently, researchers investigated relationship maintenance in family contexts. Scott Myers (2001) studied how siblings use maintenance strategies with a specific focus on the relationship between use of maintenance behaviors and sibling liking. Myers asked 257 college students to indicate how often they used the relationship maintenance strategies of positivity, openness, sharing tasks, assurances and networks with their siblings. Students indicated that sharing tasks was used the most often and openness was used the least. Additionally, this study explored potential differences in male and female sibling use of relationship maintenance behaviors. Myers found that female siblings engaged in relationship maintenance behaviors more often than either cross-sex or male dyads. He also noted that, in general, women often report feeling closer to their siblings and receiving more affection and intimacy in their sibling relationships. In a study examining the maintenance strategies employed by fathers and daughters, 250 college women and their fathers completed a survey asking them to indicate the degree to which they use various maintenance strategies (Punyanunt-Carter 2006). Results indicated that fathers are more likely than their daughters to use various maintenance strategies, with the exception of social networks.

As researchers continue to explore the different ways that partners attempt to sustain a variety of relationships, they are also turning their attention to the increasing role that technology is playing in how people maintain these associations.

COMPUTER-MEDIATED COMMUNICATION AS A MEANS OF MAINTAINING RELATIONSHIPS

Consider this—if you use email or chat programs such as AOL or instant messenger to communicate regularly with family members, friends, co-workers or a romantic partner, you are using one of the relationship maintenance strategies discussed earlier in this chapter—**computer-mediated communication (CMC)**. Not surprisingly, many Americans use CMC to meet new people or to sustain current relationships. In fact, a recent study found that nearly ninety million Americans engage in communication with others through an online group or social network (Fox et al. 2001). Among those using the Internet as a channel for interaction, the majority felt that it was a useful way to establish new connections and maintain current relationships (Fox et al. 2001). From a communication perspective, it is important to examine how CMC differs from traditional face-to-face interaction and to consider both the benefits and drawbacks of CMC.

Why has CMC become more popular as a means of establishing and maintaining relationships with others? First and foremost, more people have access to computers today and use them regularly for a variety of purposes. Also, because individuals spend more time on their computers for work or school, they also use them as a means of forming new relationships and maintaining their current ones. For individuals in established relationships who want to communicate with friends, family members and relationship partners, CMC is often less expensive and time-consuming than using the telephone or writing letters. Features of CMC which can affect interpersonal perceptions and, at

How might this conversation be different via CMC rather than in person?

the same time, alter the communication process include: limited access to nonverbal behaviors, delayed feedback, and editing ability. With CMC, there is limited exposure to nonverbal cues which shed additional insight as to the true meaning of a message. Can you recall a time when you perceived someone as being angry with you simply because his email response was short and to the point? The lack of nonverbal cues may cause you to misperceive the fact that he was in a hurry and wanted to send a quick response. Because of the asynchronous nature of email, individuals have time to formulate messages and respond to incoming messages at their own convenience. In addition, individuals who use email or chat programs can edit their messages before sending them, unlike live communication.

A benefit of CMC is that it is often used to sustain long-distance relationships. The number of individuals in long distance relationships (LDR) has been steadily climbing over the years (Rohlfing 1995). For college students who might be struggling financially, email and chat programs are a relatively inexpensive means of communicating regularly with one's long-distance relationship partner. Individuals in LDRs can use CMC as a means of communicating many of the relationship maintenance behaviors identified in this chapter—positivity, assurances, and even openness.

While the majority of relationship maintenance research conducted thus far examines the use of these strategies in face-to-face relationships, researcher Kevin Wright studied the use of relational maintenance strategies in different types of Internet relationships. Wright investigated the use of online relational maintenance strategies of college students in exclusively Internet-based and primarily Internet-based relationships (2004). "**Exclusively Internet-based (EIB) relationships** refer to relationships that are developed without any face-to-face interaction or interaction through traditional media, such as the telephone, letters, etc." (Wright 2004, 239). Conversely, **primarily Internet-based (PIB) relationships** may initially be formed online or through face-to-face interaction, could include acquaintances, friends, co-workers, or family members and often communicate through emails or instant messaging. While PIB relationships are more common than EIB relationships, the number of EIB relationships has increased dramatically as more Americans use the Internet to establish relationships.

To study differences in relationship maintenance behaviors in different types of online relationships, Wright surveyed 178 undergraduate students and asked them to report on their perceptions of the quality of communication that occurred online, frequency of relationship maintenance strategies, and type of online relationship. He found that openness and positivity were the most frequently used strategies in both EIB and PIB relationships. These strategies might be used more frequently because they are easier to employ over the Internet, or because they are perceived as more effective than other strategies (Wright 2004). Interestingly, Wright also found that individuals in EIB and PIB types of relationships did not differ significantly in the types of relationship maintenance behaviors they used. He indicates that it is difficult to tell whether individuals in these types of relationships actually prefer to use the same strategies to sustain their relationships. Perhaps, he says, the computer hinders individuals from using certain strategies online. This exploratory investigation illustrates the increased popularity of CMC as a means of sustaining interpersonal relationships.

CONCLUSIONS ABOUT RELATIONSHIP MAINTENANCE

There is an extensive body of research on strategic and routine relationship maintenance behaviors. Below, we highlight a number of significant conclusions from the relationship maintenance literature.

- Relationships are not self-sustaining and, as such, require a significant amount of time and effort.
- Individuals are most motivated to maintain relationships in which partners exhibit high amounts of trust, commitment, control mutuality and liking.
- Most individuals want to be in relationships that are perceived as equitable (inputs=outputs).
- Both routine and strategic relationship maintenance behaviors are used most frequently in equitable relationships.
- Five relationship maintenance strategies are used consistently regardless of the type of relationship, or whether the interactants communicate face-to-face or online: positivity, assurances, openness, sharing tasks, and social networks.
- Individual's use of assurances, networks and sharing tasks are consistently recognized as significant predictors of relationship commitment.
- When researchers further examined relationship maintenance behaviors in other types of relationships, additional strategies emerged, including, among others: humor, avoidance, antisocial behaviors, CMC, advice, conflict management.
- Effectiveness and frequency of strategy use depends on the type of relationship being investigated.
- Female siblings use more relationship maintenance strategies with one another than male siblings and male-female siblings.
- Individual differences such as culture affect the types of strategies used in relationships.

CONFLICT: A NATURAL COMPONENT OF ALL RELATIONSHIPS

The key to sustaining our relationships often rests in our ability to manage the conflicts that arise from time to time. To maintain stability in our relationships, it is necessary to manage conflict appropriately. Many relationship scholars have identified conflict management as an important maintenance behavior. Have you ever heard someone say, "We get along perfectly and agree on everything?" Chances are that the person wants to create a positive image of the relationship. The truth is that conflict is an inherent component of all relationships. Denying the presence of conflict in a relationship does not always indicate that the relationship is a healthy one. While our initial tendency is to view conflict as the ugly three-headed monster that destroys relationships, we need to take a step back and consider the benefits of conflict for both individuals and relationships. In the following sections we take a closer look at what conflict is, how it can be both productive and unproductive for individuals and relationships, and ways it can be effectively managed.

Definition of Conflict

Watch one episode of *Everybody Loves Raymond*, and, chances are, you will see conflict in action. But as you learn more about the characters on the show and their relationships with one another, you will soon understand that they are able to maintain the status of their relationships as a result of their ability to manage their disagreements. Regardless of whether disagreements occur between two co-workers, between husband and wife, or between two neighbors, there are aspects that all conflict episodes share. A number of definitions for conflict exist in the literature; however, we want to focus on one that approaches conflict from a communication perspective. Hocker and Wilmot (1991) define **conflict** as "an expressed struggle between at least two interdependent parties who perceive incompatible goals, scarce resources, and interference from the other party in achieving their goals" (12). To understand how and why conflict occurs, it is important to examine the main components of this definition in detail. There are five consistent aspects, or components, of conflict episodes, as listed below.

- Conflict involves an *expressed struggle*.
- Conflict parties are *interdependent*.
- Conflict parties perceive *incompatible goals*.
- Conflict parties *perceive shared resources*.
- Conflict parties perceive *interference* from one another in achieving goals.

Expressed Struggle.   The first consistent component of conflict is that it typically involves **expressed struggle** or open communication about the issue or problem. How do we know if a conflict with a friend, co-worker, or family member is really a conflict? From an interpersonal communication perspective, it is important to consider the communicative interchanges that make up the conflict episode (Hocker and Wilmot 1991).

Consider this dialogue between two roommates, Molly and Tiona:

Molly: Hey Tiona, do you want to go and get some coffee after you're done studying?

Tiona: No, thanks *(Makes no eye contact, stares at her book)*.

Molly: Is something wrong, you seem a little annoyed? I thought you said you wanted to go and get coffee later this evening?

Tiona: I did, but now I don't.

Molly: Fine, don't tell me what is wrong!

Do you think both roommates are aware that there is a problem? It is no wonder that Molly is confused! This example illustrates the importance of expressing conflict openly. When there are joint communicative representations of conflict, that is, both partners openly express their concerns or emotions, we typically say that conflict has occurred. Some individuals might feel angry or frustrated with a relationship partner but choose not to express their concerns openly. Once people openly communicate their feelings or concerns with their relationship partners, interpersonal conflict has occurred. Interpersonal communication scholars agree that communication is an essential element in all interpersonal conflict. Additionally, they stress that communication both affects, and is affected by, aspects of relationships (Canary, Cupach, and Messman 1995; Hocker and Wilmot 1991).

Interdependence.   The second key element of conflict addresses the significance of partner **interdependence**. Stated simply, if individuals rely on one another and are aware of how their decisions or behaviors affect one another, they are more likely to experience conflict than individuals who do not rely on one another. For example, on *Everybody Loves Raymond*, Debra often gets upset with her mother-in-law, Marie, for her critical comments regarding Debra's parenting style and housekeeping abilities. But Debra realizes that Marie is an important part of her husband and children's lives, and deep down she probably seeks Marie's approval. The interdependence between Debra and Marie makes it more likely that they will engage in conflict over these critical comments. If a stranger were to make the same comments, it probably would not matter to Debra. The more interdependent relationship partners are, the greater the chances are for conflict to occur (Braiker and Kelley 1979).

Goal Incompatibility.   A third factor of conflict is **goal incompatibility**. According to Hocker and Wilmot (1991) people are most likely to "engage in conflict over goals they often deny as being important to them" (17). All of us, at one time or another, will experience opposition in trying to reach a goal. Hocker and Wilmot describe two common types of goal incompatibility that can lead to conflict. One type of goal incompatibility occurs when relationship partners want the same thing. Think about two basketball players who are both competing for the same position on the team or two employees who are both contending for the same position in a company. Another type of goal incompatibility occurs when two individuals want different things. Recall the last time you and your relationship partner disagreed on the restaurant you would go to for dinner. How long did you argue about this? Do you remember how you finally decided where you would eat? Sometimes conflict is about actual differences in restaurant choices while other times it is about who gets to choose the restaurant. Whether individuals perceive their goals as similar or different, perceived incompatibility in objectives is a consistent aspect of conflict episodes (Hocker and Wilmot 1991).

Perceived Shared Resources.   A fourth component of conflict is **perceived shared resources**. Resources refer to anything that an individual identifies as valuable or meaningful and can include, among other things: people, relationships, opportunities, material objects, or time. Hocker and Wilmot (1991) point out that "The resources might be real or perceived as real by the person. Likewise, the perception of scarcity, or limitation, may be apparent or actual" (19). This is illustrated when an only child protests the addition of another sibling in the family and argues that the parents cannot possibly have enough love to go around for both children. Conflict experts say the best route to take in this situation is to try to change the child's perception of the available resource by assuring the child that there is more than enough love available for two children. Most interpersonal struggles revolve around perceived scarcity in power and self-esteem. As illustrated in the example above, the child was worried about receiving confirmation from the parents that would directly affect his or her self-esteem. Not surprisingly, when people fight or disagree, they often express sentiments which illustrate power and self-esteem struggles (Hocker and Wilmot 1991).

Interference.   The fifth and final component of conflict is **interference**. Is it possible for individuals who depend on one another and perceive incompatible goals and resources to not experience conflict? Yes it is. Hocker and Wilmot (1991) point out that even when incompatible goals and limited resources are present, individuals must perceive interference from the other in their attempt to achieve a goal. As soon as someone interferes with, or blocks, your goals, it is likely that you will experience conflict. In the *Home Improvement* episode "Back in the Saddle Shoes," Jill decides to go back to college and pursue her master's degree in counseling. Tim is less than supportive of the idea and actually presents arguments for why Jill should not go back to school. His attempts to interfere with Jill's goal of pursuing her degree lead to conflict. Eventually the truth comes out—Tim is afraid that Jill will fall for a more intelligent man if she goes back to school. When we feel like someone is trying to stand in our way of accomplishing a goal, conflict is likely to emerge.

Remember, in order for conflict to occur between individuals, the following criteria must be evident: (1) differences must be expressed openly and recognized by both partners, (2) partners must be interdependent, (3) partners must have incompatible goals, (4) partners must perceive competition for scarce resources, and (5) partners must perceive interference in goal achievement. Next, we examine how conflict can be beneficial or detrimental to maintaining stability in a relationship.

CONFLICT CAN BE PRODUCTIVE OR UNPRODUCTIVE IN RELATIONSHIPS

Depending upon how it is managed in interpersonal relationships, conflict can be productive or unproductive. When conflict is managed effectively, it can be good for both the relationship and the individuals involved. First, to establish meaningful relationships with others and survive in a social world, you must understand both the role of emotions (both your own and others') and the social and cultural norms for conflict situations. By doing so, conflict actually becomes an important part of your personal development and growth. A second benefit of experiencing and managing conflict in interpersonal relationships is that it tests the strength and character of relationships more vigorously than other types of social interaction (Canary, Cupach and Messman 1995).

When couples learn how to manage conflict effectively, they can strengthen their bond with one another and increase relationship satisfaction. Hence, individuals involved in the most rewarding relationships are able to manage conflict by using productive communication practices. For example, couples who manage conflict effectively and report higher relationship satisfaction refrain from aggression and focus more on confrontational (Cahn 1992) and collaborative communication (Sillars and Wilmot 1994).

Another way that conflict can be good for individuals is that it exposes them to different perspectives. For example, think about the last time you and your roommate argued about politics, religion, or even your favorite band. The process of actively disagreeing with another person can be personally beneficial because it exposes us to views that are different from our own. When we encounter views or perspectives that are different from ours, we usually re-examine our perspectives and reflect on why we feel or think a certain way in order to defend our views. This process of self-reflection can help individuals to either (1) develop a better understanding of their current perspective, or (2) develop a new perspective linked to the interaction with the relationship partner. Conflict can benefit individuals and relationships in a number of different ways.

When is conflict unproductive or destructive for individuals and relationships? Conflicts are typically described as unproductive, or destructive, when individuals walk away feeling frustrated or cheated by the end result. One type of destructive conflict is known as **escalatory conflict spirals**. This type of conflict is "characterized by a heavy reliance on overt power manipulation, threats, coercion and deception" (Hocker and Wilmot 1991, 34). In escalatory spirals, the conflict intensifies each time individuals communicate with one another and the conflict escalates with more destructive communication occurring each time individuals encounter each other. Individuals might also engage in unfair fighting tactics and make attempts to "get even" with one another. If you have ever watched the movie *War of the Roses*, you may recall how Oliver Rose and his wife, Barbara, focus all of their energy on increasing the intensity of the conflict surrounding their divorce. Each conflict episode builds on previous ones. At one point in the movie, Barbara decides she wants to start her own catering business. She asks Oliver to review a contract, which he berates and uses to swat a fly. Annoyed by his response, Barbara gets back at him by turning on all the appliances while Oliver is on the phone with an important client. Even their nonverbal behaviors indicate the escalating conflict experience in their relationship—during dinner they are relatively silent, but their body language speaks volumes.

When it comes to conflict situations, not everyone likes to fight it out. Rather than fight, some individuals might engage in **de-escalatory conflict spirals** that often involve flight responses (Hocker and Wilmot 1991). Some individuals avoid volatile situations and instead adopt withdrawal types of behaviors. Why do individuals avoid or withdraw from conflict situations? As we stated earlier in this section, individuals who are highly interdependent are more likely to experience conflict. Conversely, individuals who are not dependent on one another are less likely to engage in conflict. Perhaps relationship partners become bored with one another, apathetic about the relationship, or experience other problems in their relationship. If this is the case, then individuals might lose faith in the relationship, withdraw from interaction, and invest less time and effort into maintaining the relationship. Conflict in escalatory spirals is overt while conflict in de-escalatory spirals is covert. Individuals might avoid one another, or, when confronted, deny that there is a problem. When conflict is not out in the open, it cannot be addressed or managed. Thus, expressing conflict in a covert or indirect way is clearly unproductive.

TALKING ABOUT CONFLICT

The only way to improve conflict situations is to examine how we approach and communicate about them. Individuals often have difficulty managing conflict productively or collaboratively because they tend to think and talk about conflict in negative ways. People often talk about conflict using metaphors. What are some **conflict metaphors**? Examples would be using words like "explosive" or "a war" when describing the conflict process. Using these terms affects individuals' perceptions of conflict as well as their behaviors during conflict situations. Other negative metaphors used to describe conflict processes are: "conflict is a trial," "conflict is an upward struggle," "conflict is a mess," and "conflict is a game" (where one person is the winner and the other is the loser). All of these metaphors are problematic because they foster negative images of conflict, preventing people from collaborating, or working together, to manage difficult situations.

Hocker and Wilmot encourage individuals to use more positive terms to describe conflict to facilitate collaboration among individuals. For example, they suggest describing conflict as "a bargaining table," "a dance," "a balance," or a "tide." Talking about conflict using the more positive labels is productive because they emphasize collaboration among participants. Ideally, an individual will formulate the same productive images of conflict and approach conflict in the same way as the other individual involved. Thus, if you and your roommate both view conflict as a "balancing act," you recognize how important it is for the two of you to work together and keep your eye on the goal. If, however, you view conflict as a balancing act and your roommate views it as "war," you may not be able to work collaboratively toward a common goal.

CONFLICT MANAGEMENT STYLES

So if conflict can actually be healthy and productive in relationships, what are some ways to ensure that we are effective in managing it? Researchers have identified a variety of strategies that are used by individuals. The strategies can be pictured placed on a continuum, with violence at one end and collaboration at the other (Hocker and Wilmot 1991). When a conflict occurs, individuals typically decide whether they will avoid or confront it. Essentially, we make a decision to adopt various **conflict management styles** or habitual responses to conflict situations. The three most common conflict management styles individuals use to manage conflict are labeled: avoidance, competition (distributive), and collaboration (integrative). Each of these conflict management styles has unique advantages and disadvantages, depending on how and when they are used.

Avoidance

Avoidance is often used by partners who deny having a problem in the first place, or by someone who is uncomfortable at the prospect of engaging in conflict. In an effort to avoid conflict with another person, relationship partners might directly or indirectly deny there is a problem, use equivocation or evasive comments to avoid discussing issues, change topics, act noncommittal on an issue, or use jokes or humor. While occasionally avoiding conflict might not be problematic for relationships, consistently avoiding conflict has been found to be counterproductive for individuals in any type of relationship. Recall the recent conflict between former best friends Paris Hilton and Nicole Richie. Stories reported that the two stopped speaking to each other, avoided attending events where they knew the other would be, and even decided to end relationships with people who had previously been mutual acquaintances.

If you consistently avoid conflict, will the problem go away by itself?

© Philip Date, 2007, Shutterstock.

Avoidance styles of conflict management are generally not productive because they often indicate a low concern for self, others, and the relationship, and are perceived as ineffective (Hocker and Wilmot 1991). What are some of the advantages and disadvantages of avoidance as a tactical strategy? See Table 8.2 below for an overview of the advantages and disadvantages of this strategy.

It is important to think about the benefits and drawbacks of using avoidance as a means of managing conflict. There are times when conflict should not be addressed because it is not the right time or place to discuss an issue with someone. Also, depending on an individual's culture, they may be more or less predisposed to avoid conflict with others. Finally, avoiding a conflict does not make it go away. Perhaps you can recall a time when avoiding an issue with someone actually made the situation worse.

Competitive/Distributive

The second conflict management style is described as **competitive** or **distributive**. It involves the use of aggressive and uncooperative types of behaviors. Individuals using this style pursue their own goals and objectives at the expense of others (Hocker and Wilmot 1991). The primary goal when adopting this style is to win the argument using whatever means necessary. Individuals using this style view conflict as a battle or competition and address conflict situations in either assertive or aggressive ways. When individuals use a competitive style of conflict they might offer personal criticism, rejection statements, hostile remarks, jokes or questions, presumptive remarks, or denial of responsibilities. Recently, Rosie O'Donnell criticized Donald Trump on her television show *The View* for his decision to allow Miss USA 2006 to retain her crown after allegations of alcohol abuse. O'Donnell referred to Trump as a "snake oil salesman" and mocked his hairstyle by flipping her hair to one side and mocking his voice. Trump retaliated by commenting that O'Donnell is "disgraceful" and referred to her as a "loser." As you can see, both O'Donnell and Trump engaged in a competition to see who could "one-up" the other. However, this style of managing conflict is not always unproductive. What are the advantages and disadvantages of using this style to manage conflict situations?

Table 8.2   Avoidance as a Tactical Strategy

Sample Messages	Advantages	Disadvantages
Direct denial "There is no issue here, really."	Buys time to think about issues	Shows you do not care about relationship
Topic shift "Let's not talk about that right now and instead focus on dinner."	Best to use with trivial issues (don't sweat the small stuff)	Problem will not get solved
Noncommittal questions "What do you want to do about this?"	Can keep you from hurt feelings	Situation can get worse

Source: Adapted from Hocker and Wilmot 1991.

As we can see in Table 8.3 above, there are situations when using competition as a means of managing can be beneficial. For example, when an individual in a work setting is in a time crunch, lacks the time to debate all available alternatives, and feels strongly about his or her position, adopting a competitive stance to "win" an argument may be necessary. Or, if an issue has been discussed extensively and the individuals experiencing conflict have not made any progress toward resolving the disagreement, adopting a competitive stance may facilitate conflict resolution. Also, when individuals compete they often exert a great deal of energy, which sends a metamessage that the topic is important to the parties involved. However, competition can also damage relationships and isolate individuals who tend to avoid conflict situations. Unassertive or highly reticent individuals may avoid conflict situations when others adopt a competitive stance. Use of this style depends largely on the context and unique characteristics of the individuals involved.

Collaborative/Integrative

The final conflict management style, **collaborative** or **integrative**, is often described as a productive means of managing conflict because it requires open and ongoing communication. When relationship partners adopt this style, they offer descriptive and disclosive statements and, at the same time, make attempts to gain similar information from others (Hocker and Wilmot 1991). Partners work together to develop solutions to their disagreements that are mutually satisfying. Collaboration is often described as a "win-win" approach to solving relationship issues because both parties walk away satisfied with the outcome. See Table 8.4 for an overview of this strategy.

This style of conflict management is not without its own set of constraints. For example, there are times when decisions need to be made quickly. Think about a football coach arguing with his assistant coaches about which play to run to win the game; it would not be realistic for him to consult each coach before sending out the final play. Another challenge with this approach is that because it takes time and effort, people may be reluctant to use it. Also,

| **Table 8.3** | **Competitive/Distributive as a Tactical Strategy** |

Sample Messages	Advantages	Disadvantages
Criticism "You have no sense of humor."	Good in emergency situations	Can harm relationships
Hostile questions "Who works the hardest in this relationship?"	Can generate creative ideas	People get entrenched in positions
Rejection "You have no idea what you are talking about."	Useful in short-term situations	Can lead to covert conflict/games
Denial of responsibility "It is not my fault that you can't communicate with me."	Can show importance of issue	Not good if one party avoids conflict

Source: Adapted from Hocker and Wilmot 1991.

Table 8.4   Collaborative/Integrative as a Tactical Strategy

Sample Messages	Advantages	Disadvantages
Supportive remarks *"I can see why you would want to do that."*	Best when solutions must be mutually satisfying	Sometimes not worth time and effort
Concessions *"I promise to not interrupt you."*	Good for coming up with new and creative ideas	Can be used manipulatively
Soliciting criticism *"What are my communication weaknesses?"*	Preserves relationship	Everyone involved must embrace this style
Disclosive statement *"I was in a bad mood last night."*	Can lead to increased relationship satisfaction	Requires fairly strong communication skills

Source: Adapted from Hocker and Wilmot 1991.

people might feel that by soliciting feedback from everyone and getting issues out in the open, it might "open a whole other can of worms." Collaboration, by nature, encourages open expression of multiple perspectives. Sometimes encouraging others to openly express concerns can result in "tangents," lengthy discussion of unimportant or unrelated issues, and poor use of time. In other words, this approach could be viewed as time-consuming and challenging.

However, there are many benefits to using the collaborative/integrative approach to manage conflict management situations. When partners in romantic relationships report increased use of integrative styles of conflict management, relationship satisfaction increases (see, for example, Canary and Cupach 1988; Canary and Spitzberg 1989). Conversely, when partners in romantic relationships employ more distributive or avoiding styles of conflict, relationship satisfaction decreases significantly (Canary and Cupach 1988; Canary and Spitzberg 1989; Rands et al. 1981; Spitzberg et al. 1994; Ting-Toomey 1983). It should come as no surprise that those individuals who employ integrative conflict management strategies with relationship partners are generally perceived as more communicatively competent (Canary and Spitzberg 1989). Perceptions of relationship partners' competence mediate the relationship between conflict messages and relational outcomes. More specifically, Canary and Spitzberg (1989) note that "conflict messages are assessed as more or less appropriate, effective, and globally competent, and these assessments then affect relational features of trust, control mutuality, intimacy and relational satisfaction" (644). Thus, use of integrative conflict management styles, which are generally perceived as more appropriate and effective, increase relationship partners' reported satisfaction and trust.

THE DARK SIDE OF CONFLICT: VERBAL AGGRESSION

When partners lack communication skills, they are more likely to employ verbally aggressive communication behaviors, often resulting in violent episodes (deTurck 1987; Infante, Chandler and Rudd 1989; Infante, et al. 1990).

Are there times when aggressive communication is justifiable?

Verbal aggression involves assaulting or criticizing another person's sense of self and typically involves attacks on one's character, competence, background, or appearance. These types of messages not only damage an individual's perceptions of self-worth, but can also negatively affect relationship satisfaction. It is important for relationship partners to minimize the use of verbally aggressive messages during conflict episodes.

Loreen Olsen (2002) conducted a qualitative investigation of romantic couples' conflict episodes to study the relationship between communication competence and aggression. In her study, she found that partners felt that aggressive communication indicated a lack of communication competence. However, she also found there were times when individuals felt that use of aggressive communication was justifiable. For example, participants described the use of aggressive communication as a constructive way to clear the air, gain their partner's attention, and reach a resolution faster. Some participants felt aggression was appropriate in certain situations because it became a relationship-changing event and permanently altered the way the couple managed conflict episodes. Can you think of a time when an aggressive conflict episode ultimately changed the way relationship partners communicated in the future? Olsen points out that her results should be interpreted with caution because most of her participants were female European Americans and because the participants recalled a conflict event that got out of hand. Thus, while these findings might not extend to all conflict episodes, they identify descriptive accounts of when relationship partners might view aggression as appropriate. In other words, because this study had participants recall conflict events, these results suggest that in hindsight there might have been productive results from aggressive behaviors.

MANAGING CONFLICT

In the final sections of this chapter, we offer a number of useful suggestions for approaching conflict productively, regardless of the communication situation. First, when approaching a conflict situation, you should consider the advantages and disadvantages of using avoidance, competitive, or collaborative conflict management strategies. Each of these strategies requires a different set of communication behaviors and produces a variety of outcomes. From a relational perspective, collaboration is consistently viewed as the most competent way to manage conflict; often resulting in higher reported satisfaction for relationship partners. Conversely, avoidance and competition are regarded as less effective and appropriate strategies, often resulting in less relationship satisfaction.

Individuals should also consider the way they respond or react to problems in their relationships. Carl Rusbult and his colleagues (1982) found that when individuals experience problems in relationships, there are typically four different ways to react: exit, voice, loyalty, and neglect. These responses vary to the extent in which they are perceived as productive or unproductive and passive or active. **Exit** responses typically involve threats of physical separation between partners. Consider a time when you had a conflict with another person and one of you physically left the room during the episode. Did you view this as a productive way to respond to the situation? Probably not. Exit is a passive strategy that is unproductive to conflict resolution. Similarly, when relationship partners adopt a **neglect** response to conflict, they might avoid

Refusing to discuss problems is unproductive to conflict resolution.

the relationship partner, refuse to discuss problems they are experiencing, and communicate with one another in a hostile or aggressive manner. This type of response is described as active and destructive. Rusbult and his colleagues (1982) found that college couples in satisfying relationships were less likely to use neglect and exit responses.

Couples reporting higher satisfaction in their relationships were more likely to use loyalty and voice responses as a response to conflict (Rusbult 1982). When individuals adopt a **loyalty** response, they remain loyal to one another by not addressing the conflict. They may decide to "wait it out" in the hopes that by doing so, the relationship will improve on its own. Loyalty is described as a passive strategy that could be viewed as productive or unproductive, depending on the situation. On the one hand, loyalty indicates that a partner is committed to the relationship and will stick with the other partner during both good and bad times. However, because the loyalty response is passive, and the partner adopting this response to a relationship problem is not actively addressing an issue, it could also be described as an unproductive response. As mentioned previously, avoiding conflict does little to bring it to a resolution.

A more productive response to problems in relationships is the **voice** response. When individuals adopt this response, they discuss relationship concerns openly and often offer suggestions for repairing the relationship transgression. Rusbult, Johnson and Morrow (1986) noted that adopting a voice response during mild relationship transgressions assisted in stabilizing the relationship's health. Use of the voice response has been positively associated with both relationship satisfaction and commitment. Interestingly, men and women differ in the extent to which they use voice and loyalty responses. Women, more so than men, use the voice response as a means of managing minor problems and use loyalty for a wide range of problems. Men were more likely to use neglect responses than women (Rusbult et al. 1986). These gender-based differences are interesting and offer some support for the notion that many women often feel they must be the "relationship experts" or the keeper of the relationship standards.

© 2007, JupiterImages, Inc.

How do men and women typically differ in their responses to relationship problems?

A final suggestion for managing conflict effectively and appropriately has to do with using **"fair fighting"** tactics in relationships. When we use the term fair fighting, we are not referring to physical fighting in relationships. Instead, we are referring to the use of productive or competent communication practices that promote problem solving, compromise and collaboration. Table 8.5 provides additional information regarding productive and unproductive communication responses to conflict.

To manage conflict in a productive and healthy way, it is important to adopt communication patterns that create an environment in which individuals feel comfortable sharing their concerns without being belittled, embarrassed, or ridiculed. It is important to choose an appropriate time and place to discuss the problem, listen actively when the other person is talking, and refrain from using negative listening behaviors such as pseudo-listening or defensive listening.

© 2007, JupiterImages, Inc.

How can you show that you are making an effort to understand someone's concerns?

Table 8.5	Managing Conflict Effectively
Productive Communication	**Unproductive Communication**
Active listening	Pseudo-listening, defensive listening
Use of empathy	Focus on self
Choosing the right time and place (e.g., public contexts) to discuss issue problem	Choosing an inappropriate time and place (e.g., private contexts) to discuss the
Communicating with respect	Being disrespectful
Describing the problem clearly	Being ambiguous
Using I statements. For example, "I feel ___ when you ___"	Starting statements with "You are ...!"
Stay in the present	Bringing up the past
Focusing on relevant issues only	Kitchensinking—throwing everything into the argument [including?] the kitchen sink!

Also, it is important be empathetic when communicating with the other person. Make an attempt to understand the other person's feelings. Individuals often experience problems in their relationships because they do not really listen to one another. It is important to show individuals that you are listening by using active listening behaviors, paraphrasing their messages, and asking relevant questions to help understand their perspective.

SUMMARY

Relationships require work and effort! In this chapter we explored reasons for maintaining relationships, identified various maintenance strategies, and discussed the outcomes of strategy use. Because more people are using the Internet as a means of maintaining their relationships, we discussed the benefits and drawbacks of using CMC to maintain our relationships. In the last sections of this chapter, we focused on managing conflict effectively as a means of stabilizing our relationships. More specifically, we focused on the definition of conflict, different types of conflict management strategies, conflict responses, and using productive communication during conflict episodes.

APPLICATIONS

Discussion Questions

A. Relationship maintenance strategies are used in virtually all relationships. The research on relationship maintenance has focused primarily on strategies used in platonic and romantic relationships. However, it is likely that individuals use strategies to maintain their work or professional relationships. Identify several relationship maintenance strategies that you use to sustain your work relationships. Are they similar to those identified in the chapter?

B. Burleson and Samter state that maintaining relationships with others typically involves mastery of specific communication skills. Can you identify five or more skills needed to effectively maintain relationships with family members, friends, or romantic partners?

C. Reflect on a recent conflict that you may have experienced with a friend, roommate, or co-worker. What was your approach to this situation? What conflict management style did you use? What was the outcome of this situation? In retrospect, do you feel that you could have handled this situation more effectively? What would you have done differently?

REFERENCES

Ayres, J. 1983. Strategies to maintain relationships. *Communication Quarterly, 31*, 62–67.

Braiker, H. B., and H. H. Kelley. 1979. Conflict in the development of close relationships. In R. L. Burgess and T. L. Huston (Eds.), *Social Exchange in Developing Relationships*. New York: Academic Press.

Burgoon, J. K., and J. L. Hale. 1984. The fundamental topoi of relational communication. *Communication Monographs, 51*, 19–41.

Burleson, B., and W. Samter. 1994. A social skills approach to relationship maintenance: How individual differences in communication skills affect the achievement of relationship functions. In D. J. Canary and L. Stafford (Eds.), *Communication and relational maintenance* (61–90). New York: Academic Press.

Cahn, D. 1992. *Conflict in intimate relationships* (72–112). New York: The Guilford Press.

Canary, D. J., and B. H. Spitzberg. 1989. A model of perceived competence of conflict strategies. *Human Communication Research, 15*, 630–649.

Canary, D. J., and L. Stafford. 1992. Relational maintenance strategies and equity in marriage. *Communication Monographs, 59*, 243–267.

———. 1994. Maintaining relationships through strategic and routine interaction. In D. J. Canary and L. Stafford (Eds.), *Communication and relational maintenance* (pp. 3–22). San Diego, CA: Academic Press.

———. 2001. Equity in the preservation of personal relationships. In J. H. Harvey and A. Wenzel (Eds.), *Close romantic relationships: Maintenance and enhancement* (pp. 133–151). Mahwah, NJ: Lawrence Erlbaum Associates, Publishers.

Canary, D. J., and W. R. Cupach. 1988. Relational and episodic characteristics associated with conflict tactics. *Journal of Social and Personal Relationships, 5*, 305–325.

Canary, D. J., L. Stafford, K. S. Hause, and L. A. Wallace. 1993. An inductive analysis of relational maintenance strategies: Comparison among lovers, friends, relatives, and others. *Communication Research Reports, 10*, 5–14.

Canary, D. J., W. R. Cupach, and S. J. Messman. 1995. *Relationship conflict*. Thousand Oaks, CA: Sage Publications.

Cialdini, R. B. 2003. *Influence: Science and practice (4th ed.)*. International Edition (country or state?): Allyn and Bacon.

Dainton, M. 2000. Maintenance behaviors, expectations for maintenance and satisfaction: Linking comparison levels to relational maintenance strategies. *Journal of Social and Personal Relationships, 17*, 827–842.

Dainton, M., and B. Aylor. 2002. A relational uncertainty analysis of jealousy, trust, and maintenance in long-distance versus geographically close relationships. *Communication Quarterly, 49*, 172–188.

Dainton, M., and L. Stafford. 1993. Routine maintenance behaviors: A comparison of relationship type, partner similarity, and sex differences. *Journal of Personal and Social Relationships, 10*, 255–272.

deTurck, M. A. 1987. When communication fails: Physical aggression as a compliance gaining strategy. *Communication Monographs, 51*, 106–112.

Diggs, R. C., and L. Stafford. 1998. Maintaining marital relationships: A comparison between African American and European American individuals. In V. J. Duncan (Ed.), *Towards achieving MAAT.* (192–292). Dubuque, IA: Kendall Hunt.

Dindia, K., and D. J. Canary. 1993. Definitions and theoretical perspectives on maintaining relationships. *Journal of Social and Personal Relationships, 10*, 163–173.

Dindia, K., and L. Baxter. 1987. Strategies for maintaining and repairing marital relationships. *Journal of Social and Personal Relationships, 4*, 143–158.

Duck, S. 1988. *Relating to others*. Buckingham, PA: Open University Press.

Eldrige, N. S., and L. A. Gilbert. 1990. Correlates of relationship satisfaction in lesbian couples. *Psychology of Women Quarterly, 14*, 43–62.

Fox, S., L. Rainie, E. Larsen, J. Horrigan, A. Lenhart, T. Spooner, and C. Carter. 2001. The Pew Internet and American life project. www.pewinternet.org/

Haas, S. M., and L. Stafford. 1998. An initial examination of maintenance behaviors in gay and lesbian relationships. *Journal of Social and Personal Relationships, 15,* 846–855.

Hocker, J. L., and W. W. Wilmot. 1991. *Interpersonal Conflict* (4–42, 103–144). Dubuque, IA: Wm C. Brown Publishers.

Infante, D. A., T. A. Chandler, and J. E. Rudd. 1989. Test of an argumentative skill deficiency model of interspousal violence. *Communication Monographs, 56,* 163–177.

Infante, D. A., T. C. Sabourin, J. E. Rudd, and E. A. Shannon. 1990. Verbal aggression in violent and nonviolent disputes. *Communication Quarterly, 38,* 361–371.

Jones, R. W., and J. E. Bates. 1978. Satisfaction in male homosexual couples. *Journal of Homosexuality, 3,* 217–224.

Messman, S. J., D. J. Canary, and K. S. Hause. 2000. Motives to remain platonic, equity, and the use of maintenance strategies in opposite-sex friendships. *Journal of Social and Personal Relationships, 17,* 67–94.

Myers, S. 2001. Relational maintenance behaviors in the sibling relationship. *Communication Quarterly, 49,* 19–37.

Myers, S., and K. Weber. 2004. Preliminary development of a measure of sibling relational maintenance behaviors: Scale development and initial findings. *Communication Quarterly, 52,* 334–347.

Olsen, L. 2002. "As ugly and as painful as it was, it was effective": Individuals' unique assessment of communication competence during aggressive conflict episodes. *Communication Studies, 53,* 171–188.

Punyanunt-Carter, N. M. 2006. Evaluating the effects of attachment styles on relationship maintenance behaviors in father-daughter relationships. *Family Journal, 14,* 135–143.

Ragsdale, J. D. 1996. Gender, satisfaction level, and the use of relational maintenance strategies in marriage. *Communication Monographs, 63,* 354–369.

Rands, M., G. Levinger, and G. D. Mellinger. 1981. Patterns of conflict resolution and marital satisfaction. *Journal of Family Issues, 2,* 297–321.

Rohlfing, M. 1995. "Doesn't anybody stay in the same place anymore?" An exploration of the understudied phenomenon of long-distance relationships. In J. Wood and S. Duck (Eds.) *Communication and relational maintenance* (23–44). New York: Academic Press.

Rusbult, C. E., D. J. Johnson, and G. D. Morrow. 1986. Determinants and consequences of exit, voice, loyalty, and neglect: Responses to dissatisfaction in adult romantic involvements. *Human Relations, 39,* 45–63.

Rusbult, C. E., I. M. Zembrodt, and L. K. Grunn. 1982. Exit, voice, loyalty, and neglect: Responses to dissatisfaction in romantic involvements. *Journal of Personality and Social Psychology, 43,* 1230–1242.

Sillars, A. L., and W. W. Wilmot. 1994. Communication strategies in conflict and mediation. In J. A. Daly and J. M. Wiemann (Eds.), *Strategic interpersonal communication* (163–190). Hillsdale, NJ: Lawrence Erlbaum.

Spitzberg, B. H., D. J. Canary, and W. R. Cupach. 1994. A competence based approach to the study of interpersonal conflict. In D. D. Cahn (Ed.), *Conflict in personal relationships* (183–202). Hillsdale, NJ: Lawrence Erlbaum.

Stafford, L., and D. J. Canary. 1991. Maintenance strategies and romantic relationship type, gender and relational characteristics. *Journal of Social and Personal Relationships, 8,* 217–242.

Ting-Toomey, S. 1983. An analysis of verbal communication patterns in high and low marital adjustment groups. *Human Communication Research, 9,* 306–319.

Wright, K. 2004. Online relational maintenance strategies and perceptions of partners within exclusively internet-based and primarily internet-based relationships. *Communication Studies, 55,* 239–253.

Terminating Relationships
Knowing When to Throw in the Towel

OBJECTIVES

- Recall common reasons platonic friendships terminate
- Discuss the strengths and weaknesses of using indirect versus direct methods of terminating relationships
- Identify four common reasons romantic relationships terminate
- Describe Duck's four phases of relationship termination
- Explain Knapp's model of relationship dissolution. Describe each stage of coming apart and offer an example of typical communication that occurs in each stage
- Explain the five tactics used during relationship disengagement
- Identify several strategies you can employ to "remain friends" with ex-romantic partners
- Offer examples of strategies individuals can use to survive relationship dissolution

© Alex Brosa, 2007, Shutterstock.

KEY TERMS

social exchange theory
indirect methods
direct methods
infidelity
commitment
dissimilarity
outside pressure
self determination
 theory
fundamental
 attribution error

equity theory
intrapsychic phase
dyadic phase
social phase
grave dressing phase
differentiating
circumscribing
stagnating
avoiding
terminating
positive tone messages

de-escalation messages
withdrawal/avoidance
 tactics
justification tactics
negative identity
 management
closure
granting forgiveness
self-forgiveness
reframing

OVERVIEW

From the old "Greensleeves" (Alas, my love, you do me wrong to cast me off discourteously . . .) to gleeful songs like "Already Gone," from most of Garth Brooks' repertoire to rock songs like Hoobastank's "The Reason," we are as concerned with the end as with the beginning. Romantic relationships are hardly exclusive; throughout life, relationships of different forms will be left as closed books. How?

We have discussed how our interpersonal relationships are initiated, maintained, and, in some instances, how they turn dark. In this chapter, we turn to the process of relationship disengagement for all types of relationships. Not surprisingly, the research, like Neal Sedaka's song, notes that "Breaking up is hard to do," and usually results in pain for one or both partners. Throughout this chapter, we examine the most common reasons for ending both platonic and romantic relationships. We also take an in-depth look at research involving both potentially aggravating and mitigating strategies used by individuals in relationship termination. We then face the aftermath of relationship disengagement, exploring suggestions for surviving relationship disengagement and ultimately moving on.

Why do some friendships tend to outlast others?

When they graduate and go their separate ways, will this friendship end?

TERMINATING FRIENDSHIPS

Friendships are some of the most enduring relationships we have. There are friendships that we have had since youth with a shelf life of "forever." There are other friends who tend to drift in and out of our lives like last season's shoes. Why do some friendships tend to outlast others? Often, friendships are forged from commonalities in our life. For example, we meet certain people in a class who live in the same dorm, have the same major, work at the same job, share the same religion or social group, or share the same enemy or mutual friend. Friendships may terminate because the very thing that brought them together no longer exists. People move away, change jobs, or move on to a different life stage (i.e., marriage, children, etc.) and no longer share the proximity and closeness that once protected the relationship. The *Friends* are all singles in New York; the *Desperate Housewives* share Wisteria Lane; the Dundler Mifflin employees on *The Office* work together, as do the *Grey's Anatomy* interns. Remove the binding element and friendships may fade. Consider how, when not killed off, characters are removed from shows, particularly the cast-rotating *ER*. Whether for career, love, or family, a resident leaves the hospital and Chicago and, as a result, is detached from the life of the colleagues previously seen daily. While employed as a plot device to remove a character, such occasions illustrate an aspect of reality.

There are a number of reasons individuals end friendships. The most common reasons reported for terminating a friendship were less affection (22.8 percent), friend or self changed (21 percent), no longer participate in activities or spend time together (15.4 percent), and increase in distance (13 percent). (Johnson, Wittenberg, Haigh, Wigley, Becker, Brown and Craig 2004). Additional findings suggest that male same-sex friendships tend to dissolve for different reasons than female same-sex friendships. Females were more likely to terminate friendships due to a conflict situation, whereas males were more likely to terminate friendships as a result of fewer common interests.

The way that someone ends a friendship depends on the intimacy, or closeness, experienced in the relationship. Another study compared the differences in dissolution between casual and best friends (Rose and Serafica 1986). Researchers found that proximity was a stronger predictor of dissolution in casual friends, while decreased affection was more important in best friends. One reason reported for best and close friendships dissolving was the interface from other relationships, such as romantic relationships. This plays a particularly detrimental role in female friendships. When one individual begins to spend more time interacting with her romantic partners' male friends than with her own friends, the neglected female friends are likely to become frustrated with her behavior.

As a friendship grows apart, we can neglect the responsibilities of the relationship by choosing to provide less of our time, energy, trust, understanding, and support. When an individual is neglecting the responsibilities of the friendship, individuals may start weighing the costs and rewards of the relationship. Recall our discussion of Social Exchange Theory in Chapter Six. To review, **Social Exchange Theory** refers to an assessment of costs and rewards in determining the value of pursuing or continuing a relationship (Thibaut and Kelley 1959). Rewards consist of behaviors or aspects of the relationship that are desirable, and that the recipient perceives as enjoyable or fulfilling. In friendships, rewards are how much fun you have with the person, and the extent to which he or she is trustworthy, honest, sincere, helpful, and supportive. By contrast, costs are perceived as undesirable behaviors or outcomes. Costs in friendships may be characterized as "toxic" behaviors: the extent to which a friend may be controlling, demanding, depressing, self-absorbed, deceitful, and unfair. Also, friendships take time and energy, which may be perceived as costs when we have less time and energy to devote to them. According to Social Exchange Theory, when the costs of the relationship outweigh the rewards, we contemplate ending the friendship. We may use indirect or direct methods to end a friendship.

© Jason Stitt, 2007, Shutterstock.

A friendship reward is having fun when you're together.

Using Indirect Methods to End a Friendship

Indirect methods work best if your goal is to decrease the intensity of the friendship by increasing the emotional and physical distance between you and your friend. Indirect methods reflect your intentions of gradually letting go of the relationship. Examples of indirect methods include calling the friend less, sending fewer emails, blocking the friend from your Buddy List or switching your screen name, and spending less time with the friend.

There are drawbacks to using indirect methods to gradually weaken relationship bonds. For example, giving excuses for not hanging out may backfire. Florence Isaacs, author of *Toxic Friends/True Friends: How Your Friends Can Make or Break Your Health, Happiness, Family, and Career* (1999), suggests that giving excuses allows the other person an opportunity to overcome your refusal; he or she may answer your "Oh, I can't afford the gas to get out there," with "That's okay, I can pick you up."

In addition, because indirect methods are not the most honest approach, the friend is often left confused about your true feelings. Often he or she will keep trying and will not understand your indirect attempts to slow down, or even end, the friendship. If this is the case, it may be time to move to more direct approaches of ending the relationship.

Using Direct Methods to End a Friendship

Direct methods work best if your friend does not recognize the intent of your indirect attempts or if you are interested in terminating the friendship abruptly (due to some hurtful circumstance). As you can imagine, direct approaches are specifically telling the friend how you honestly feel. Sometimes this is not an easy task, but there are some tools you can use to ease this uncomfortable situation. First, use "I" statements. For example, "I'm very busy with my new girlfriend and with work so I cannot hang out with you every weekend," or "I was really hurt by your comment at dinner the other night and I'm not interested in being friends with someone who doesn't respect me." Direct methods leave little room for misinterpretation. While they are effective, they can be hurtful and sometimes shocking to hear from the perspective of the receiver. If you choose to engage in this approach, be prepared to be assertive and provide a valid reason for why you are ending the friendship.

TERMINATING ROMANTIC RELATIONSHIPS

"There must be fifty ways to leave your lover," and though Paul Simon suggests mainly variations on "slipping out the back," some individuals prove highly creative in their personal spins on "it's not you, it's me." The common causes of relationship disengagement, however, are more limited. There are several significant reasons individuals have provided for terminating romantic relationships. Typically, the decision to leave a romantic partner is a difficult and arduous task. In this section, we examine four common reasons individuals leave romantic relationships (adapted from Cupach and Metts 1986). These include: (1) infidelity, (2) lack of commitment, (3) dissimilarity, and (4) outside pressures.

Infidelity

Infidelity can be defined as behaving in a way that crosses the perceived boundary and expectation of an exclusive relationship. Infidelity can take many forms, including physical (holding hands), sexual (kissing and other activities), and emotional (sharing intimate conversation) (Spitzberg and Tafoya 2005). Research suggests that men are more likely to be upset with a partner's sexual infidelity, while women tend to be more upset with a partners' emotional infidelity (Glass and Wright 1985). Studies have also shown that infidelity is more likely to exist inside marriages with marital instability, dishonesty, arguments about trust, narcissism, and time spent apart (Atkins, Yi, Baucom and Christensen 2005). While approximately ninety-nine percent of married persons expect sexual fidelity from their spouse (Treas and Giesen 2000), not many couples are meeting those expectations.

Although infidelity statistics are difficult to measure, we report some interesting findings that describe the pervasiveness of infidelity. Atwood and Schwartz (2002) estimate that fifty to sixty percent of married men and forty-five to fifty-five percent of married women engage in some form of extramarital affair at some point in their marriage. The *Washington Post* reported that, according to counselor Janis Abrahms Spring, author of *After the Affair*, affairs affect one of every 2.7 couples. Other interesting findings suggest that ten percent of extramarital affairs last one day. Of those that last more than one day:

- Ten percent last less than a month
- Fifty percent last more than a month but less than a year
- Forty percent last two or more years.

According to Spring's statistics, few extramarital affairs last longer than four years.

Additionally, a longitudinal study found that infidelity is the most frequently cited cause of divorce (Amato and Rogers 1997). Another study found that forty percent of divorced individuals reported at least one extramarital sexual contact during their marriage (Janus and Janus 1993). These alarming statistics imply that although not many condone infidelity, there is a significant proportion of people engaging in these types of behaviors.

Our culture has both romanticized and rebuked infidelity. The archetypical story of Tristan and Isolde, wherein a young queen cheats on her kind husband with the knight she truly loves, was turned into a hit 2006 film of the same title by Ridley Scott. Guinevere and Lancelot's doomed love that betrays the noble King Arthur, whom they both care deeply for, is continually retold in musical form. *Walk the Line* was another recent movie dealing with the relationship between Johnny Cash and June Carter, which caused the dissolution of Cash's previous marriage. Movies like *Fatal Attraction* and *What Lies Beneath*, however, offer deadly punishment for adultery. According to research, relationships in which one or both individuals have potential alternative partners with highly attractive qualities are "particularly vulnerable" to dissolution (Simpson 1987), and when a relationship's rewards fall below the expected rewards of an alternative relationship, it is most likely to end (Thibaut and Kelley 1959). Hollywood, California, where attractive individuals live in extremely close proximity, seems to be a natural hub for infidelity in all three of its forms.

Lack of Commitment

Another reason individuals provide for terminating romantic relationships is a lack of commitment. Although infidelity is one way to demonstrate an individuals' lack of commitment, other ways include: not spending enough time together, not prioritizing the relationship, not valuing the other's opinion, experiencing power struggles, and not nurturing the maintenance and development of the relationship. Lack of **commitment** in a relationship can foster feelings of abandonment and loneliness. Some relationship experts argue that partners' commitment to the relationship is a stronger predictor of relationship stability than feelings of love (Lund 1985). Researcher Mary Lund studied heterosexual dating relationships in an attempt to determine whether love or

High commitment to a relationship is a strong predictor of its stability.

commitment served as a stronger predictor of relationship stability. She found that couples with higher levels of commitment were more likely to continue the relationship than those with high levels of love and low levels of commitment. In this study, couples' expectations of staying together proved to be more important to relationship stability than their feelings of love for one another.

Lack of commitment to the relationship may be a catalyst for more damaging outcomes, such as infidelity; couples often attempt therapy to resolve these issues. One study found two characteristics that identified unsuccessful couples in therapy. They are "inability or unwillingness to change" and "lack of commitment" (Whisman, Dixon, and Johnson 1997). Another report found that the most significant problems for couples who attended therapy are a lack of loving feelings and lack of communication, power struggles, extramarital affairs, and unrealistic expectations (Whisman, Dixon, and Johnson 1997).

Can previous relationship experiences affect an individual's willingness to commit to future relationships? Communication researchers explored how past relationship solidarity was related to current relationship commitment, satisfaction, and investment among college students in dating relationships. They found that an individual's past relationship experiences may be to blame for a current relationships' lack of commitment with, specifically, a negative relationship between participants' past relationship solidarity and current relationship commitment and satisfaction. It is important to note that these relationships were only significant for the female participants in the study. Researchers argue that these findings may be based on the different ways in which "men and women cope with break-ups and how these differences might have affected their retrospective reports of their past relationships" (Merolla Weber, Myers, and Booth-Butterfield 2004, 261). Women may be more in tune with their physical and emotional closeness in past relationships than males. Males, on the other hand, may be more inclined to employ emotional distraction techniques after break-ups to avoid dealing with their feelings (Merolla et al. 2004).

Dissimilarity

Scholars have identified similarity as one of two components that relationship dyads consider when deciding whether to stay together or to break up (Hill, Rubin, and Peplau 1976). A longitudinal study suggested that couples who were most similar in educational plans, intelligence, and attractiveness were most likely to remain together, whereas couples that were different in the levels of these aspects were more likely to break up. Some may say, "opposites attract," but the truth is, **dissimilarity** creates more problems than solutions. Having differences in backgrounds (religion, family values), intelligence (educational goals, IQ), attitudes concerning family roles, ethics, and communicating about conflicts, and temperament (argumentativeness, assertiveness) can contribute to conflict situations and misinterpretations of behavior.

Couples who share similar beliefs and interests are more likely to stay together.

A communication concept that is strongly linked to similarity is interpersonal solidarity. Lawrence Wheeless defined interpersonal solidarity as feelings of closeness between people that develop as a result of shared sentiments, similarities and intimate behaviors (1978). With that in mind, it makes sense that solidarity increases as relationships become more intimate, and it decreases as relationships turn toward termination (Wheeless, Wheeless, and Baus 1984). As solidarity increases in romantic relationships, so do individuals' levels of trust, reciprocity, and self-disclosures (Wheeless 1976). Also, the closer we feel to our partner, the more likely we are to provide emotional support (Weber and Patterson 1996). It makes sense to say that if individuals in romantic relationships perceive differences between themselves, there will be less trust, reciprocity, and emotional support, and fewer self-disclosures will be shared.

Writers often use a lack of interpersonal solidarity as the basis to break up fictional couples, particularly in cases when infidelity would be seen as out of character. On *Gilmore Girls*, for instance, Rory Gilmore ultimately breaks up with her devoted boyfriend when his lack of interest in books and of drive to strive beyond the community college in their town runs contrary to her love for literature and dream to attend Harvard. The contrast is made acute by a boy friend of hers who shares her interests in intellectual debate and matches her fast-paced banter. This sense of a widening gap between two individuals will commonly terminate a relationship.

Outside Pressures

External or **outside pressure** from friends, family, or occupations may negatively impact relationship satisfaction. Family members may put pressure on romantic relationships when they ask questions like "When are you two getting married?" or make comments such as, "You should save your money for a house!" and "I want to be a grandparent!" Friends also may exert pressure on romantic relationships by hinting that not enough time is spent with them, pressuring you to do things without your significant other. For couples in the public eye, the paparazzi acts as the external pressure peering over the hedge, demanding details and pushing theories of engagement, pregnancy, etc., on the pair.

According to **self determination theory**, people have an innate psychological need to feel autonomous, or self-governing, in one's behavior (Deci and Ryan 1985, 2000, 2002). In other words, we want to feel free to choose our own path in relationships, rather than be coerced or pressured into certain behaviors. Ultimately, this self-initiated behavior will lead to better personal and social adjustment. Trait autonomy, or the extent to which we are self-determined, is related to feelings of well-being and security in relationships (La Guardia et al. 2000). Hence, those who report feeling responsible for, and in control of, their own decisions are also more secure and positive about their relationships with others.

Work relationships or job stressors can impact the satisfaction in our romantic relationship. An increase in job demands, hours, and travel requirements are examples of significant occupational pressures that may affect relationship stability. The time-consuming career of a doctor, for instance, can be seen in the media as being a challenge to relationships lasting, particularly on shows like *ER*, wherein constant relationship disengagement occurs.

© Elena Elisseeva, 2007, Shutterstock.

Stressful career demands can impact the satisfaction in relationships.

HOMOSEXUAL VERSUS HETEROSEXUAL RELATIONSHIP DISSOLUTION

Although scant research has addressed gay and lesbian relationship termination, Lawrence Kurdek has found that cohabitating gay or lesbian partners are more similar than different when compared to married heterosexual partners (Kurdek 1992; 1998). In his 1998 longitudinal study, he examined relationship satisfaction among partners from gay, lesbian, and heterosexual married couples over five annual assessments. He found that neither gay nor lesbian partners differed from heterosexual partners in both the trajectory of change and the level of relationship satisfaction over time and that all three groups showed a similar decrease in satisfaction over the five years. However, some differences were detected. Both gay and lesbian partners reported more frequent relationship dissolution compared to married spouses. Additionally, gay and lesbian partners reported more autonomy than married people. Furthermore, lesbian partners reported significantly more intimacy and equality than married individuals (Kurdek 1998).

ASSESSING RELATIONSHIP PROBLEMS

When considering whether to stay in a relationship or not, we often assess the trouble occurring in the relationship and the explanations for these problems. For example, we ask ourselves questions such as, Why does he act that way? Why did she say that to me? or Why would he or she hurt me? To address these questions, it is necessary to recall our discussion of attribution theory and the Fundamental Attribution Error from Chapter Five. These theories provide a framework for understanding how we explain our own and others' behaviors. Recall our discussion of the **fundamental attribution error** which holds that people tend to attribute others' behaviors to internal, rather than external, causes. Rather than consider external or situational causes for others' behavior, which are also not always readily available, we often tend to take the "easy" way out and attribute others' behaviors to internal, or stable, factors, such as personality traits.

Not surprisingly, appraisals of our relationship partner's intentions relate to how satisfied we are in the relationship. Researchers have identified a consistent link between the attributions, or explanations, about relationship partners' intentions and reported relationship satisfaction (Fincham 1994; Waldinger and Schulz 2006). Much of the research on attributions in romantic relationships has examined how an assessment of a partner's accountability for a relationship transgression affects relationship satisfaction (Waldinger et al. 2006). It is natural to want to understand why our partner is acting a certain way, and eventually, these judgments influence our evaluation of our partner.

When relationship partners offer consistently negative attributions or explanations for a partner's behavior, they are more likely to report lower relationship satisfaction (Fincham and Bradbury 1993; Miller and Bradbury 1995). Thus, when a relationship partner forgets to buy a birthday present or forgets to recognize an important date, the offended partner may offer negative explanations for the behavior, especially if the negative behavior has been repeated over time. The offended partner may say, "He didn't get me a present because he is lazy," or "She didn't remember our anniversary because she is so self-absorbed." When individuals view a partner's behavior as selfishly motivated and intentional, they are more likely to view their partner in a negative way and to report decreased relationship satisfaction (Fincham, Harold, and Gano-Phillips 2000). Recent research indicates that relationship satisfaction can also affect the types of attributions partners make about each other's behavior, with less satisfied partners being more inclined to provide negative attributions for a partner's behaviors. Thus, the relationship between attribution processes and relationship satisfaction is described as a bidirectional one, which makes this somewhat challenging for researchers to study (Fincham et al. 2000).

Anita Vangelisti (1992) interviewed dating couples to determine the association between relationship problems and relational dissatisfaction. In her study, she recognized a problem as significant for relationship partners when it meets at least two of the following criteria: (1) the behavior must be negatively valenced on the relationship, (2) it must occur with some degree of frequency, and (3) it must be salient enough for one or both partners to remember it and recall it as a continuing source of dissatisfaction within the relationship. This makes sense, because if it is an annoying habit (such as not looking at your partner while listening) and it is consistent over time, it may reach the point where it becomes a relational problem. However, a salient behavior (such as kissing a colleague at happy hour) may only have to happen once, but is prominent enough to continually cause displeasure in the relationship, even though the behavior was never repeated. This study found that the most frequently reported communicative problem was withholding expression of negative feelings; the feelings of anger, fear, distress, disgust and shame.

Once we assess the relational problems, we may conclude that there is some form of inequity. **Equity theory** suggests that couples are happiest in relationships when there is a balance of inputs and outputs. If you perceive you are receiving too little from the relationship compared to what you are contributing, this will impact your satisfaction. Alternatively, if you are receiving more outputs from the relationship than you are contributing, you will feel a sense of guilt from the imbalance. However, this is highly subjective in terms of one's personal view of inputs, outputs, and fairness.

DECISION MAKING DURING RELATIONSHIP TERMINATION

Now we turn our attention to Duck's (1982) four-phase model of decision-making during relationship termination to understand how individuals determine whether or not to end a relationship.

Intrapsychic Phase

When one partner recognizes that something is wrong in a relationship and that he or she is no longer happy, feelings of frustration set in. The individual begins to consider the costs and rewards of the relationship and to explore the possibilities of alternative relationships. The "leaver" finds fault and places blame on the partner until finally, enough justification to withdraw from the relationship has accumulated. This initial phase in the relationship termination process is the **intrapsychic phase**. During this phase, the leaver spends considerable time contemplating whether the relationship is worth saving.

Dyadic Phase

When the leaver officially announces to the partner that he or she is leaving or thinking of leaving, the **dyadic phase** begins. This phase opens the flood gates for discussion and justifications. This often emotionally exhaustive phase is characterized by long talks and rationalizations of how the partnership "got to this place." During this phase, the other partner may make attempts to reconcile the relationship and to illustrate the costs of withdrawing. This phase typically continues until someone admits, "I have had enough."

Social Phase

If the relationship cannot be salvaged, the relationship termination then goes public. When the relationship termination is focused less on the relationship and more on the relationship partners' friends and family, it is a sign that we have moved to the **social phase**. For example, the question, What are we going to tell people? is often negotiated in this phase. Stories, blaming, and accounts of situations are articulated to friends and family. At this time, friends will often choose sides. In terms of the relationship partners, the rules and roles of their post break-up status are discussed. In other words, questions like, Can we still be friends? or Can I still call you? are negotiated.

Grave Dressing

The last phase is **grave dressing**. This phase is called grave dressing because partners typically "dress up" the dead relationship (or grave) by promoting a positive image of their role in their particular version of the relationship. Grave dressing also refers to "officially burying" the relationship. Partners are able to articulate the explanation of the termination and create their own versions of the relationship, whether truthful or not. Some people in this stage will have a ceremonial burying phase by burning pictures and returning, giving away, or selling items given to them by their "ex."

FIVE STAGES OF RELATIONSHIP DISSOLUTION

Knapp's model of relationship dissolution is both similar to and different from the model presented by Steve Duck (1982). Mark Knapp's model of relationship dissolution focuses more on what happens between the relationship partners and less on how the partners interact with their social circles (Vangelisti 2002). You may recall our discussion of Knapp's (1978) stages of coming together in Chapter Six; he also developed a five-stage model that depicts how relationships typically come apart, or dissolve. The five stages of dissolution are labeled: differentiating, circumscribing, stagnating, avoiding, and terminating. Remember our earlier discussion of stage models; it is possible that (1) partners are not in the same stage together, (2) some stages last longer than others do, and (3) partners often skip stages. It is important to note that this model seems to depict what actually happens when relationships deteriorate, not what should happen (Knapp 1978).

Differentiating

While in the stages of coming together, couples tend to emphasize hobbies, interests, and values that they have in common; in the **differentiating** stage, partners highlight their differences. Individuals accentuate their unique attributes and use more "I" and "me" statements. During this phase of relationship dissolution partners may engage in a great deal of conflict that often emphasizes all of the ways they differ from one another. For example, if someone says she likes eating out, the partner expresses a preference for cooking at home. If an individual tells his partner that he likes action movies, the partner immediately states her affinity for romantic comedies. One's independence from the relationship is the central focus of this stage, which has both positive and negative implications. On one hand, when individuals reassert their individual needs, they may choose to do things on their own, spend more time with friends, and reestablish their identity. This process can be healthy for a relationship. For example, let us say before two individuals entered into a relationship, he enjoyed playing hockey and she enjoyed participating in a yoga class. But as the relationship developed, there was less time for each person to enjoy his or her personal activity due to favoring more collaborative activities with the partner. In due course, these interests were neglected. In the differentiating stage, those roots may be returned to, with hockey or yoga classes being taken up again. This may provide a "spark" needed in the relationship and provide alternative topics for the partners to discuss. On the other hand, if the individual taking part in the activity excludes the significant other from his or her feelings and experiences, this independence may ultimately create more emotional distance in the relationship. If the partner is kept involved in emotional travels, this stage may have beneficial outcomes.

Circumscribing

When there is not a conscious decision to keep the partner involved, the relationship may drift apart. The next stage of relationship dissolution is labeled the **circumscribing** stage. During this stage, the communication between the relationship partners is often described as restricted, controlled, or constrained. Akin to the "don't talk about politics or religion" standard, relationship partners choose to talk about safe topics that will not lead to some type of argument (Vangelisti 2002). Both the quality and quantity of information exchanged between the relationship partners deteriorates as partners attempt to avoid sensitive subject matter. Relationship partners discuss "safe" topics such as plans for the day, current events, and the weather, which are barely deeper or warmer than material used in conversation with an acquaintance.

Stagnating

The third stage of relationship dissolution is the **stagnating** stage. This stage is often described as two people who are merely "going through the motions" in their relationship because their communication has come to a virtual standstill. There is very little interaction within the relationship and partners continue to do things separately. When they think of bringing up any issues regarding the relationship they tell themselves, "It will just turn into an argument,"

When couples resort to holding things inside to avoid conflict, communication is stagnant.

© iofoto, 2007, Shutterstock.

so they resort to holding things inside to avoid a conflict. They conserve their energy for their daily activities and do not exert any energy on preserving the relationship. Roommates, friends, and even family members may feel stagnant in their relationships with one another. Extended time in this stage can be particularly problematic as individuals may lose their motivation to fix the relationship. Over time, the thought of having to face the partner may become arduous. Therefore, it is often easier to just avoid the partner.

Avoiding

The fourth stage of coming apart is accurately labeled the **avoiding** stage. During this stage, relationship partners will actively fill their schedules to avoid seeing their partners. Vangelisti (2002) describes this stage as particularly difficult, noting that when the partners do talk to one another, "they make it clear that they are not interested in each other or in the relationship" (666). Relationship partners will arrive early to work and come home late in an effort to avoid one another. The idea of seeing the relationship partner is exhausting and any dialogue with this person is short, to the point, and often superficial. On the inside, individuals are exhausted from creating activities to avoid their partner and have increased disdain for him or her.

Termination

As we grow increasingly disappointed in a relationship and in our partner, we reach a threshold and we want to move on. This is when we reach the final stage of coming apart, the **termination** stage, which marks the end of the relationship. Relationship partners may choose to divorce the partner, move out, or call an end to any type of formal or contractual commitment with the partner. When relationship partners do communicate during this stage, they make attempts to put physical and/or psychological distance between themselves and their relationship partner. Relationship partners will also make attempts to disassociate themselves from their relationship partner. Some married individuals will disassociate themselves from their partners by using their maiden names or explicitly stating to friends, co-workers, and family members, "We are not a couple anymore." See Table 9.1 for examples of typical communication that occur during the stages of coming apart.

Table 9.1   Typical Communications in Knapp's Stages of Coming Apart

Stage	Communication Example
Differentiating	*"You always stare at my sister!"*
	"You are just so different from me!"
	"I hate when you don't wash the dishes!"

Stage	Communication Example
Circumscribing	*"It's going to rain tomorrow."*
	"Did you let the dog out yet?"
	"I am not going to answer that because it will just lead to a fight!"
Stagnating	*"Oh, you're home."*
	"What is the point of discussing this anymore?"
	"I know, I know. The usual."
Avoiding	*"I have to work nights all this week."*
	"I will not be home for dinner."
	"What time are you going?"
Terminating	*"I don't want to be in this relationship."*
	"Sorry, but we can't date anymore."
	"I'm moving out."

STRATEGIES USED TO TERMINATE RELATIONSHIPS

Determining how one should end a relationship can be quite stressful. Whether you are terminating a relationship with a romantic partner, a roommate, or a neighbor it can create much anxiety. When we are stressed we often turn to easily accessible solutions that are not always effective. However, we recommend that you do not employ any of the romantic relationship break-up lines provided in Table 9.2 below.

Once the leaver decides to verbalize his or her intentions, he or she typically relies on relational disengagement tactics. During the relational disengagement period, there is obviously a great deal of conflict. Leavers will use different strategies, depending on the type of the relationship and the timing of the disengagement. For example, more polite and face-saving tactics are typically used in the beginning of the relationship termination phase. However, if the rejected partner does not respond to these tactics, or if the leaver is in a dangerous relationship and immediate action is needed, more forceful and direct tactics may be necessary. Researchers have studied what people specifically

Table 9.2   Worst Break-Up Lines

1. I think we both know this is not working out.
2. I think one of us knows this is not really working out.
3. I am trouble, baby, with a capital T.
4. My wife is having a bigger problem with us dating than I thought she would.
5. It is not you, it is me.
6. It is not me, it is you.
7. Buh-bye.

Source: Adapted from www.esquire.com/features/articles. Ted Allen and Scott Omelianuk

recall saying during a break-up (Baxter 1982; Cody 1982) and they have identified five tactics used during relational disengagement.

Positive Tone Messages

First, **positive tone messages** are created to ease the pain for the rejected partner. These messages have a strong emotional tone and usually imply that the leaver would like to see less of the other person, but not entirely end the relationship. When individuals employ this strategy they usually want to try to end the relationship in a positive and pleasant way. An example of a positive tone message would be, "I really like you as a person, but I do not feel as strongly about you, as you do me." In other words, the classic "It's not you, it's me." Here the leaver tries to ease the pain of the break-up by suggesting that he or she still likes the rejected partner and is interested in a friendship.

De-escalation Messages

The second tactic also involves reducing the amount of time spent with the partner. **De-escalation messages** are less emotional than positive tone messages and typically provide a rationale for wanting to see less of the rejected partner. For example, "I think we need a break," or "My feelings for you have changed since the start of this relationship," would both be de-escalation messages. This strategy may be problematic because it is only perceived as a partial or temporary type of relationship termination strategy. Individuals who want to end the relationship for good may want to follow up with a more direct strategy for ending the relationship.

Withdrawal or Avoidance

A third tactic, **withdrawal** or **avoidance**, refers to actively spending less time with the person. This includes dodging phone calls, blocking IMs, and rerouting daily activities in order to avoid the individual. When you do run into the person, conversations are kept brief and shallow. This strategy is very indirect and can affect the individuals' ability to maintain a friendship in the future.

© Alex Brosa, 2007, Shutterstock.

When the relationship is not working, you may feel justification to end it.

Justification Tactic

A fourth way to disengage from a relationship involves the **justification tactic**. This tactic has three important elements. First, the relationship partner states that he or she needs to stop seeing the other person. Next, the relationship partner provides a reason for ending the relationship with the other person. Finally, the relationship partner recognizes that the relationship is not salvageable and may even become worse if the relationship continues. An example of this tactic is, "This relationship is not giving me what I need so we need to stop seeing each other." A person might say to his roommate, "I cannot live with you anymore because all we do is fight and argue and I do not see things getting any better. I am worried that if we stay roommates, things will get even worse than they are now!"

The last tactic is typically used as a last resort to terminate a relationship or when relationship partners are in need of immediate disengagement.

Negative Identity Management Tactic

A strategy which is used to hurry the disengagement process and has little consideration for the rejected partner is called the **negative identity management** tactic. Manipulation is often part of this tactic. For example, the leaver may spark a disagreement with the partner to create an unpleasant situation and then suggest, "See, this isn't working . . . we should see other people."

REDEFINING THE RELATIONSHIP AFTER THE BREAK-UP: REMAINING "JUST FRIENDS"

After a break-up, we often want to remain friends with our "ex." This makes sense because we have self-disclosed personal information to each other, relied on this person for emotional support and guidance, and have a number of things in common. Think about everything that drew you two together in the first place. But what are the chances that this new definition of your relationship will be successful? Some research suggests that a couple is much more likely to stay friends when the man has been the one who precipitated the break-up (or when the break-up was mutual) than when the woman initiated the break-up (Hill, Rubin, Peplau 1976).

Other research studies suggest that if the romantic couple were friends prior to the romantic involvement, their chances of returning to a friendship is significantly higher than those who never maintained a friendship (Metts, Cupach, and Bejlovec 1989). Additionally, if the partners were still receiving rewards or resources from the relationship, these could influence the impact of a partner's satisfaction with the post break-up friendship (Busboom, Collins, and Givertz 2002).

Certain relationship disengagement strategies are more effective in creating a positive post break-up relationship. When we ask our students how they would prefer to end a romantic relationship, most agree that they would desire an honest and direct strategy. Negative disengagement strategies, such as withdrawal, neglecting, or avoidance have been identified as inhibiting post-dating relationship quality (Metts et. al. 1989; Banks et al. 1987; Busboom, Collins, and Givertz 2002). If relationship partners would like to remain friends, it is a good idea to use positive tone messages, direct strategies or other tactics that protect the other person's feelings.

Although it is certainly possible to remain friends after a break-up, it is important that both parties agree with the new relational "rules." Discuss the boundaries of the relationship and be open about what is appropriate and inappropriate behavior. It is not unusual for post break-up friendships to cross the friendship boundaries in times of distress due to the familiarity, comfortableness, and security of the relationship (think Ross and Rachel from the television show *Friends*). It is important to remember you broke up for a reason!

After a break-up, keep yourself busy with family or friends you may have neglected during the relationships.

© digitalskillet, 2007, Shutterstock.

METHODS OF COPING WITH RELATIONSHIP DISSOLUTION

Scholars also note that the dissolution of a romantic relationship can be one of the most painful and stressful experiences people endure in their personal lives (Feeney and Noller 1992; Simpson 1987). This section will discuss methods of coping with relationship dissolution and creating closure.

Because ending a relationship can be one of the most emotionally charged events we experience, often there is no easy or painless way. No two relationships are identical in nature and there are no scripts to terminate relationships. We are flooded with different emotions including sadness, anger, fear, denial, guilt, and confusion. Sometimes we are relieved that the relationship is over and we are anticipating more rewarding relationships. Here are some methods of coping with relationship dissolution:

1. Recognize that relationship dissolution is a process. Allow yourself time to feel a range of emotions. This is normal and healthy. Do not reject your feelings or hide them behind negative coping strategies such as binge eating (or refusing to eat), binge drinking, or drug use. Also, do not rush into another romantic relationship without properly healing from the past.
2. Rely on your support network. Discuss your feelings with friends and family. Engage in activities that were neglected during your romantic relationship. Stay busy and redirect your attention. For example, find a new hobby or go on vacation with some of your friends.
3. If you feel you are burdening your friends and family, or you continue to feel depressed or angry, talking with a professional can help. Often, counseling is covered by health insurance. Most university counseling services are provided free of charge to students; take advantage of resources that are included in your tuition. Discussing issues with a third party that has no personal involvement in your existing relationships can provide a fresh perspective.

CLOSURE AND FORGIVENESS

Closure refers to a level of understanding, or emotional conclusion, to a difficult life event, such as terminating a romantic relationship. In this situation, closure often includes the rationale for the break-up. Some research suggests that individuals need a certain level of closure of their break-up before they can effectively move on (Weber 1998). The purpose of closure is to discuss things that "worked" in the relationship as well as to discuss the challenges of the relationship in order to learn from them. Remember, the purpose of this discussion is to make future relationships more effective, and not to resurrect the terminated relationship. Therefore, blaming, accusations, and name-calling are anti-productive. If properly executed, closure is helpful in understanding what went wrong in the relationship, providing some direction for future relationships.

Granting forgiveness is one strategy used during closure. Forgiveness does not mean you forget, accept, understand, or excuse the behavior; it simply implies that you will not hold your partner in debt for his or her wrongdoing. Granting forgiveness is a powerful tool. When you forgive someone that you are terminating a relationship with, you set yourself and your partner free from harboring negative feelings toward each other and perceptions of the relationship.

Self-forgiveness refers to you giving yourself permission to heal and move forward. You give yourself permission to shed yourself of the burden, guilt, pain, and anger that is held inside of you. Once you grant yourself forgiveness you can focus on how to become a better person and make healthier choices in the future.

Creating closure optimally involves getting together with your "ex" face-to-face to discuss the good times and the bad. In most situations, this option is impossible because either it is too difficult to sit in the same room or a partner has physically moved away. Therefore, closure is often difficult and not easily attainable. One way to create an emotional conclusion to a relationship is to reframe the event. Frequently, this is a way individuals can create a sense of closure without relying on the ex-partner. **Reframing** is a psychological process in which you change the way you look at the romantic termination in order to foster a more productive resolution. For example, if you are angry and hurt that your partner cheated on you, you may reframe the event by thinking about how dishonest the partner was. Instead of focusing on your hurt and anger, you psychologically emphasize that untruthfulness is not a characteristic of a person you want to share a romantic relationship with. You focus on recognizing signs of the cheating behavior and predictors of his or her behavior so you can be more aware in future relationships. By reframing the event, you are looking at the event in a different light, which enables you to move forward.

SUMMARY

In Hoobastank's hit song "The Reason," the singer apologizes for the choices he made in their relationship. "I've found a reason for me/ To change who I used to be . . . and the reason is you," he claims, suggesting he has learned from the mistakes made in the relationship and has grown as an individual. Although there are countless break-up songs, we deliberately chose this one because it demonstrates that relationship dissolution can be a learning experience. This chapter reviewed the indirect and direct ways individuals dissolve relationships. We reviewed the four-phase process of decision-making during relationship termination: intrapsychic phase, dyadic phase, social phase, and grave dressing phase, and also explored the five stages of relationship deterioration: differentiating, circumscribing, stagnating, avoiding, and terminating. Furthermore, we identified the five tactics used to terminate romantic relationships: positive tone messages, de-escalation messages, withdrawal tactics, justification tactics, and negative identity management tactics. Finally, we discussed consequences of relationship dissolution, including closure, forgiveness, and reframing the event.

APPLICATIONS

Exercise to Forgive Yourself

1. Write down with pen and paper all of the things that you have done wrong. It is imperative that you *write*. Word processing is not the same.
2. Read the list.
3. Now say "I did the best that I could with the knowledge that I had at the time. I now forgive myself and go free."
4. Destroy the list (burn, shred, do not eat).
5. Repeat the exercise for each of the other people who have hurt you.
6. Now begin anew to live your life without the burden of unforgiven pain.

Once you are able to talk about difficult subjects, you might try the following exercise.

From "Forgiveness as a Key to the Future" by Steven Martin & Catherine Martin, www.positive-way.com. Reprinted with permission of The Positive Way.

Exercise to Forgive a Partner

1. Set an agenda to work on one issue at a time. You both must agree that you are ready to talk about that issue.
2. Using active listening techniques and ground rules that you have agreed to, discuss the pain and concerns that you have about the issue. The object is to understand how you each *feel* about the issue. Do not point the finger and do not place blame, but try to understand the consequences of each other's actions. You must show respect and care for each other.
3. The offender asks for forgiveness. Apologies are extremely powerful. Understand the pain and feelings of the offended person.
4. The offended person agrees to forgive. Commit the issue to the past without getting even or holding the offender in debt. The issue will not be used as a weapon in future conflicts.
5. The offender agrees to change his or her behavior as appropriate.
6. You both move forward with a commitment to create a better future.

REFERENCES

Abrahms Spring, J. 1997. *After the affair: Healing the pain and rebuilding trust when a partner has been unfaithful.* New York: Harper Collins.

Amato, P. R., and S. J. Rogers. 1997. A longitudinal study of marital problems and subsequent divorce. *Journal of Marriage and the Family, 59*, 612–624.

Atkins, D. C., J. Yi, D. H. Baucom, and A. Christensen. 2005. Infidelity in couples seeking marital therapy. *Journal of Family Psychology, 19*, 470–473.

Atwood, J. D., and L. Schwartz. 2002. Cyber-sex: The new affair treatment considerations. *Journal of Couple and Relationship Therapy, 1*, 37–56.

Banks, S. P., D. M. Altendorf, J. O. Green, and M. J. Cody. 1987. An examination of relationship disengagement: Perceptions, breakup strategies and outcomes. *The Western Journal of Speech Communication, 52*, 19–41.

Baxter, L. 1982. Strategies for ending relationships: Two studies. *Western Journal of Speech Communication, 46*, 233–242.

Busboom, A. L., D. M. Collins, and M. D. Givertz. 2002. Can we still be friends? Resources and barriers to friendship quality after romantic relationship dissolution. *Personal Relationships, 9,* 215–223.

Cody, M. 1982. A typology of disengagement strategies and an examination of the role intimacy reactions to inequity and relational problems play in strategy selection. *Communication Monographs, 49,* 148–170.

Cupach, W. R., and S. Metts. 1986. Accounts of relational dissolution: A comparison of marital and non-marital relationships. *Communication Monographs, 53,* 311–334.

Deci, E. L., and R. M. Ryan. 1985. *Intrinsic motivation and self determination in human behavior.* New York: Plenum Press.

_____. 2000. The "what" and "why" of goal pursuits: Human needs and the self-determination of behavior. *Psychological Inquiry, 11,* 227–268.

_____. 2002. Self-determination research: Reflections and future directions. In E. L. Deci and R. M. Ryan (Eds.), *Handbook of self-determination research* (431–441). Rochester, NY: University of Rochester Press.

Duck, S. W. 1982. A topography of relationship disengagement and dissolution. In S. W. Duck (Ed.), *Personal relationships 4: Dissolving personal relationships* (1–30). London: Academic Press.

Feemey, J. A., and P. Noller. 1992. Attachment style and romantic love: Relationship dissolution. *Australian Journal of Psychology, 44,* 69–74.

Fincham, F. D. 1994. Cognition in marriage: Current status and future challenges. *Applied and preventative psychology: Current scientific perspectives, 3,* 185–198.

Fincham, F. D., and T. N. Bradbury. 1993. Marital satisfaction, depression and attributions: A longitudinal analysis. *Journal of Personality and Social Psychology, 64,* 442–452

Fincham, F. D., G. T. Harold, and S. Gano-Phillips. 2000. The longitudinal association between attributions and marital satisfaction: Direction of effects and role of efficacy expectations. *Journal of Family Psychology, 14,* 267–285.

Glass, D. P., and T. L. Wright. 1985. Sex differences in type of extramarital involvement and marital dissatisfaction. *Sex Roles, 12,* 1101–1120.

Hill, C. T., Z. Rubin, and L. A. Peplau. 1976. Breakups before marriage: The end of 103 affairs. *Journal of Social Issues, 32,* 147–168.

Isaacs, F. 1999. *Toxic friends/true friends: How your friends can make or break your health, happiness, family and career.* Scranton: William Morrow & Co.

Janus, S. S., and C. L. Janus. 1993. *The Janus report on sexual behavior.* New York: Wiley.

Johnson, A. J., E. Wittenberg, M. Haigh, S. Wigley, J. Becker, K. Brown, and E. Craig. 2004. The process of relationship development and deterioration: Turning points in friendships that have terminated. *Communication Quarterly, 52,* 54–67.

Knapp, M. L. 1978. *Social intercourse: From greeting to goodbye.* Boston: Allyn & Bacon.

Kurdek, L. A. 1998. Relationship outcomes and their predictors: Longitudinal evidence from heterosexual married, gay cohabiting, and lesbian cohabiting couples. *Journal of Marriage and the Family, 60,* 553–568.

_____. 1992. Relationship stability and relationship satisfaction in cohabiting gay and lesbian couples: A prospective longitudinal test of the contextual and interdependence models. *Journal of Social and Personal Relationships, 9,* 125–142.

La Guardia, J. G., R. M. Ryan, C. E. Couchman, and E. L. Deci. 2000. Within-person variation in security of attachment: A self-determination theory perspective on attachment, need fulfillment, and well-being. *Journal of Personality and Social Psychology, 79,* 367–384.

Lund, M. 1985. The development of investment and commitment scales for predicting continuity of personal relationships. *Journal of Social and Personal Relationships, 2,* 3–23.

Merolla, A. J., K. D. Weber, S. A. Myers, and M. B. Booth-Butterfield. 2004. The impact of past dating relationship solidarity on commitment, satisfaction, and investment in current relationships. *Communication Quarterly, 52,* 251–264.

Metts, S., W. R. Cupach, and R. A. Bejlovec. 1989. "I love you too much to ever start liking you": Redefining romantic relationships. *Journal of Social and Personal Relationships, 6,* 259–274.

Miller, G. E., and T. N. Bradbury. 1995. Refining the association between attributions and behavior in marital interaction. *Journal of Family Psychology, 9,* 196–208.

Rose, S., and F. C. Serafica. 1986. Keeping and ending casual, close, and best friendships. *Journal of Social and Personal Relationships, 3,* 275–288.

Simpson, J. A. 1987. The dissolution of romantic relationships: Factors involved in relationship stability and distress. *Journal of Personality and Social Psychology, 53,* 683–692.

Spitzberg, B., and M. Tafoya. 2005. Explorations in communicative infidelity: Jealousy, sociosexuality, and vengefulness. Paper presented at the International Communication Association annual meeting in New York, NY.

Thibault, J. W., and H. H. Kelley. 1959. *The Social Psychology of Groups.* New York: Wiley.

Treas, J., and D. Giesen. 2000. Sexual infidelity among married and cohabiting Americans. *Journal of Marriage and the Family, 62*, 48–60.

Vangelisti, A. L. 2002. Interpersonal processes in romantic relationships. In M. L. Knappand J. A. Daly. (Eds.), *Handbook of interpersonal communication* (643–679). Thousand Oaks, CA: Sage Publications.

———. 1992. Communicative problems in committed relationships: An attributional analysis. In J. H. Harvery, T. L. Orbuch, and A. L. Weber (Eds.), *Attributions, accounts, and close relationships* (144–164). New York: Springer-Verlag.

Waldinger, R. J., and M. S. Schulz. 2006. Linking hearts and minds in couple interactions: Intentions, attributions, and overriding sentiments. *Journal of Family Psychology, 20*, 494–504.

Weber, A. L. 1998. Losing, leaving, and letting go: Coping with nonmarital breakups. In B. H. Spitzberg and W. R. Cupach (Eds.), *The dark side of close relationships* (267–306). Mahwah, NJ: Erlbaum.

Weber, K., and B. R. Patterson. 1996. Construction and validation of a communication based emotional support scale. *Communication Research Reports, 13*(1), 68–76.

Wheeless, L. 1976. Self-disclosure and interpersonal solidarity: Measurement, validation, and relationships. *Human Communication Research, 3*(1), 47–61.

———. 1978. A follow-up study of the relationships among trust, disclosure, and interpersonal solidarity. *Human Communication Research, 4*(2), 143–157.

Wheeless, L. R., V. E. Wheeless, and R. Baus. 1984. Sexual communication, communication satisfaction, and solidarity in the developmental stages of intimate relationships. *Western Journal of Speech Communication, 48*, 217–230.

Whisman, M. A., A. E. Dixon, and B. Johnson. 1997. Therapists' perspectives of couple problems and treatment issues in couple therapy. *Journal of Family Psychology, 11*, 361–366.

Wilmont, W. W., D. A. Carbaugh, and L. A. Baxter. 1985. Communicative strategies used to terminate romantic relationships. *Western Journal of Speech Communication, 49*, 204–216.

The Dark Side of Interpersonal Relationships

OBJECTIVES

- Understand what is meant by the "dark side" of communication
- Define *deception*
- Explain Interpersonal Deception Theory
- Discuss the three potential deceptive responses
- Describe five fundamental dimensions that deceivers use to manage information
- Discuss three possible methods of deception detection
- Identify three sets of key questions used to contemplate telling a lie
- Explain three reasons embarrassment occurs in social situations
- Identify three roles associated with embarrassment
- Provide three potential responses to embarrassing communication
- Define *jealousy* and identify the six types of jealousy
- Explain the six jealousy-related goals
- Distinguish between the five bases of power
- Describe the three levels of influence
- Distinguish between argumentativeness and aggressiveness
- Explain the four levels of aggression
- Define *Obsessive Relational Intrusion* (ORI)
- Recognize potential risks for ORI as a result of computer-mediated communication

© Marcin Balcerzak, 2007, Shutterstock.

KEY TERMS

dark side of communication
deception
Interpersonal Deception Theory (IDT)
falsification
concealment
equivocation
completeness
relevance/directness
clarity
personalization

veridicality
leakage cues
positive relational deceptive strategies
third-party information
solicited vs. unsolicited confessions
embarrassment
agent
recipients
observer

accounts
apologies
joking
jealousy
friend jealousy
family jealousy
romantic jealousy
power jealousy
activity jealousy
intimacy jealousy
compensatory restoration
power

reward power
coercive power
legitimate power
referent power
expert power
compliance
identification

internalization
dominance
argumentativeness
verbal aggression
low aggression
moderate aggression
high aggression

severe aggression
Employee Emotional
   Abuse (EEA)
obsessive relational
   intrusion

OVERVIEW

Yoda warns us in *Star Wars* about the symbolic dangers of the "dark side." He identifies anger, fear, and aggression as characteristics of this dark place. In the past two chapters we have discussed how we initiate and sustain relationships. But the stark reality is this—our interpersonal relationships can, and often *do*, experience a dark side. Friends and family members can deceive us, romantic partners may lie and cheat, and our colleagues and supervisors could attempt to abuse their power. As a result of these negative behaviors in our relationships, we can become angry, fearful, and perhaps even aggressive towards others. Although most of the research in communication is devoted to discussing appropriate and effective behavior to foster positive communicative outcomes, William Cupach and Brian Spitzberg challenged academic scholars to tackle problematic and disruptive communication patterns in their 1994 book, *The Dark Side of Interpersonal Communication*. What exactly is the dark side of communication? The **dark side of communication** is defined as, "an integrative metaphor for a certain perspective toward the study of human folly, frailty and fallibility" (Cupach and Spitzberg 1994, 240). Some examples of **dark communication** that have been studied are: deception or lying, conflict, jealousy, intentionally hurtful messages, relationship termination, embarrassment, loneliness, co-dependency, and obsession, or stalking (Spitzberg 2006). This chapter recognizes that interpersonal relationships are not always filled with sunshine and smiles. People can, and do, lie, deceive, abuse power, and cheat in all types of relationships.

Beware of the dark side. Anger . . . fear . . . aggression. The dark side of the Force are they. Easily they flow, quick to join you in a fight.

Star Wars: Episode V The Empire Strikes Back directed by George Lucas, 2 hrs. 4 min., LucasFilm, 1980.

The goal of this chapter is to recognize the dark side of communication and to understand the motivation behind these behaviors. Although we cannot possibly attempt to discuss all of the communication behaviors that have been identified as potentially negative or dark, we have selected a few which most students in interpersonal communication are likely to encounter. Specifically, we will explore the how and why individuals in romantic or platonic relationships deceive each other, become jealous, deal with social embarrassment, engage in aggressive behavior, and abuse relationships. Further, we will discuss the role that dark communication plays in online interactions. To assist you in understanding how these concepts have been examined, we will discuss various studies that provide a clearer picture of these destructive forms of communicating. We will also provide suggestions on how to cope if you encounter these circumstances.

DECEPTION AND INTERPERSONAL RELATIONSHIPS

In 2004, a study conducted by Britain's *That's Life!* magazine examined the prevalence of lies in relationships. The magazine surveyed 5,000 women and discovered that ninety-four percent of them admitted to lying. While thirty-four percent of them reported that they tell "white lies" daily, seventy-six percent of the women revealed to researchers that they have told life-changing lies (Knox, Schact, Holt, and Turner 1993). While your initial reaction may be one of shock at the high percentage of women who admitted to lying, stop for a minute and recall the last time that you failed to tell the complete and honest truth. Perhaps your significant other asked what you thought about a meal he had cooked or how she looked in an outfit. Or maybe you lied to your boss about why you called off work or needed to switch shifts. What do we lie about? Most people admit to lying about everything from what they ate for breakfast to why they were late for work. Married couples may even lie to one another about their finances. In 2006, the *New Zealand Herald* reported results of a poll taken by a bank which discovered that forty-two percent of women and thirty-five percent of men lie to their partners about their financial situation. **Deception** is defined as, "a message knowingly transmitted by a sender to foster a false belief or conclusion by a receiver" (Buller and Burgoon, 1996, 209). While we would like to believe that our relationships are built on truth and honesty, the reality is that friends, family members, and romantic partners deceive each other from time to time. Consider this scenario:

> Jack has been in love with Shawna since their freshman year of college. He was always extremely nervous about speaking with her and he came to terms with the fact that they would probably never be together. In the meantime, Jack started dating Shawna's roommate, Tina. After three months, Jack really started to fall for Tina. One evening, Shawna asked Jack for a ride to the library. He agreed. In the car, Shawna started expressing feelings for Jack. Jack was stunned. He just could not believe that this day had come. His heart raced as he tried to think of an appropriate reply. However, out of respect to his relationship with Tina, he reluctantly told Shawna that he did not have feelings for her.

In this example, Jack protects his current relationship with Tina by deceiving Shawna about his true feelings. Of course, we know that not all deception is done with such honorable intentions. David Buller and Judee Burgoon (1996) proposed **Interpersonal Deception Theory** (IDT) to explain the strategic choices made when engaging in deceptive communication (1996). While a person may attempt to be strategic in creating a deceptive message, there are cues that alert the other person that the individual is being less than honest. At the same time, the receiver of the message attempts to mask, or hide, his knowledge of the deception. Rather than directly accuse the person who is lying, the person may nod their head, offer verbal prompts ("I see!" or "So what else happened?"), and generally behave in ways designed to keep the source from seeing his suspicion. In essence, it is a back-and-forth game between relational partners. The source tries to mask the deception and the receiver tries to hide his suspicion of the deception. Now, consider this example:

> Julie and Robbie have been dating for two years. During the fall semester of their junior year, Julie decided to study abroad in Scotland.

Although, Robbie was not happy that Julie was leaving, he was excited for her. At first, Julie was extremely homesick and spoke with Robbie every evening. As time passed, she met several new friends in Scotland and enjoyed going out dancing every night. Some evenings she had a little too much to drink and would end up kissing other men on the dance floor. Robbie continued to call Julie each night. He was becoming increasingly suspicious of Julie's behavior abroad. One evening he asked Julie, "Have you been with anyone since you have been there?"

There are three potentially deceptive responses that Julie can give. She can tell an outright lie or resort to **falsification:** "No, I have been completely faithful." Oftentimes this requires the source to create a fictional story to explain the lie. Alternatively, Julie might partially tell the truth while leaving out important details. This refers to **concealment:** "Well, when I go out I do dance with other guys." We typically do this when we want to hide a secret. Or Julie could engage in **equivocation,** or be strategically vague: "Just because I go out dancing does not necessarily mean I have to hook up with someone." This type of response is used to avoid the issue altogether.

In addition to managing the deceptive responses discussed previously (falsification, concealment, equivocation), Interpersonal Deception Theory also suggests that deceivers manipulate their verbal and nonverbal behavior to appear more credible (Burgoon et al. 1996). This manipulation is accomplished by varying the message along five fundamental dimensions.

Completeness

First, deceivers may vary on the **completeness** or extent of message details. The deceiver knows that an appropriate amount of information needs to be provided in order to be perceived truthful by the receiver. The more practiced deceiver also realizes that specific details are probably best kept to a minimum; there is less for the receiver to challenge. When interpreting the completeness of a message, receivers may become suspicious if the information provided is too brief or vague.

Relevance/Directness

A second fundamental dimension on which deceptive messages are manipulated is its **relevance** or **directness.** This refers to the extent to which the deceiver produces messages that are logical in flow and sequence, and are pertinent to the conversation. The more direct and relevant the message, the more it is perceived as truthful. Two indicators of potential deception are when a person goes off on a tangent in response to a question or is cautious in his or her response.

Clarity

The extent to which the deceiver is clear, comprehensible, and concise is a third dimension of message manipulation. The **clarity** dimension varies along a continuum from very clear to completely ambiguous. The more evasive or vague a message is, the more cause there is for a receiver to probe for additional information and clarification.

Personalization

A fourth dimension involves the **personalization** of the information. The extent to which the deceiver takes ownership of the information may vary. If the deceiver relies on verbal distancing or non-immediate communication, he will be perceived as less truthful. For example, the suggestions "everyone goes out during the week here" and "I just miss you so much that I am just trying to keep myself busy," are two examples that disassociate the deceiver with the behavior.

Veridicality

The last dimension is the extent to which the deceiver appears to be truthful, or the **veridicality** of the message. This dimension is twofold. First, the message is constructed based on the objective truth value reported by the source. In other words, to what extent does the deceiver believe the message is truthful? Next, the believability of the message is judged by the receiver. In evaluating the truthfulness of a message, receivers often rely on nonverbal cues that are the result of our body language. Examples of behaviors believed to signal deception include increased blinking, speech errors, higher voice pitch and enlarged pupils (Zuckerman and Driver 1985). These unconscious behaviors are often referred to as **leakage cues,** and while deceptive individuals attempt to control these behaviors, others may be able to detect their dishonesty.

People often tell lies to make themselves seem more attractive to someone new.

WHY DO WE LIE?

Based on the high percentage of people who report engaging in deception, the question becomes, why are we so prone to lying? When asked, most people suggest that they lie to make themselves appear more admirable. In Chapter Six we discussed the role of physical attraction in initiating relationships. Thus, it comes as no surprise that one study revealed that we lie to attract an attractive date (Rowatt, Cunningham and Druen 1999). In the study, participants reported lying about their own personal attributes such as appearance, personality, income, career, grades and past relational outcomes in an attempt to attract another person. In fact, twenty-five percent of respondents indicated that they engage in this type of deception in initial encounters with someone they are attracted to.

Consider the following conversation from the *Friends* episode "The One the Morning After." Ross debates whether he should be honest with Rachel about sleeping with another woman during the time that he and Rachel were apart.

Ross tells Chandler and Joey that Rachel wants to work on their relationship and worries about how she will react to hearing that he slept with another woman. They can't believe Ross is even considering telling Rachel about it . . . how stupid can he be?

But Ross believes that he needs to be completely honest with Rachel if there is any hope to rebuild their relationship. Joey agrees that being honest is best, as long as it doesn't cause any problems! And Chandler points out that it will only hurt Rachel. There won't be anything left to save if Ross tells her.

Ross still isn't completely convinced that he should keep quiet. Chandler concedes, saying that at least Ross should wait until the time is right to tell Rachel . . . and that would be when he's on his deathbed.

According to the deception literature, there are three types of lies that people tell (Camden, Motley, and Wilson 1984; DePaulo, Kashy, Kirkendale, Wyer, and Epstein 1996). These include lies to: (1) harm others, (2) protect self, and (3) spare others.

Lying to Harm Others

The first type of deceptions, lying to harm others, is often the most damaging type of lie in interpersonal relationships. These types of lies are done to intentionally hurt others by distorting information, fabricating stories, or deliberately omitting important information. Perhaps the best example of lies designed to harm others are those seen during political campaign ads. Specific information about one's opponent is strategically distorted and manipulated in an attempt to damage their candidacy.

Lying to Protect Self

A more egotistical goal refers to lying to protect self. The goal of this type of lie is to make oneself look good. This can be accomplished by exaggerating praise and/or omitting weaknesses. In a study that examined sexual lies among college students, lying about the number of previous sexual partners emerged as the most frequently told lie (Knox et al. 1993). Regardless of whether the number of sexual partners was inflated to appear more experienced, or reduced to appear more "pure," the goal of the lie was to enhance one's image.

Spare Others

The most common type of lie is to spare others. In the movie *A Few Good Men*, Jack Nicholson's character, Colonel Nathan R. Jessep, states, "You can't handle the truth." In this situation, Col. Jessep emphasizes that sometimes we lie in order to spare or protect others from the truth. Perhaps we want to avoid hurting the other person's feelings or damaging his self-esteem. At other times we may "stretch the truth" or omit details for the good of the relationship. Consider the earlier example of Ross' lie to Rachel. Joey and Chandler try to help justify the deception by pointing out that the truth would end up hurting Rachel and would eliminate any chance of a potential future together.

ARE THERE GOOD REASONS FOR LYING?

While the definition of deception indicates that a source intentionally designs the message with the goal of instilling a false belief in the receiver, it is important to take a step back and consider the potential benefits of deception in relationships (Knapp and Vangelisti 2006). Dan O'Hair and Michael Cody (1994) distinguish between positive or negative deceptive strategies. They suggest that strategies that enhance, escalate, repair, and improve

relationships can be considered **positive relational deceptive strategies.**
These include responses to the inevitable questions, "How do you like my
new outfit?" or "What do you think of my new haircut?" In these situations
we often respond with a white lie in order to foster liking, or positive affect.
In other words, we are motivated to deceive to preserve the relationship, to
avoid hurting the other person's feelings, to avoid a conflict, or even to protect a third party. In other instances, we may decide that the deception is not
worth the risk. Consider the following example when it was determined that
the potential consequences of deception outweighed the benefits. In the film
The Pursuit of Happyness, Will Smith portrays a homeless man who is seeking
an internship with a stock brokerage firm. After spending the night in jail for
unpaid parking tickets, Smith rushes to his interview at Dean Witter. As he
enters the room in a tshirt and jeans spattered with paint, he says, "I've been
sitting outside trying to think up a good story of why I would show up for
such an important interview dressed like this. And I couldn't think of a good
story. So I finally decided it was probably best to just tell the truth." In the
end, his character's honesty impresses the interviewers, and he is offered the
internship.

Have you ever lied about
a friend's appearance to
avoid hurt feelings?

DETECTING DECEPTION

Understanding the ways in which messages are manipulated is one way to
enhance your ability to detect deception. Earlier we described some of the nonverbal cues associated with deception. But there are several verbal cues that
can tip us off about lies as well. In a recent study on deceptive communication practices (Park et al. 2002), 202 college students were asked to recall a
time when they had caught another person being deceptive. While a variety of
discovery mechanisms were identified in the study, the three most prominent
ones include the strategies labeled third party information, physical evidence,
and confessions.

Third-Party Information

Third-party information involves information being revealed by a person outside the relationship. Suppose a teenager wants to go to a party while his parents are out of town, but he knows his parents would not approve. He lies to
his parents and tells them that he is spending the night at his friend's house in
case they call home while he is at the party. When his mother speaks with the
friend's mother a few days later and thanks her for allowing him to stay at their
house, the friend's mother reveals that he never spent the night. Thus the lie is
revealed by an outside party.

Physical Evidence

Sometimes we are able to detect deception by doing our best Sherlock Holmes
impression and looking for physical evidence. For instance, on an episode of
Grey's Anatomy, Addison, Dr. Shepherd's wife, discovered a pair of black panties
that clearly did not belong to her in her husband's tuxedo pocket. The physical

evidence swiftly revealed Derek's betrayal and finally ended the fragile marriage. The classic lipstick-on-the-collar shtick is another familiar Hollywood portrayal of deception detection.

Confessions

Another method by which deception is detected is via confessions made by the deceiver. **Solicited confessions** are often offered as the result of direct questioning or confrontation. Suppose you heard that your best friend went on a ski trip with a group of people the same weekend that the two of you had planned to go to a professional hockey game. Initially, he told you that he could not go to the game because he was swamped with homework. When you follow up and tell him that you heard he had gone skiing that same weekend, he feels guilty and confesses his lie. While some confessions are solicited, at other times these declarations come from out of the blue. Suppose your significant other spontaneously confesses that she has been reading your emails without your knowledge. Nothing caused you to suspect that she was engaging in this behavior, yet she decided to make an **unsolicited confession.** An important point to note is that we are often able to detect deception using a combination of cues—in fact, many people report a combination of verbal and nonverbal signals as tipping them off about dishonesty.

TO LIE OR NOT TO LIE: THAT IS THE QUESTION

Deception and lying are multidimensional constructs. Key components to consider when analyzing a deceptive message include: the importance of the relationship, the importance of the information to the relationship, and the costs and rewards associated with the lie. When deciding whether it is to your benefit to tell a lie, consider the following three sets of questions posed by Knapp and Vangelisti (2006):

1. What is the potential outcome of the lie? Can it potentially benefit our relationship, or one of us, individually?
2. Based on the rules we have established for our relationship, is it reasonable and just for me to tell a lie? Or am I violating one of the spoken or unspoken expectancies that we have for our relationship? What lies would we agree upon that are acceptable versus unacceptable?
3. Am I telling a lie in an attempt to protect my partner from being harmed? If I were to be caught telling the lie, would my partner understand my justification for telling the lie?

What is the most important determinant in ending a relationship as a result of deception? Knapp and Vangelisti (2006) state that the more importance the receiver attaches to the information being lied about, the greater the chance that he or she will decide to end the relationship.

Now that you have a better understanding of the concept of deception and of the reasons why people lie, it is our hope that you will be strategic in your analysis of the appropriateness of deceptive messages.

EMBARRASSMENT: WHY DID I SAY THAT?

Can you remember a time when you had a huge crush on someone, and when you finally had the opportunity to talk to them and make that great first impression, something went horribly wrong and you ended up putting your foot in your mouth? Or have you ever told a joke at a party and nobody laughed? In these types of situations, we often experience social embarrassment. Recall our discussion in Chapter Two regarding the role of self-presentation in relationships. When we perceive that our self-esteem has been threatened or if we have presented what we perceive to be a negative view of the self to others, **embarrassment** occurs. Our sense of identity is at stake if the response to our behavior is not what we expected. Gross and Stone (1964) proposed that embarrassment emerges as the result of three factors that occur in social interactions. First, misrepresentations or cognitive shortcomings may cause us to feel embarrassment. Have you ever called someone by the wrong name or forgotten how you know someone? Losing confidence in our role or ability in a social situation can also cause us to experience discomfort. Sometimes we script out an interaction, such as the all-important first phone call to an attractive person, and the conversation does not turn out like we had anticipated. Finally, a loss of dignity, or composure, can cause us to become "red-faced." Examples of this may include tripping as you are making your big entrance into the campus hangout, or discovering that your pants are unzipped after you have just had a conversation with your boss.

Our Role in Embarrassment

It is easy to see why we would be embarrassed in any of these situations, even as we were in control of our own behavior. We can just as easily become uncomfortable in those situations where we are the silent observer. Sattler (1965) identified three roles that exist in embarrassing social situations: agent, recipient, and observer. As an **agent,** we are responsible for our own embarrassment, perhaps by accidentally swearing in front of your grandmother or unexpectedly burping during an important interview lunch. In other situations, we are the **recipients,** or targets, of embarrassing communication. Examples of this type of embarrassment might include your best friend revealing to your secret crush that you are attracted to him and your mother telling your friend about the time you ran naked around the neighborhood when you were three years old. Finally, it is likely that you can recall a situation where you were simply a bystander, or **observer,** of another's embarrassment and experienced feelings of discomfort yourself. In these situations, we often offer an awkward comment, express a reassuring remark, or simply attempt to ignore the situation.

Responding to Embarrassment

Building on Goffman's theory of face-saving and identity management, Edelmann (1985) identified three primary types of messages individuals use in response to embarrassing encounters. These include accounts, apologies, and jokes. **Accounts** provide a potential explanation for the cause of the embarrassing situation. Suppose you arrive at class only to discover that you forgot an important assignment that was due. You decide to speak with your instructor

Sometimes one embarrassing moment seems like it will last forever.

© Andrew Taylor, 2007, Shutterstock.

and explain that you have been overwhelmed with group projects in two other classes and with searching for a job. In some instances, we may feel the need to apologize for the embarrassing behavior. **Apologies** are attempts to identify the source of blame for the incident. Suppose you accidentally revealed to your friend that she has not been included in the group's plans for the weekend. As you stumble over your words, you might comment, "I'm sorry. I didn't realize until now that you weren't invited," or "I didn't make the plans. They invited me along and I just assumed you were included." These responses are made with the hope that your friend will forgive you for the non-invitation. **Joking** involves using humor to create a more light-hearted response to a situation. At the 2006 Academy Awards, Jennifer Garner tripped over her dress as she approached the podium. To cover her embarrassment, she joked, "I do all my own stunts." According to arousal relief theory (Berylne 1969), use of humor in embarrassing or difficult situations often evokes positive affective responses which can help individuals diffuse anxiety or stress.

The next time that you find yourself becoming embarrassed in a social situation, remember—everyone experiences this discomfort at one time or another. While at the time it may appear to be a black cloud that hangs over your head, it is likely that these feelings will be temporary and short-lived. However, there are other dark aspects of interpersonal communication whose impact may not be so minimal on our interactions and relationships.

JEALOUSY IN INTERPERSONAL RELATIONSHIPS

Another aspect of interpersonal relationships that has received a lot of attention in the literature is jealousy. Chances are that you have heard jealousy described as the "green-eyed monster." In the movie *Terms of Endearment*, a mother's jealousy over her daughter's relationships wreaks havoc in their own relationship. Jealousy causes us to experience a variety of emotions and sometimes causes us to communicate or react in ways that we normally would not. Consider some of the things that can cause us to experience jealousy:

- Your best friend recently went away to college. He sends you text messages describing all the fun he is having with his new roommate and other friends he has made in the dorm.
- A co-worker talks about all the activities that she does with her young children. You wonder how she is able to find the time to finish her work and spend so much time with her kids, especially because you see yourself as a neglectful parent.
- Your relationship partner has been spending a great deal of time lately with a new friend and has expressed repeatedly how much he likes this friend.

In situations like those described in the scenarios above, it is normal to experience feelings of anger or sadness. Maybe we even feel a little bit envious or resentful. **Jealousy** has been defined as, "a protective reaction to a perceived threat to a valued relationship, arising from a situation in which the partner's involvement with an activity and/or another person is contrary to the jealous person's definition of their relationship" (Hansen 1985, 713). It is important to point out that this definition addresses the fact that jealousy can be experienced in various types of relationships, not just romantic, and can be induced by various issues or situations.

Types of Jealousy in Relationships

Jennifer Bevan and Wendy Samter (2004) used this definition as the foundation for their study, which examined six different types of jealousy, three that are experienced as a result of the type of the relationship, and three that are based on the issues experienced between partners. The types identified in this study include: (1) friend jealousy, (2) family jealousy, (3) romantic jealousy, (4) power jealousy, (5) intimacy jealousy, and (6) activity jealousy. The first two types, **friend jealousy** and **family jealousy,** are typically the result of an individual's relationship with another friend or family member. In this situation, we often become frustrated and perceive them as being "taken" away from us. **Romantic jealousy** is also the result of a partner's relationship with another person, and is associated with perceived intimacy between two people. Consider the following example:

> Justin noticed that his wife, Nicole, had been spending more and more time at work. One evening, he decided to surprise her by taking dinner to her office. As he approached her office, he noticed that she was engrossed in a quiet conversation with an attractive man. Angry, Justin stormed out of the building without saying a word. For the next several days, Justin was very curt in his conversations with Nicole. Finally she asked him what was bothering him. Justin exploded, "So who is the new guy at work? And why didn't you tell me that you're spending so much time together?" Nicole was dumbfounded and responded, "I don't know what you're talking about." Justin mentioned that he had stopped by to bring her dinner and had seen them talking quietly in her office. Finally, Nicole understood who he was referring to and responded, "That was Marcus, the consultant who was brought in from Seattle to help with this project. He saw the picture of the kids on my desk and wanted to talk about how much he's missing his own kids since he's been away from them for the past two weeks."

In this scenario, romantic jealousy caused Justin to perceive a potential relationship between Nicole and her co-worker. It should come as no surprise that this type of jealousy has received the most attention in literature. Therefore, many of the studies discussed in this section will refer to romantic jealousy.

The last three types of jealousy examined by Bevan and Samter (2004) involve issues experienced by relational partners. **Power jealousy** is often associated with perceptions that a partner's other relationships or obligations are viewed as more important than your relationship with the person. If a friend changes plans and cannot spend time with you, or decides to invite others to go to the game with the two of you, you may question whether outside issues are more important to her than your relationship. **Activity jealousy** emerges when our relational partner dedicates time to various hobbies or interests. Have you ever become frustrated by the amount of attention that a friend dedicates to PlayStation, fraternity or sorority activities, or sports? In these

An attempt to make yourself appear more "attractive" than the competition may just make you look insecure.

© Fat, 2007, Shutterstock.

instances, the activities are perceived as a threat to your relationship. Finally, **intimacy jealousy** is the result of the exchange of intimate or private information that a partner may share with a third party, someone not in the relationship. Suppose your significant other reveals to his best friend that he is undergoing a series of medical tests, but says nothing to you. Your discovery of the "concealed" information results in feelings of intimacy jealousy. Later, you may discover that your partner simply did not want you to worry, and decided not to tell you until the results of the test were returned.

Why Does Jealousy Occur?

What causes us to experience feelings of jealousy? Laura Guerrero and Peter Anderson (1998) suggest that there are at least six jealousy-related goals. An extensive body of research on this topic has concluded that individuals evoke or suppress feelings of jealousy to obtain a variety of goals or objectives in their personal relationships. In the next sections we examine the six jealousy-related goals identified by researchers.

Maintain the Primary Relationship.   First, we become jealous in situations where we wish to maintain the primary relationship. Specifically, we are concerned with preserving the relationship. When individuals are interested in maintaining a current relationship, they will often compare themselves to a rival and try to appear more rewarding to their partner by compensating for any perceived shortcomings (Guerrero and Afifi 1999). Making oneself appear more "attractive" than the competition (also referred to as **compensatory restoration,** see table 10.1) may be an effective maintenance strategy—up to a point. Making incessant comparisons to rivals may cause your partner to perceive you as being desperate or insecure.

Preserving One's Self-Esteem.   A second goal associated with jealousy is focused on preserving one's self-esteem. This jealousy goal is concerned with maintaining one's pride, and with feeling good about oneself. Individuals who are concerned about protecting their self-esteem rarely seek out circumstances that may threaten how they view themselves (Kernis 1995). Therefore, it comes as no surprise that the more an individual is focused on preserving his or her self-esteem, the more likely he or she is to avoid or deny jealous situations (Guerrero and Afifi 1999). Since jealousy has a negative connotation in our culture and is related to perceptions of "weakness," it makes sense that these individuals are less likely to question or scrutinize their partners' behavior or to communicate jealous feelings.

Reducing Uncertainty about the Relationship.   Another goal of jealousy is to reduce uncertainty about the relationship. The purpose of this type of jealousy is to help an individual learn where one stands in the relationship, predict the future of the relationship, and understand how the other partner perceives the relationship. This was the only goal found to predict open and non-aggressive communication between partners (Guerrero and Afifi 1999). If the purpose of jealousy is to reduce uncertainty and learn more about the partner, it makes sense that open and direct communication are essential to accomplishing this goal.

Reducing Uncertainty about a Rival Relationship.   A fourth goal involves reducing uncertainty about a rival relationship. This jealousy goal determines the threat of the competition, or how serious the rival relationship is. Individuals who focus on this goal often resort to indirect strategies, such as spying, checking up on the partner, or questioning the rival about the situation (Guerrero and Afifi 1999). They may do this to save face with their partners so they are not perceived as "jealous" people.

Re-assess the Relationship.   When individuals are questioning the status of a relationship, they may use jealousy in an attempt to re-assess the relationship. This goal is concerned with comparing the cost with the benefits associated with the relationship. When analyzing this goal, Guerero and Afifi (1999) found that individuals typically engage in indirect strategies such as avoidance, distancing, or making the partner feel jealous. When we are evaluating a relationship, we typically step back to reconsider our own perceptions of autonomy (see our discussion of the relationship stages of coming apart in Chapter Ten). Therefore, it may make sense to give the relationship space.

Restoring Equity through Retaliation.   Do you know anyone who purposely evoked jealousy to get back at someone or to make his or her partner feel bad? The last goal of jealousy refers to this idea of restoring equity through retaliation. The purpose of evoking this type of jealousy response is to show the partner what it is like to experience negative emotions and to hurt the person as retribution for something the partner has done.

There are clearly a number of different reasons that relationship partners attempt to evoke jealousy responses from their partners. Not surprisingly, experiencing heightened amounts of jealousy in relationships negatively affects relationship satisfaction (Guerrero and Eloy 1992). Thus, it is important for you to understand the reasons why we evoke feelings of jealousy in others and, at the same time, to refrain from using tactics or strategies that cause others to feel jealous.

Characteristics Associated with Jealousy

Researchers have examined many questions associated with jealousy, including: How does someone become jealous? What types of relationships are more likely to evoke jealousy? What are the results of feeling jealous? Studies have revealed that psychological predictors of jealousy are low levels of self-esteem and feelings of insecurity (Mcintosh 1989). Another study found that jealousy is more likely to occur in relationships of shorter duration (for less than one year) than in those of longer duration (more than one year) (Knox, Zusman, Mabon, and Shriver 1999). What conditions are most likely to elicit jealous reactions? A 1999 study (Knox et al.) found that talking to or about a previous partner is the action or topic that is most likely to evoke jealousy. So are you guilty of attempting to make others feel jealous? Complete the Evoking Jealousy Scale on the next page to help you identify your own tendencies.

Gender Differences and Jealousy

Studies have found no significant differences between males and females with regard to one gender being more likely to emerge as a primary source of jealousy (Knox, Zusman, Mabon, and Shriver 1999). Further, no significant sex

The attractiveness of perceived competition plays a role in determining the amount of jealousy experienced.

differences have been found with regard to the frequency, duration, or intensity of jealousy (Pines and Friedman 1998). However, while males and females do not necessarily differ in their amount of expressed jealousy, research has shown that they do experience jealousy for different reasons, or as the result of the specific characteristics associated with the threat. For example, males are more likely to become jealous as a result of sexual infidelity, whereas females become more jealous over emotional infidelity (Buss et al. 1992). Recent studies have found that, regardless of biological sex, the reactions to different types of jealousy are similar for males and females (Dijkstar and Buunk 2004). That is, emotional infidelity typically evoked responses of anxiety, worry, distrust, and suspicion, while responses to sexual infidelity were associated with feelings of sadness, rejection, anger, and betrayal. The physical or social attractiveness of the perceived competition also plays a role in determining the amount of jealousy experienced. Women experience more jealousy in response to a physically attractive threat, while men become more jealous when the threat is perceived as being more socially dominant (Dijkstra and Buunk 1998). Evolutionary psychologists argue the reason for this gender difference is due to the fact that our society typically rates a female's value in a relationship as determined by her physical attractiveness, whereas the relationship value of males is often evaluated by their status or dominance (Townsend and Levy 1990).

Evoking Jealousy Scale

Directions: Rate how often you have attempted the following items using the scale below:

1 = Never
2 = Almost never
3 = Sometimes
4 = Neutral
5 = Often
6 = Almost always
7 = Always

"I have tried to make my partner jealous by . . ."

_____ 1. Dancing with someone else while he or she is around.

_____ 2. Dressing nicely when going out.

_____ 3. Telling him or her someone flirted with me.

_____ 4. Telling him or her I found a person attractive.

_____ 5. Acting like it does not matter what he or she does.

_____ 6. Pretending to be interested in another person.

_____ 7. Talking to an ex-boyfriend or ex-girlfriend.

_____ 8. Wearing clothing that highlights my features.

_____ 9. Spending time doing activities without him or her.

_____ 10. Talking about activities I have been involved in.

_____ 11. Doing things he or she wants to do, but cannot.

_____ 12. Going out and not inviting him or her.

_____ 13. Talking with his or her friends.

_____ 14. Talking about a person of the opposite sex.

_____ 15. Having a person of the opposite sex answer the phone.

_____ 16. Telling him or her how much fun I had with a person of the opposite sex.

_____ 17. Having an opposite sex friend stop by when he or she is there.

_____ 18. Flirting with members of the opposite sex.

Coping with Jealousy

The way people initially express feelings of jealousy to a partner will ultimately influence how the partner responds. Stephen Yoshimura (2004) found that responses such as integrative communication and negative affect expression (e.g., crying) were perceived as evoking positive emotional responses by the partner (see Table 10.1). In other words, expressing your feelings openly and directly with your partner and appearing hurt by the threat produces positive emotional and behavior outcomes. This same study also found that negative emotional outcomes were more likely to produce violent behavior and manipulation attempts by the other partner. See Table 10.1 for a complete list of the ways people respond to feelings of jealousy.

Table 10.1   Communicative Responses to Jealousy

Strategy	Definition/Examples
1. Negative affect expression	Nonverbal expressions of jealousy-related affect that the partner can see. *Examples:* acting anxious when with the partner, appearing hurt, wearing "displeasure" on face, crying in front of the partner
2. Integrative communication	Direct, nonaggressive communication about jealousy with the partner. *Examples:* disclosing jealous feelings to the partner, asking the partner probing questions, trying to reach an understanding with the partner, reassuring the partner that we can "work it out"
3. Distributive communication	Direct, aggressive communication about jealousy with the partner. *Examples:* accusing the partner of being unfaithful, being sarcastic or rude toward the partner, arguing with the partner, bringing up the issue over and over again to "bombard" the partner
4. Active distancing	Indirect, aggressive means of communicating jealousy to the partner. *Examples:* giving the partner the "silent treatment," storming out of the room, giving the partner cold or dirty looks, withdrawing affection and sexual favors

(continued)

Table 10.1   Communicative Responses to Jealousy

Strategy	Definition/Examples
5. Avoidance/ denial	Indirect, nonagressive communication that focuses on avoiding the jealousy-invoking issue, situation, or partner. *Examples:* denying jealous feelings when confronted by the partner, pretending to be unaffected by the situation, decreasing contact with the partner, avoiding jealousy-evoking situations
6. Violent communication/ threats	Threatening or actually engaging in physical violence against the partner. *Examples:* threatening to harm the partner if they continue to see the rival, scaring the partner by acting as if they were about to hit the partner, roughly pulling the partner away from the rival, pushing or slapping the partner
7. Signs of possession	Publicly displaying the relationship to others so they know the partner is "taken." *Examples:* putting an arm around the partner and saying "he or she is taken," constantly introducing the partner as a "girl/boy friend," telling potential rival of plans to be married, kissing the partner in front of potential rival
8. Derogating competitors	Making negative comments about potential rivals to the partner and to others. *Examples:* "bad mouthing" the rival in front of the partner and his or her friends, expressing disbelief that anyone would be attracted to the rival
9. Relationship threats	Threatening to terminate or de-escalate the primary relationship or to be unfaithful. *Examples:* threatening to end the relationship if the partner continues to see the rival, threatening infidelity
10. Surveillance/ restriction	Behavioral strategies designed to find out about or interfere with the rival relationship. *Examples:* spying or checking up on the partner, looking through the partner's belongings for evidence of a rival relationship, pressing the redial button to see who the partner called last, restricting the partner's access to rivals at parties
11. Compensatory restoration	Behavior aimed at improving the primary relationship and/or making oneself more desirable. *Examples:* sending the partner gifts or flowers, keeping the house cleaned and nice, trying to present oneself as better than the rival, trying to appear more physically attractive
12. Manipulation attempts	Moves to induce negative feelings in the partner and/or shift responsibility for communicating about the problem to the partner. *Examples:* flirting with others to make the partner jealous, inducing guilt, calling the partner's "bluff" by daring him to break-up and go off with the rival, bring the rival's name up in conversation to check for a reaction, asking a friend to talk to the partner about the situation
13. Rival contacts	Direct communication with the rival about the jealousy situation, rival relationship, or partner. *Examples:* telling the rival to stop seeing the partner, informing the rival that the partner is "already in a relationship," saying something "mean" to the rival, asking the rival about the relationship without revealing one's identity, making negative comments about the partner in order to discourage the rival from pursuing the partner
14. Violent behavior	Directing violence toward objects, either in private or in the presence of others. *Examples:* slamming doors, breaking dishes, throwing the partner's possessions

Source: Adapted from Guerrero and Anderson 1998; Guerrero, Anderson, Jorgensen, Spitzberg, and Eloy 1995.

While we have explored some of the reasons for becoming jealous and have proposed some methods for managing situations that cause the green-eyed monster to emerge, let us take a moment to consider the role that perceived influence and power can play in causing us to experience envy.

INTERPERSONAL POWER AND AGGRESSION

A possible factor contributing to our tendency to encounter jealousy in relationships may be explained by the interpersonal power perceived by relational partners. In this section, we will take a closer look at the potential implications of power in relationships and explore power's relationship to verbal aggression and violence. **Power** can be defined as one's ability to influence others to behave in ways they normally might not. Popular television shows such as *Super Nanny* and *Nanny 911* often identify power as the key issue affecting families. What types of power impact our relationships with others?

Types of Power

French and Raven (1960) identified five types of power that individuals typically use when they are attempting to influence others. The five classic power bases are explained below.

Reward Power.   **Reward power** is based on a person's perception that the source of power can provide rewards. Example: *I'll clean up the apartment and maybe my roommate will invite me to go with him on the ski trip with his family this weekend.*

Coercive Power.   **Coercive power** focuses on the perceived ability of the source to punish or to enact negative consequences. Example: *I have to finish this report today or I know my boss will make me come in this weekend.*

Legitimate Power.   **Legitimate power** is centered on the perception that the source has authority because of a particular role that she plays in the relationship or a title that she holds. Example: *Because I'm the mommy, and I said so.*

Referent Power.   **Referent power** is based on a person's respect, identification and attraction to the source. Example: *No matter how ridiculous I feel, I will dress up in a costume and go to this Halloween party because I am really attracted to you and want you to like me.*

Expert Power.   **Expert power** is grounded in the perception that the source possesses knowledge, expertise, or skills in a particular area. Example: *I will listen to what she says about our household budget because she is the financial wizard in the family.*

French and Raven propose that it is the perception of the receiver of the message that is the key to analyzing power. Consider our earlier discussions about interpersonal communication in Chapters One and Two. We stated that effective interpersonal communication is receiver-based. Thus, it is important to consider the receiver's perception of the source to predict

© 226552472‚ 2007, Shutterstock.

In the role of a parent, one holds legitimate power in the relationship.

future interactions. But do individuals have power if we do not give it to them? Based on the important role that receiver perception plays in the communication process, probably not. Consider the following scenario:

> Alan had very little respect for his mother. At thirteen years old, he was completely out of control. He skipped school, ignored his mother's rules, and even hit his mother on several occasions when she attempted to discipline him. Finally, his mother had reached the breaking point. One night she caught Alan doing drugs with his friends in the basement. She reported Alan to the authorities and hoped that it would help him get back on track. But his misbehavior continued.

In this instance, Alan's mother should have legitimate power over him. However, his behavior is an obvious indicator that he does not perceive her to have any power in the relationship. Even when his mother attempts to utilize coercive power by calling the police, it does nothing to change Alan's perception. His inability to view his mother as having reward, coercive, or legitimate power even results in Alan's occasional use of physical violence. If you do not perceive your relational partner as having the power, then it is unlikely that you would comply with any requests he or she makes.

In Chapter Six we discussed the role of attraction in interpersonal relationships. Understanding the relationship between attraction and power may help explain why some influence attempts are successful whereas others fail. Depending on the perceived power base, receivers will alter their perceptions of the source's attractiveness and determine the level of acceptance or resistance in response to the request. Suppose your best friend uses a threat, or coercive power, in an attempt to influence you. This will typically decrease your level of perceived attraction for your friend, and chances are that you will resist their request. On the other hand, if you perceive that the friend has the power to reward you as a result of the request, it is likely that you would find them more attractive and would have minimal resistance to the request. These same principles can be applied in a variety of relationships. What if your mother told you that if you cleaned your room she would reward you with $5.00 and a trip to the movies? You would be more willing to agree to her request and you would find her to be more interpersonally attractive than if she would have said, "If you don't clean your room, you will have to pay me $5.00 to do it for you, and you'll be grounded from the movies for the next week." Threats and coercive behavior typically breed resentment and result in higher levels of resistance.

Relationship between Power and Interpersonal Influence

To better understand the impact of power in our decisions of whether to comply with requests made in our interpersonal relationships, we look at the three levels of influence that can be achieved. These include compliance, identification, and internalization (Kelman 1961). **Compliance** occurs when an individual agrees to a request because he can see a potential reward or punishment for doing so. This level of influence is likely to persuade someone to do something, but his motivation is typically low and the change in the behavior is usually quite temporary. When you tell your roommate that she can have your car for the weekend if she drives you to the airport and she later complies with your request, you have influenced her at the compliance level. In this example, the only reason the roommate complies with the request is to obtain a reward.

If a person decides to agree to an influence attempt because she recognizes the potential benefits of doing so, or perhaps she wishes to establish a relationship with the source, then **identification** has occurred. A student agrees to his teacher's recommendation that he take honors level courses next semester to help prepare him for college instead of "cruising" in the regular classes with his friends. In this instance, individuals are typically more motivated to comply because they agree with the source's goals, interests and values. The last level of influence, **internalization**, is employed when an individual adopts a behavior because it is internally rewarding. In other words, it feels like the right thing to do. This type of influence is successful because the person sees the requested behavior as fitting within his or her existing value system. The individual agrees to the behavior because he intrinsically believes it should be done, not just because someone told him to do so. An example of this might be a spouse who takes on the responsibility of extra household or childcare duties in order to assist a partner who is experiencing a difficult time at work. In this instance, the person agrees to the request because of the value placed on family and the level of commitment made to the relationship. Table 10.2 summarizes the level of influence that can be achieved as a result of each of the five types of power.

Power versus Dominance in Relationships

What is the difference between power and dominance? Burgoon and Dillman (1995) argue, "Because power is broadly defined as the ability to exercise influence by possessing one or more power bases, dominance is but one means of many for expressing power" (65). In other words, power is the potential to influence another's behavior, whereas **dominance** is a mechanism typically associated with attempts to express power and take control in a relationship. What is the relationship between talking and influence? One study found that the more an individual talks, the more opportunities he has to gain influence over others (Daly, McCroskey, and Richmond 1977). A separate study suggests

Table 10.2   **Power and Impact on Levels of Influence**

Types of Power	Levels of Influence		
	Compliance	Identification	Internalization
Reward	X		
Coercive	X		
Legitimate	X		
Referent	X	X	X
Expert	X	X	X

Source: Adapted from Kelman 1961; Richmond, McCroskey, and McCroskey 2005.

that managing what individuals talk about and "controlling the floor" are perceived as forms of interpersonal dominance or control (Palmer 1989).

VERBAL AGGRESSION

Perhaps one of the most vivid examples of verbal aggression in action can be witnessed in the movie and book, *The Devil Wears Prada*. As she attempts to navigate her way in the fashion magazine industry, Andrea Sachs learns that dealing with verbal attacks from her boss and co-workers is part of the "game," and something she must endure if she wishes to pursue a career in the field. She encounters both direct and indirect influence attempts. Miranda, her boss, prefers an influence style that attacks Andy's self-esteem. She bluntly tells Andy that she has "no style" and publicly criticizes Andy's work in front of her colleagues. To make matters worse, Emily, a co-worker, refers to Andy as being "hopeless." Nigel, the photographer who befriends Andy, eventually convinces her that she needs to change in order to make it in the business. He provides her with logical facts and arguments containing tips to help her succeed in the industry. It becomes apparent that Nigel's approach of presenting arguments was much more effective in helping Andy comply, and ultimately succeed, than the aggressive approach used by Miranda and Emily.

Attempts to gain influence over others are often made in one of two ways. First, rational arguments can be presented for why compliance should occur. A second strategy is to attack the other person's self-esteem or character. As you can see, one of these strategies is positive, and the other is negative and potentially damaging to relationships. So why do some individuals choose to present rational arguments while others choose to attack? The explanation rests in the distinction between communication traits known as argumentativeness and verbal aggression. **Argumentativeness** refers to the extent to which an individual challenges a position or issue (Infante and Rancer 1982). A person can question or debate whether they should comply with a request without directly addressing the personal characteristics of the person making the request. When a request is addressed with a response that attacks the self-confidence, chararacter, and/or intelligence of another person, **verbal aggressiveness** is being used (Infante and Wigley 1986). Suppose your best friend asks you to let him borrow your car to drive to a concert, but you do not wish to comply with his request. An argumentative person might respond with statements such as, "It's probably not a good idea, since you aren't insured to drive my car. Besides, I don't want to rack up miles on it since it's a lease." The request is addressed with logical, rational points. An example of a verbally aggressive response might be, "Are you stupid? Why in the world would you be crazy enough to think that I would trust you with my car?" In this instance, the person's intelligence, sanity, and trustworthiness have been attacked. Examples of verbally aggressive messages might include attacks on one's character or competence, teasing or ridiculing, or even making threats or jokes about another's appearance.

Loreen Olson suggests that there are four levels of aggression that are experienced in our interpersonal encounters (2004). **Low aggression** is characterized by yelling, crying, refusing to talk, or stomping out of the room. **Moderate aggression** involves more intense acts of verbal aggression such as verbal insults, swearing at the other, and indirect physical displays of anger such as kicking, hitting, throwing inanimate objects, or threatening to engage in these behaviors. Next, **high aggression** refers to intensive face threatening, and verbal belittling, and direct physical contact with the other person in the form of slapping, shoving, or pushing. The most severe level, **severe aggression,** includes intense verbal abuse and threats and involves physical attacks that include kicking, biting, punching, hitting with an object, raping, and using a weapon. Not only can verbally aggressive acts occur before relational conflicts, they occur as a consequence to partner aggression and also serve to escalate the conflict. In relationships, struggles for power and control are often at the heart of reciprocated and escalating aggression between partners (Olson 2004).

While our first tendency is to assume that aggression and violence are often restricted to close relationships with romantic partners or family members, this is not the case. Researchers have examined their presence and impact in a variety of relational contexts.

Verbal Aggression in the Classroom

Since verbal aggression is perceived as a negative communication behavior, it should come as no surprise that researchers have identified several negative outcomes associated with teachers who use words to attack students in the classroom. Students who perceive their instructors as being verbally aggressive report that they are less motivated in that class (Myers and Rocca 2001). Also, they evaluate the teacher as being less competent and as behaving inappropriately (Martin, Weber, and Burant 1997). In an environment where a student fears becoming the target of verbal abuse, less learning occurs (Myers 2002) and the chances are greater that students will choose to avoid the situation by skipping class (Rocca 2004). When you consider that aggressiveness fosters a negative learning experience, the power of a teacher's communication becomes apparent. The same principles hold true in other instructional contexts. In the movie *Kicking and Screaming,* Phil (Will Farrell) volunteers to coach his son's soccer team. In the beginning of the film, Phil's coaching style and communication are patient and nurturing—he even goes so far as to bring the boys finches as rewards for their hard work. Eventually, Phil's competitive nature emerges, and his interactions with the boys and their parents become verbally aggressive. At one point he taunts a young player who misses a goal by screaming at him in front of the entire team, "You've just been served a plate of humiliation!" While the purpose of these athletic experiences is to provide training, the aggressive communication could have serious negative implications.

Workplace Bullying

Another context that has been the target of research on verbal aggression is the workplace. Because it is likely that all of you either have been employed, or will be at some point in your life, it is important to understand the potential for verbal aggression and emotional abuse to occur in this environment. Approximately ninety percent of adults report that they have been a victim of workplace bullying at some point during their professional career (Hornstein 1996). Workplace bullying, intimidation, employee humiliation and organizational manipulation are all considered to be **Employee Emotional Abuse (EEA).**

The vast majority of workplace bullies are bosses.

EEA is defined as repeated, targeted, unwelcome, destructive communication by more powerful individuals toward less empowered individuals in the organization, which results in emotional harm (LutgenSandvik 2003). In February 2006, a Vallejo, California high school teacher agreed to an out-of-court settlement after suing the state administrator and other district officials for alleged harassment and discrimination. The school district agreed to pay the teacher $225,000, to compensate her for the emotional distress she experienced at work.

So who is most likely to engage in bullying at work? The results may surprise you. According to the United States Hostile Workplace Survey in 2000:

- Women comprised fifty percent of the bullies.
- Women bullies target other women an overwhelming eighty-four percent of the time; men bullies target women in sixty-nine percent of the cases; women are the majority (seventy-seven percent) of targets.
- The vast majority of bullies are bosses (eighty-one percent); they have the power to terminate their targets at will.
- Approximately forty-one percent of targets were diagnosed with depression.
- More than eighty percent of targets reported effects that prevented them from being productive at work (severe anxiety, lost concentration, sleeplessness, etc.).
- Post-Traumatic Stress Disorder (PTSD) symptoms afflicted thirty-one percent of the women who experienced workplace bullying; twenty-one percent of the men who had been bullied reported PTSD symptoms.

OBSESSIVE RELATIONAL INTRUSION

In some cases, verbal aggression and violence have been linked to instances of obsessive relational intrusion (ORI). William Cupach and Brian Spitzberg (1998) developed the concept of ORI to address the interpersonal aspect of stalking. All of us have heard stories in the news of celebrities who have been stalked: prior to his death in 1980, John Lennon was stalked by Mark Chapman; tennis champion Monica Seles was stabbed by a stalker who was a fan of her opponent, Steffi Graf. Cupach and Spitzberg (1998) distinguish ORI from stalking in the sense that ORI occurs out of a desire to initiate a relationship, whereas stalking often has a purpose of harming, and possibly even destroying, another person. The communication that takes place in ORI is typical of most relationships, the exchange of messages via phone calls, letters, or gifts. Many of these communicative behaviors are an attempt to either initiate or escalate a relationship; however, one person often becomes jealous and sometimes even possessive.

Obsessive relational intrusion is defined as the "repeated and unwanted pursuit and invasion of one's sense of physical or symbolic privacy by another person, either stranger or acquaintance, who desires and/or presumes an intimate relationship" (Cupach and Spitzberg 1998, 235). In a study of 341 college students, nineteen percent of the men and ten percent of the women indicated that they had obsessively pursued another person using various methods and strategies. As far as gender differences in the types of tactics used to communicate an interest in another, there were no significant differences found.

© Jaimie Duplass, 2007, Shutterstock.

Examples of the most frequently reported tactics by both men and women include the following:

- Sending/communicating unwanted messages
- Expressing exaggerated affection
- Giving or sending unwanted gifts
- Monitoring the other person's actions
- Intruding in the interactions of the other person
- Intruding on the other person's friends and/or family
- Covertly obtaining information about the person

Perhaps as you read this description of ORI, you may discover that you or someone you know has experienced this dark aspect of interpersonal relationships. To understand how victims of ORI manage these unwanted advances, Spitzberg and Cupach (2001) conducted an analysis of the coping strategies identified across a variety of studies. A summary of these coping strategies is presented in Table 10.3 on page 266.

Unfortunately, relational obsession and stalking are not restricted to face-to-face interactions. As more and more people use the Internet as a forum for initiating and building relationships, it is important to understand the potential dangers associated with these types of relationships. Cyberstalking refers to harassment, or obsessive communication, via the Internet. Several television news shows have recently conducted in-depth investigations regarding this phenomenon, focusing on the use of online communication by pedophiles to form relationships with children and minors. It is important to note that cyberstalkers often obtain personal information about their targets that is disclosed on the Internet and may use this information to harm others.

While you may be thinking that obsessive relationships are the result of posting personal information to online dating sites, consider the information that is posted on a variety of social networking websites that are gaining in popularity. More than 100 million people engage in interactions via online social communities where personal information is exchanged. Two of the most popular sites among college students and teenagers are MySpace and Facebook. Why have these online sites gained so much popularity in recent years? A study conducted at Carnegie Mellon University by students revealed that individuals join Facebook for several reasons: (1) as a result of peer pressure by friends encouraging them to create an online profile, (2) to maintain relationships at a distance, (3) to form new relationships, or (4) to get assistance with classes (Govani and Pashley 2005). While students report that they turn to these sites to assist in initiating and maintaining relationships, the harsh reality is that online behaviors have actually damaged many relationships. Incidences of students posting pictures depicting themselves in sexually provocative ways, or while engaging in illegal or excessive drinking have prompted university officials to use sites such as Facebook to identify improper and illegal behavior. Table 10.4 highlights some of the ways in which colleges and universities have used the Facebook site to monitor and discipline students.

While it is important to be aware of the potential dangers and risks of exchanging and revealing personal information online, the more critical issue involves learning how to manage and use these

© 6454881632, 2007, Shutterstock.

As more relationships are initiated via the Internet, it is important to understand the potential dangers.

new communication mediums appropriately. In Chapter Fourteen we present a detailed overview of computer-mediated communication (CMC) research and provide suggestions for using CMC effectively and appropriately as a means of social networking. It is important to be selective in the information that you choose to share via CMC. Also, realize that people can and do lie about themselves in both face to face and computer mediated contexts. These issues will be discussed in much greater depth in Chapter Fourteen.

Table 10.3   Summary of Obsessive Relational Intrusion Coping Strategies

Coping Strategy	Examples
Moving inward	Ignore or deny the problem and hope it goes away Blame yourself Engage in self-destructive means to escape (e.g., alcohol, drugs, suicide)
Moving outward	Seek sympathy from others Seek social support from friends and/or family Seek legal assistance (e.g., police, attorney)
Moving away	Control interactions with the person (e.g., maintain a closed body position, avoid eye contact) Use verbal avoidance or escape tactics (e.g., make excuses) Restrict accessibility (e.g., change schedule, switch work shifts, obtain caller ID, change email address, use pseudonyms online)
Moving toward	Diminish seriousness of the situation (e.g., joke or tease the pursuer) Employ problem-solving tactics or negotiation Mutually negotiate relationship definition (e.g., discuss your preferences for the type of relationship you would like with the other)
Moving against	Issue verbal warnings/threats Build a legal case (e.g., save emails, letters, keep a record of calls) Use protective responses (e.g., email blocker, restraining order)

Aggression and Violent Behavior by PERGAMON. Reproduced with permission of PERGAMON in the format reuse in a book/textbook via Copyright Clearance Center.

Table 10.4   Facebook in the News

April 2005	University of Mississippi students were threatened with a civil lawsuit for leading a Facebook group that devoted their desire to sleep with a certain female professor. They made a public apology. (*www.dukechronicle.com* 03/08/2006)
May 2005	LSU swimmers were kicked off the team after athletics officials discovered they belonged to a Facebook group that posts disparaging comments about swim coaches (usa.com-athletes sound over athletes Facebook time, 03/08/2006)
September 2005	Northern Kentucky men's basketball coach found Facebook photos of his underage athletes with alcohol. They were let off with a warning. (usa.com-athletes sound over athletes Facebook time, 03/08/2006)

October 2005	North Carolina State University resident advisor reported nine of her students for underage drinking when she found evidence in one resident's Facebook photo album (*www.dukechronicle. com* 03/08/2006)
	Penn State University police used Facebook as a tool to identify students who rushed the football field after the Ohio University game. *(http://www.thepost.ohiou.edu)*
December 2005	Florida State athletes were given ten days to cleanse their profiles. (usa.com-athletes sound over athletes facebook time, 03/08/2006)
	Loyola University of Chicago athletic director forbids his athletes to join to protect them from gamblers or sexual predators who can learn more about them (usa.com-athletes sound over athletes facebook time, 03/08/2006)
	Colorado athletes were accused of sending a racially threatening Facebook message to a fellow athlete. Campus police issued tickets for harassment. (usa.com-athletes sound over athletes facebook time, 03/08/2006)
January 2006	Kentucky athletic director told athletes to scrub their profiles of anything that could shed a bad light on the school. (www. usatoday.com-athletes sound over athletes Facebook time, 03/08/2006)
February 2006	Students at the University of Kansas living in the scholarship hall were written up for pictures uploaded to Facebook.com that indicated a party violating the alcohol policy. (Kansan.com)

SUMMARY

While the topics discussed in this chapter may not be particularly pleasant, it is important to address their role in our communication with others. Not all relationships are enjoyable. To use the analogy of a roller coaster, virtually all relationships experience ups and downs. In this chapter we have discussed the concept of interpersonal deception and explored the potential impact of telling lies on the future of our relationships. In addition, we discussed the potential embarrassment that pops up from time to time and causes us to become "red-faced" in our interactions. In keeping with color analogies, relationships often encounter the "green-eyed monster" when jealousy emerges and causes us to respond in ways that we might not otherwise. We identified power and influence as a potential source of jealousy and as something that can affect our interactions with others. The distinction between argumentativeness and aggressiveness was made, as we offered a glimpse into the ugly side of power, when it results in verbal attack against others. Finally, we discussed the concept of obsession in relationships and presented the concept of obsessive relational intrusion. We concluded this discussion by addressing the dark side of relationships and computer mediated communication. While at first glance social networking sites like Facebook and Myspace may seem beneficial, there is a dark side to these as well.

Oftentimes we hear the phrase, "Communication is the key to success." The purpose of this chapter was to introduce a few communication situations in which communication was not part of the solution, but was, in fact, part of the problem. It is important to remember that communication is a tool that can be used for good or evil purposes. It is up to us to understand how to effectively use communication to accomplish our goals and to become more competent in our interactions with others. By offering you a glimpse into the "dark side" of communication, it is our hope that your relationships will encounter more "ups" than "downs."

APPLICATIONS
Discussion Questions

A. Most people would agree that there are times when it is okay to deceive a friend, family member, or romantic partner. Have you ever been in a particular situation where you felt it was okay to deceive someone? Describe the situation and your reasons.

B. What are some ways to make sure that your partner does not feel jealous in regard to your romantic relationship? What are some suggestions for dealing with someone that often reports jealous feelings?

C. What is the best way to influence a friend or family member to change a problematic behavior? What type of persuasion and social influence tactics could you employ to get the friend or family member to change? Describe the tactics that you would use and those that you would avoid.

D. Provide three examples of types of information that should not be disclosed on social networking sites such as Facebook and Myspace.

REFERENCES

Berlyne, D. E. 1969. Laughter, humor and play. In G. Lindzey and E. Aronson (Eds.), *Handbook of Social Psychology,* Vol. 3, (795–813). Reading, Mass.: Addison-Wesley.

Bevan, J. L., and Samter, W. 2004. Toward a broader conceptualization of jealousy in close relationships: Two exploratory studies. *Communication Studies, 55,* 14–28.

Buller, D. B., and J. K. Burgoon. 1996. Interpersonal deception theory. *Communication Theory, 6,* 203–242.

Burgoon, J. K., D. B. Buller, L. K. Guerrero, W. Afifi, and C. M. Feldman. 1996. Interpersonal deception XII: Information management dimensions underlying types of deceptive messages. *Communication Monographs, 63,* 50–69.

Burgoon, J. K., and L. Dillman. 1995. Gender, immediacy and nonverbal communication. In P. J. Kalbfleisch and M. J. Cody (Eds.), *Gender, power, and communication in human relationships.* (63–81). Hillsdale, NJ: Lawrence Erlbaum Associates.

Buss, D. M., R. J. Larsen, D. Westen, and J. Semmelroth. 1992. Sex differences in jealousy: Evolution, physiology, and psychology. *Psychological Science, 3,* 251–255.

Camden, C., M. T. Motley, and A. Wilson. 1984. White lies in interpersonal communication: A taxonomy and preliminary investigation of social motives. *The Western Journal of Speech Communication, 48,* 309–325.

Cayanus, J. L., and M. Booth-Butterfield. 2004. Relationship orientation, jealousy, and equity: An examination of jealousy evoking and positive communication responses. *Communication Quarterly, 52,* 237–250.

Cupach, W. R., and B. H. Spitzberg. 1994. *The dark side of interpersonal communication.* Hillsdale, NJ: Lawrence Erlbaum.

———. 1998. Obsessive relational intrusion and stalking. In B. H. Spitzberg, and W. R. Cupach (Eds.), *The dark side of close relationships* (233–263). Hillsdale, NJ: Erlbaum.

Daly, J. A., J. C. McCroskey, and V. P. Richmond. 1977. Relationship between vocal activity and perception of communicators in small group interaction. *Western Journal of Speech Communication, 41,* 175–187.

DePaulo, B. M., D. A. Kasy, S. E. Kirkendale, M. M. Wyer, and J. A. Epstein. 1996. Lying in everyday life. *Journal of Personality and Social Psychology, 70,* 979–995.

Dijkstra, P., and B. P. Buunk. 1998. Jealousy as a function of rival characteristics: An evolutionary perspective. *Personality and Social Psychology Bulletin, 24,* 1158–1166.

Edelmann, R. J. 1985. Social embarrassment: An analysis of the process. *Journal of Social and Personal Relationships, 2,* 195–213.

French, J. P. R., and B. Raven. 1960. The bases of social power. In D. Cartwright and A. Zander (Eds.), *Group Dynamics* (607–623). New York: Harper and Row.

Govani, T. and H. Pashley. November 21, 2006 Student awareness of the privacy implications when using Facebook. *<http://lorrie.cranor.org/courses/fa05/tubzhlp.pdf>*

Gross, E., and G. P. Stone. 1964. Embarrassment and the analysis of role requirements. *American Journal of Sociology, 70,* 1–15.

Guerrero, L. K., and W. A. Afifi. 1999. Toward a goal-oriented approach for understanding communicative responses to jealousy. *Western Journal of Communication, 63,* 216–248.

Guerrero, L. K., and P. A. Anderson.1998. Jealousy experience and expression in romantic relationships. In P. A. Anderson and L. K. Guerrero (Eds.), *Handbook of communication and emotion* (155–188). San Diego, CA: Academic Press.

Guerrero, L. K., P. A. Anderson, P. F. Jorgensen, B. H. Spitzberg, and S. V. Eloy. 1995. Coping with the green-eyed monster: Conceptualizing and measuring communicative responses to romantic jealousy. *Western Journal of Communication, 59,* 270–304.

Guerrero, L. K. and S. V. Eloy. 1992. Relationship satisfaction and jealousy across marital types. *Communication Reports, 5,* 23–41.

Hansen, G. L. 1985. Dating jealousy among college students. *Sex Roles. 12,* 713–721.

Hornstein, H. A. 1996. *Brutal bosses and their prey. How to overcome and identify abuse in the workplace.* New York: Riverhead Books.

Infante, D. A., and A. S. Rancer. 1982. A conceptualization and measure of argumentativeness. *Journal of Personality Assessment, 46,* 72–80.

Infante, D. A., and C. J. Wigley. 1986. Verbal aggression: An interpersonal model and measure. *Communication Monographs, 53,* 61–69.

Kelman, H. C. 1961. Processes of opinion change. *Public Opinion Quarterly, 25,* 58–78.

Kernis, M. H. 1995. *Efficacy, agency and self-esteem.* New York: Plenum Press.

Knapp, M. L., and A. L. Vangelisti. 2006. Lying. In K. M. Galvin and P. J. Cooper (Eds.), *Making connections* (247–252). Los Angeles, CA: Roxbury.

Knox, D., C. Schact, J. Holt, and J. Turner. 1993. Sexual lies among university students. *College Student Journal, 27,* 269–272.

Knox, D., M. E. Zusman, L. Mabon, and L. Shriver. 1999. Jealousy in college student relationships. *College Student Journal, 33,* 328.

Lutgen-Sandvik, P. 2003. The communicative cycle of employee emotional abuse. *Management Communication Quarterly, 16,* 471–502.

Martin, M. M., K. Weber, and P. A. Burant. 1997. *Students' perceptions of a teacher's use of slang and verbal aggressiveness in a lecture: An experiment.* Paper presented at the Eastern Communication Association Convention, Baltimore, MD.

McIntosh, E. G. 1989. An investigation of romantic jealousy among black undergraduates. *Social Behavior and Personality, 17,* 135–141.

Myers, S. A. 2002. Perceived aggressive instructor communication and student state motivation, learning and satisfaction. *Communication Reports, 15,* 113–121.

Myers, S. A., and K. A. Rocca. 2001. Perceived instructor argumentativeness and verbal aggressiveness in the college classroom: Effects on student perceptions of climate, apprehension, and state motivation. *Western Journal of Communication, 65,* 113–137.

O'Hair, H. D., and M. J. Cody. 1994. Everyday deception. In W. R. Cupach and B. Spitzberg (Ed.), *The dark side of interpersonal communication* (181–213). Hillsdale, NJ: Lawrence Erlbaum Associates.

Olson, L. N. 2004. Relational control-motivated aggression: A theoretically-based typology of intimate violence. *Journal of Family Communication, 4,* 209–233.

Palmer, M. T. 1989. Controlling conversations: Turns, topics and interpersonal control. *Communication Monographs, 56,* 1–18.

Park, H. S., T. R. Levine, S. A. McCornack, K. Morrison, and M. Ferrara. 2002. How people really detect lies. *Communication Monographs, 69,* 144–157.

Pines, A. M., and A. Friedman. 1998. Gender differences in romantic jealousy. *The Journal of Social Psychology, 138,* 54–71.

Richmond, V. P., J. C. McCroskey, and L. L. McCroskey. 2005. *Organizational communication for survival, making work, work.* Boston: Allyn and Bacon.

Rocca, K. A. 2004. College student attendance: Impact of instructor immediacy and verbal aggression. *Communication Education, 53,* 185–195.

Rowatt, W. C. 1999. Lying to get a date: The effectiveness of facial physical attractiveness on the willingness to deceive prospective dating partners. *Journal of Social and Personal Relationships, 16,* 209–223.

Sattler, J. M. 1965. A theoretical, developmental, and clinical investigation of embarrassment. *Clinical Psychology Monographs, 71,* 19–59.

Spitzberg, B. H. 2006. A struggle in the dark. In K. M. Galvin and P. J. Cooper (Eds.), *Making connections* (240–246). Los Angeles, CA: Roxbury.

Spitzberg, B. H., D. J. Canary, and W. R. Cupach. 1994. A competence based approach to the study of interpersonal conflict. In D. D. Cahn (Ed.), *Conflict in personal relationships* (183–202). Hillsdale, NJ: Lawrence Erlbaum.

Spitzberg, B. H., and W. R. Cupach. 2001. Paradoxes of pursuit: Toward a relational model of stalking-related phenomena. In J. Davis (Ed.), *Stalking, stalkers and their victims: Prevention, intervention, and threat assessment.* Boca Raton, FL: CRC Press.

_____. 2003. What mad pursuit? Obsessive relational intrusion and stalking related phenomena. *Aggression and Violent Behavior, 8,* 345–375.

Townsend, J. M., and G. D. Levy. 1990. Effects of potential partners' costume and physical attractiveness on sexual and partner selection. *Journal of Psychology, 124,* 371–389.

Yoshiimura, S. M. 2004. Sex differences in the contexts of extreme jealousy. *Personal Relationships, 11,* 319–328.

Zuckerman, M., and R. Driver. 1985. Telling lies: verbal and nonverbal correlates of deception. In A. Siegman and S. Feldstein (Eds.), *Multichannel integrations of nonverbal behavior,* (129–148). Hillsdale, NJ: Lawrence Erlbaum.

Intercultural Communication

OBJECTIVES

- Understand three reasons for studying the impact of diversity on interpersonal relationships
- Increase awareness of four basic core concepts: knowledge, understanding, acceptance, and skills
- Define culture
- Differentiate the co-cultural categories of ethnicity, race, region, and social class
- Identify three characteristics of culture
- Discuss factors which affect our perceptions of others: needs, beliefs, values, and attitudes
- Identify three steps in the process of forming stereotypes
- Recognize how stereotypes and prejudice influence interpersonal relationships
- Describe three forms of prejudice
- Explain the three functions that prejudices fulfill in our interpersonal relationships
- Evaluate the impact of Hofstede's four dimensions of cultural values on interpersonal communication
- Recognize five strategies to enhance effective interpersonal communication in diverse relationships

© 2007, JupiterImages Corporation.

KEYTERMS

knowledge
uncertainty reduction
  theory (URT)
passive strategies
active strategies
interactive
  strategies
self-disclosure
understanding
acceptance
ethnocentrism
skills
culture

diversity
socialization
ethnicity
race
regional differences
social class
homophily
explicit learning
implicit learning
perception
personal orientation
  system
needs

beliefs
values
attitudes
stereotyping
racial profiling
prejudice
racism
race
ageism
sexism
verbal abuse
discrimination
violence

acceptance   individualism/   masculine/feminine
high/low context   collectivism   cultures
cultures   power distance   uncertainty avoidance

On July 28, 2006, actor Mel Gibson was pulled over while speeding on Pacific Coast Highway in Malibu, California. As officers were questioning Gibson, he began yelling at them, making anti-Semitic and sexist comments toward the arresting officers.

In October 2006, *Grey's Anatomy* actor Isaiah Washington got into a fight with fellow actor Patrick Dempsey over an alleged gay slur that Washington made about their colleague, T. R. Knight. Even though the incident eventually faded from the spotlight, Washington publicly made an anti-gay comment at the 2007 Golden Globe awards a few months later as he attempted to defend his earlier actions to members of the press.

In November 2006, *Seinfeld* actor Michael Richards erupted into a series of racial epithets targeted toward two African American men attending his performance at the Laugh Factory in Los Angeles. Richards claimed that he was angry at the men for heckling him and allegedly disturbing his comedy routine.

What causes individuals to engage in such negative behavior? Why do people exchange such hurtful words and actions? One reason may be the inability to engage in effective interpersonal communication with those who are different. We make decisions on how to communicate with others based on our beliefs, our values, and our attitudes. As a result, if our beliefs or attitudes toward another individual or group are negative, our communication with them may be negative as well. Why is it that some people fear and apprehend communication with diverse others instead of embracing differences as the added "spice" of interpersonal relationships? In this chapter we will explore a variety of concepts that help explain how our attitudes, beliefs, and values both shape and are shaped by our interactions with others.

OVERVIEW

Throughout this text, we have discussed various aspects of interpersonal communication and the roles they play in initiating and sustaining relationships. As we approach the end of the journey of exploring the specifics of interpersonal communication, we would be remiss if we failed to discuss the one variable that *all* interpersonal relationships have in common—they are comprised of diverse individuals. Typically, discussions of diversity focus on things that we can see: race, ethnicity, and gender being the most commonly identified elements when defining diversity. Focusing attention on the obvious differences may cause us to fail to recognize that cultural attitudes, values, and norms also play a role in our interpersonal relationships. These are only a few of the less apparent factors that create challenges for relational partners when trying to achieve shared meaning. Consider friends who get upset with one another simply because they differ in their beliefs of how to spend their first weekend out of school. One might want to hang out with family members who were visiting from out of town instead of going out to the exclusive "Summer

Relationships are comprised of individuals who are diverse in many ways.

© Stephen Coburn, 2007, Shutterstock.

Kickoff Party" at the hot new nightclub that the other friend had received an exclusive invitation to attend. Differing values for family relationships and friendships contribute to the diversity encountered in this relationship. Maybe you have had a difficult time getting a teacher to understand that your questions are not intended to "challenge his authority," but are attempts to better understand the information being presented in class.

Diversity comes in many shapes and forms. While knowledge of the traditional views of cultural diversity can help you to understand the challenges you may encounter in your own relationships, it is important to focus on the source of many of our communication behaviors and to understand how cultural perceptions impact our view of relationships and communication. We can use the analogy of a coach and a team to understand the influence of diversity on interpersonal relationships and the role communication plays in the process. A good coach would not send a team out on the playing field without preparing them for the game. Plays are taught and rehearsed; team members know what to expect from one another. Practice sessions are conducted so that these preferred ways of acting and reacting can be learned and refined. Sure, there are times when the game plan does not work as planned. The coach and team may become frustrated. They regroup, communicate, and develop an alternate plan. However, if the team continues to run exactly the same play every single game, the chances for success will be slim. Becoming a competent communicator across cultures requires you to develop a similar game plan. You need to be aware of the characteristics that can lead to misunderstandings when communicating with people from diverse backgrounds. Knowing that each person's communication is guided by his unique set of values, beliefs, and attitudes will prepare you for differences in your approaches to conversations. Just as a team needs to study plays, people need to study and understand the various elements that create confusion and miscommunication in cross-cultural encounters. This chapter will help you to develop a personal game plan for becoming a competent communicator in diverse interpersonal relationships. Four core concepts which are essential to enhancing competence include: knowledge, understanding, skills, and acceptance. Let us examine each of these concepts more closely.

THE IMPACT OF CULTURAL DIVERSITY ON INTERPERSONAL RELATIONSHIPS

As buzz words such as "diversity" and "cultural sensitivity" continue to permeate discussions regarding relationships in the workplace, the classroom, and our personal lives, there is a need to increase the understanding of both diversity and communication, and their influence on personal relationships. This is an extremely exciting time in our history. Changes in political and social policy, evolving demographics, and technological advances have provided us with vast opportunities for forming relationships with diverse others. Three specific reasons for exploring the impact of cultural diversity on communication in interpersonal relationships are (1) increased awareness of self, (2) appreciation for technological transformations, and (3) understanding of demographic transitions.

© Laurence Gough, 2007, Shutterstock.

Now more than ever, we have opportunities to form relationships with many different people.

Understanding the Self

Perhaps the simplest and most overlooked reason for studying the impact of diversity on our relationships is the opportunity it provides for exploring and understanding our own cultural background and identity. By delving into the cultural factors which influence communication patterns, we begin to gain an awareness of our own reasons for thinking and behaving as we do.

A woman had lived in a small town with a population of 350 all of her life. The population was entirely Caucasian, and the overwhelming majority was Methodist and middle-class. Upon moving to a large metropolitan area, she found the challenges of understanding the cultural differences to be phenomenal. Her knowledge of initiating relationships was limited to experiences in a small, cohesive community. Shortly after moving into her new apartment, she encountered her next door neighbor struggling to bring several bags of groceries from the parking lot to the building. While introducing herself, she attempted to take a couple of bags from her neighbor's car. She was quickly told that her assistance was not needed. She discussed the incident with a roommate. The roommate pointed out, "You have to understand that people in large cities don't just walk up and help one another. Don't be offended. City folks just don't trust people as easily as people you're accustomed to." As she found the first few weeks in the city to be frustrating, her focus was on how "strange" other people were, not on understanding how her own cultural background influenced her perceptions and expectations of others' behavior.

In Chapter Two, the impact of individual identity on our communication in relationships was discussed. When considering the impact they have on our identity formation, our first instinct may be to focus on interactions with family members and peers. Communication with significant others plays a large role in shaping our sense of self. However, it is essential that we examine the role that culture has played in the process as well. After all, it is likely that the rules and expectations that our family and friends have for our communication behaviors are derived from cultural expectations. Many unspoken guidelines are within different cultural influences.

How have cell phones impacted the way we communicate?

© Tad Denson, 2007, Shutterstock.

Technological Transformations

In the 1960s, Marshall McLuhan introduced the notion of a "global village" (McLuhan and Powers 1989). He predicted that mass media and technology would bring the world closer together, a notion considered to be farfetched at that time. But a quick inventory of today's technologies, which provide opportunities for forming diverse relationships, reveals that McLuhan's vision was quite accurate. Airline travel, television, cell phones, and the Internet are just a few of the technologies that have changed the way we communicate. Humans now have the capability to travel around the world in a matter of hours, simultaneously view events as they occur in other cities and countries, and concurrently interact with persons from around the globe.

Opportunities provided by technology for forming relationships with diverse persons have increased exponentially over the past twenty years. A 2005 survey revealed that nearly 1 billion people worldwide have access to the Internet (*http://www.internetworldstats.com/america.htm*). In the United States alone, nearly 250 million people use the World Wide Web to find information and to form relationships with others. Teenagers are forming and maintaining relationships via the computer at increasing rates due to social networking sites such as MySpace and Facebook. Some schools encourage students to communicate with intercultural email partners in a variety of subject areas. Internet chat rooms and discussion boards enable individuals to form friendships with others from almost anywhere. An examination of one teen chat site revealed that there were students communicating with one another from seven different states as well as from Canada, Great Britain, and Puerto Rico. As corporate America expands its boundaries to include many overseas partners, work teams will be comprised of members from diverse cultures. People come to the workplace with diverse beliefs, experiences, and expectations about the role of communication in relationships at work. Gergen (1991) emphasizes the fact that new technology has eliminated the barriers of space and time which previously inhibited relationships from forming with diverse individuals. Technology provides opportunities to communicate with persons who come from backgrounds entirely different than our own. Understanding the factors that influence communication will enhance our appreciation of these opportunities.

Influence of Demographic Transitions

Over the past twenty years, the demographic composition of the United States has changed dramatically. And predictions for the twenty-first century indicate that the life expectancy of the population will be longer and that the racial and ethnic composition will be more diverse than ever. Medical advancements have extended the life expectancy of Americans. Immigration patterns have changed dramatically since the 1960s, before then most immigrants came primarily from European countries. Today, nearly ninety percent of immigrants arrive from Latin American and Asian nations. By the middle of the twenty-first century, the majority of the U.S. population will be comprised of today's racial and ethnic minorities. Over the past decade, the number of interracial and interdenominational marriages has increased, and the U.S. workplace has seen a shift from the predominance of white male employees to a more diverse workforce that is also comprised of women and racial and ethnic groups. Opportunities to expand our linguistic, political, and social knowledge abound.

However, not all intercultural encounters are viewed as opportunities. While these demographic shifts create opportunities for diverse relationships, it is important to recognize that they present communication challenges as well. Some intercultural encounters are approached with fear and apprehension. Uncertainty about other individuals creates tension. In July 2005, a series of bombs exploded on subways and a bus in London. Since that time, reporters have pointed to the mistrust, misunderstanding, and fear that have caused members of this city (which once prided itself on its racial, ethnic, and religious diversity), to be more cautious in their interactions with others.

© Juriah Mosin, 2007, Shutterstock.

The demographic composition of the United States will continue to change and become more diverse.

Consequences of changing demographics are being felt in many social institutions. Schools are faced with issues such as bilingualism, differences in learning styles, and challenges of conflict among diverse groups. The Los Angeles school system reported that more than 100 different languages were spoken in classrooms across the county. Yet language is only one piece of a cultural code to be deciphered; other factors include understanding the perceptions and motivations that influence relationships in the home culture. Administrators at Taylor County High School in Georgia were faced with the challenge of how to address a group of students who wanted to host a "white-only" prom:

> Even after schools were integrated in the South, many rural areas still held separate proms for blacks and whites, and Taylor County High School was no exception. The first integrated prom in 31 years was organized by the school's Junior class because they collectively decided they all wanted to be together as a complete group. Every year before that, students and their parents planned separate dances. The proms weren't organized by the school itself, as school officials were concerned about potential interracial dating issues. The year after the first integrated prom, a small group of white students announced that they also wanted a separate dance. One of the students who had initiated the integrated dance said she was bitterly disappointed to hear that some students wanted to go back to the old ways after they had succeeded in bringing about such a change in the school.

Now more than ever, relationship success depends on the ability to demonstrate communication competence across cultures. Achieving communication competence is the ultimate goal in our interpersonal relationships. When the source and receiver are from diverse backgrounds and have unique expectations of communication, this goal may be perceived as difficult to achieve.

COMMUNICATION COMPETENCE: FOUR CORE CONCEPTS

Knowledge

Knowledge refers to the theoretical principles and concepts that explain behaviors occurring within a specific communication context. In other words, increasing your knowledge of communication theories and the concepts used to explain the challenges faced in intercultural relationships will enhance your ability to understand and accept those differences. In addition, knowledge will enhance your interpersonal skills when communicating with diverse others. You have already increased your knowledge base as a result of reading this textbook up to this point. Each of the concepts and theories that have been introduced has enhanced your understanding of the factors that impact communication in interpersonal relationships. Throughout this chapter we will take a second look at some of the theories introduced earlier in the text that have direct implications for intercultural encounters.

Uncertainty Reduction Theory. Berger and Calabrese's **uncertainty reduction theory** (URT) helps us understand how knowledge can assist us in forming effective interpersonal relationships by predicting the attitudes, behaviors, and emotions of others. As we initiate new relationships, our goal is to reduce our level of uncertainty about the other person (Berger and Calabrese 1975). When crossing cultural lines, alleviating this ambiguity becomes a bit trickier. For example, the notion of what constitutes acceptable disclosures in interpersonal relationships in the U.S. might differ from what is considered proper in other cultures. Is it acceptable to ask about another person's occupation? About her family? How does the other person view status differentials and what rules does he or she adopt for communicating with someone of different status? Berger (1979) identified three primary communication strategies used to reduce uncertainty in relationships. These are: passive strategies, active strategies, and interactive strategies.

Passive strategies typically involve observation and social comparison. We observe members of other cultures and make assessments as to the differences that exist. When one of your authors arrived in Hong Kong to teach summer classes, she did not speak Chinese. She spent many hours during her first weekend there sitting at the busy harbor, browsing through shopping areas, and walking around campus to observe how people interacted with one another. Through her observations, she learned the cultural rules for personal space, noticed styles of dress and forms of nonverbal greetings, and became familiar with the protocol for communication between students and teachers on campus.

Active strategies require us to engage in interactions with others to learn additional information about the other person. Suppose your professor assigns you to have weekly conversations with an international partner during the semester. Prior to your first meeting, you may decide to ask other international students what they know about your conversation partner's culture, or you may go online and participate in chat rooms that have members from the conversation partner's culture.

Interactive strategies typically involve a face-to-face encounter between two individuals to reduce uncertainty. Typically, partners engage in **self-disclosure** as a means of sharing information about themselves with others. When examining cultural differences in disclosure, it was found that American college students disclose about a much wider range of topics, and to more people outside the family, whereas college students in Korea selfdisclose mostly to immediate family members (Ishii, Thomas and Klopf 1993). Consider the following example:

Alicia was excited to learn that she had been selected to live with an international student in the dorm during her freshmen year. She had been fortunate enough to travel with her parents on business trips to various countries for the past several years and found learning about other cultures to be fascinating. Her new roommate, Kyon, was from Korea. As they were unpacking their things, Alicia told Kyon about her hometown, her summer vacation to Hilton Head Island, and about all of her friends from high school who were attending their college. She shared how frightened she was about the first day of classes, and she laughed as she told Kyon how she had taken her schedule and walked around campus to locate her classrooms for the first day of class. Eventually, Alicia noticed that she had been doing all the talking, so she began asking Kyon questions. While Kyon was willing to discuss the classes she would be taking and the plane trip from Korea, she seemed reluctant to talk about her family, friends, or even her fears about starting college.

Without knowledge of cultural differences in communication styles, Alicia may have become easily frustrated by Kyon's lack of disclosure. After all, in the United States it is common to engage in question-asking and selfdisclosure to reduce our uncertainty about others. But understanding that expectations for self-disclosure in Korea are different from those held by Americans will help alleviate the potential frustration and hurt feelings that could occur otherwise.

Knowledge of one's own culture is learned. Cultures teach their members preferred perceptual and communication patterns just as a coach teaches a team the plays. Beginning at a very young age, this learning process instills knowledge about the culture's accepted behaviors. As children enter kindergarten in the U.S., they learn that they need to raise their hand to ask a question in class and to listen quietly while the teacher is speaking. Communication is the channel for teaching these lessons. Members of a culture practice the preferred behaviors and, if they deviate from the endorsed mannerisms they will probably find that they are unsuccessful in their communication. Consider the following example:

Young children learn quickly that listening quietly to the teacher is the accepted behavior for school.

© PhotoCreate, 2007, Shutterstock.

A student from Ethiopia shared this story about his experiences in American classrooms. During his high school years, he lost class participation points because of his unwillingness to speak out in class. While he was confused about his low grade, he did not approach the teacher and ask for clarification. Rather, he accepted the teacher's evaluation of his performance. However, what the teacher did not know was that in his culture students are not active participants in class. The teacher is viewed as the authority and the students are expected to listen and learn. Further, to question a teacher's authority would be viewed as extremely disrespectful.

As we engage in relationships with diverse persons, the knowledge of what constitutes competent communication behaviors is learned. Recent articles have focused on the need for cultural and social knowledge among U.S. armed service workers (McFate 2005; McFate and Jackson 2005). As U.S. military personnel travel overseas for service, it is important that they have a solid understanding of the cultural beliefs and norms that are expected. While the mission of the troops may be to restore order, respect for cultural expectations must still be demonstrated. Even the simple act of eating and drinking could be perceived as being offensive without proper knowledge of cultural norms. Soldiers training for duty in Iraq need to understand that members of Muslim cultures do not eat or drink during the day during the month of Ramadan. By refraining from eating or drinking in front of members of the Muslim culture during this period, U.S. soldiers can display respect for the Muslim culture. Studying the role of values, beliefs, attitudes, and needs in shaping and sustaining relationships can be invaluable. New knowledge can remove some of the barriers that can create communication challenges in relationships with diverse people. But knowledge in and of itself is insufficient for achieving competence. We also need to gain an understanding of why others communicate the way they do.

Understanding

Understanding involves applying knowledge to specific situations in an attempt to explain the behaviors that are occurring. While you may know how uncertainty reduction theory (URT) is defined, it is important to gain an understanding of how it impacts a particular interaction. Understanding involves exploring the roots, or sources of communication, rather than simply explaining the behavior. Imagine this scenario. You attend the funeral of the mother of your close friend who is Jewish. At the end of the ceremony, Jewish tradition calls for friends and family members to shovel dirt onto the coffin, but you are not aware of this tradition. This act makes you extremely uncomfortable, and you decide not to participate in the tradition; you end up offending your friend. Knowledge of the Jewish cultural customs would have assisted you in understanding the negative reaction that resulted from your refusal to participate in the ceremony.

As the twenty-first century opens, the cultural composition of the United States is becoming increasingly diverse. A recent Associated Press news article suggests that the term "minority" may no longer be an accurate descriptor for various U.S. co-cultures *(http://www.diversityinc.com/public/16722print.cfm)*. Non-Latino whites currently encompass less than fifty percent of the population of Texas, and it is predicted that more than one-third of all Americans will soon live in a state where groups formerly considered minority groups will outnumber Caucasians. Changes in demographics provide more opportunities for individuals to interact with individuals who are from diverse cultural backgrounds. Consider the various relationship contexts we have discussed in this text. The chances are greater than ever before that you will form relationships with teachers, physicians, and co-workers who are from diverse backgrounds.

Broadening our understanding of diversity to understand the influence of a variety of elements such as race, ethnicity, language differences, and religious beliefs is essential for relationship success. In many classrooms across the U.S., Caucasians are no longer the majority. On the surface, twenty-five students may appear to be similar, based on their racial or ethnic status, but it is quite possible that there are twenty-five different cultural backgrounds represented. One aspect of their diverse backgrounds may be seen in the language that is spoken in each of their homes. Nearly seventeen percent of elementary and secondary school students speak a language other than English in their homes *(http://www.census.gov/prod/2004pubs/04statab/educ.pdf)*. Even where racial and ethnic diversity may be minimal, students come from different geographical locations and religious backgrounds and are impacted by their unique family backgrounds. Understanding how each of these elements impacts individual decisions to communicate in relationships is essential. For example, Jack was confused when he saw his friend Adam place a rock on the grave of a close friend who had recently passed away after a car accident. He did not understand that Adam's behavior was guided by an old Jewish custom of placing a rock on a loved one's grave as a sign of respect. According to tradition, the rocks were originally used as a way to mark gravesites. As more people visited the site, they added rocks to demonstrate how many people loved and respected the person.

© PhotoCreate, 2007, Shutterstock.

A room full of students appearing to be similar on the surface could have many different cultural backgrounds.

It is important to understand that what works in one relationship may not work in all. Consider our earlier example of the coach and his team. Just as it would be ineffective to run the same play over and over again in a game, communicating with diverse persons in the same manner would not result in satisfying relationships. While this chapter will assist you in building knowledge and understanding of communication differences, acceptance of differences is also key to interpersonal success.

Acceptance

Acceptance refers to our awareness of the feelings and emotions involved in diverse approaches to relationships and communication. It encompasses our willingness to understand the behavior of others. Accepting differences in behavior enables us to be less judgmental and to reject ethnocentric thinking. **Ethnocentrism** refers to the tendency to perceive our own ways of behaving and thinking as being correct, or acceptable, and judging the behaviors of others as being "strange," incorrect, or inferior. Challenges in our interactions are often attributed to external, rather than cultural factors. Consider two coworkers who attempt to influence one another on a project on which they are collaborating. Joe tries to persuade Maynae by directly disagreeing with her proposal and engaging in assertive communication. Maynae's cultural background is one that values saving face. Thus, she avoids directly disagreeing with Joe—rather, she nods her head and proceeds with the project as she planned. Both of them end up frustrated. Joe cannot understand why Maynae did not follow their game plan. Had she not nodded her head and agreed with him? Joe attributes Maynae's actions to her shyness. Maynae is frustrated by Joe's confusion. Did he not understand that she did not want to embarrass him in front of their colleagues? She deduces that he must be in a bad mood and was not paying attention. As they continue to disagree about how to proceed with the project, they attribute the communication difficulty to the other person's mood or to shyness, both reasons being external to cultural factors. In reality, they may have diverse cultural expectations for how to influence others.

Skills

We have discussed many of the specific skills that are central to interpersonal communication throughout this text. **Skills** are the specific communication behaviors which contribute to competent and effective interpersonal communication. Effective listening, assertiveness, responsiveness, nonverbal sensitivity, language comprehension, and conflict management are only a few of the many skills required when interacting in diverse relationships. It is important to note that there is a difference between knowing how to communicate effectively across cultures, and actually being able to engage in the appropriate behaviors. You might understand that the Chinese culture values silence, but because you are an extremely talkative person and are ineffective in practicing silence you may be perceived as being rude when interacting with members of the Chinese culture. While language is an important skill to enhance communication competence, practicing nonverbal skills can also assist in producing effective interpersonal encounters. For example, when dining with friends from Japan, it is appropriate to make loud slurping sounds while eating a meal. The act of slurping is a behavior that is considered to be a compliment to the cook in Japan as it communicates that the food is delicious. But what if you feel very uncomfortable and do not know how to demonstrate the proper slurping behavior because you have never been encouraged to do so? Remaining silent while eating is perceived as an insult in these cultures, but your lack of slurping skills inhibit your ability to communicate your appreciation for the meal.

CULTURE AND DIVERSITY DEFINED

Culture has been defined by scholars in a number of different ways. In fact, one book identified more than 200 different definitions of culture (Kroeber and Kluckhohn 1952). In the fifty years since these definitions were compiled, attention to the increasing diversity of our world has prompted scholars to create even more. Anthropologists have broadly defined culture as being comprised of perceptions, behaviors, and evaluations. This definition was expanded to include shared ideas of a group which incorporates ethical standards as well as other intellectual components. Other researchers have adopted a descriptive approach to explaining culture. Their definitions include characteristics such as knowledge, morals, beliefs, customs, art, music, law, and values. In this text, we define **culture** as shared perceptions which shape the communication patterns and expectations of a group of people.

Diversity refers to the unique qualities or characteristics that distinguish individuals and groups from one another. The following is a list of characteristics that contribute to diversity in our interpersonal relationships.

- Age
- Educational background
- Ethnicity
- Family status
- Gender
- Income
- Military experience
- National, regional, or other geographical areas of origin
- Ownership of property and assets
- Physical and mental ability
- Race
- Sexual orientation
- Social class
- Spiritual practice
- Work experience

Diversity takes into consideration specific elements that have tremendous potential for our relationships. Consider the characteristics that you share with your closest friend. Chances are that you formed a relationship based on similarities in some of the areas listed above. Perhaps you are close in age and have similar educational backgrounds. Stop for a moment and consider the relationship implications when there are differences across these characteristics. A couple with different spiritual backgrounds may need to negotiate whose religious beliefs will be followed in raising their children. A daughter who is a lesbian may find it difficult communicating her feelings about her relationship

What characteristics do close friends share?

with her heterosexual parents. Or a soldier may be challenged to convey his beliefs about war and his value of freedom with his friends back home who have not served in the military. When considering the many characteristics of diversity, it is easy to see why many relationships encounter stumbling blocks as individuals attempt to navigate differences in knowledge, experiences, beliefs, and values.

One of the first steps in becoming competent in our relationships involves recognizing the unique characteristics that each relationship partner possesses. Recall the discussion in Chapter Five about the role perception plays in shaping communication in our relationships. Our culture shapes our perception and society teaches us the preferred ways of behaving. The American value for democracy is shared by many members of this country. Beginning in elementary school, we are taught the meaning of democracy. As we grow up, we see people defending their rights to free speech. Thus, our culture begins shaping our perceptions at a very young age. Perception influences and forms our values, beliefs, and attitudes. These shared perceptions are both consciously taught and unconsciously learned. **Socialization** refers to the process of learning about one's cultural norms and expectations. This is critical for an individual to become a functioning member of society. Sources of socialization include parents, peers, teachers, celebrities, political leaders, workplace colleagues, educational materials, and mass media. Perceptions are highly individualized, so much so that we may not realize that others see things differently. It may be easy to overlook the impact that diversity has on our communication patterns. Communication behaviors are often unique to a culture, allowing us to easily identify members of various cultural groups. For example, an employee from Georgia assigned to work on a project with a team from Ohio is likely to be identified by her accent. Forms of address, such as when a child refers to an adult as "Miss Sarah," may also indicate a southern background. Culture is not only reflected in our behavior, it also influences our expectations. We form assumptions about how individuals should behave and what we should expect in our relationships with them. Japan is considered to be a collectivistic culture which values and encourages the accomplishments of groups over individual achievement. A student from Japan may experience difficulty in the U.S. where individualism is valued. He may be uncomfortable in situations where he is "singled out" for his individual academic achievements, preferring to be acknowledged with his class.

Americans typically learn to value democracy at a young age.

© Stephanie Davis, 2007, Shutterstock.

While we each have diverse characteristics that make us unique, we also share some aspects in common with other members of our larger culture. These shared characteristics allow us to identify with various groups and help shape our identity.

CO-CULTURES WITHIN THE UNITED STATES

Within the larger cultural context, numerous co-cultures exist, each distinguishable by unique characteristics. It is important to note that individuals are members of more than one co-culture. Consider this. An employee may claim membership as a member of the organization, in addition to being an adult, male, African-American Texan with Republican views, and of the Methodist faith. A total of seven co-cultures are claimed. Multiple memberships may contribute to confusion and miscommunication that occurs in relationships. Suppose you assume that because a teammate on your soccer team likes sports, she would not be interested in classical music or the theatre. As you pass a poster announcing the upcoming cultural arts series on your campus, you make some negative comments about people who attend musical and theatrical events. What you do not know is that your teammate has been a student of classical music since a young age, and that her mother is a trained opera singer. While this scenario is an extremely simplified example, assuming that membership in one group precludes an individual from having interests in other groups can lead to embarrassing situations that can impact relationships. Some examples of co-cultural classifications follow.

Ethnicity

While the terms "race" and "ethnicity" have often been used synonymously, these two categories are unique. **Ethnicity** refers to the common heritage, or background, shared by a group of people. Categories may be established to identify the culture from which one's ancestors came. These include Irish-American, Polish-American, or Mexican-American. While there has been some debate over the connotations associated with the labeling of some of these groups, the intention of naming is simply for identification purposes.

Race

Race is the term used to refer to genetically inherited biological characteristics such as hair texture and color, eye shape, skin color, and facial structure. Terms used to describe different racial categories include Caucasian, African American, and Asian. One situation which impacts our classification of groups results from the increasing number of intercultural marriages and relationships. Previously there were no categories on the U.S. census form to allow individuals to indicate their identification with more than one racial classification. This changed on the 2000 census with the addition of the category "other" to allow citizens to report their racial identification. As a result, individuals can now identify themselves as members of multiple racial groups rather than being restricted to only one racial identity.

Regional Differences

Within a given culture, speech patterns, attitudes, and values may differ significantly depending on the geographic location that an individual calls home. Northern Germans express values which are quite different from those of southern Germans. Those who reside in northern Brazil communicate using nonverbal gestures which are unrecognizable to those from southern Brazil. Accents within a culture also vary depending on the geographic region. Japanese spoken in Okinawa takes on different tones when spoken in Tokyo. English spoken by those who live in the Amish region of Pennsylvania is used differently by Texans. Dodd (1998) observed a variety of **regional differences** in communication styles within the boundaries of the United States. These include variety in the amount of animation, perceived openness, informal rapport, and rate of speech delivery. Even when examining the values of urban versus rural cultures, differences in values are obvious. Rural cultures appear to approach decisions more cautiously and simplistically. Members of urban cultures are more willing to take risks and reach decisions more quickly.

When we initiate relationships, we choose to be with people who share our common interests.

Social Class

Cultures often find that members stratify themselves on the basis of educational, occupational, or financial backgrounds, resulting in classifications and status differentials. Those whose careers produce high financial gain are usually awarded greater power and status in the American culture. Other cultures are more concerned with the amount of education that a person has completed. Stratification often occurs on the basis of **homophily,** the idea that we choose to be with people who are similar to us. Thus, when initiating relationships, we seek out those in similar careers, with similar educational experiences, and of similar financial status.

In some cultures, it is possible to move from one social class category to another. For example, a person in the U.S. can easily move from one category to another as a result of their economic or educational status. Graduating from college may enable a person to gain a more prestigious job, and thereby allow him to achieve a higher social standing. Other cultures adhere to a philosophy of ascribed roles in society; an individual is born into a particular social class and there is nothing that can be done to warrant movement to a higher level. The caste system in India is one that restricts members from gaining social status. Relationships in these cultures are restricted to those who are in the same social class.

CHARACTERISTICS OF CULTURE

In the next sections we explain the three primary characteristics of culture: 1) it is learned, 2) it is dynamic, and 3) it is pervasive.

Culture Is Learned

The preferred ways of behaving as a member of a society are learned at a young age. Consider the learning experiences of children. Adults teach them how to say words, which foods can be eaten with the fingers and which should be eaten with utensils, and songs and rituals that are part of the culture. They may be taught that profanity is not acceptable and they are rewarded for saying the Pledge of Allegiance. Children are even taught biases and prejudices. Expectations about the nature of relationships and communication are also learned at a young age. For example, in the United States it is viewed as unacceptable for male friends to hold hands. In some Arab cultures it is not uncommon to see two men engage in this behavior. Society teaches us the behaviors that are accepted by most members of the culture, and, at the same time, instills within us a response mechanism for reacting to violations of cultural norms.

What is acceptable behavior in a culture is learned both explicitly and implicitly. **Explicit learning** involves actual instructions regarding the preferred way of behaving. A school may print a brochure that specifies the dress code that is required of all students, or a teacher may instruct students to raise their hand before speaking in class. In our families, we learn expectations for communication in relationships. For example, a young girl whose mother has experienced negative relationships with former spouses might be taught to "never trust men" and may find it difficult to engage in disclosure and to form relationships with males. **Implicit learning** occurs via observation. We are not directly told what behaviors are preferred; rather they are learned by observing others. Our choices of what to wear for a first date or the first day of work are influenced by observing what others wear or by what we have learned from the media. We learn the preferred ways of dressing so as to be accepted by our peers.

Culture Is Dynamic

Over time, events occur that cause change; cultures do not remain static. Consider changes in relationships that occurred after the events of September 11th. In the days and months following the tragedy, people reported that they engaged in more frequent communication with friends and family members. People were more willing to engage in open expressions of affection. Cultures and their members also change as a result of "borrowing" aspects from other cultures. It is quite common to open a fashion magazine and see examples of trends being borrowed from other cultures. For example, many stores and catalogues showcase Asian-inspired t-shirts and jewelry that include Chinese or Japanese writing. It is also quite common to see clothing adopting cultural styles such as the recent style of women in the U.S. wearing kimono style dresses.

Depending on a culture's approach to uncertainty, the encouragement and acceptance of change may occur at different rates. Within the last decade, change has occurred at a rapid rate within the United States. Technological advances make some computers obsolete a year or two after purchase. Food and exercise trends also appear to go through changes as new diet fads are constantly introduced to the culture. In 2003, the Atkins diet gained popularity in the United States and carbohydrates were declared to be taboo. Not only did people begin to alter their dietary habits, restaurants altered their menus by designing and promoting dishes that were "Atkins-friendly." Eventually, doctors began questioning the health issues associated with the Atkins diet, and in 2005, the U.S. Department of Agriculture revised the traditional food pyramid to include six dimensions recommended for a healthy diet. Not only do cultures change with regard to food and clothing styles, but popular culture also undergoes transitions. The popularity of television shows change as new shows are introduced. What is "hot" one season may be "out" the next.

While you may initially question what impact these changes in various cultural aspects has on our interpersonal relationships, consider the amount of time we spend discussing aspects of culture with others. Friends gather around the water cooler and in dorm rooms to discuss the previous night's episode of *Survivor* or *Desperate Housewives*. They analyze the reasons for changes in the cafeteria menu to accommodate society's low carb trend. Changes in our culture provide many topics for discussion and debate in our personal relationships. However, not all cultures embrace change. In fact, some cultures are reluctant to implement change. For example, Germany scores high on uncertainty avoidance. This high score is reflective of the culture's reluctance to change as well as the desire to have strict rules and guidelines in place to maintain order. Some countries, such as Argentina, may find that their members adopt similar religious beliefs. When the majority of a culture's members practice the same religion, there is very little uncertainty about the beliefs held by individuals.

Culture Is Pervasive

Culture is everywhere. Take a moment and look around you. Chances are that you see numerous examples of your culture's influence with one simple glance. Is there a computer on your desk? Perhaps there are posters, photos, or artwork on the walls. Is there a television turned on or music playing? Maybe you are on campus and there are other students nearby. Take a look at the style of their clothes and listen to the words that they are saying to one another. Each of these things demonstrates the pervasive nature of culture. It surrounds us—in fact, we cannot escape the influence of our culture. If one were to adopt a descriptive definition of culture, this prevalence could be seen as influencing everything: our expectations for relationships, the clothing we wear, the language we speak, the food we choose, and even our daily schedules. Culture is represented not only in our material possessions, but also in the values, beliefs, and attitudes that comprise our personal orientation system. It shapes virtually every aspect of our lives and influences our thoughts and actions. Culture also affects how we initiate and maintain our interpersonal relationships. In many European cultures, it is common for teenagers to go out on large "group" dates, while females in Australia may ask out males and offer to split the cost of a date.

Culture surrounds our lives and its influence is everywhere.

In China and Japan, dating is typically reserved for those who are older, typically in their twenties. Dating was discouraged in India until recently. Families were expected to introduce couples and help them get to know one another socially in preparation for marriage. While online dating has grown in popularity in the U.S. and many European countries, this method of initiating romantic relationships would be frowned upon in cultures that view dating as a time for getting to know one's potential future in-laws.

By taking a moment to consider the impact that culture has on our lives, it becomes clear that culture and communication are inseparable. Our verbal and nonverbal messages are shaped by our culture's influence, and we learn about our culture through the messages we receive from others. Given the level of influence that culture and communication have on one another, it should come as no surprise that the diversity that exists among members of a culture impacts the relationships that they form with one another.

HOW DIVERSITY IMPACTS INTERPERSONAL RELATIONSHIPS

Think about the first day in a new school or at a new job. Consider some of the thoughts that may go through your mind. Probably many expectations are formed about the people you see as you walk through the door. Some of the differences may be visible simply by looking at the other person, such as their gender, race, or age. In addition, many "hidden" differences also exist, such as their beliefs, values, and attitudes. Once the realization sets in that we are expected to communicate with someone whose cultural makeup is likely different from our own, we quickly search for any information, or cues, to help us make sense of how to interact in the particular situation. The process which helps us to organize the stimuli that bombards us in a potential communication encounter is known as perception.

In Chapter Five, we defined **perception** as the process of selecting, organizing, and interpreting stimuli into something that makes sense or is meaningful. Our perception causes us to view relationships and communicate in ways that are potentially different from the ways of others. The perception process may be explained in this way. Think about all the possible things that you could identify by using all five of your senses. Consider all the possible things that you could see, touch, feel, taste, and smell. Literally hundreds of stimuli compete for your attention at a given time! It would be virtually impossible to perceive all of the stimuli at the same time, so we pick and choose which things to pay attention to and ignore the others. Because individuals are selective in what they pay attention to and how they interpret it, each person forms their own perception of behaviors and events. As a result, we each have our own unique view of the world.

The role of selective interpretation was also discussed in Chapter Five. Because of our cultural influences, we may assign different meanings to behaviors. If we do not take the time or make the effort to see what is truly behind our interpretation, serious barriers to effective communication may occur. Imagine the reaction of a teacher who traveled to Hong Kong and, at a celebration dinner, was presented with an appetizer of chicken feet! She perceived the consumption of chicken feet to be disgusting, and her nonverbal behavior of wrinkling her nose and her refusal of the appetizer offended her hosts. The teacher regretted her reaction of obvious disgust, especially after she considered the fact that individuals of other cultures might view her favorite food (a cheeseburger), as disgusting due to their perception of the cow being sacred.

PERSONAL ORIENTATION SYSTEM

Each individual has a set of predispositions which serves as a guide for thoughts, actions, and behaviors. These predispositions are comprised of one's needs, beliefs, values, and attitudes and are commonly referred to as one's **personal orientation system.** Communication plans and relationship expectations are developed and organized based on these characteristics. Many of the components of the personal orientation system are learned within the cultural context. Messages are transmitted from parents, teachers, and friends who teach the younger members of society to perceive certain actions as good or bad, fair or unfair. For example, Chinese children are taught to value history and tradition, and stories of the past are viewed as lessons to guide their behavior. Children in the U.S. tend to view stories of the past as entertaining, but instead of following tradition, they are encouraged to find new and innovative ways of doing things. When faced with decisions regarding the proper way to respond in situations, our needs, beliefs, values, and attitudes assist us in guiding our perception of a situation.

Needs

All individuals have **needs,** strong feelings of discomfort or desire which motivate them to achieve satisfaction or comfort. A strong relationship exists between needs and interpersonal communication, with communication serving as the primary mechanism through which we satisfy needs. If a student needs to have an assignment explained more clearly, he or she must communicate that need to the instructor. If an employee needs assistance in obtaining a copy of a company report, communication with the human resources director or with a supervisor can satisfy the need.

Everyone has a need to love and be loved.

© Lee Morris, 2007, Shutterstock.

Maslow's hierarchy of needs (1954) organizes the needs which humans must fulfill. A hierarchical structure helps us to understand the importance and priority of having some needs achieved before others. At the most basic level are the physiological needs of humans. These include the need for food, clothing, and shelter. While most cultures are able to devote adequate attention to meeting these needs, others cannot. The next level includes safety needs. Individuals possess a motivation to feel safe and secure in their surroundings. However, cultures differ in their methods for satisfying this need. At the middle of the hierarchy are affection needs. Schutz (1958) identified three basic needs across cultures: affection, control, and inclusion. We have a need to love and to be loved. Esteem needs are located at the next level of Maslow's hierarchy. Humans have a need to feel good about themselves. Interpersonal communication with others is one mechanism for meeting this need. Things that cultural members say and do impact the fulfillment of these needs. At the highest level of Maslow's hierarchy is self-actualization. This level is achieved when an individual feels that he or she has accomplished all that can be achieved in a lifetime. As the U.S. Army's motto implies, self-actualization is fulfilled when an individual feels that the goal "be all that you can be" has been met.

When applying Maslow's hierarchy to our interpersonal relationships, it becomes apparent that communication is the mechanism through which we meet some of our most basic needs, as well as fulfilling higher levels of need. Communication is the key to understanding individuals' needs and in comprehending the value placed on need fulfillment. Understanding what needs individuals have and their importance enables us to interact more effectively and to avoid misunderstandings. While one person may have a need for power and status, another may possess a strong need for friendship and affection. The intensity with which each of these needs is experienced may cause these two people to interact in very different ways.

Beliefs

A second component of culture which guides our thoughts and behaviors is our belief system. **Beliefs** are an important part of understanding our interactions with diverse others because they not only influence our conscious reactions to situations, but dominate our subconscious thoughts as well. We are constantly influenced by our beliefs. They are our personal convictions regarding the truth or existence of things. In Chapter Two we discussed how interactions with others shape our view of self. Through our interpersonal communication, we form beliefs about ourselves and our relationships. Based on positive interactions with your family members and teachers, you may believe that you are destined to succeed in college. Less supportive interactions might result in the belief that you will accomplish very little in life. Ultimately, these beliefs impact our communication with others. The formation of the central substance of our belief system begins at a very early age and continues to evolve as we grow and form relationships with others.

When crossing cultural borders, an examination of the beliefs possessed by a culture's members yields some fascinating differences. People from Malaysia believe that it is bad luck to touch someone on the top of the head as it is believed to be the location of the center for spiritual energy. Hawaiians possess a number of beliefs about the messages indicated by the appearance of a rainbow. Consider the superstitious beliefs held by members of the American culture. Walking under a ladder, having a black cat cross your path, and the groom seeing the bride on the wedding day prior to the ceremony are all believed to be signs of bad luck. Our beliefs impact our interpersonal communication.

Because most people do not question social institutions, many of the beliefs of a culture are perpetuated from generation to generation without any thought being given to the reasons for the existence of the beliefs. Some individuals have reported that reactions to their questioning of beliefs have been so negative that they feared rejection in their relationships and simply adopted the accepted beliefs into their own personal orientation system.

Values

Values serve as the guide for an individual's behavior. They dictate what we should and should not do. Kluckhohn (1951) describes **values** as a personal philosophy, either explicitly or implicitly expressed, that influences the choice of alternative actions which may be available to an individual. This definition highlights the relationship between values and communication in that values are communicated both explicitly and implicitly through our behaviors. The majority of our actions are reflective of the values which are firmly established in our personal orientation system.

Values are often communicated explicitly through verbal communication. Some cultural values are evident in the proverbs shared among people. "A stitch in time saves nine" communicates the value placed on addressing issues or problems when they are small rather than waiting until they grow bigger. Practicality and being satisfied with what you have is expressed in the proverb, "A bird in the hand is worth two in the bush." The Swedish proverb, "Friendship doubles our joy and divides our grief" describes the value placed on friendships. In his book, *A Pirate Looks at Fifty*, Jimmy Buffett communicates his value for family relationships and friendships when he states, "I have always looked at life as a voyage, mostly wonderful, sometimes frightening. In my family and friends I have discovered treasure more valuable than gold."

Nonverbal communication may be a more subtle means for communicating values. Many Asian cultures practice the custom of giving a gift to demonstrate the value for reciprocity and friendship. It is not unusual for students to offer their teachers gifts in exchange for the

© Galina Barskaya, 2007, Shutterstock.

Friendships are often the most valued things in peoples' lives.

lessons that are learned. In the American culture, many teachers would be extremely uncomfortable accepting these gifts, resulting in confusion in the student-teacher relationship, possibly making subsequent interactions uncomfortable. It is important to gain an understanding not only of the values held by a culture's members, but also the ways in which individuals communicate these values. By doing so, misunderstandings may be avoided.

Attitudes: Stereotyping and Prejudice

Throughout our lives, each of us develops learned predispositions to respond in favorable or unfavorable ways toward people or objects. These tendencies are known as **attitudes.** A primary goal of this chapter is to assist you in identifying your responses to differences as well as to help you to understand your internal orientations guiding these reactions. If ever we interpret another's cultural customs or actions as being wrong or offensive, it is important to understand our own attitudes and how our culture has influenced their formation. Failure to understand these tendencies can result in irrational attitude formation, producing negative results in interpersonal relationships with diverse others. Two attitude formations to avoid are stereotypes and prejudices.

Stereotyping.   Stereotyping results from the inability to see and appreciate the uniqueness of individuals. When generalizations about a group are made and are then attributed to any individuals who either associate with, or are members of, the group, the process of **stereotyping** is evolving. Three steps have been identified in the process of stereotyping.

The first step involves categorizing a group of people based on observable characteristics that they have in common. An international student from Scotland commented that she thought that all Americans would be like the people she saw on Beverly Hills 90210—tan, attractive, and extremely materialistic. As a result, she reported that she was initially apprehensive about forming relationships with many of her American classmates and socialized mainly with other international students.

The second step involves assigning characteristics to a group of people. An example of this step would be a popular magazine characterizing mothers who are employed outside the home as being less dedicated to their children.

Finally, we apply those characteristics to any individual that is a member of that group. An example would be the teacher who assumes that a student-athlete is not serious about academic studies. Following the events of 9/11, some members of Arab cultures have reported that they have been subjected to racial profiling. **Racial profiling** occurs when law enforcement or other officials use race as a basis for investigating a person of criminal involvement. This is a result of applying the single characteristic of race in determining whether a person should be viewed as threatening.

While stereotyping can be irrational, it is actually quite normal. Because humans are uncomfortable with uncertainty, stereotyping enables us to make predictions about our potential interactions with others. In order to become more competent in our interactions with diverse others, it is important to realize that stereotypes *can* and *do* impact our perceptions and our communication.

Prejudice.   Another form of attitude which involves negative reactions toward a group of people based on inflexible and inaccurate assumptions is commonly known as **prejudice.** In essence, prejudice involves "pre-judging" individuals. Some of the most common forms of prejudice in the U.S. include racism, sexism, and ageism.

Racism. Racism refers to prejudice against an individual or group based on their racial composition. **Race** is a term used to refer to inherited biological characteristics such as skin color, eye color, hair texture, and facial structure.

> In her 1995 film entitled *Blue Eyed*, Jane Elliott shares with viewers a diversity training session conducted with adults of various racial and ethnic backgrounds in Kansas City. Blue-eyed members of the group are told that they are inferior to the rest of the group simply based on their eye color. As the film unfolds, it is amazing to watch the confusion, mistrust, lack of confidence, and fear of communication that emerges among members of the group. Elliott explains that while some may consider her decision to discriminate simply on the basis of eye color to be irrational, it is not much different than choosing to treat someone differently on the basis of skin color. She points out that the chemical which produces eye color is the same one that produces skin color.

Ageism. Negative communication toward persons based on their age is referred to as **ageism.** In our culture, some people assume that senior citizens are incapable of making contributions to society and can be considered helpless. In 1967, Congress passed the ADEA (Age Discrimination in Employment Act) to protect older workers against age discrimination. According to the law, an employer cannot replace an employee over the age of forty with a younger person if the current employer is able to satisfactorily perform her or his job. Sue Sewell, age fifty-one, expresses her frustration of ageism in the workplace:

> "Society is missing out on the talent and a wealth of experience of the older worker. I have recently returned to the workplace after a spell at home and have noticed that some younger workers and management are not tolerant of the older worker. I think the older worker is stereo-typed as being slow and less likely to be able to pick up new ideas and be able to use new technology. I, like many others in my age bracket, cannot give up work as we have mortgages, bills to pay, and depend-ents to support. I actually also enjoy being out in the world of work; it makes me feel more a part of society. If the retirement age is to be 70 and beyond as is being mooted at present, then we must have more opportunities for people to be employed whatever their age." (*http://www.maturityworks.co.uk/uploads/files/matwrksreport.qxd1.pdf*)

Ageism is also communicated when negative prejudices are harbored by adults against teenagers based on the attitude that teens are rude and unruly. While some equate college students on Spring Break with partying and drinking, recent programs have been developed on college campuses to provide students with opportunities to complete community service projects during their break from studies. In 2006, thousands of college students traveled to post-Hurricane Katrina Mississippi and New Orleans and spent their Spring Break vacations assisting in the clean-up process.

Sexism. Sexism refers to negative communication directed toward persons of a particular sex. In the United States, sexist attitudes have traditionally been directed toward females. As a result, females have experienced discrimination in the workplace and in other walks of life. While stories of sexism frequently focus on the prejudices against females, men also are subject to sexist behaviors. Consider the father who stays at home and raises the children. As he shops for groceries with the children in the cart or plays with them at the park on a sunny weekday afternoon, he may hear a comment such as, "It's so nice that he's babysitting the children!" Not surprisingly, he may become offended because it is assumed that he is not capable of being the primary caregiver for his children.

COMMUNICATING PREJUDICE

There are three primary means for communicating prejudice. **Verbal abuse** refers to the process of engaging in comments or jokes that are insulting or demeaning to a targeted group. Consider the impressions that we form of people as a result of their negative verbal behaviors toward others. The racist comments made by *Seinfeld*'s Michael Richards may have caused some Kramer fans to question their positive attitudes toward the actor. **Discrimination** involves denying an individual or group of people their rights. While prejudice involves negative cognitions, or thoughts, discrimination is displayed when behaviors are used to express one's negative cognitions. Typically, discrimination is expressed through negative verbal comments made toward a group or an individual, with physical avoidance being the ultimate goal. The most severe form of prejudice is **violence.** On April 29, 1992, the verdict in the trial involving the 1991 beating of Rodney King by four Los Angeles police officers was read. Only one of the four officers was found guilty of using excessive force; the others were cleared of all charges against them. As word of the verdict was spread, riots erupted throughout Los Angeles. During the next three days, television viewers witnessed physical attacks, arson, and looting throughout the city. In the end, more than 4,000 people were injured, more than fifty were killed, and the city suffered over $1 billion in damages. This violence demonstrates the potentially extreme outcome of prejudice.

Fortunately, a 2004 study of 2,000 teens conducted by Teenage Research Unlimited (TRU) in Illinois points to changing trends among young Americans. Nearly sixty percent of teenagers reported that they have close friends of different races. Friendships of diverse religious or political beliefs and economic backgrounds are also prominent among today's teens. TRU President Michael Wood summarized the changing views of this generation as, "Teens still prefer to hang out with peers who share common ground with them. But that no longer means that their friends have to necessarily *look* the part. It's all about attitudes and actions—about *who* you are and what you *do*, not *what* you are" (*http://www.teenresearch.com/PRview.cfm?edit_id=278.*) Additional research points to the benefits of multicultural interactions that occur among college students. A 1997 study found that college students who have frequent interactions with students of different racial backgrounds and engage in positive discussions about race and ethnicity tend to have a higher self-concept and report that they are more satisfied with college (Smith and Associates, 1997).

© William Frederick Lawson, 2007, Shutterstock.

Teens prefer to have friends who share their interests, regardless of their backgrounds.

Functions of Prejudice

While prejudice is often based on false, irrational, and inflexible generalizations, it is often considered "normal." Why do individuals form prejudice? Three primary reasons for forming prejudice have been identified.

Acceptance. **Acceptance** is when a person communicates negative feelings toward a particular group in order to fit in within a desired group. An example of this is when a fraternity member expresses hatred for another fraternity's members. When asked why he has these strong feelings, the only reason offered is "because all Alpha Betas dislike them."

Defend the Ego. Another reason for communicating prejudice is to defend the ego. By expressing negative feelings and attitudes toward a group of people, individuals create a scapegoat for their own misfortunes. An employee was overheard expressing his prejudice against women being selected for administrative positions. Upon further questioning, he admitted that he did not actually harbor any ill feelings toward women supervisors. Rather, he was frustrated by the fact that a woman had been offered the position rather than him.

Provide Information. A final reason for prejudice is to provide information. As was stated earlier, humans have a need to reduce uncertainty. Unfortunately, many individuals form prejudice as a means for forming knowledge about a group of people with whom little or no contact has been made. Recall our earlier example of the student from Scotland who was reluctant to interact with American students because of the stereotypes formed as a result of watching *Beverly Hills 90210*. Because limited information was available, the student experienced high levels of uncertainty about how to interact with American college students. Prejudices were formed as a means to reduce the level of uncertainty and to provide a framework for building expectations. By forming these negative predispositions, an information base was constructed on which to form expectations about potential interactions.

Cultural Value Orientations

To understand the values shared by a culture's members, a number of scholars have developed models for studying value orientations. These models pose questions designed to measure the intensity with which a culture's members value specific characteristics.

Kluckhohn and Strodbeck (1961) developed one of the first models of cultural value orientation, and it is still being used in research today. Questions are designed to gain insight into such perceptions regarding relationships between humans and humans and nature. Sample questions include:

- What is the basic nature of human beings? Are they inherently evil and incapable of being trusted, or do most humans have a good heart?
- How are social relationships organized? Are relationships viewed as being hierarchical with divisions of power? Or should equal rights be present in all social relationships?

Hall's model of cultural values (1976) represents a continuum of characteristics associated with high-context and low-context cultures. These differences are characterized by distinct differences in communication styles. Cultures which fall at the **low-context** end of the continuum exhibit high verbal tendencies. This style is associated with a direct approach and verbal expressiveness. A philosophy of "say what you mean" is embraced. **High-context** cultures, on the other hand, prefer a more indirect style; cues about the intended message are interpreted through nonverbal channels. Whereas persons from a low-context culture expect messages to be direct, those from a high-context culture search the environment for cues. Rather than asking a person whether he or she is happy, high-context cultures would infer these feelings from other cues such as posture, facial expressions, and disposition. Consider the difficulties experienced by a couple who have different cultural backgrounds:

> Alec was confused. He and Miki had been living together for the past year and were engaged to be married in a few months. One evening, Miki was silent as they ate dinner. He knew something was upsetting her, but she kept insisting that things were fine. Miki was extremely frustrated as well. Why did Alec always insist that she tell him what was wrong? Did she always have to put her feelings into words? Why couldn't Alec be more in tune with her nonverbal behaviors and understand that things were not quite right?

This example illustrates the difference between the influence of the low-context approach of the U.S. on Alec's behavior and the high-context approach of Miki's Japanese upbringing. Miki expects Alec to be more aware of the messages that are being communicated via nonverbal channels, while Alec expects Miki to say what is bothering her.

A final model of cultural values is presented by Hofstede (1980). Four dimensions of values were identified by examining the attitudes of employees in more than forty cultures. These dimensions include individualism/collectivism, power distance, masculinity/femininity, and uncertainty avoidance.

Individualism/Collectivism.

Individualism/collectivism describes the relationship between the individual and the groups to which he or she belongs. **Individualistic** cultures, such as in the United States, focus on individual accomplishments and achievements. **Collectivism,** or value and concern for the group, is the primary value of many Asian cultures. Consider the cultural differences portrayed in the automobile manufacturing plant in the film *Gung Ho*. Asian managers took great pride in their work as their performance ultimately reflected on their group. They did not dream of taking time off for personal reasons. The American workers, on the other hand, whose behaviors reflected individualism, placed their individual needs over those of the company. Employees would take time off to be at the birth of a child or to keep a medical appointment. These differences in the values of the group versus the self had disastrous outcomes, with the company facing the risk of closing as a result of conflicting cultural values.

Power Distance.

Power distance refers to the distribution of power in personal relationships as well as within organizations. Low power distance cultures have a flat structure with most individuals being viewed as equals. The tendency to show favoritism to individuals based on their age, status, or gender is minimized. High power cultures are depicted by a tall hierarchical structure with distinct status differences. Imagine the frustration experienced by a young intercultural couple who had been married for only a few months.

The husband, who was Hispanic, was raised in a culture that places the man as the head of the household (high power distance). His wife, who was raised by a single working mother in New York City, valued her independence. The power differential in her family of origin was low, thus she anticipated that her husband would view her as an equal partner in their relationship. As a result of their differing values for status and power based on their roles as husband and wife, the couple experienced many arguments.

Masculine/Feminine.   Prevalence of masculine and feminine traits in a culture characterizes Hofstede's (1980) dimensions of masculinity and femininity. **Masculine** cultures demonstrate a preference for assertiveness, ambition, and achievement. Characteristics of responsiveness, nurturance, and cooperation are associated with cultures at the **feminine** end of this dimension. Gender roles in these cultures are perceived to be more equal. Cultures such as those found in Japan and Mexico exhibit more masculine tendencies, while those found in Brazil, Sweden, and Taiwan are more feminine.

Uncertainty Avoidance.   **Uncertainty avoidance** refers to the willingness of a culture to approach or to avoid change. Cultures high in uncertainty avoidance demonstrate a preference for avoiding change. They embrace tradition and order. China and Germany are examples of countries with cultures that avoid uncertainty and embrace tradition. Cultures low in uncertainty avoidance welcome the possibility of change and are more willing to take risks. The United States and Finland are more open to change and are more tolerant of taking risks and adopting new and innovative approaches.

Understanding these dimensions can provide cues as to which values are promoted among members of a culture. This information is useful for determining the appropriate methods to approach interpersonal communication and for providing valuable information that assists in checking the accuracy of one's perceptions.

SUGGESTIONS FOR SUCCESSFUL INTERPERSONAL RELATIONSHIPS WITH DIVERSE OTHERS

As shown throughout this chapter, perceptions can be faulty. But there are strategies which can enhance accuracy in perception. Each of the suggestions below involves understanding and practicing better interpersonal communication.

- Engage in careful listening and clear communication. Focus on listening for what is really being said, not what you want to hear. Be clear and explicit in your communication. Refrain from using slang or idioms.
- Refrain from judging people based on observable differences such as race, ethnicity, or gender.
- Do not misjudge people based on verbal (e.g., accent or grammar) or non-verbal differences.
- Be patient with yourself. Remember that becoming an effective crosscultural communicator requires skills and knowledge. It takes time to practice those skills. You may make mistakes, but there are lessons to be learned from those faux pas.

- Practice patience with others. Cultural influences are powerful, and making the transition from one culture's way of thinking and behaving to another's takes time.
- Check for understanding. Do not be afraid to ask for clarification or to ensure that you understood what was being communicated. One simple question now can save offending someone later.

SUMMARY

Throughout this chapter we have discussed the prevalence of diversity in *all* of our interpersonal relationships. While diversity is most frequently identified based on observable characteristics such as race, ethnicity, or sex, it is important to consider additional variables that influence our communication choices as we interact with others. Individual beliefs, attitudes, and values have a significant impact on the messages we send as well as on our reactions to the messages that we receive. At this point we would like to reiterate the importance of studying and understanding the impact of cultural diversity on our interpersonal interactions—by taking a moment to enhance your own knowledge and skills, you are better equipped to understand the reasons underlying your own communication preferences as well as the communication choices of others.

APPLICATIONS

Discussion Questions

1. Interview a friend, co-worker, or family member who has traveled to another country for an extended period of time. What did this individual learn about his own culture? Ask this individual to describe how our culture differs in attitudes, beliefs, values, and practices from the one that he or she visited.

2. Cite several examples of how intercultural communication competence is related to personal and professional success.

3. Discuss five ways that individuals are diverse and how these differences may lead to miscommunication.

4. Provide explicit and implicit examples of how you learned about your culture.

REFERENCES

Antonio, A. L., M. Chang, K. Hakuta, D. Kenny, S. Levin, and J. Milem. 2004. Effects of racial diversity on complex thinking in college students. *Psychological Science, 15,* 507–510.

Berger, C. 1979. Beyond initial interactions: In H. Giles and R. St. Clair (Eds.), *Language and social psychology* (122–144). Oxford: Basil Blackwell.

Berger, C., and R. Calabrese. 1975. Some explorations in initial interaction and beyond: Toward a developmental theory of interpersonal communication. *Human Communication Research, 1,* 99–112.

Buffet, Jimmy. *A Pirate Looks at Fifty.*

CNN.com May 2003. Georgia high school students plan white-only prom. Retrieved September 13, 2007 http://www.cnn.com/2003/EDUCATION/05/02/separate.proms.ap/

Dodd, C. 1998. *Dynamics of intercultural communication (5th ed.)*. San Francisco, CA: McGraw-Hill.

Gergen, K. 1991. *The saturated self: Dilemmas of identity in contemporary life.* New York: Harper Collins Basic Books. Hall, E. T. 1976. *Beyond culture.* Garden City, NY: Anchor.

Hofstede, G. 1980. Motivation, leadership, and organizations: Do American theories apply abroad? *Organizational Dynamics, Summer,* 42–63.

http://www.internetworldstats.com/america.htm

http://www.diversityinc.com/pbhz/16722pont.cfm

Ishii, S., C. Thomas, and D. Klopf. 1993. Self-disclosure among Japanese and Americans. *Otsuma Review, 26,* 51–57.

Kluckhohn, C. 1951. Values and value-orientation in the theory of action. In T. Parsons and E. Shils (Eds.), *Toward a general theory of action* (388–433). Cambridge, MA: Harvard University Press.

Kluckhohn, C., and F. Strodbeck. 1961. *Variations in value orientations.* Evanston, IL: Row, Peterson.

Kroeber, A. L., and C. Kluckhohn. 1952. *Culture: A critical review of concepts and definitions.* Cambridge, MA: Harvard University Press.

Maslow, A. 1954. *Motivation and personality.* New York: Harper.

McFate, M. 2005. The military utility of understanding adversary culture. *Joint Force Quarterly, 38,* 42–48.

McFate, M., and A. Jackson. 2005. An organizational solution for DOD's cultural knowledge needs. *Military Review, 85,* 18–21.

McLuhan, M., and B. Powers. 1989. *The global village: Transformations in world life and media in the 21st century.* New York: Oxford University Press.

Schutz, W. 1958. *FIRO: A three dimensional theory of interpersonal behavior.* New York, NY: Holt, Rinehart & Winston.

Smith, D. and Associates. 1997. *Diversity works: The emerging picture of how students benefit.* Washington, DC: Association of American Colleges and Universities.

The Maturity Works Report. June 2003. *The Social Impact of Workplace Ageism.* Retrieved June 3, 2007. http://www.maturityworks.co.uk/uploads/files/matwrksreport.qxd1.pdf.

Teen Research Unlimited. November 2004. *Diversity in Word and Deed: Most Teens Claim Multicultural Friends.* Retrieved July 29, 2007. http://www.teenresearch.com/PRview.cfm?edit_id=278.

Family Communication

© digitalskillet, 2007, Shutterstock.

OBJECTIVES

- List three types of family relationships (marital, parent-child, sibling) and discuss communication issues experienced in each type of relationship
- Distinguish between content versus relational expectations as they relate to marital satisfaction
- Identify six sibling relational maintenance strategies
- Apply the central elements of systems theory to family interactions
- Explain family communication patterns theory
- List the four family types identified by Koerner and Fitzpatrick
- Recall the three underlying assumptions of symbolic interaction theory as it relates to families
- Discuss ways in which families form their own identity (stories, myths, metaphors, themes)
- Distinguish between confirmation, rejection, and disconfirming messages
- Discuss the ABCX model of stress as it applies to family interactions

KEY TERMS

voluntary and involuntary relationships
content expectations
relational expectations
traditional couples
separate couples
independent couples
launching stage
deidentification
family systems theory
wholeness
interdependence
hierarchy
boundaries
ambiguous boundaries
calibration

equifinality
family communication patterns theory
conversation orientation
conformity orientation
pluralistic families
consensual families
laissez-faire families
protective families
symbolic interactionism
family stories
birth stories
courtship stories
stories of survival
myths

metaphors
themes
confirmation
rejection
disconfirmation
intimacy
ABCX model
internal stressor
external stressor
normative stressor
non-normative stressor
voluntary stressor
involuntary stressor
chronic stressor
acute stressor

OVERVIEW

We begin this chapter by advancing an important question about family communication: What makes family relationships unique from the other types of interpersonal relationships we experience in a lifetime? Vangelisti (2004) describes the significance of the family by labeling it "the crucible of society" (p. ix). Family relationships are unique from other types of interpersonal relationships because they are described as both voluntary and involuntary and play a significant role in shaping self-perceptions. Our family relationships usually offer our first glimpse of what it means to form an intimate connection with another person.

> *"The family. We were a strange little band of characters trudging through life sharing diseases and toothpaste, coveting one another's desserts, hiding shampoo, borrowing money, locking each other out of our rooms, inflicting pain and kissing to heal it in the same instant, loving, laughing, defending, and trying to figure out the common thread that bound us all together."*
>
> Erma Bombeck. *Family: The Ties That Bind…And Gag!* New York: McGraw-Hill, 1987, p. 9.

Erma Bombeck wrote for three decades, chronicling absurdities encountered in life, such as families. Families contain unique communicative features. Each of us has a frame of reference for understanding communication in families since these are the first and often the longest-lasting relationships formed in our lives. Perhaps the best way to understand family relationships is to take a look at the role of interpersonal communication in the family and how it shapes our sense of identity and serves as a model for communication choices. Even in situations where relationships with family members have become strained, the bonds have likely shaped an individual's sense of self, served as a model for desirable or undesirable communication, and shaped expectations for future relationships. In this chapter we examine some of the classic and contemporary family communication research, theories and concepts. We will also address interpersonal communication concepts as they apply across the family life span, focusing on both the positive and challenging aspects of these interactions.

DEFINITION OF FAMILY

Most family relationships are involuntary because we don't choose who to include.

If you were asked to list the number of people you consider to be part of your family, would you include in-laws, close family friends, close personal friends, neighbors, siblings' spouses, stepfamilies, co-workers? Would you include only those relatives related by blood or marriage? When students are asked this question, they often include a wide range of individuals in their list of family members. Most family relationships are described as **involuntary** types because we do not get to choose our parents, siblings, cousins, aunts, uncles, grandparents, and so on. Some family relationships may be formed of **voluntary** members. For example, the television series *Friends* shows how non-biological relationships can fulfill family roles. As we grow older, our choices of who we include in our "family" expand. Voluntary families

© Pascale Wowak, 2007, Shutterstock.

are created as a result of conscious decisions made to include others in the familial relationship. For example, we select our spouse or life partner. We all have experience with family relationships, but have you considered the unique nature of these bonds? A scene from the 2005 film *The Family Stone* illustrates this obligation. Sarah Jessica Parker portrays a young woman struggling to be accepted by her fiancé's close-knit family. At one point she becomes frustrated and asks her future mother-in-law, "What's so great about you guys?" Diane Keaton replies, "Uh, nothing … it's just that we're all that we've got." Each family member recognizes other family members' idiosyncrasies, but also realizes that the strength of the family bond surpasses all other relationships.

TYPES OF FAMILY RELATIONSHIPS

It is difficult to describe a "typical" family in the twenty-first century. Over the years, the structure of the typical American family has changed. The *Handbook of Family Communication* explores several different family forms such as intact families, divorced or single parent families, stepfamilies, and the families of lesbian women or gay men. But while the forms may have changed, core relationships continue to exist and have provided scholars with opportunities to take a glimpse into how communication develops in these relationships. While we do not have the space to discuss all family forms, three specific interpersonal relationships that exist in the family structure will be discussed: marital relationships, parent-child relationships, and sibling relationships.

Marital Relationships

In a recent issue of *Psychology Today* anthropologist Helen Fisher wrote "I have long been captivated by one of the most striking characteristics of our species: We form enduring pair bonds. The vast majority of other mammals—some 97 percent—do not" (Fisher, 2007, 78). These enduring pair bonds, or marriages, often provide individuals with a great deal of social support, happiness, personal fulfillment and satisfaction. According to family communication researchers Turner and West (2002), "marriage is often seen as the most important intimate relationship two people can share" (232). Some research indicates that individuals in healthy marriages tend to be both healthier and happier than unmarried individuals or those in unhealthy relationships. The longstanding question posed by researchers from a variety of academic and professional fields has always been how to obtain and maintain an enduring marital relationship.

Each life partner brings his or her own set of expectations to the marital relationship. If you have ever tuned into a television talk show, you have probably seen a couple asking the host to solve their marital problems. It is not unusual for the host to identify differing expectations as the root of the problem. Earlier in this text, we mentioned that messages have both content and relational dimensions. The same is true of our expectations for relationships—couples hold content expectations and relational expectations for their partnership.

© sonya etchison, 2007, Shutterstock.

Individuals in healthy marriages tend to be healthier and happier than others.

Content Expectations.

Content expectations focus on how the relationship is defined by the role each partner plays. Roles are defined by the expectations held for a position in family. The popular ABC television show *Wife Swap* focuses on the role expectations established for wives in two different types of families. In each episode, the wives switch families for two weeks. Clashes ensue over differing content expectations for husbands' and wives' roles in housekeeping and child-rearing. It is important to note that one of the difficult tasks involved in the marital relationship is ensuring that the two sets of expectations are congruent.

Relational Expectations.

Relational expectations refer to the similarity, or correspondence, of the emotional, or affective, expectations each partner has for defining the relationship. In one episode of *Wife Swap*, the Kraut and Hardin wives exchange households. One wife spends considerable time shopping and focusing on the current fashion trends, while her husband tends to the household duties. The other wife expects all family members to participate in household chores, and the couple has formed the expectation that the role of the wife will include being responsible for home schooling the children. When the two families swap wives for the two-week period, they discover that their relational expectations are incongruent in the new environment. This often causes the sparks to fly! When the wives are in their own homes, communication is more satisfying because their spouses and children have congruent expectations for the relationship. They understand what their family roles are, and they have become comfortable with the communication expectations associated with these roles. Marital satisfaction is greater in relationships where couples discuss their expectations for the relationship—failure to talk about expectancies is often equated to playing "guess what's inside my mind."

To explain the various expectations that couples have for communication and for the relationship, Fitzpatrick (1987) developed a model to distinguish each couple type and how they view role conventionality, interdependence, and approach to conflict. Three couple types were identified: traditionals, separates, and independents (see also Table 12.1).

© Losevsky Pavel, 2007, Shutterstock.

Traditional couples adopt conventional sex roles in their marriages.

Traditionals.

Those who exhibit a high level of interdependence and sharing are considered **traditional couples**. Conventional sex roles are adopted in traditional couples, with

---

⚡ Table 12.1   Description of Marital Types

Marital Type of Couples	Characteristics
Traditionals	Demonstrate a high amount of interdependence and sharing; adopt traditional or conventional sex roles
Separates	Emphasize each other's individual identity over relational maintenance; typically avoid conflict
Independents	Respect the need for autonomy; negotiate a high level of communication and sharing; adopt nonconventional sex roles (husband stays home and wife works outside of home)

males performing tasks such as lawn care, automobile maintenance, and taking out the garbage. Women fulfill the role of nurturing caregiver and are responsible for housekeeping and childcare duties. In her research, Fitzpatrick (1987) found that traditionals tend to be the most satisfied of the three couple types.

Separates.   **Separate couples** tend to emphasize each individual's identity and independence over maintaining the relationship. In addition to maintaining conventional sex roles in the relationship, this couple is characterized by their avoidance of conflict. As is evident, this couple type typically reports a low level of marital satisfaction.

Independents.   **Independent couples** simultaneously respect the need for autonomy and engage in a high level communication and sharing with one another. Sex roles in the independent relationship are nonconventional or nonexistent. While it may appear that independents enjoy a happily married relationship, research shows that many independent couples report low levels of satisfaction. By applying this model to our examination of marital communication, we see that one of the characteristics that distinguish the various couple types from one another is their expectations for sex roles and their approach to conflict situations.

Parent-Child Relationships

The first family relationship formed is between a parent and a child. As well as having a legal responsibility to care for and protect their children, parents are responsible for the moral and character development of their children—not an easy task. In his book, *Family First*, Dr. Phil McGraw (2004) discusses the role that parents play in preparing children for life's challenges, and points out that parents need to realize the influence they have as a result of the messages they communicate to their children. A parent's role is complicated; biological and emotional attachments create a special bond that makes communication both rewarding and frustrating at times. Television shows such as *Nanny 911* and *Super Nanny* provide parents with advice for managing interactions with their children. They also provide a glimpse into the parenting challenges experienced by others, offering support to parents who can see that others are enduring the same, or worse, situations.

Over the course of the family life cycle, communication between parents and children evolves as new events occur. It is during this time that the dialectical tensions between autonomy and connection are perhaps the strongest. In the beginning of their lives children are totally dependent on the parents to provide for them and look out for their best interests. In the United States, many parents begin teaching children at a young age to become independent. Children are encouraged to learn to eat by themselves, pick out their own clothes, and to explore their individual interests in sports and other extracurricular activities. But even while encouraging independence, many parents simultaneously reinforce the message that they are still connected to their children. Providing children with cellular telephones is one

© Suzanne Tucker, 2007, Shutterstock.

Young children assert their independence as they "do it all by myself."

strategy currently used by parents to stay connected as their children explore autonomy.

In her article *"Putting Parents in Their Place: Outside Class,"* (see page 294) Valerie Strauss (2006) illustrates how "too much parent involvement can hinder students' independence" as she explains parent involvement with the "millennial generation."

As children progress through adolescence, a new set of communication issues needs to be considered. Up to this point, children have been encouraged to become independent, but eventually the dialectical tension between autonomy and connection kicks in and parents may begin to feel that children are becoming too independent. Adolescence is often a difficult transition period for both children and parents alike, and it is not uncommon for conflicts to occur during this time in the family life cycle. A common communication issue during this period involves the negotiation of rules, with new guidelines for behavior being added on a regular basis as parents and children clash over preferences for clothes, manners, curfews, and activities. As the occurrence of parent-child conflict increases during adolescence, issues that once seemed unimportant now take on new relevance. Consider the issues you and your parents disagreed on during your adolescence. Why do you think communication surrounding these issues was so problematic?

As children grow up, identify their aspirations, and pursue their goals, families may find that their time is divided, and this provides yet another source of tension in the household. One recent study found that parents and their teenage children spend less than one hour per day talking to one another *(http://www.familycommunication.org/)* and the number of families who report that they share meals at the dinner table each day has dwindled over the years.

While many adult privileges are granted to children when they reach the age of eighteen, parents and children view and negotiate the transition to adulthood in different ways. The period when children begin the separation process from their parents is often referred to as the **"launching" stage.** However, this term is often misleading because many families continue to experience a sense of interdependence in their lives for a period of time after the child reaches legal age. For example, after returning to college after Christmas break, one student was overheard saying, "It was kind of nice being back home and knowing that my mom would stay up and wait for me to come in at night. I guess I have to admit that I missed that during my first semester at college." While some may find comfort in the old routines, others may find that new rules need to be negotiated during the launching stage. Adult children who live in their parent's home while getting started in their careers may find that while they are independent in terms of their professional life, they are still dependent on their parents for need fulfillment in their personal life. Daily chores, financial contributions, and respect for household rules often emerge as topics requiring negotiation.

Divorce and remarriage create additional issues to consider in parent-child interactions. Stepfamilies face unique challenges that revolve around issues relating to discipline, resources, and ties to the biological family unit. An estimated one-third of Americans are likely to experience life in a stepfamily (Bumpass et al. 1995). Should stepfamilies

© Galina Barskaya, 2007, Shutterstock.

During adolescence, issues that once were insignificant can create conflict.

Putting Parents in Their Place: Outside Class

They are needy, overanxious and sometimes plain pesky—and schools at every level are trying to find ways to deal with them.

No, not students. Parents—specifically parents of today's "millennial generation" who, many educators are discovering, can't let their kids go.

They text message their children in middle school, use the cellphone like an umbilical cord to Harvard Yard and have no compunction about marching into kindergarten class and screaming at a teacher about a grade.

To handle the modern breed of micromanaging parent, educators are devising programs to help them separate from their kids—and they are taking a harder line on especially intrusive parents.

At seminars, such as one in Phoenix last year titled "Managing Millennial Parents," they swap strategies on how to handle the "hovercrafts" or "helicopter parents," so dubbed because of a propensity to swoop in at the slightest crisis.

Educators worry not only about how their school climates are affected by intrusive parents trying to set their own agendas but also about the ability of young people to become independent.

"As a child gets older, it is a real problem for a parent to work against their child's independent thought and action, and it is happening more often," said Ron Goldblatt, executive director of the Association of Independent Maryland Schools.

"Many young adults entering college have the academic skills they will need to succeed but are somewhat lacking in life skills like self-reliance, sharing, and conflict resolution," said Linda Walter, an administrator at Seton Hall University in New Jersey and co-chairman of the family portion of new-student orientation.

Educators say the shift in parental engagement coincides with the rise of the millennial generation, kids born after 1982.

"They have been the most protected and programmed children ever—car seats and safety helmets, play groups and soccer leagues, cellphones and e-mail," said Mark McCarthy, assistant vice president and dean of student development at Marquette University in Milwaukee. "The parents of this generation are used to close and constant contact with their children and vice versa."

Strauss, Valerie. 2006. Putting Parents in Their Place: Outside Class; Too Much Involvement Can Hinder Students' Independence, Experts Say. *Washington Post,* **March 21.**

DISCUSSION QUESTION
How is the "millennial generation" parent different in terms of parent-child communication than the parents of past generations?

and stepchildren expect communication and relationships to be similar to those between biological parents and children? Family communication scholars describe the experience of entering a stepfamily as similar to starting a novel halfway through the book (Coleman, Ganong, and Fine 2004). One student recently described the experience of joining a stepfamily as similar to reading the description of a movie on the back of a DVD and then making a decision about whether or not you will like the movie. Based on the brief description, the movie seems like a good choice. However, once you begin watching the movie, you learn that it is not at all what you expected. Similarly, individuals enter stepfamily situations and often expect them to function like intact families when often this is not the case (Coleman et al. 2004).

Images of stepfamilies portrayed in stories and the media often depict these relationships as filled with challenges and negative communication. In the 1998 film *Stepmom*, a conversation between the biological mother (Jackie) and her daughter (Anna) about her stepmother (Isabel) illustrates one of many potential communication issues associated with stepfamily relationships.

Anna: I think Isabel's pretty.

Jackie: Yeah, I think she's pretty too … if you like big teeth.

Anna: Mom?

Jackie: Yes sweetie?

Anna: If you want me to hate her, I will. (*Stepmom* directed by Chris Columbus, 2hr. 4 min.,1492 Pictures, 1998.)

Anger or guilt can impact communication about the relationship, and both children and parents may find it difficult to be open about their true feelings. Another communication hurdle faced in the stepparent-stepchild relationship is the use of names to refer to the relationship. In a 2003 interview on Moviehole.net, Jada Pinkett Smith revealed that she refers to her stepson as her "bonus child," and Demi Moore's daughters refer to stepdad, Ashton Kutcher, as "MOD" which stands for "My Other Dad." (*http://people.aol.com/people/articles/0,19736,1090617,00.html*).

Maintenance in Parent-Child Relationships.   Parents and children often find the need to increase efforts in maintaining their relationship as children grow older and gain more autonomy. Activities, new friends, and, eventually, the process of starting a new family can detract from the time and energy available for relationships with parents. In some instances, the onset of these maintenance challenges begins much earlier when parents decide to divorce. Non-custodial parents are faced with identifying new strategies to maintain the relationship with their children in the absence of the close physical proximity they once shared. While many strategies used to maintain the relationship are similar to those found in other types of relationships, in a 1999 study Thomas-Maddox identified several strategies unique to this context. Non-custodial parents indicated that they depend on mediated communication (sending letters, emails, phone calls) and material/monetary offerings (sending gifts, taking children on "exciting" trips) to maintain their relationship. Responses from children revealed that there are additional strategies they initiate to maintain a relationship with their non-custodial parents. Strategies listed most frequently by children include mediated communication, proximity (living with non-custodial parent during summer vacations and breaks by choice), and suggesting joint activities (proposing ideas such as going to the movies). While being physically separated as a result of this difficult decision may not be easy for parents and children, there are communication strategies that are used to continue the relationship from a distance.

Sibling Relationships

Relationships with siblings generally last the longest, given that our brothers and sisters are often still with us long after our parents are gone. Approximately eighty percent of individuals have siblings and, with the exception of first-born children, sibling relationships are simultaneously formed with parent relationships. In their younger years, siblings often spend more time playing and interacting with one another than they do with their parents. But that does not necessarily mean these relationships are always positive. One minute siblings may be collaborating to "team up" against their parents, and the next minute they may be fighting like cats and dogs.

© Terrie L. Zeller, 2007, Shutterstock.

During younger years, siblings often spend more time together than with their parents.

Communication in the sibling relationship often reflects both negative and positive aspects. As family resources such as time, parent's attention, or physical objects are perceived to be scarce, siblings may engage in conflict or competition.

Studies have shown that same-sex siblings tend to be more competitive than opposite-sex siblings. In some instances, siblings may be expected to fulfill the role of teacher or "co-parent." If you have siblings, chances are you have probably been instructed to "Watch out for your brother (or sister)" at some point in time. Often this occurs in single-parent families or in families where both parents are employed outside the home.

As siblings approach adolescence, their relationship experiences new transformations. Perhaps the competition for resources may become more intense, or siblings experience frustration when they are compared to one another. In these instances, a sibling may seek deidentification from other siblings. **Deidentification** is defined as an individual's attempt to create a distinct identity that is separate from that of their siblings. Have you ever had a teacher compare you to an older sibling? Or perhaps you have had friends at school who point out how similar or different you are compared to your brother or sister. When siblings are constantly evaluated against one another, they may experience a desire to create a unique identity and sense of self. Perhaps your ability to play soccer was often compared to one of your siblings that also played soccer. In an effort to distinguish yourself from your sibling, you quit playing soccer and started wrestling instead.

Maintenance in Sibling Relationships

Recall our discussion of the importance of relationship maintenance in Chapter Seven. Relational maintenance is of particular importance in the sibling relationship as the relationship between brothers and sisters typically lasts longer than any other family relationship. In a study designed to investigate unique maintenance strategies employed by siblings, six behaviors were identified

Siblings often maintain their connections through participation in family events.

(Myers and Weber 2004). These include confirmation, humor, social support, family visits, escape, and verbal aggression.

Confirmation. Confirmation strategies consist of messages used to communicate the importance or value of siblings in one's life. Statements such as, "I'm lucky to have you as my brother" or "I really appreciate having you here to support me" are often viewed as validating the relationship.

Humor. Often siblings use humor as a way to bring amusement or enjoyment to their relationship. Sharing private jokes about family members or making fun of their behaviors are ways siblings use humor to strengthen their bond.

Social Support. Siblings provide social support to one another by using verbal and nonverbal comforting strategies to assist one another through difficult times. Asking a sibling for advice or sharing information about difficulties in other relationships illustrates the trust that is present in the relationship.

Family Events. Siblings often maintain and strengthen their relationships with each other and other family members through participation in family events. They may agree to visit their parents at the same time during the summer or holidays to spend time together.

Escape. Sometimes we view our relationships with our siblings as an escape during difficult situations. Have you ever agreed to attend a family wedding or reunion only because your sibling agreed to attend? Doing so solidifies the bond by communicating the dependence that you have on one another to provide an outlet during difficult times.

Verbal Aggression. While the final strategy, verbal aggression, may seem counterintuitive to maintaining a relationship, this maintenance mechanism allows siblings to vent their frustrations with one another. Over the years, they may have discovered that yelling at one another is the most effective method for having their concerns heard.

FAMILY COMMUNICATION THEORIES

Several theories can be applied to the study of communication in family relationships. Recall the definition of interpersonal communication: a process which occurs in a specific context and involves an exchange of verbal or nonverbal messages between two connected individuals with the intent to achieve shared meaning. The family is one context of connected individuals in which these interactions occur. Scholars of family communication have applied a variety of interpersonal theories to explain these interactions. In essence, virtually any theory of interpersonal communication could be applied to the study of families. Three theories which have implications for the family relationship in particular are systems theory, family communication patterns theory, and symbolic interactionism.

Systems Theory

Systems theory has been employed by family scholars to explore a variety of interactions, including children's attitudes about their single parent dating (Marrow-Ferguson and Dickson 1995), family involvement in addressing children's problems at school (Walsh and Williams 1997), and adolescent abuse of their parents (Eckstein 2004). **Family systems theory** is one of the most frequently used theories in family communication scholarship (Stamp 2004). The basic premise behind this theory is that family relationships can be treated as systems and can include the study of systemic qualities such as wholeness, interdependence, hierarchy, boundaries, calibration, and equifinality (Stamp 2004). Each of the elements of systems theory is particularly relevant in explaining how and why family members relate to one another.

Wholeness.   **Wholeness** implies that a family creates its own personality or culture, and that this personality is unique from that of each family member. Many studies that have applied systems theory recognize that in order to understand the dynamics of families, the role of individual family members must be considered as well.

Interdependence.   **Interdependence** proposes that the family system is comprised of interrelated parts, or members. A change experienced by one family member is likely to result in changes that impact all other family members. Suppose a child catches the flu and cannot attend school for several days. If both parents work outside the home, one will have to make adjustments to his work schedule to stay at home with the child. To protect other family members from being exposed to the illness, family routines such as sharing dinner or watching television together may be altered.

Hierarchy.   All systems have levels, or a **hierarchy,** present. Typically, parents take on the powerful roles in the family and are responsible for seeing that children's needs are fulfilled and that discipline and control are maintained in the system. Perhaps the system element that has gained the most attention in family studies is boundaries.

Boundaries.   Families create **boundaries** to communicate to members who are to be considered part of the system. These boundaries are often flexible as the family expands to include friends and pets. **Ambiguous boundaries** often create confusion about who family members perceive as being part of the system. In the movie *While You Were Sleeping*, Lucy (Sandra Bullock) discovers that the man the family refers to as Uncle Saul (Jack Warden) is included in the family's boundaries due to their strong friendship. Uncle Saul says, "Lucy, the Callaghans, well, they took me in as part of their family. I'd never let anyone hurt them." Even though the family bonds are not biological, he communicates that he is dedicated to protecting the family and views them as an important part of his life.

Calibration.   The system element of **calibration** is the mechanism that allows the family to review their

© HTuller, 2007, Shutterstock.

Typically the parents are responsible for taking care of children and maintaining the powerful roles in the family.

relationships and communication and decide if any adjustments need to be made to the system. Television shows such as *Nanny 911* provide examples of families that can be used as a basis for comparison. Feedback communicated through messages received from others can also be taken into consideration. While waiting in line at the grocery store, a mother might be complimented on how well-behaved her children are. This provides her with feedback to gauge her performance as a mother.

Equifinality.   The final systems element, **equifinality,** refers to families' abilities to achieve the same goal by following different paths or employing different communication behaviors. For example, one family may teach the children independence by communicating the expectation that the children are responsible for getting themselves up and getting ready for school in the morning. In another family, the mother might enter the bedroom and gently sing "Good Morning" to the children, lay out their school clothes, and have breakfast ready for them. Both families accomplish the same goal: working through the morning routine of getting to school on time. However, each family has a different method for accomplishing the goal.

Family Communication Patterns Theory

Perhaps one of the most complicated phenomena to factor into the family communication equation is the role that intrapersonal communication plays in the process. **Family communication patterns theory** is a comprehensive theory that focuses on the cognitive processes used to shape and guide our interpersonal interactions. Originally developed by McLeod and Chaffee (1972, 1973) as a way for explaining family members' interactions associated with television viewing, the goal of the theory was to explain how parents help children to understand messages received from multiple sources through mediated channels. But consider for a moment all of the different messages received from outside the family that are processed on a daily basis. Ritchie and Fitzpatrick (1990) expanded the focus of this theory beyond mediated messages to focus on how a variety of messages are processed and discussed within the family to create shared meaning. This revised theory identified two primary orientations used by families: conversation and conformity.

Conversation.   **Conversation orientation** refers to the level of openness and the frequency with which a variety of topics are discussed. Families who adopt a high conversation orientation encourage members to openly and frequently share their thoughts and feelings with one another on a wide variety of topics. It is rare that a topic is "off limits" for discussion in families who have a high conversation orientation. On the other hand, families with low conversation orientation experience less frequent or less open interactions, and sometimes there are limits with regard to what topics can be discussed.

Conformity.   The second dimension of the communication pattern analysis focuses on the family's conformity orientation. **Conformity** refers to the degree to which a family encourages autonomy in individual beliefs, values, and attitudes. Families who emphasize a high level of conformity in interactions encourage family members to adopt similar ways of thinking about topics, often with the goal of avoiding conflict and promoting harmony in the family. At the other end of the conformity continuum, family members are encouraged to form independent beliefs and attitudes, and these differing opinions are often perceived as having equal value in discussions and decisionmaking. To explain the interrelationship between conversation orientation and conformity orientation, Koerner and Fitzpatrick identified four different family types (2002). These include pluralistic, consensual, laissez-faire, and protective families. See Table 12.2 for an integration of the family types into the two family orientations.

Parents who encourage their children to form relationships outside the home and couples who believe that each partner should pursue his own network of friends typically do so in an effort to broaden the perspectives of individuals within the family. Use the scale in Table 12.3 to find out what you perceive your family orientation to be.

Pluralistic.   **Pluralistic families** adopt a high conversation orientation and a low conformity orientation. Almost anything goes in this family! A wide range of topics are discussed, and family members are encouraged to have their own opinions without feeling the pressure to agree with one another. Children in pluralistic families are often encouraged to participate in decisionmaking on topics ranging from where the family should go for vacation to the establishment of family rules.

Consensual.   **Consensual families** adopt both a high conversation and a high conformity orientation. These families often encourage members to be open in their interactions with one another, but they expect that family members will adopt similar opinions and values. Parents in consensual families promote open conversations, but they still believe that they are the authority when it comes to decisions in the family.

Laissez-Faire.   **Laissez-faire families** adopt both a low conversation and low conformity orientation. Rarely will family members talk with one another, and when conversations do occur, they are focused on a limited number of

Table 12.2   Family Types as Identified by Family Communications Patterns Theory

	High Conformity	Low Conformity
HIGH CONVERSATION	CONSENSUAL Strong pressure towardagreement; encouragement to take interest in ideas without disturbing power in family hierarchy	PLURALISTIC Open communication anddiscussion of ideas is encouraged but with little emphasis on social constraint; fosters communication competence as well as independence of ideas
LOW CONVERSATION	LAISSEZ-FAIRE Little parent-child interaction; child relatively more influenced by external social settings (e.g., peer groups)	PROTECTIVE Obedience is prized; little concern for conceptual matters; child is not well-prepared for dealing with outside influences and is easily persuaded

Table 12.3   The Revised Family Communication Pattern Instrument

Respond to the following statements as they apply to your communication with your parents while you were growing up. Place a number on the line that best describes your agreement with the statements below, using the following scale:

5 = Strongly Agree, 4 = Agree, 3 = Neither Agree nor Disagree, 2 = Disagree, 1 = Strongly Disagree

_____ 1. My parents often said things like, "You'll know better when you grow up."

_____ 2. My parents often asked my opinion when the family was talking about something.

_____ 3. My parents often said things like, "My ideas are right and you should not question them."

_____ 4. My parents encouraged me to challenge their ideas and beliefs.

_____ 5. My parents often said things like, "A child should not argue with adults."

_____ 6. I usually told my parents what I was thinking about things.

_____ 7. My parents often said things like, "There are some things that are just not to be talked about."

_____ 8. I can tell my parents almost anything.

_____ 9. When anything really important was involved, my parents expected me to obey without question.

_____ 10. In our family we often talk about our feelings and emotions.

_____ 11. In our home, my parents usually had the last word.

_____ 12. My parents and I often had long, relaxed conversation about nothing in particular.

_____ 13. My parents felt that it was important to be the boss.

_____ 14. I really enjoyed talking with my parents, even when we disagreed.

_____ 15. My parents sometimes became irritated with my views if they were different from theirs.

_____ 16. My parents often say something like "you should always look at both sides of an issue."

_____ 17. If my parents don't approve of it, they don't want to know about it.

_____ 18. My parents like to hear my opinions, even when they don't agree with me.

_____ 19. When I am at home, I am expected to obey my parents' rules.

_____ 20. My parents encourage me to express my feelings.

_____ 21. My parents tended to be very open about their emotions.

_____ 22. We often talk as a family about things we have done during the day.

_____ 23. In our family we often talk about our plans and hopes for the future.

_____ 24. In our family we talk about topics like politics and religion where some persons disagree with others.

_____ 25. My parents often say something like "Every member of the family should have some say in family decisions."

_____ 26. My parents often say something like "You should give in on arguments rather than risk making people mad."

SCORING DIRECTIONS:

Items 1, 3, 5, 7, 9, 11, 13, 15, 17, 19, 26 represent the Conformity items. Add these items and divide by 11 to determine your Conformity score.

Items 2, 4, 6, 8, 10, 12, 14, 16, 18, 20, 21, 22, 23, 24, 25 represent the Conversation items. Add these items and divide by 15 to determine your Conversation score.

Scoring—Your scores will range from 1–5 and the higher score is more likely to be the perceived communication pattern in your family.

topics. Children are encouraged to make their own decisions, often with little or no guidance or feedback from their parents in the laissez-faire family.

Protective.   **Protective families** score low on conversation orientation and high on conformity. The phrase "Children should be seen but not heard" is characteristic of this family type. Parents are considered to be the authority, and children are expected to obey the family rules without questioning them.

Identifying and understanding the approaches used to communicate and to promote autonomy and independence is beneficial to understanding how these interactions shape both individual and family identities.

Symbolic Interaction Theory

Symbolic interactionism is perhaps one of the most widely applied theories in the study of family life. In Chapter Three we discussed the role that symbols and messages play in assigning meaning to our experiences, others, and ourselves. Mead's (1934) five concepts of symbolic interactionism (mind, self, I, me, and roles) are particularly useful in understanding the impact that family interactions have on shaping one's identity. In his discussion of the concept of "mind," Mead explains the role that symbols play in creating shared meaning. Children interact with family members and learn language and social meanings associated with words. Similarly, Mead points out that one's sense of "self" is developed through interactions with others. Families are influential in shaping this view of self through the messages and reactions to one another. Family members gain a sense of how they are viewed by others from messages that are exchanged. Statements such as "You're such a good husband!" or "He's such a rotten kid" shape how individuals see themselves.

It is important to note that individual differences, such as personality traits or communication predispositions, may cause family members to view the same situation in very different ways. Consider the following scenario.

Kaija was quiet as Jay drove up the driveway. Jay smiled at her and said, "Trust me, they'll love you!" Kaija was meeting Jay's family for the first time since he had proposed. As they entered the front door, she was bombarded with hugs and kisses from various aunts, uncles, grandparents, and cousins. During dinner the talking never stopped! Kaija felt so left out—and nobody even seemed to care enough to ask her questions about herself. At one point, she slipped out on the back patio just to have a few moments of peace and quiet. As they drove back to campus, Jay commented, "Wasn't it a great evening! Everyone thought you were awesome!" Kaija couldn't believe what she had just heard. How could Jay have come to the conclusion that his family liked her? After all, they didn't take the time to find out anything about her. And the hugs and kisses were so intimidating. Kaija's family would have never shown such open displays of affection the first time they met Jay. She was confused—how could Jay have thought the evening went so great when she thought it had been horrible?

Who was correct in his or her assessment of the evening's events? Symbolic interactionism would indicate that both Jay and Kaija formed accurate perceptions. Each of them had formed his own meaning of the event based on his interpretation of the messages and behaviors. We learn in the scenario that Kaija's family would not have displayed affection so openly, while Jay's family background shaped his acceptance of effusive greetings. Our experiences in our family of origin shape our meanings of events, messages, and behaviors. The fact that Jay's family did not ask Kaija about herself caused her to perceive them as being uninterested. But suppose Jay had shared with his family that Kaija was an only child and tended to be shy around large groups. He may have asked them to refrain from bombarding her with questions that might cause her to feel uncomfortable. To better understand how symbolic interactionism applies to this scenario, it might be useful to examine the three underlying assumptions of the theory (LaRossa and Reitzes 1993).

First, *our interactions with family members influence the meanings we assign to behaviors and messages.* Children determine if they should evaluate experiences as being positive or negative by watching the reactions of family members to various events and messages. A child whose parents avoid conflict may believe that conflict is a negative behavior that should be avoided at all costs. Coming from a family that shows caring through conversation, Kaija assigned a negative meaning to Jay's family's failure to ask her questions about herself.

Next, *individuals create a sense of self which serves as a guide for selecting future behaviors.* We assess situations and take into consideration whether others will perceive behaviors and messages in a positive or negative way. This assumption goes beyond our own evaluation of events to include the perceptions of others. A child whose father has told him "You're a rotten kid" and "You'll never amount to anything" has learned to misbehave. As the negative messages are repeated, he comes to believe that others expect him to misbehave.

Finally, symbolic interactionism posits that the *behavior of family members is influenced by culture and society.* Perhaps this assumption sheds light on the reasons families are reluctant to admit that they experience conflict from time to time. Based on media portrayals of family life and from listening to the happy stories of other families, an expectation has been established that "normal" families do not fight.

CREATING A FAMILY IDENTITY

While individual family members form their own identities, the family as a unit also creates a collective identity. Communication is the primary mechanism for creating this family identity, with various messages and behaviors providing insight as to how the family views itself as a group. Four ways that families create and sustain an identity as a unit are through stories, myths, themes, and metaphors. As we discuss each of these elements, reflect on your own family of origin and how these communicative acts shaped your sense of what it means to be a part of your family.

Family Stories

Family stories are narratives recounting significant events that have been shared by members. In essence, family life is comprised of a series of stories. Because they are about shared experiences, these stories are often personal and emotional; they may evoke positive or negative feelings in family members. Individuals often use these stories to shape their own sense of identity. One of the authors of your text had a difficult time gaining confidence in her driving ability. Do you think it might be due in part to the fact that her family members enjoyed telling and retelling the story of how she was responsible for wrecking the family car when she was four years old?

Three types of family stories that have been studied by family scholars in an attempt to explain how families define their experiences are birth stories, courtship stories, and stories of survival. **Birth stories** describe how each person entered the family and can define how members "fit" into the system. One woman shared a story of enduring a forty-two hour labor prior to the birth of her son. She stated, "I guess I should have known then that he would always be chal-

Families share special stories of a child's birth to connect the child within the family.

lenging me because he gave me such a difficult time from the beginning!" **Courtship stories** provide a timeline for tracing romance in the family. They are often used to describe how parents and grandparents met and how they decided that they were right for one another. A young woman who was engaged to be married asked her grandfather how he met her grandmother. He explained that she was working in the fields on her family farm and that it was love at first sight. He joked, "I knew she was a hard worker, so I asked her to marry me!" But he went on to explain that he knew she was devoted to helping her family and knew that she would be dedicated to her own family. **Stories of survival** are narratives used to explain how family members have overcome difficult times, and they are often told to help family members cope with challenges they face. Three sisters who, at a young age, were physically abused by their father, discussed sharing their stories with one another as well as with other young girls to assist them in coping with similar experiences. While some might perceive the retelling of these stories as being too painful, the sisters viewed the stories as therapeutic and reinforced the notion that if they could survive the abuse of their father, they were strong enough to face any situation.

Family Myths

Family **myths** are created to communicate the beliefs, values, and attitudes held by members to represent characteristics that are considered important to the family. These myths are often fictional as they are based on an ideal image the family wishes to convey to others. Consider the following example:

> "I couldn't believe what I was hearing! At my grandfather's funeral, my dad's family members were all talking about what a great man my grandfather was and how much they would miss him. My grandmother sobbed as she whispered, 'He was such a loving and caring man. I don't know what I'll do without him.' After the service, I asked my father why they were all referring to my grandfather that way. For years I had heard stories of the physical abuse that had taken place in the family during my dad's childhood, and I had heard my grandfather yell at my grandmother on numerous occasions. My dad

responded, 'It's just easier on your grandmother if we all remember him in a positive way.' "

In this scenario, the family creates a myth that portrays the grandfather as a loving, caring man. Doing so enables them to protect the grandmother and to perpetuate the belief that he was a good father and husband. In the movie, *Doing Time on Maple Drive*, a family goes to great lengths to portray the image of the "perfect family" to their friends and neighbors. At one point, the son reveals to his parents that he attempted to commit suicide because he would rather be dead than admit to them that he is gay. This scene illustrates the power of family myths and the tremendous amount of pressure placed on family members to live up to the expectations communicated in these myths.

Metaphors

Sometimes families create **metaphors** to assist in communicating how family life as a system is experienced by members. Family metaphors make reference to specific objects, events, or images to represent the family experience and a collective identity. The metaphor of a "three-ring circus" may be used to describe the chaos and disorganization that exists within one family, while the "well-oiled machine" can depict the emphasis on control and organization that is the norm for another family. Metaphors can provide those within the family and outside of the family with an understanding of what behaviors are valued as well as how family members are expected to behave. A person from a "well-oiled machine" family can use the metaphor to understand the expectations associated with being a member of the family.

Themes

Family **themes** represent important concerns regarding the expected relationship between family members and can assist family members in understanding how to direct their energy as a family unit. These themes often emerge from two primary sources—the background or experience of parents, and the dialectical pulls experienced by the family. Suppose Joe and Marnie are having a difficult time managing the tensions of autonomy and connection as their children grow older, begin dating, and spend more time with friends than with family members. In an attempt to communicate their concern for the growing independence of family members, they remind the children that "Blood is thicker than water" and "Friends may come and go, but family is forever." These themes are intended to remind the children that while they may form many relationships outside the unit, the strongest ties should be reserved for those in their family.

CONSEQUENCES OF FAMILY RELATIONSHIPS

Throughout this text, various communication variables have been identified as being both beneficial and harmful to our interpersonal relationships. Because families play such a vital role in the development of our self-identity, understanding how specific communication behaviors can enhance and damage our relationships and our sense of self is important.

Families can serve as the primary source of understanding and support for individuals. As we grow older, we receive messages that let us know that we are cared for and accepted. These perceptions are often shaped by the types of verbal and nonverbal cues we receive from others and are often linked to the formation of our sense of self. Three types of messages are often used to indicate whether family members view us in the same way we see ourselves.

Offering encouragement fosters development of a more intimate relationship.

Confirmation

Confirmation occurs when we treat and communicate with family members in a way that is consistent with how they see themselves. A child who perceives himself to be independent is confirmed when a parent gives him responsibility and allows him to make his own decisions.

Rejection

Rejection occurs when family members treat others in a manner that is inconsistent with how they see themselves. Can you recall a time when you felt like you were "grown up" but your parents treated you as though you were still a child? Perhaps you felt you were responsible enough to be left alone while your parents went out for the evening, but they hired a babysitter to stay with you. At times, family members communicate with one another in a way that is disconfirming.

Disconfirmation

Disconfirmation occurs when family members fail to offer any type of response. This behavior can be viewed as lack of acknowledgement for how they view other family members. We often get caught up in our busy schedules and fail to communicate with family members. Even though our response is neither positive nor negative, it can cause others to feel dissatisfied with the relationship. A parent who fails to comment on a child's report card, or a wife who fails to acknowledge the efforts of her husband's attempts at cooking dinner are examples of disconfirming responses. Understanding and supportive communication are related to family satisfaction. If we perceive family members as being there for us, we are more willing to exert energy toward developing a more intimate relationship.

COMMUNICATING INTIMACY

Earlier in this text we discussed the concept of intimacy in romantic and marital relationships. Our first experience in developing intimacy in relationships is often a result of our interactions with parents, siblings, and other family members. **Intimacy** refers to close relationships in which two or more people share personal and private information with one another. Young children are often more willing to disclose their fears and goals with family members than with others, and this is often the result of the perceived trust and affection associated with these relationships. How do you show affection for your family members? Chances are that the most basic way this is demonstrated is through our willingness to share disclosures. While we know that intimacy is fostered through our self-disclosures, these revelations are not necessarily exchanged equally between family members. Studies of disclosure in families have found that wives engage in disclosures more often than husbands, and both male and female children report disclosing more information to their mothers than to their fathers. As children grow older, their disclosure patterns often change. College students often disclose more to friends than to their parents. Consider the changes in your own disclosure patterns with your parents. As you get older, you may discover that you are more willing to share negative and honest information about yourself with your friends than you are with parents.

DIFFICULT COMMUNICATION

We have addressed the positive and supportive aspects of interpersonal communication in family relationships, but it is important to note that families are not immune to difficult communication. Just as romantic partners and friends experience highs and lows in relationships, so do families. Because families evolve as members grow and encounter new life experiences, additional communication challenges emerge. The key to effectively managing these issues and maintaining a positive relationship is to understand the role of communication in guiding us through the muddy waters.

Family Stress

Reuben Hill developed the **ABCX model** to study the stress experienced by families during war (1958). Each component of this model provides a glimpse into how different families cope with stress. To begin, "A" represents the stressor event and resulting hardship. "B" refers to the resources a family has available to manage the stress. Given that different families define stress in unique ways, "C" is used to explain how the family defines the stress. Depending on how a family defines "A" "B" and "C," the perception of an event as a crisis is represented by "X." The model is useful for understanding how and why families label situations as stressful and cope with stressors.

"A" represents the stressor event of a young mother stationed with the U.S. military in Iraq. In this story, extended family members serve as resources to assist with the care of a three-year old child in the absence of his mother, in this case representing the "B." The confusion experienced by the grandmother as she tries to help her grandson cope with the separation causes her to define the stressor as emotionally draining (C). While the family knows that the daughter will return home eventually, they also understand that she chose to serve her country and realize the danger associated with this responsibility. This may keep the family from evaluating the stress as crisis (X). Take a look at Table 12.4 to review each step of the ABCX model.

Stressor events can take many forms; Boss (1988) developed a typology of stressors that families face. These include stressors that are internal versus external, normative versus non-normative, voluntary versus involuntary, and

Table 12.4 The ABCX Model of Family Stress

A	Event producing the stress	Parent of a small child stationed overseas in the military
B	Resources a family has available	Extended family members (grandparents) assist with child care back home in the U.S.
C	Meaning family assigns to the stress	Grandmother finds the child's questions to be emotionally draining, to cause sadness
X	Perception of ability to manage stress (crisis or manageable)	Knowledge that parent chose to go overseas to serve in military; knowledge that this situation will eventually end keeps family from perceiving this as a "crisis"

chronic versus acute. **Internal stressors** are those that evolve from a family member. Examples might include a daughter's upcoming wedding or a teen who has tried to run away from home. **External stressors,** on the other hand, are often the result of an event that occurs outside the family, such as a hurricane destroying a family's home or even just an increase in the price of gasoline.

Normative stressors are those that are expected to occur at some point during the course of the family life cycle. The birth of a child or the death of an elderly parent is are events that families anticipate dealing with at some point in time. **Non-normative stressors** are unpredictable and often catch families "off guard." While most people think that winning the lottery would be a great stressor to experience, families do not typically anticipate coming into such a large sum of money and have difficulty dealing with new challenges posed by their good fortune.

Voluntary stressors are those events that family members seek out, such as changing careers and moving to a new city or deciding to run for political office. **Involuntary stressors** are events that simply occur—a family member being injured in a car accident or the announcement of an unplanned teen pregnancy.

Illnesses such as cancer or alcoholism are examples of **chronic stressor** events that require families to cope with the situation for an extended period of time. **Acute stressors** are relatively short-lived and include events such as a student getting suspended for misbehaving or losing the only set of keys to the family car.

Violence and Abuse in Families

Some of us learn at a young age that family is a source of caring and support and will be throughout our lives, but this is not always the case. Often family members encounter stress in their lives and turn to alcohol, drug abuse, or domestic violence as a means to escape from their problems. In these situations, the sad reality is that family members often hurt the ones they love the most. In 1998, nearly one million incidents of violence against a former spouses, boyfriends, or girlfriends were reported (U.S. Dept. of Justice 1998). Unfortunately, abusive behavior often follows a pattern in families, with fifty percent of men who admitted to assaulting their wives reporting that they also frequently abused their children (Strauss, Gellas, and Smith 1990). Abuse may come in the form of physical violence, or verbal and psychological mistreatment. While spousal or child abuse are the forms most often discussed, it is important to note that there are numerous occurrences of elder abuse as well as incidents of abuse in same-sex couples. Disclosures may serve as a mechanism through which family reports reveal abuse, but often the abuse goes unreported.

As children gain more power in the family, incidents of parental abuse by adolescent children have increased (Eckstein 2004). The parent-child relationship is not meant to be equal. Parents need to have control and authority in this dependent relationship. However, in some instances, the reverse is true, with children assuming power in the relationship. Three forms of parental abuse have been identified: physical, psychological, and financial. Physical abuse involves hitting, slapping, and pushing parents. In a 1989 study, nearly fourteen percent of parents reported being physically abused by their adolescent children at least once (Agnew and Huguley). Children may also engage in psychological forms of abuse. Examples of this type of abuse would be creating a sense of fear and include making threats to run away or hurt themselves, or name-calling. A final form of mistreatment is financial abuse. Children who steal from their parents, make demands for things beyond the family's budget, or damage the family's home or possessions are guilty of this type of abuse.

So what mechanisms are available to help family members through these damaging and harmful situations? Before any other step, family members need to admit abuse occurs and to seek assistance in dealing with the situation. Family members often feel ashamed or perceive that the family is a failure by admitting that there is physical or psychological abuse in the home. Seeking professional assistance is a crucial first step in resolving these potentially harmful issues.

SUMMARY

While we form countless interpersonal relationships throughout our lifetime, the relationships and interactions with family members are perhaps the most influential. Beginning at a young age, messages received from family members shape our identity and influence our own choice of communication behaviors. In addition to the individual identities that are shaped by these interactions, the family itself begins to create an identity that is shared by members. Throughout this chapter we have discussed the importance of interpersonal communication throughout the family life cycle. Various interpersonal theories can be applied to the study of family communication to illustrate the dynamic nature of these relationships. While we often assume that "family is forever," it is important to recognize that just as other types of interpersonal relationships experience a "dark side," family relationships can experience turbulent times as well. By exploring the role that interpersonal communication plays in families, we are better able to understand our own tendencies for interacting with others.

APPLICATIONS

Discussion Questions

A. Talk about the definition of the term **family** with several other students. Who would you include in your family? Explain why these individuals are included. What individual differences affect how you define this term (e.g., sex, culture, age, your family of origin, relationship experiences) and who you include in your family?

B. Identify a family from one of your favorite television shows. Use systems theory to analyze the characters' communication patterns and relationships with one another (e.g., interdependence, wholeness, etc). Would you describe the family members' communication and relationships as healthy or unhealthy? Defend your response to this question and be sure to use specific examples to support your arguments.

REFERENCES

Agnew, R., and S. Huguley. 1989. Adolescent violence toward parents. *Journal of Marriage and the Family, 51,* 699–711.
Boss, P. 1988. *Family stress management.* Newbury Park, CA: Sage.
Bumpass, L. L., R. K. Raley, and J. Sweet. 1995. The changing character of stepfamilies: Implications of cohabitation and nonmarital childbearing. *Demography, 32,* 425–436.
Coleman, M., L. Ganong, and M. Fine. 2004. Communication in stepfamilies. In A. Vangelisti (Ed.), *Handbook of family communication.* (215–232). Lawrence Erlbaum Associates: Mahwah, NJ.
Eckstein, N. 2004. Emergent issues in families experiencing adolescent to parent abuse. *Western Journal of Communication, 68,* 365–388.
Fisher, H. 2007. The laws of chemistry. *Psychology Today. 76–81.*
Fitzpatrick, M. A., 1987. Marital interaction. In C. Berger and S. Chaffee (Eds.), *Handbook of communication science* (564–618). Newbury Park, CA: Sage.
Hill, R. 1958. Generic features of families under stress. *Social Casework, 49,* 139–150.
Koerner, A. F., and M. A. Fitzpatrick. 2002. Toward a theory of family communication. *Communication Theory, 12,* 70–91.
LaRossa, R., and D. C. Reitzes. 1993. Symbolic interactionism and family studies. In P. G. Boss, W. J. Doherty, R. LaRossa, W. R. Schumm, and S. K. Steinmetz (Eds.), *Sourcebook of family theories and methods: A contextual approach* (135–163). New York, NY: Plenum Press.
Marrow-Ferguson, S., and F. Dickson. 1995. Children's expectations of their single-parent's dating behavior: A preliminary investigation of emergent themes relevant to single-parent dating. *Journal of Applied Communication Research, 23,* 1–17.
McGraw, P. 2004. *Family first: Your step-by-step plan for creating a phenomenal family.* New York, NY: Free Press.
McLeod, J. M., and S. H. Chaffee. 1972. The construction of social reality. In J. Tedeschi (Ed.), *The social influence process* (50–59). Chicago, IL: Aldine-Atherton.
_____. 1973. Interpersonal approaches to communication research. *American Behavior Scientist, 16,* 469–499.
Mead, G. H. 1934. *Mind, self and society.* Chicago: University of Chicago Press.
Myers, S. A., and K. D. Weber. 2004. Preliminary development of a measure of sibling relational maintenance behaviors: Scale development and initial findings. *Communication Quarterly, 52,* 334–346.
Ritchie, L. D. 1990. Family communication patterns: Measuring interpersonal perceptions of interpersonal relationships. *Communication Research, 17*(4), 523–544.
Ritchie, L. D., and M. A. Fitzpatrick. 1990. Family communication patterns: Measuring interpersonal perceptions of interpersonal relationships. *Communication Research, 17,* 523–544.
Sansone, K. 2005. *Woman first, family always.* Des Moines, IA: Meredith Books.
Smith, P. B., and D. R. Pederson. 1988. Maternal sensitivity and patterns of infant-mother attachment. *Child Development, 59,* 1097–1101.
Stafford, L., and D. J. Canary. 1999. Maintenance strategies and romantic relationship type, gender, and relational characteristics. *Journal of Social and Personal Relationships, 8,* 217–242.
Stamp, G. H. 2004. Theories of family relationships and a family relationships theoretical model. In A. Vangelisti (Ed.), *Handbook of family communication.* (1–30). Lawrence Erlbaum Associates: Mahwah, NJ.
Strauss, M. A., R. J. Gelles, and C. Smith. 1990. *Physical violence in American families; Risk factors and adaptations to violence in 8,145 families.* New Brunswick: Transaction Publishers.
Thomas-Maddox, C. 1999. *Keeping the relationship alive: An analysis of relational maintenance strategies employed by noncustodial parents and their children following divorce.* Paper presented at the National Communication Association convention. Chicago, IL.
Turner, L. H., and West, R. 2002. *Perspectives on Family Communication.* McGraw-Hill: Boston, MA.

U.S. Department of Justice. 1998. *Violence by intimates: Analysis of data on crimes by current or former spouses, boyfriends, and girlfriends.* Washington, DC.

Ungricht, Margo. (2006, February 17) MSNBC Citizen Journalist Reports: Stories from front line families. Retrieved from http://msnbc.com/id/7012316/.

Vangelisti, A. 2004. *Handbook of family communication.* Lawrence Erlbaum Associates: Mahwah, NJ.

Walsh, W. M., and R. Williams. 1997. *School and family therapy: Using systems theory and family therapy in the resolution of school problems.* Springfield, IL: Charles C. Thomas.

Health Communication

OBJECTIVES

1. Understand the role communication plays in physical and mental health.

2. Explain the health communication cycle.

3. Distinguish health communication concerns between health contexts.

KEY TERMS

audience analysis
audience profile
channels
communication
  channels
communication
  objectives
communication
  strategies

communication
  vehicles
community
  development
health communication
health disparities
health equity
intended audiences
key groups

program outcomes
situation analysis
social determinants of
  health
stakeholders
underserved
  populations
vulnerable
  populations

Health communication is an evolving and increasingly prominent field in public health, health care, and the non-profit and private sectors. Therefore, many authors and organizations have been attempting to define or redefine it over time. Because of the multidisciplinary nature of health communication, many of the definitions may appear somewhat different from each other. Nevertheless, when they are analyzed, most point to the role that health communication can play in influencing, supporting, and empowering individuals, communities, health care professionals, policymakers, or special groups to adopt and sustain a behavior or a social, organizational, and policy change that will ultimately improve individual, community, and public health outcomes.

Understanding the true meaning of health communication and establishing the right context for its implementation may help communication managers and other public health, community development, and health care professionals identify early on the training needs of staff, the communities they serve, and others who are involved in the communication process. It will also help create the right organizational mind-set and capacity that should lead to a successful use of communication approaches to reach group-, stakeholder-, and community-specific goals.

CHAPTER OBJECTIVES

This chapter sets the stage to discuss current health communication contexts. It also positions the importance of health communication in public health, health care, and community development as well as the nonprofit and private sectors. Finally, it describes key elements, action areas, and limitations of health communication, and introduces readers to "the role societal, organizational, and individual factors" play in influencing and being influenced by public health communication (Association of Schools of Public Health, 2007, p. 5) and communication interventions in clinical (Hospitals and Health Networks, 2012) and other health-related settings.

DEFINING HEALTH COMMUNICATION

There are several definitions of health communication, which for the most part share common meanings and attributes. This section analyzes and aims to consolidate different definitions for health communication. This analysis starts from the literal and historical meaning of the word *communication*.

What Is Communication?

An understanding of health communication theory and practice requires reflection on the literal meaning of the word *communication*. *Communication* is defined in this way: "1. *Exchange of information*, between individuals, for example, by means of speaking, writing, or using a common system of signs and behaviors; 2. *Message*—a spoken or written message; 3. *Act of communicating*; 4. *Rapport*—a sense of mutual understanding and sympathy; 5. *Access*—a means of access or communication, for example, a connecting door" (*Encarta Dictionary*, January 2007).

In fact, all of these meanings can help define the modalities of well-designed health communication interventions. As with other forms of communication, health communication should be based on a two-way exchange of information that uses a "common system of signs and behaviors." It should be accessible and create "mutual feelings of understanding and sympathy" among members of the communication team and **intended audiences** or **key groups** (all groups the health communication program is seeking to engage in the communication process.) In this book, the terms *intended audience* and *key group* are used interchangeably. Yet, the term *key group* may be better suited to acknowledge the participatory nature of well-designed health communication interventions in which communities and other key groups are the lead architects of the change process communication can bring about. For those who always have worked within a participatory model of health communication interventions, this distinction is concerned primarily with terminology-related preferences in different models and organizational cultures. Yet, as *audience* may have a more passive connotation, using the term *key group* may indicate the importance of creating key groups' ownership of the communication process, and of truly understanding priorities, needs, and preferences as a key premise to all communication interventions.

Finally, going back to the literal meaning of the word *communication* as defined at the beginning of this section, **channels** or **communication channels** (the means or path, such as mass media or new media, used to reach out to and connect with key groups via health communication messages and materials) and messages are the "connecting doors" that allow health communication interventions to reach and engage intended groups.

Communication has its roots in people's need to share meanings and ideas. A review of the origin and interpretation of early forms of communication, such as writing, shows that many of the reasons for which people may have started developing graphic notations and other early forms of writing are similar to those we can list for health communication.

One of the most important questions about the origins of writing is, "Why did writing begin and for what specific reasons?" (Houston, 2004, p. 234). Although the answer is still being debated, many established theories suggest that writing developed because of state and ceremonial needs (Houston, 2004). More specifically, in ancient Mesoamerica, early forms of writing may have been introduced to help local rulers "control the underlings and impress rivals by means of propaganda" (Houston, 2004, p. 234; Marcus, 1992) or "capture the dominant and dominating message within self-interested declarations" (Houston, 2004, p. 234) with the intention of "advertising" (p. 235) such views. In other words, it is possible to speculate that the desire and need to influence and connect with others are among the most important reasons for the emergence of early forms of writing. This need is also evident in many other forms of communication that seek to create feelings of approval, recognition, empowerment, or friendliness, among others.

Health Communication Defined

One of the key objectives of **health communication** is to engage, empower, and influence individuals and communities. The goal is admirable because health communication aims to improve health outcomes by sharing health-related information. In fact, the Centers for Disease Control and Prevention (CDC) define *health communication* as "the study and use of communication strategies to inform and influence individual and community decisions that enhance health" (CDC, 2001; US Department of Health and Human Services, 2012a). The word *influence* is also included in the *Healthy People 2010* definition of health communication as "the art and technique of informing, influencing, and motivating individual, institutional, and public audiences about important health issues" (US Department of Health and Human Services, 2005, pp. 11–12).

Yet, the broader mandate of health communication is intrinsically related to its potential impact on vulnerable and underserved populations. **Vulnerable populations** include groups who have a higher risk for poor physical, psychological, or social health in the absence of adequate conditions that are supportive of positive outcomes (for example, children, the elderly, people living with disability, migrant populations, and special groups affected by stigma and social discrimination). **Underserved populations** include geographical, ethnic, social, or community-specific groups who do not have adequate access to health or community services and infrastructure or information. "Use health communication strategies … to improve population health outcomes and health care quality, and to achieve health equity," reads *Healthy People 2020* (US Department of Health and Human Services, 2012b). **Health equity** is providing every person with the same opportunity to stay healthy or to effectively cope with disease and crisis, regardless of race, gender, age, economic conditions, social status, environment, and other socially determined factors. This can be achieved only by creating a receptive and favorable environment in which information can be adequately shared, understood, absorbed, and discussed by different communities and sectors in a way that is inclusive and representative of vulnerable and underserved groups. This requires an in-depth understanding of the needs, beliefs, taboos, attitudes, lifestyle, socioeconomics, environment, and social norms of all key groups and sectors that are involved—or should be involved—in the communication process. It also demands that communication is based on messages that are easily understood. This is well characterized in the definition of *communication* by Pearson and Nelson (1991), who view it as "the process of understanding and sharing meanings" (p. 6).

A practical example that illustrates this definition is the difference between making an innocent joke about a friend's personality trait and doing the same about a colleague or recent acquaintance. The friend would likely laugh at the joke, whereas the colleague or recent acquaintance might be offended. In communication, understanding the context of the communication effort is interdependent with becoming familiar with intended audiences. This increases the likelihood that all meanings are shared and understood in the way communicators intended them. Therefore, communication, especially about life-and-death matters such as in public health and health care, is a long-term strategic process. It requires a true understanding of the key groups and communities we seek to engage as well as our willingness and ability to adapt and redefine the goals, strategies, and activities of communication interventions on the basis of audience participation and feedback.

Health communication interventions have been successfully used for many years by public health and nonprofit organizations, the commercial sector, and others to advance public, corporate, clinical, or product-related goals in relation to health. As many authors have noted, health communication draws from numerous disciplines and theoretical fields, including health education, social and behavioral sciences, community development, mass and speech communication, marketing, social marketing, psychology, anthropology, and sociology (Bernhardt, 2004; Kreps, Query, and Bonaguro, 2007; Institute of Medicine, 2003b; World Health Organization [WHO], 2003). It relies on different communication activities or action areas, including interpersonal communication, mass media and new media communication, strategic policy communication and public advocacy, community mobilization and citizen engagement, professional medical communications, and constituency relations and strategic partnerships (Bernhardt, 2004; Schiavo, 2008, 2011b; WHO, 2003).

Table 13.1 provides some of the most recent definitions of health communication and is organized by key words most commonly used to characterize health communication and its role. It is evident that "sharing meanings or information," "influencing individuals or communities," "informing," "motivating individuals and key groups," "exchanging information," "changing behaviors," "engaging," "empowering," and "achieving behavioral and social results" are among the most common attributes of health communication.

Another important attribute of health communication should be "to support and sustain change." In fact, key elements of successful health communication interventions always include long-term program sustainability as well as the development of communication tools and steps that make it easy for individuals, communities, and other key groups to adopt or sustain a recommended behavior, practice, or policy change. If we integrate this practice-based perspective with many of the definitions in Table 13.1, the new definition on page 327 emerges.

Table 13.1   Health Communication Definitions

Key Words	Definitions
To inform and influence (individual and community) decisions	"Health communication is a key strategy to *inform* [emphasis added throughout table] the public about decisions health concerns and to maintain important health issues on the public agenda" (New South Wales Department of Health, Australia, 2006).
	"The study or use of communication strategies *to inform and influence* individual and community decisions that enhance health" (CDC, 2001; US Department of Health and Human Services, 2005).
	Health communication is a "means to disease prevention through behavior modification" (Freimuth, Linnan, and Potter, 2000, p. 337). It has been defined as "the study and use of methods to *inform and influence* individual and community decisions that enhance health" (Freimuth, Linnan, and Potter, 2000, p. 338; Freimuth, Cole, and Kirby, 2000, p. 475).
	"Health communication is a process for the development and diffusion of messages to specific audiences in order to *influence* their knowledge, attitudes and beliefs in favor of healthy behavioral choices" (Exchange, 2006; Smith and Hornik, 1999).
	"Health communication is the use of communication techniques and technologies to (positively) *influence* individuals, populations, and organizations for the purpose of promoting conditions conducive to human and environmental health" (Maibach and Holtgrave, 1995, pp. 219–220; Health Communication Unit, 2006). "It may include diverse activities such as clinician-patient interactions, classes, self-help groups, mailings, hot lines, mass media campaigns, and events" (Health Communication Unit, 2006).
Motivating individuals and key groups	"The art and technique of informing, influencing and *motivating* individual, institutional, and public audiences about important health issues. Its scope includes disease prevention, health promotion, health care policy, and business, as well as enhancement of the quality of life and health of individuals within the community" (Ratzan and others, 1994, p. 361).
	"Effective health communication is the art and technique of *informing, influencing, and motivating* individuals, institutions, and large public audiences about important health issues based on sound scientific and ethical considerations" (Tufts University Student Services, 2006).
Change behavior, achieve social and behavioral results	"Health communication, like health education, is an approach which attempts to *change a set of behaviors* in a large-scale target audience regarding a specific problem in a predefined period of time" (Clift and Freimuth, 1995, p. 68),
	"There is good evidence that public health communication has affected health behavior … In addition, … many public agencies assume that public health communication is a powerful tool for *behavior change*" (Hornik, 2008a, pp. xi–xv).
	"… *behavior change* is credibly associated with public health communication …" (Hornik, 2008b, p.1).
	"… health communication strategies that are collaboratively and strategically designed, implemented, and evaluated can help to improve health in a significant and lasting way. Positive results are achieved by empowering people *to change their behavior* and by facilitating *social change*" (Krenn and Limaye, 2009).

(continued)

Table 13.1   Health Communication Definitions (*continued*)

Key Words	Definitions
	Health communication and other disciplines "may have some differences, but they share a common goal: creating *social change* by changing people's attitudes, external structures, and/ or *modify or eliminate certain behaviors*" (CDC, 2011a).
Increase knowledge and understanding of health-related issues	"The goal of health communication is to *increase knowledge and understanding* of health-related issues and to improve the health status of the intended audience" (Muturi, 2005, p. 78).
	"Communication means a process of *creating understanding* as the basis for development. It places emphasis on people interaction" (Agunga, 1997, p. 225).
Empowers people	"Communication *empowers people* by providing them with knowledge and understanding about specific health problems and interventions" (Muturi, 2005, p. 81).
	"… transformative communication… seek[s] not only to educate people about health risks, but also to facilitate the types of social relationships most likely to *empower* them to resist the impacts of unhealthy social influences" (Campbell and Scott, 2012, pp. 179–180).
	"Communication processes are central to broader *empowerment* practices through which people are able to arrive at their own understanding of issues, to consider and discuss ideas, to negotiate, and to engage in public debates at community and national levels" (Food and Agriculture Organization of the United Nations and others, 2011, p. 1).
Exchange, interchange of information, two-way dialogue	"A process for partnership and participation that is based on *two-way dialogue,* where there is an interactive *interchange of information,* ideas, techniques and knowledge between senders and receivers of information on an equal footing, leading to improved understanding, shared knowledge, greater consensus, and identification of possible effective action" (Exchange, 2005).
	"Health communication is the scientific development, strategic dissemination, and critical evaluation of relevant, accurate, accessible, and understandable health *information communicated to and from intended audiences* to advance the health of the public" (Bernhardt, 2004, p. 2051).
Engaging	"One of the most important, and largely unrecognized, dimensions of effective health communication relates to how *engaging* the communication is" (Kreps, 2012a, p. 253).
	"To compete successfully for audience attention, health-related communications have to be polished and *engaging*" (Cassell, Jackson, and Cheuvront, 1998, p. 76).

Health communication is a multifaceted and multidisciplinary field of research, theory, and practice. It is concerned with reaching different populations and groups to exchange health-related information, ideas, and methods in order to influence, engage, empower, and support individuals, communities, health care professionals, patients, policymakers, organizations, special groups and the public, so that they will champion, introduce, adopt, or sustain a health or social behavior, practice, or policy that will ultimately improve individual, community, and public health outcomes.

HEALTH COMMUNICATION IN THE TWENTY-FIRST CENTURY: KEY CHARACTERISTICS AND DEFINING FEATURES

Health communication is about improving health outcomes by encouraging behavior modification and social change. It is increasingly considered an integral part of most public health interventions (US Department of Health and Human Services, 2012a; Bernhardt, 2004). It is a comprehensive approach that relies on the full understanding and participation of its intended audiences.

Health communication theory draws on a number of additional disciplines and models. In fact, both the health communication field and its theoretical basis have evolved and changed in the past fifty years (Piotrow, Kincaid, Rimon, and Rinehart, 1997; Piotrow, Rimon, Payne Merritt, and Saffitz, 2003; Bernhardt, 2004). With increasing frequency, it is considered "the avant-garde in suggesting and integrating new theoretical approaches and practices" (Drum Beat, 2005).

Most important, communicators are no longer viewed as those who write press releases and other media-related communications, but as fundamental members of the public health, health care, nonprofit, or health industry teams. Communication is no longer considered a skill (Bernhardt, 2004) but a science-based discipline that requires training and passion, and relies on the use of different **communication vehicles** (materials, activities, events, and other tools used to deliver a message through communication channels; Health Communication Unit, 2003b) and channels. According to Saba (2006):

> In the past, and this is probably the most prevalent trend even today, health communication practitioners were trained "on-the-job." People from different fields (sociology, demography, public health, psychology, communication with all its different specialties, such as filmmaking, journalism and advertising) entered or were brought into health communication programs to meet the need for professional human resources in this field. By performing their job and working in teams, they learned how to adapt their skills to the new field and were taught by other practitioners about the common practices and basic "lingo" of health communication. In the mid-90s, and in response to the increasing demand for health communication professionals, several schools in the United States started their own curricular programs and/or "concentrations" in Health Communication. This helped bring more attention from the academic world to this emerging field. The number of peer-reviewed articles and several other types of health communication publications increased. The field moved from in-service training to pre-service education.

As a result, there is an increasing understanding that "the level of technical competence of communication practitioners can affect outcomes." A structured approach to health communications planning, a spotless program execution, and a rigorous evaluation process are the result of adequate competencies and relevant training, which are supported by leading organizations and agendas in different fields (Association of Schools of public Health, 2007; US Department of Health and Human Services, 2012b; American Medical Association, 2006; Hospitals and Health Network, 2012; National Board of Public Health

Examiners, 2011). "In health communication, the learning process is a lifetime endeavor and should be facilitated by the continuous development of new training initiatives and tools" (Schiavo, 2006). Training may start in the academic setting but should always be influenced and complemented by practical experience and observations, and other learning opportunities, including in-service training, continuing professional education, and ongoing mentoring.

Health communication can reach its highest potential when it is discussed and applied within a team-oriented context that includes public health, health care, community development, and other professionals from different sectors and disciplines. Teamwork and mutual agreement, on both the intervention's ultimate objectives and expected results, are key to the successful design, implementation, and impact of any program.

Finally, it is important to remember that there is no magic fix that can address health issues. Health communication is an evolving discipline and should always incorporate lessons learned as well as use a multidisciplinary approach to all interventions. This is in line with one of the fundamental premises of this book that recognizes the experience of practitioners as a key factor in developing theories, models, and approaches that should guide and inform health communication planning, implementation, and assessment.

Table 13.2 lists the key elements of health communication, which are further analyzed in the following sections.

People-Centered

Health communication is a long-term process that begins and ends with people's needs and preferences. In health communication, intended audiences should not be merely a *target* (even if this terminology is used by many practitioners from around the world primarily to indicate that a communication intervention will focus on, benefit, and engage a specific group of people that shares similar characteristics—such as age, socioeconomics, and ethnicity. It does not necessarily imply lack of audience participation) but an active participant in the process of analyzing and prioritizing the health issue, finding culturally appropriate and cost-effective solutions, and becoming effectively engaged as the lead change designer in the planning, implementation, and assessment of all interventions. This is why the term *key group* may better

---

Table 13.2   Key Characteristics of Health Communication

- People-centered
- Evidence-based
- Multidisciplinary
- Strategic
- Process-oriented
- Cost-effective
- Creative in support of strategy
- Audience- and media-specific
- Relationship building
- Aimed at behavioral and social results
- Inclusive of vulnerable and underserved groups

represent the role communities, teachers, parents, health care professionals, religious and community leaders, women, and many other key groups and stakeholders from a variety of segments of society and professional sectors should assume in the communication process. Yet, different organizations may have different cultural preferences for specific terminology even within the context of their participatory models and planning frameworks.

In implementing a people-centered approach to communication, researching communities and other key groups is a necessary but often not sufficient step because the effectiveness and sustainability of most interventions is often linked to the level of engagement of their key beneficiaries and those who influence them. Engaging communities and different sectors is often accomplished in health communication practice by working together with organizations and leaders who represent them or by directly involving members of a specific community at the outset of program design. For example, if a health communication intervention aims to reach and benefit breast cancer survivors, all strategies and key program elements should be designed, discussed, prioritized, tested, implemented, and evaluated together with membership organizations, patient groups, leaders, and patients who can speak for survivors and represent their needs and preferences. Most important, these groups need to feel invested and well represented. They should be the key protagonists of the action-oriented process that will lead to behavioral or social change.

Evidence-Based

Health communication is grounded in research. Successful health communication interventions are based on a true understanding not only of key groups but also of situations and sociopolitical environments. This includes existing programs and lessons learned, policies, social norms, key issues, work and living environments, and obstacles in addressing the specific health problem. The overall premise of health communication is that behavioral and social change is conditioned by the environment in which people live and work, as well as by those who influence them. Several socially determined factors (also referred to as **social determinants of health**)—including socioeconomic conditions, race, ethnicity, culture, as well as having access to health care services, a built environment that supports physical activity, neighborhoods with accessible and affordable nutritious food, health information that's culturally appropriate and accurately reflects literacy levels, and caring and friendly clinical settings—influence and are influenced by health communication (Association of Schools of Public Health, 2007). This requires a comprehensive research approach that relies on traditional, online, and new media-based research techniques for the formal development of a **situation analysis** (a planning term that describes the analysis of individual, social, political, environmental, community-specific, and behavior-related factors that can affect attitudes, behaviors, social norms, and policies about a health issue and its potential solutions) and **audience analysis** (a comprehensive, research-based, participatory, and strategic analysis of all key groups' characteristics, demographics, needs, preferences, values, social norms, attitudes, and behavior). The **audience profile,** a report on all findings, is the culminating step of a process of effective engagement and participation that involve all key groups and stakeholders in the overall analysis). Situation and audience analyses are fundamental and interrelated steps of health communication planning (the audience analysis is described in this book as a component of the situation analysis), which should be participatory and empowering in their nature, and are described in detail in Chapter Eleven.

Multidisciplinary

Health communication is "transdisciplinary in nature" (Bernhardt, 2004, p. 2051; Institute of Medicine, 2003b) and draws on multiple disciplines (Bernhardt, 2004; WHO, 2003). Health communication recognizes the complexity of attaining behavioral and social change and uses a multifaceted approach that is grounded in the application of several theoretical frameworks and disciplines, including health education, social marketing, behavioral and social change theories, and medical and clinical models (see Chapter Two for a comprehensive discussion of key theories and models). It draws on principles successfully used in the nonprofit and corporate sectors and also on the people-centered approach of other disciplines, such as psychology, sociology, and anthropology (WHO, 2003). It is not anchored to a single specific theory or model. With people always at the core of each intervention, it uses a case-by-case approach in selecting those models, theories, and strategies that are best suited to reach their hearts; secure their involvement in the health issue and, most important, its solutions; and support and facilitate their journey on a path to better health.

Piotrow, Rimon, Payne Merritt, and Saffitz (2003) identify four different "eras" of health communication:

> (1) The *clinic era*, based on a medical care model and the notion that if people knew where services were located they would find their way to the clinics; (2) the *field era*, a more proactive approach emphasizing outreach workers, community-based distribution, and a variety of information, education, and communication (IEC) products; (3) the *social marketing era*, developed from the commercial concepts that consumers will buy the products they want at subsidized prices; and, (4) ... the era of *strategic behavior communications*, founded on behavioral science models that emphasize the need to influence social norms and policy environments to facilitate and empower the iterative and dynamic process of both individual and social change, (pp. 1–2)

More recently, health communication has evolved toward a fifth "era" of strategic communication for behavioral and social change that rightly emphasizes and combines behavioral and social science models and disciplines along with marketing, medical, and social norms-based models, and aims at achieving long-lasting behavioral and social results. However, even in the context of each different health communication era, many of the theoretical approaches of other periods still find use in program planning or execution. For example, the situation analysis of a health communication program still uses commercial and social marketing tools and models—even if combined with community dialogue and other participatory or new media-based methods (see Chapters Two and Ten for a detailed description)—to analyze the environment in which change should occur. Instead, in the early stages of approaching key opinion leaders and other key **stakeholders** (all individuals and groups who have an interest or share responsibilities in a given issue, such as policymakers, community leaders, and community members), keeping in mind McGuire's steps about communication for persuasion (1984; see Chapter Two), may help communicators gain stakeholder support for the importance or the urgency of adequately addressing a health issue. This theoretical flexibility should keep communicators focused on key groups and stakeholders and always on the lookout for the best approach and planning framework to achieve behavioral and social results by engaging and empowering people. In concert with the other features previously discussed, it also enables the overall communication process to be truly fluid and suited to respond to people's needs.

The importance of a somewhat flexible theoretical basis, which should be selected on a case-by-case basis (National Cancer Institute, 2005a), is already supported by reputable organizations and authors. For example, publications by the US Department of Health and Human Services (2002), and the National Cancer Institute at the National Institutes of Health (2002) points to the importance of selecting planning frameworks that "can help [communicators] identify the social science theories most appropriate for understanding the problem and the situation" (National Cancer Institute at the National Institutes of Health, 2002, p. 218). These theories, models, and constructs include several theoretical concepts and frameworks (see Chapter Two) that are also used in motivating change at individual and interpersonal levels or organizational, community, and societal levels (National Cancer Institute at the National Institutes of Health, 2002) by related or complementary disciplines.

The goal here is not to advocate for a lack of theoretical structure in communication planning and execution. On the contrary, planning frameworks, models, and theories should be consistent at least until preliminary steps of the evaluation phase of a program are completed. This allows communicators to take advantage of lessons learned and redefine theoretical constructs and **communication objectives** (the intermediate steps that need to be achieved in order to meet program goals and outcome objectives; National Cancer Institute, 2002) by comparing **program outcomes,** which measure changes in knowledge, attitudes, skills, behavior, and other parameters, with those that were anticipated in the planning phase. However, the ability to draw on multiple disciplines and theoretical constructs is a definitive advantage of the health communication field and one of the keys to the success of well-planned and well-executed communication programs.

Strategic

Health communication programs need to display a sound strategy and plan of action. All activities need to be well planned and respond to a specific audience-related need. Consider the example of Bonnie, a twenty-five-year-old mother who is not sure about whether to immunize her newborn child. Activities in support of a strategy that focuses on facilitating communication between Bonnie and her health care provider make sense only if evidence shows all or any of the following points: (1) Bonnie is likely to be influenced primarily, or at least significantly, by her health care provider and not by family or other new mothers; (2) there are several gaps in the understanding of patients' needs that prevent health care providers from communicating effectively; (3) providers lack adequate tools to talk about this topic with patients in a time-effective and efficient manner; (4) research data have been validated by community dialogue and other participatory methods that are inclusive of Bonnie and her peers; and (5) Bonnie and her peers and organizations that represent them have participated in designing all interventions.

Communication strategies (the overall approach used to accomplish the communication objectives) need to be research-based, and all activities should serve such strategies. Therefore, we should not rely on any workshop, press release, brochure, video, or anything else to provide effective communication without making sure that its content and format reflect the selected approach (the strategy), and that this is a priority to reach people's hearts. For this purpose, health communication strategies need to respond to an actual need that has been identified by preliminary research and confirmed by the intended audience.

Process-Oriented

Communication is a long-term process. Influencing people and their behaviors requires an ongoing commitment to the health issue and its solutions. This is rooted in a deep understanding of key groups, communities, and their environments, and aims at building consensus among affected groups, community members, and key stakeholders about the potential plan of action.

Most, if not all, health communication programs change or evolve from what communication experts may have originally envisioned due to the input and participation of communities, key opinion leaders, patient groups, professional associations, policymakers, community members, and other key stakeholders.

In health communication, engaging key groups on relevant health issues as well as exploring suitable ways to address them is only the first step of a long-term, people-centered process. This process often requires theoretical flexibility to accommodate people's needs, preferences, and priorities.

While in the midst of many process-oriented projects, many practitioners may have noticed that health communication is often misunderstood. Health communication uses multiple channels and approaches, which, despite what some people may think, include but are not limited to the use of the mass media or new media. Moreover, health communication aims at improving health outcomes and in the process help advance public health and community development goals or create market share (depending on whether health communication strategies are used for nonprofit or for-profit goals) or encourages compliance to clinical recommendations and healthy lifestyles. Finally, health communication cannot focus only on channels, messages, and media. It also should attempt to involve and create consensus and feelings of ownership among intended audiences.

Exchange, a networking and learning program on health communication for development that is based in the United Kingdom and has multiple partners, views health communication as "a process for partnership and participation that is based on two-way dialogue, where there is an interactive interchange of information, ideas, techniques, and knowledge between senders and receivers of information on an equal footing, leading to improved understanding, shared knowledge, greater consensus, and identification of possible effective action" (2005). This definition makes sense in all settings and situations, but it assumes a greater relevance for health communication programs that aim to improve health outcomes in developing countries. Communication for development often needs to rely on creative solutions that compensate for the lack of local capabilities and infrastructure. These solutions usually emerge after months of discussion with local community leaders and organizations, government officials, and representatives of public and community groups. Word of mouth and the ability of community leaders to engage members of their own communities is often all that communicators have at hand.

Consider the case of Maria, a mother of four children who lives in a small village in sub-Saharan Africa together with her seventy-five-year-old father. Her village is almost completely isolated from major metropolitan areas, and very few people in town have a radio or know how to read. Maria is unaware that malaria, which is endemic in that region, poses a higher risk to children than to the elderly. Because elderly people benefit from a high hierarchical status in that region, if Maria is able to find money to purchase mosquito nets to protect someone in her family from mosquito bites and the consequent threat of malaria, she would probably choose that her father sleep under them, leaving her children unprotected. This is despite the high mortality rate from malaria among children in her village. If her village's community leaders told her to do otherwise, she would likely change her practice and protect her children. This may be the first building block toward the development and adoption of new social norms not only by Maria but also her peers and other community members.

Involving Maria's community leaders and peers in the communication process that would lead to a potential change in her habits requires long-term commitment. Such effort demands the involvement of local organizations and authorities who are respected and trusted by community leaders, as well as an open mind in listening to suggestions and seeking solutions with the help of all key stakeholders. Because of the lack of local capabilities and limited access to adequate communication channels, this process is likely to take longer than any similar initiative in the developed world. Therefore, communicators should view this as an ongoing process and applaud every small step forward.

Cost-Effective

Cost-effectiveness is a concept that health communication borrows from commercial and social marketing. It is particularly important in the competitive working environment of public health and nonprofit organizations, where the lack of sufficient funds or adequate economic planning can often undermine important initiatives. It implies the need to seek solutions that allow communicators to advance their goals with minimal use of human and economic resources. Yet, communicators should use their funds as long as they are well spent and advance their evidence-based strategy. They should also seek creative solutions that minimize the use of internal funds and human resources by seeking partnerships, using existing materials or programs as a starting point, and maximizing synergies with the work of other departments in their organization or external groups and stakeholders in the same field.

Creative in Support of Strategy

Creativity is a significant attribute of communicators because it allows them to consider multiple options, formats, and media channels to reach and engage different groups. It also helps them devise solutions that preserve the sustainability and cost-effectiveness of specific health communication interventions. However, even the greatest ideas or the best-designed and best-executed communication tools may fail to achieve behavioral or social results if they do not respond to a strategic need identified by research data and validated by key stakeholders from intended groups. Too often communication programs and resources fail to make an impact because of this common mistake.

For example, developing and distributing a brochure on how to use insecticide-treated nets (ITNs) makes sense only if the intended community is already aware of the cycle of malaria transmission as well as the need for protection from mosquito bites. If this is not the case and most community members still believe that malaria is contracted by bathing in the river or is a complication of some other fevers (Pinto, 1998; Schiavo, 1998, 2000), the first strategic imperative is disease awareness, with a specific focus on the cycle of transmission and subsequent protective measures. All communication materials and activities need to address this basic information need before talking about the use of ITNs and reasons to use them as an alternative to other potential protection methods. Creativity should come into play in devising culturally friendly tools to start sharing information about malaria and to engage community members in designing a community-specific communication intervention that would encourage protective behaviors and would benefit the overall community. In a nutshell, we should refrain from using creativity to develop and implement great, sensational, or innovative ideas when these do not respond to people's needs and key strategic priorities of the health communication intervention.

Audience- and Media-Specific

The importance of audience-specific messages and channels became one of the most important lessons learned after the anthrax-by-mail bioterrorist attacks that rocked the United States in October 2001. At the time, several letters containing the lethal agent *Bacillus anthracis* were mailed to senators and representatives of the media (Jernigan and others, 2002; Blanchard and others, 2005). The attack also exposed government staff workers, including US postal workers in the US Postal Service facility in Washington, DC, and other parts of the country, to anthrax. Two workers in the Washington facility died as a result of anthrax inhalation (Blanchard and others, 2005).

Communication during this emergency was perceived by several members of the medical, patient, and worker communities as well as public figures and the media to be often inconsistent and disorganized (Blanchard and others, 2005; Vanderford, 2003). Equally important, postal workers and US Senate staff have reported erosion of their trust in public health agencies (Blanchard and others, 2005). Several analyses point to the possibility that the *one message-one behavior approach* to communication (UCLA Department of Epidemiology, 2002)—in other words, using the same message and strategic approach for all audiences, which is likely to result in the same unspecific behavior that may not be relevant to specific communities or groups—led to feelings of being left out among postal workers, who in the Brentwood facility in Washington, DC, were primarily African Americans or individuals with a severe hearing impairment (Blanchard and others, 2005). They also point to the need for public health officials to develop the relationships that are needed to communicate with groups of different racial and socioeconomic backgrounds as well as "those with physical limitations that could hinder communication, such as those with hearing impairments" (Blanchard and others, 2005, p. 494; McEwen and Anton-Culver, 1988).

The lessons learned from the anthrax scare support some of the fundamental principles of good health communication practices. Messages need to be key group-specific and tailored to channels allowing the most effective reach, including among vulnerable and underserved groups. Because it is very likely that communication efforts may aim at producing multiple key group-appropriate behaviors, the one message-one behavior approach should be avoided (UCLA Department of Epidemiology, 2002) even when time and resources are lacking. As highlighted by the anthrax case study, in developing audience-specific messages and activities, the contribution of local advocates and community representatives is fundamental to increase the likelihood that messages will be heard, understood, and trusted by intended audiences.

Relationship Building

Communication is a relationship business. Establishing and preserving good relationships is critical to the success of health communication interventions, and, among other things, can help build long-term and successful partnerships and coalitions, secure credible stakeholder endorsement of the health issue, and expand the pool of ambassadors on behalf of the health cause.

Most important, good relationships help create the environment of "shared meanings and understanding" (Pearson and Nelson, 1991, p. 6) that is central to achieving social or behavioral results at the individual, community, and population levels. Good relationships should be established with key stakeholders and representatives of key groups, health organizations, community-based organizations, governments, and many other. critical members of the extended health communication team. A detailed discussion of the dos and don'ts as well as the development of successful partnerships and relationship-building efforts is found in Chapters Eight and Thirteen.

Aimed at Behavioral and Social Results

Nowadays, we are transitioning from the "era of strategic behavior communications" (Piotrow, Rimon, Payne Merritt, and Saffitz, 2003, p. 2) to the *era of behavioral and social impact communication*. Several US and international models and agenda (for example, *Healthy People 2020*, COMBI, Communication for Development; see Chapter Two) support the importance of a behavioral and social change-driven mind-set in developing health communication interventions. Although the ultimate goal of health communication has always been influencing behaviors, social norms, and policies (with the latter often being instrumental in institutionalizing social change and norms), there is a renewed emphasis on the importance of establishing behavioral and social objectives early on in the design of health communication interventions.

"What do you want people to do?" is the first question that should be asked in communication planning meetings. Do you want them to immunize their children before age two? Become aware of their risk for heart disease and behave accordingly to prevent it? Ask their dentists about oral cancer screening? Do you want local legislators to support a stricter law on the use of infant car seats? Or communities and special groups to create an environment of peer-to-peer support designed to discourage adolescents from initiating smoking? Or encourage people from different sectors (for example, employers, clinicians, etc.) to provide social support and tools to members of underserved communities so they are more likely to adopt and sustain a healthy lifestyle? Answering these kinds of questions is the first step in identifying suitable and research-based objectives of a communication program.

Although different theories (see Chapter Two) may specifically support the importance of either behavioral or social results as key outcome indicators, these two parameters are actually interconnected. In fact, social change typically takes place as the result of a series of behavioral results at the individual, group, community, social, and political levels.

Inclusive of Vulnerable and Underserved Groups

With a precise mandate from *Healthy People 2020* and the fact that several international organizations, such as UNICEF, have been investing overtime in rolling out an equity-based approach to programming, health communication is increasingly considered a key field that can contribute to a reduction of **health disparities** ("diseases or health conditions that discriminate and tend to be more common and more severe among vulnerable and underserved populations" [Health Equity Initiative, 2012b]; or overall differences in health outcomes) and an advancement of health equity. Therefore, health communication programs need to be mindful and inclusive of vulnerable and underserved populations. Such inclusiveness is not only limited to making sure that programs intended for the general population or specific communities also have a measurable impact on disadvantaged groups but it also entails that such groups are involved in the planning, implementation, and evaluation of all interventions so that their voices are heard and considered as part of the overall communication process. This is also important to build leadership capacity among vulnerable and underserved groups so they can adequately address current and future health and community development topics and find their own solutions to pressing issues.

THE HEALTH COMMUNICATION ENVIRONMENT

When looking at the health communication environment where change should occur and be sustained (Figure 13.1), it becomes clear that effective communication can be a powerful tool in seeking to influence all of the factors that are highlighted in the figure. It is also clear that regardless of whether these factors are related to the audience, health behavior, product, service, social, or political environment, all of them are interconnected and can mutually affect each other. At the same time, health communication interventions can tip the existing balance among these factors, and change the weight they may have in defining a specific health issue and its solutions as well as within the living, working, and aging environment of the people we seek to reach and engage in the health communication process.

Figure 13.1 also reflects some of the key principles of marketing models as well as the socioecological model (Morris, 1975), behavioral and social sciences constructs, and other theoretical models (VanLeeuwen, Waltner-Toews, Abernathy, and Smit, 1999) that are used in public health, health care, global health, and other fields to show the connection and influence of different factors (individual, interpersonal, community, sociopolitical, organizational, and public policy) on individual, group, and community behavior as well as to understand the process that may lead to behavioral and social results. Health communication theoretical basis is discussed in detail in Chapter Two.

Figure 13.1   The Health Communication Environment

Communicatioin and Other Key Groups
Healthy beliefs, attitudes, and behaviour
Gender-related factors
Literacy levels
Risk factors
lifestyle issues
Socioeconomic factors
Living and working environments
Access to service and information

Political Environment
Policies,laws
Political willingness
and commitment
Levels of priority in
Political agenda

**HEALTHA
COMMUNICATION**

**Recommended Health or social
Behaviour,Service,or Product**
Benefits
Risks
Disadvantages
Price or lifestyle trade-off
Availability and access
Cultural and social acceptance

Social Environment
Stakesholders'beliefs, attitudes, and practices
Social norms and practies
Social structure
Social support
Existing initiatives and programs

HEALTH COMMUNICATION IN PUBLIC HEALTH, HEALTH CARE, AND COMMUNITY DEVELOPMENT

Prior to the recent call to action by many federal and multilateral organizations, which encouraged a strategic and more frequent use of communication, health communication was used only marginally in a variety of sectors. It was perceived more as a skill than a discipline and confined to the mere dissemination of scientific and medical findings by public health and other professionals (Bernhardt, 2004). This section reviews current thinking on the role of health communication in public health, health care settings, and community development, and also serves as a reminder of the need for increased collaboration among these important sectors.

Health Communication in Public Health

Health communication is a well-recognized discipline in public health. Many public health organizations and leaders (Bernhardt, 2004; Freimuth, Cole, and Kirby, 2000; Institute of Medicine, 2002, 2003b; National Cancer Institute at the National Institutes of Health, 2002; Piotrow, Kincaid, Rimon, and Rinehart, 1997; Rimal and Lapinski, 2009; US Department of Health and Human Services, 2005,2012b) understand and recognize the role that health communication can play in advancing health outcomes and the general health status of interested populations and special groups. Most important, there is a new awareness of the reach of health communication as well as its many strategic action areas (for example, interpersonal communication, professional medical communications, community mobilization and citizen engagement, and mass media and new media communication).

As defined by *Healthy People 2010* (US Department of Health and Human Services, 2005), in the US public health agenda, the scope of health communication in public health "includes disease prevention, health promotion, health care policy, and the business of health care as well as enhancement of the quality of life and health of individuals within the community" (p. 11–20; Ratzan and others, 1994). Health communication "links the domains of communication and health" (p. 11–13) and is regarded as a science (Freimuth and Quinn, 2004; Bernhardt, 2004) of great importance in public health, especially in the era of epidemics and emerging diseases, the increasing toll of chronic diseases, the aging of large segments and percentages of the population of many countries, urbanization, increased disparities and socioeconomic divides, global threats, bioterrorism, and a new emphasis on a preventive and patient-centered approach to health. Finally, *Healthy People 2020* establishes health communication as a key discipline in contributing to advance health equity (US Department of Health and Human Resources, 2012b).

Health Communication in Health Care Settings

Health communication has an invaluable role within health care settings. Although provider-patient communications—which is perhaps the best known and most important use of communication within health care settings—is discussed in detail within Chapter Four, it is worth mentioning here that communication is also used to coordinate the activities of interdependent health care providers, encourage the widespread use of best clinical practices, promote the application of scientific advancements, and overall to administer complex and multisectoral health care delivery systems (see Chapter Seven and other relevant sections throughout this book).

As *Healthy People 2020* suggests, by combining effective health communication processes and integrating them with new technology and tools, there is the potential to

- Improve health care quality and safety.
- Increase the efficiency of health care and public health service delivery.
- Improve the public health information infrastructure.
- Support care in the community and at home.
- Facilitate clinical and consumer decision-making.
- Build health skills and knowledge (US Department of Health and Human Services, 2012b).

Among other things, *Healthy People 2020's* recommendations reflect the support many reputable voices and organizations—in the United States and globally—have lent to the need for effective integration of the work and strategies from our public health and health care systems.

Health Communication in Community Development

As previously mentioned, health is influenced by many different factors and is not only the mere absence of illness. Health is a state of well-being that includes the physical, psychological, and social aspects of life, which in turn are influenced by the environment in which we live, work, grow, and age.

Community development refers to a field of research and practice that involves community members, average citizens, professionals, grant-makers, and others in improving various aspects of local communities. More traditionally, community development interventions have been dealing with providing and increasing access to adequate transportation, jobs, and other socioeconomic opportunities, education, and different kinds of infrastructure (for example, parks, community centers, etc.) within a given community or population. Yet, because all of these interventions or factors are greatly connected to people's ability to stay healthy or effectively cope with disease and emergency, many organizations have been calling for increased collaboration among the community development, health care, and public health fields (Braunstein and Lavizzo-Mourey, 2011).

Health communication can play a key role in moving forward such a collaborative agenda. It can help bridge organizational cultures and showcase relevant synergies among the works of public health, health care, and community development organizations and professionals; increase awareness on how key social determinants of health influence health outcomes; establish "good health," and more in general health equity, as key determinants of socioeconomic development; and engage and mobilize professionals from different sectors to take action. Health communication can be instrumental in empowering community members and professionals from different sectors to implement such cross-sectoral collaborative agenda, which would benefit different communities and populations in the United States and globally. We will continue to explore this important theme throughout the book.

THE ROLE OF HEALTH COMMUNICATION IN THE MARKETING MIX

As mentioned, health communication strategies are integral to a variety of interventions in different contexts. In the private sector, health communication strategies are primarily used in a marketing context. Still, many of the other behavioral and social constructs of health communication—and definitely the models that position people at the center of any communication intervention—are considered and used at least at an empirical level. As in other settings (for example, public health), health communication functions tend to be similar to those described in the "What Health Communication Can and Cannot Do" section of this chapter.

Many in the private sector regard health communication as a critical component of the marketing mix, which is traditionally defined by the key four Ps of social marketing (see Chapter Two for a more detailed description): product, price, place, and promotion—in other words, "developing, delivering, and promoting a superior offer" (Maibach, 2003). Chapter Two includes a more detailed discussion of marketing models as one of the key theoretical and practical influences of health communication.

OVERVIEW OF KEY COMMUNICATION AREAS

Global health communication is a term increasingly used to include different communication approaches and action areas, such as interpersonal communication, social and community mobilization, and advocacy (Haider, 2005; Waisbord and Larson, 2005). Well-planned health communication programs rely on an integrated blend of different action areas that should be selected in consideration of expected behavioral and social outcomes (WHO, 2003; O'Sullivan, Yonlder, Morgan, and Merritt, 2003; Health Communication Partnership, 2005a). Long-term results can be achieved only through an engagement process that involves key groups and stakeholders, implements participatory approaches to research, and uses culturally appropriate action areas and communication channels. Remember that there is no magic fix in health communication.

Message repetitiveness and frequency are also important factors in health communication. Often the resonance effect, which can be defined as the ability to create a snowball effect for message delivery by using multiple vehicles, sources, and messengers, can help motivate people to change by reminding them of the desired behavior (for example, complying with childhood immunization requirements, using mosquito nets for protection against malaria, attempting to quit smoking) and its benefits. To this end, several action areas are usually used in health communication and are described in detail in the topic-specific chapters in Part Two:

- *Interpersonal communication*, which uses interpersonal channels (for example, one-on-one or group meetings), and is based on active listening, social and behavioral theories, as well as the ability to relate to, and identify with, the audience's needs and cultural preferences and efficiently address them. This includes "personal selling and counseling" (WHO, 2003, p. 2), which takes place during one-on-one encounters with members of key groups and other key stakeholders, as well as during group events and in locations where materials and services are available. It also includes provider-patient communications—which has been identified as one of the most important areas of health communication (US Department of Health and Human Services, 2005) and should aim at improving health outcomes by optimizing the relationships between providers and their patients, and community dialogue, which is an example of interpersonal communication at scale and is used in research and practice to solicit community input and engage and empower participants throughout the communication process.
- *Mass media and new media communication*, which relies on the skillful use of culturally competent and audience-appropriate mass media, new media, and social media, as well as other communication channels to place a health issue on the public agenda, raise awareness of its root causes and risk factors, advocate for its solutions, or highlight its importance so that key stakeholders, groups, communities, or the public at large take action.
- *Community mobilization and citizen engagement*, a bottom-up and participatory process that at times more formally includes methods for public

consultations and citizen engagement. By using multiple communication channels, community mobilization seeks to involve community leaders and the community at large in addressing a health issue, participating in determining key steps to behavioral or social change, or practicing a desired behavior.

- *Professional medical communications,* a peer-to-peer approach intended to reach and engage health care professionals that aims to (1) promote the adoption of best medical and health practices; (2) establish new concepts and standards of care; (3) publicize recent medical discoveries, beliefs, parameters, and policies; (4) change or establish new medical priorities; and (5) advance health policy changes, among other goals.

- *Constituency relations and strategic partnerships in health communication,* a critical component of all other areas of health communication as well as a communication area of its own. Constituency relations refers to the process of (1) creating consensus among key stakeholders about health issues and their potential solutions, (2) expanding program reach by involving key constituencies, (3) developing alliances, (4) managing and anticipating criticisms and opponents, and (5) maintaining key relationships with other health organizations or stakeholders. Effective constituency relations often lead to strategic and multisectoral partnerships.

- *Policy communication and public advocacy,* which include government relations, policy briefing and communication, public advocacy, and media advocacy, and use multiple communication channels, venues, and media to influence the beliefs, attitudes, and behavior of policymakers, and consequently the adoption, implementation, and sustainability of different policies and funding streams for specific issues.

THE HEALTH COMMUNICATION CYCLE

The importance of a rigorous, theory-driven, and systematic approach to the design, implementation, and evaluation of health communication interventions has been established by several reputable organizations in the United States and globally (Association of Schools of Public Health, 2007; US Department of Health and Human Services, 2012b; WHO, 2003). Chapter Two includes examples of theory-driven planning frameworks used by different types of organizations in a variety of professional settings.

As previously mentioned in the book's introduction, Part Three provides detailed step-by-step guidance on health communication planning, implementation, and evaluation and at the same time also highlights the cyclical and interdependent nature of different phases of health communication interventions. Although a comprehensive overview of the health communication cycle and strategic planning process can be found in Chapter Ten, Figure 13.2 briefly describes key phases of health communication planning and introduces the basic planning framework that is discussed in detail in Part Three. Figure 13.2 also shows how strategic Banning is directly connected to the other two stages of the health communication cycle (program implementation and monitoring, and evaluation, feedback, and refinement).

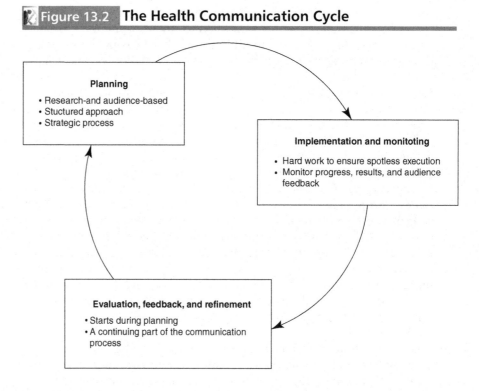

Figure 13.2 The Health Communication Cycle

WHAT HEALTH COMMUNICATION CAN AND CANNOT DO

Health communication cannot work in a vacuum and is usually a critical component of larger public health or community development interventions or corporate efforts. Because of the complexity of health issues, it may "not be equally effective in addressing all issues or relaying all messages" (National Cancer Institute at the National Institutes of Health, 2002, p. 3), at least in a given time frame.

Health communication cannot replace the lack of local infrastructure (such as the absence of appropriate health services or hospitals or other essential services that would provide communities with enhanced opportunities to stay healthy, as, for example, parks, adequate transportation systems, recreational facilities, bike-sharing programs, and stores that sell nutritious food) or capability (such as an inadequate number of health care providers in relation to the size of the population being attended). It cannot compensate for inadequate medical solutions to treat, diagnose, or prevent any disease. But it can help advocate for change and create a receptive environment to support the development of new health services or the allocation of additional funds for medical and scientific discovery, or access to existing treatments or community services, or the recruitment of health care professionals in new medical fields or underserved geographical areas. In doing so, it helps secure political commitment, stakeholder endorsement, and community involvement to encourage change, devise community-specific solutions, and improve health outcomes.

Because of the evolving role of health communication, other authors and organizations have been defining the potential contribution of health communication to the health care and public health fields. For example, the US National Cancer Institute at the National Institutes of Health (2002) has a homonymous section, which partly inspired the need for this section, in one of its publications on the topic.

Understanding the role and the potential impact of health communication is important to take full advantage of the contribution of this field to health and related social outcomes as well as to set realistic expectations on what can be accomplished among team members, program partners, key groups, and stakeholders. Table 13.3 provides examples of what health communication can and cannot do.

Table 13.3   What Health Communication Can and Cannot Do

Health Communication Can Help...	Health Communication Cannot...
Raise awareness of health issues and their root causes to drive policy or practice changes	Work in a vacuum, independent from other public health, health care, marketing, and community development interventions
Engage and empower communities and key groups	
Influence research agendas and priorities and support the need for additional funds for medical and scientific discovery	Replace the lack of local infrastructure, services, or capability
Increase understanding of the many socially determined factors that influence health and illness so they can be adequately addressed at the population and community levels	Compensate for the absence of adequate treat ment or diagnostic or preventive options and services
Encourage collaboration among different sectors, such as public health, community development, and health care	"Be equally effective in addressing all issues or relaying all messages," atleast in the same time frame (National Cancer Institute at the National Institutes of Health, 2002, p. 3)
Secure stakeholder endorsement of health and related social issues	
"Influence perceptions, beliefs and attitudes that may change social norms" (National Cancer Institute at the National Institutes of Health, 2002, p. 3)	
Promote data and emerging issues to establish new standards of care	
"Increase demand for health services" (National Cancer Institute at the National Institutes of Health, 2002, p. 3) and products	
Show benefits of and encourage behavior change	
"Demonstrate healthy skills" (National Cancer Institute at the National Institutes of Health, 2002, p. 3)	
Provoke public discussion to drive disease diagnosis, treatment, or prevention	
Suggest and "prompt action" (National Cancer Institute at the National Institutes of Health, 2002, p. 3)	

(continued)

 **Table 13.3   What Health Communication Can and Cannot Do (*continued*)**

Health Communication Can Help...	Health Communication Cannot...
Build constituencies to support health and social change across different sectors and communities	
Advocate for equal access to existing health products and services	
Strengthen third-party relationships	
Improve patient compliance and outcomes	

KEY CONCEPTS

- Health communication is a multifaceted and multidisciplinary field of research, theory, and practice. It is concerned with reaching different populations and groups to exchange health-related information, ideas, and methods in order to influence, engage, empower, and support different groups so that they will champion, introduce, adopt, or sustain a health or social behavior, practice, or policy that will ultimately improve individual, community, and public health outcomes.
- Health communication should be inclusive and representative also of vulnerable and underserved groups.
- Health communication is an increasingly prominent field in public health, health care, community development, and the private sector (both nonprofit and corporate).
- Health communication can play a key role in advancing health equity.
- Several socially determined factors (also referred to as *social determinants of health)* influence and are influenced by health communication.
- One of the key characteristics of health communication is its multidisciplinary nature, which allows the theoretical flexibility that is needed to consider and approach each situation and key group for their unique characteristics and needs.
- We are now in the era of behavioral and social impact communication. In fact, several US and international models and agendas support the importance of a behavioral and social change-driven mind-set in developing health communication interventions.
- Health communication is an evolving discipline that should always incorporate lessons learned and practical experiences. Practitioners should take an important role in defining theories and models to inform new directions in health communication.
- It is important to be aware of key features and limitations of health communication (and more specifically what communication can and cannot do).
- Health communication relies on several action areas.
- Well-designed programs are the result of an integrated blend of different areas that should be selected in light of expected behavioral and social outcomes.

FOR DISCUSSION AND PRACTICE

1. Did you have any preliminary idea about the definition and role of health communication prior to reading this chapter? If yes, how does it compare to what you have learned in this chapter?

2. In your opinion, what are the two most important defining features of health communication and why? How do they relate to the other key characteristics of health communication that are discussed in this chapter?

3. Can you recall a personal experience in which a health communication program, message, or health-related encounter (for example, a physician visit) has influenced your decisions or perceptions about a specific health issue? Describe the experience and emphasize key factors that affected your decision and health behavior.

4. Did you ever participate in the development or implementation of a health communication intervention? If yes, what were some of the key learnings and how do they relate to the attributes of health communication as described in this chapter?

5. Can you think of examples of health communication interventions that seek to benefit and address the needs of vulnerable and underserved groups in your neighborhood, community, city, and country? If yes, did you observe any results or impact among these groups?

CPSIA information can be obtained
at www.ICGtesting.com
Printed in the USA
FSOW04n0213040817
37209FS